— ON —
BENTLEY

ON BENTLEY SINCE 1919

Introduction by Warren Allport

BAY
VIEW
BOOKS

Published 1988 by
Bay View Books Ltd
13a Bridgeland Street
Bideford, Devon EX39 2QE

Distributed by
Chris Lloyd Sales and Marketing Services
P.O. Box 327, Poole, Dorset BH15 2RG

ISBN 1-870979-03-6

Printed in Hong Kong

Acknowledgments

The publishers are grateful to the following who have helped
in the compilation of this book: Warren Allport, Peter Garnier,
Jon Pressnell and David Preston. For pictures reproduced in
this book, acknowledgments are due to *Autocar*, Haymarket
Motoring Photo Library, Quadrant Picture Library and Rolls-
Royce Motors Ltd.

Compiler's note

The forerunner of this book was *Bentley 1919-1931*, compiled
by Peter Garnier and published by IPC Transport Press in 1978,
and some of the *Autocar* articles that were reproduced in it
appear again here. Peter had planned to trace the great
marque's history since 1931 in a companion book but that did
not take shape as he retired, so in the spirit of that first volume
the whole history of Bentley has been covered in a similar
form.

It is not covered consistently, because Bentley history is
not consistent year on year, but the stories of the early and
recent years are vigorous. So the book has a positive beginning
and because of the welcome resurgence of the 1980s a much
more positive open-end than could have been foreseen at the
end of the 1970s.

Some of the contemporary journal features are
representative rather than definitive. For example, the S2
Continental that was road tested in 1960 was primarily
intended for town use and consequently had the lower back
axle ratio of normal saloons, so that its top speed was
presumably lower than a true-specification Continental. But
that points towards individuality, which adds interest to any
marque history – and gives critics opportunities to take
compilers to task . . .

To put contemporary reports, descriptions and reviews into
perspective, Warren Allport, *Autocar's* Rolls-Royce and Bentley
guru for many years, has brought his journal article on the first
60 years of the marque up to date, to form an erudite
introduction to this Bentley story, 1919-1988.

David Hodges 5.5.88

Contents

Bentley since 1919

From the first 3-litre chassis of 1919 to the 1988 Turbo R

By Warren Allport

THE ORIGINS of the Bentley car go back to January 1919 and the formation of Bentley Motors Ltd, but it was to be October of that year before the first engine designed by W.O. Bentley, Harry and F.T. Burgess actually ran on the bench in the little mews off Baker Street. By then W.O. Bentley had acquired considerable engineering and design experience. He had served a premium apprenticeship with the Great Northern Railway at Doncaster, had assisted in the running of a fleet of 250 Unic cabs operated in London by the National Cab Co. Ltd, and with his brother, H.M. Bentley, had sold and raced the French DFP car for which Bentley and Bentley had the London agency. All this was before the First World War, during which W.O. served in the Royal Naval Air Service and designed the Bentley rotary aero engine. Wartime service brought W.O. into contact with F.T. Burgess, head designer at Humbers, S.C.H. Davis, an admiralty inspector, and "Nobby" Clarke, a chief petty officer in the RNAS. All three were later to become involved with the Bentley car.

Today it may seem surprising that one of the first things W.O. did to the 3-litre chassis was to reduce the noise, coming chiefly from the straight tooth gears and the scavenger oil pump. Wet sump lubrication and a camshaft with three cams and separate rockers were substituted, and a second magneto was added. The Claudel carburettor was replaced by a five-jet Smith. Just 367 days after design work started, the first 3-litre was road tested by *The Autocar* in January 1920. The result was

a flood of sales enquiries which Bentley Motors had neither the factory nor the staff to supply. It was not until September 1921 that Noel van Raalte took delivery of the first chassis supplied to a customer though very few 3-litres were delivered from the new factory at Cricklewood before 1922. One of the problems facing the company was the expense of having all the parts made by outside suppliers. At that time the 117.5in wheelbase chassis cost £1,050, so it was by no means cheap.

After the war, the formation of Bentley Motors was the outward sign of W.O. Bentley's determination to design his own sports car to race instead of trying to improve the DFP. Three litres might seem a large engine size by today's standards for a first model, but in those days engines were far less efficient and also a large capacity resulted in plenty of low speed torque – something that was needed at a time when gear changing was by no means easy for the average motorist. In fact, the 2,996cc four-cylinder engine developed only about 65bhp at 3,500rpm, despite four valves and two sparking plugs per cylinder. Typical of many engines of the day was its long stroke of 149mm for a bore of only 80mm. Magneto ignition, a pre-war Claudel carburettor and dry sump lubrication were other features. With no factory of their own to manufacture the parts needed Bentley Motors were entirely reliant on outside suppliers to provide the parts for the first engine. This was unfortunate at a time when there was a terrific boom in car sales

W.O. Bentley in the first 3-litre car, in January 1920, and the Crewe-built Turbo R of the late 1980s

F.C. Clement in one of the 1922 TT cars; he finished second in the race, best placed of the three team cars. W.D. Hawkes in one of the TT cars, modified for the 1922 Indianapolis 500

and many component suppliers had more work than they could cope with without bothering about a new and untried car. Prodigious efforts by the Bentley Motors staff, who then also included "Nobby" Clarke, Clive Gallop and Jimmy Enstone, resulted in the first engine being installed in a chassis in time for the 1919 Olympia Show in November. However, although outwardly the new model appeared finished, the crankcase and cam case were made of wood and there was no valve gear.

Racing was to be associated with the Bentley name right from the very earliest days because W.O. knew the publicity value that a win brought from his pre-war experiences racing and selling DFPs. Brooklands was the scene for the second experimental car's racing debut on 7 May 1921 in the hands of Frank Clement followed on 16 May by the first Bentley win in a race at the Brooklands Whitsun meeting. 1922 brought further success for the 3-litre when W.D., Hawkes came thirteenth in the Indianapolis 500 at an average speed of 75mph, and was followed by a team win for three cars driven by W.O. Hawkes and Clement in the Isle of Man Tourist Trophy Race on 22 June. The direct result of this win was a faster Tourist Trophy Replica model with higher compression costing £1,295.

The first Le Mans

For 1923 a longer 130in wheelbase chassis was offered costing £1,100 to meet demand from customers for a roomier closed body – something never intended – and this was to form the basis of 3-litre production right up to 1929. John Duff had taken a number of class records at Brooklands with a short chassis 3-litre in 1922, and in 1923 approached Bentley Motors and asked them to prepare his car for the new Le Mans 24-hour race and provide him with a mechanic and co-driver. W.O. Bentley thought the whole idea completely mad as he didn't see how any car could last the race. Duff was very persuasive and the result was that the car was prepared, Clement was loaned as co-driver and two mechanics were provided. In the end W.O. and sales manager A.F. Hillstead went over to see the race and witnessed Clement setting a new lap record of 66.69 mph and the car finishing fourth. The following year Duff and Clement recorded the first Bentley win at Le Mans at an average speed of 53.78 mph, front wheel brakes were added to the production car and the Speed Model 3-litre was introduced.

By 1924 it had become obvious that more power was needed to cope with the closed bodies which many customers were fitting. An experimental 4¼-litre six-cylinder car was running and W.O. combined a test run with a visit to the French Grand Prix. A chance encounter on the return journey resulted in a "race" with the prototype Rolls-Royce Phantom I also on test in France. There was nothing in top speed between the two cars, and back at Cricklewood W.O. decided that to keep ahead

of Rolls-Royce they had better increase the engine capacity to 6½ litres. Thus the 6½-litre six cylinder Bentley was born, and in 1925 was offered with a wheelbase of 132, 145.3 or 153.3in. It was another long stroke (140mm) design with a 100mm bore and a single Smith carburettor fed all six cylinders. The variety of chassis lengths meant that at last it was possible to provide the luxury saloon coachwork demanded by Bentley customers and still have 75 mph performance. Financial problems were never far away from Bentley Motors and it was in 1925 that millionaire Woolf Barnato assumed financial control.

W.O. Bentley's policy was to enter only races which suited the car and which they stood a good chance of winning. This is why Le Mans with its long straights which allowed the big cars to use their performance became so important for Bentley. Encouraged by the win in 1924, a team of two 3-litres was entered in 1925 and three cars in 1926. Unfortunately none of the cars stayed the distance.

The 4½-litre Bentley

By the time the 1927 Le Mans race came round there was a new Bentley on the market. This was the famous 4½-litre ohc four-cylinder which was in effect a 6½ minus two cylinders and had a capacity of 4,398cc. Standard wheelbase was 130in although eight cars were produced with a 117.5in wheelbase. The 4½ was introduced to meet the demand from customers who wanted a 3-litre with more room, performance and flexibility. A single 4½, driven by Clement and Callingham, backed up by two 3 litres were the Bentley team entries for Le Mans 1927. The famous crash at White House Corner involving all three cars put the 4½ and one of the 3 litres out of the race. It was left to Dr J.D. Benjafield and Sammy Davis, then sports editor of *The Autocar*, to nurse the remaining battered Bentley home for the second Bentley victory at the Sarthe Circuit. The publicity value of that win was enormous and more Bentley racing successes followed. A team of three 4½ cars was entered for the 1928 Le Mans race and Woolf Barnato won. A year later came the best ever Bentley team win with the green cars taking the first four places. This was Woolf Barnato's second Le Mans win, not because as chairman of Bentley Motors he had the best car but because he was one of the finest drivers of the day. While driving for the Bentley team he never made a mistake, drove absolutely to the book observing the maximum permitted engine revs and obeyed the instructions of the team manager.

The BARC Six Hours Race in June 1929 was also won by the 6½, crewed by Barnato and Dunfee and this race marked the first appearance of Tim Birkin in the supercharged 4½-litre car. Amherst Villiers rebuilt the engine and fitted a supercharger driven at engine speed off the crankshaft. W.O. disapproved of this move but Birkin persuaded Barnato that a team of blowers, as the supercharged cars were called, should

John Duff's winning 3-litre at Le Mans in 1924

A famous victory was scored by Benjafield and Davis in the 1927 Le Mans 24-hour Race. Their battered 3-litre is rounding the Pontlieue hairpin towards the end of the race

The third-placed Bentley during a night pit stop at Le Mans in 1929, when the marque enjoyed a 1-2-3-4 clean sweep

be entered for the 1929 Irish Grand Prix and Tourist Trophy. In spite of the considerable increase in engine power there were no Bentley wins. In fact the blower 4½ never won a major race, suffered many mechanical failures and brought Bentley Motors a lot of the wrong sort of publicity. Birkin persuaded the Hon Dorothy Paget to put up the money to set up a factory at Welwyn to build the supercharged cars which he was racing in direct competition with the works team. Even more unfortunate was Barnato's decision to let Birkin enter a team of three blower 4½s for the 1930 Le Mans race because this meant that 50 cars had to be built for sale to the public.

Two other changes in 1929 were the end of 3-litre production and the introduction of the short chassis Speed Six with a higher lift camshaft and twin SU carburettors. It was the finest touring car the company had built up to that time and in the first half of 1929 Bentley Motors made their first ever profit.

A 4½-litre supercharged car with Gurney Nutting body, built for Woolf Barnato

The 8-litre
W.O.'s finest model, the 8-litre, was announced at the end of 1930, but by then the effects of the slump had hit car sales hard and luxury car sales like the Bentley had dwindled to a mere trickle. The 8-litre actually made money for the company but the works could not exist on the few sales that were made. In spite of the fact that the 8-litre offered real luxury motoring with 100 mph performance superior to the big Rolls-Royce Phantom II, the writing was on the wall by 1931. As a last desperate attempt to revive sales the Bentley Motors board decided to launch a smaller 4-litre car to compete with the Rolls-Royce 20/25 hp. Harry Ricardo designed the pushrod 3,915cc engine with bore and stroke of 85x115mm as W.O. would have nothing to do with it. All might still have been well if this engine had not been installed in the massive 8-litre chassis. The result was a car that did not have the performance the Bentley clientele expected and which did not sell.

In July 1931 Woolf Barnato's financial advisers persuaded him not to meet two mortgages totalling £65,000 in favour of

An 8-litre carrying rather ponderous bodywork

The 1931 4-litre was an undistinguished car, using the 8-litre chassis and a new pushrod engine

Woolf Barnato at the wheel of the first production 3½-litre to be built after the Rolls-Royce takeover. The handsome Vanden Plas body is particularly well suited to the 'silent sports car'

the London Life Association and the receiver was called in. In September 1931 Bentley Motors was in voluntary liquidation. While this had been going on W.O. Bentley had been having talks with Napiers with a view to their taking over the company and producing the 8-litre as a Napier-Bentley. Negotiations were all but concluded and required only court approval when Rolls-Royce outbid Napier and took over the company. The reasons for this were obvious, Rolls-Royce's own luxury car sales were in decline and they did not want to see the 8-litre back in production and competition with the Phantom II.

The 3½-litre Derby Bentley
It is greatly to the credit of Rolls-Royce that having acquired Bentley Motors together with all the trade marks and W.O., they did not let the Bentley marque die. Bentley Motors (1931) Ltd. was formed on 14 December 1931, but none of the old models were to reappear. Soon after this Royce was working on a 2½-litre supercharged car which the sales department thought might make a Bentley replacement, but like the blower Bentleys it proved none too reliable. In the meantime the experimental department at Derby had been trying out a baby Rolls Royce 18 hp, with a 2,364cc engine and no supercharger.

Called the Peregrine this was to form the basis of the new Bentley after W.A. Robotham had found that the existing 20/25 hp engine and gearbox could be made to fit the chassis. This not only restored the performance when fitted with a higher compression and twin SU carburettors but the chassis also handled. Sir Henry Royce gave his blessing to this rearrangement of components – all of which he had designed – but did not live to see the announcement of the 3½-litre Bentley as The Silent Sports Car in 1933. The silence of the 3½ nearly prevented it being marketed as Rolls-Royce managing director Arthur Sidgreaves did not think it sounded noisy enough for a sports car. Fortunately dealers such as the late Jack Barclay and A.H. Pass thought otherwise.

Whereas W.O. Bentley had raced his cars to sell them, the new company actually forbade their customers to race but in 1934 Sidgreaves was persuaded by Eddie Hall, a 3½-litre customer, to provide works support for a private entry in the Tourist Trophy Race at Ards. In the event Hall finished second at an average speed of 78.4 mph. Entries in 1935 and 1936 were again works supported and again Eddie Hall finished second, which helped Bentley sales considerably.

By 1936 customers were fitting heavier bodies to the chassis and the performance was suffering, so the engine was bored out from 3,669 to 4,257cc and the resulting model became known as the 4¼-litre. By the time it was on the market there was considerable activity in the experimental department at Derby, a six-cylinder engine with single chain-driven overhead camshaft was being developed as was independent suspension and there was considerable work on bearings following a spate of failures caused by high speed driving on the Continent with associated high oil temperatures. New aluminium alloy bearings were used with some success and the situation was further improved by the standardisation of a gearbox with an overdrive top incorporated. Final development of the model came with the arrival of the Mark V in 1939 with independent front suspension.

The Corniche

Rolls-Royce was very conscious of the need to provide good performance for the Bentley and investigations into reducing body weight and streamlining had been going on for some time when in 1938 Rolls-Royce Paris manager Walter Sleator persuaded Andre Embiricos to buy a 4¼-litre chassis and have a special streamlined body fitted. Georges Paulin designed the two-door body which was built by Pourtout. With a top speed of over 100 mph, this car created considerable interest and was used by Rolls-Royce for publicity purposes at Brooklands and on the Continent. The result was a decision to build a modified production version, based on the later Mark V chassis and with a streamlined four-door saloon body designed by Paulin. This car was called the Corniche and had a body by Van Vooren of Paris, though it was intended that Park Ward would build the production bodies. A 15,000-mile Continental test was run on the Corniche prototype in the summer of 1939 but a serious accident put an end to testing. The chassis returned to Derby for rebuilding but the special body was repaired locally and later destroyed by a bomb on the quayside at Dieppe. It had been planned to exhibit several examples of the Corniche, with bodies by Van Vooren, at the 1939 London and Paris motor shows which were never held.

Post-war cars

All Bentley production had stopped by early 1940, but just before the war a number of new models had been designed as a rationalised Rolls-Royce and Bentley range using many common components to reduce cost. There were four-, six- and eight-cylinder engines with an F-head inlet over exhaust configuration in a rationalised new chassis intended to be offered with a steel body. The war prevented this but in 1946

A 1934 four-door sports saloon by Mann Egerton on the 3½-litre chassis

E.R. Hall's works-prepared but independently-entered 3½-litre in the 1934 Tourist Trophy

A James Young bodied 4¼-litre of 1938

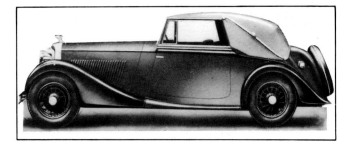

The standard 1939 coupé

The Mk VI was the first post-war Bentley and the first to be marketed with a standard steel body as a complete car

after running prototypes for an extensive mileage on wartime work, a modified six-cylinder car with hydraulic front brakes did go into production as the Bentley Mark VI. It was the first model produced by Rolls-Royce to be fitted with a standard Pressed Steel body, although chassis were available, and therefore was built entirely in the Crewe factory where post-war car manufacture was based. Until 1947, the Bentley was the only model emerging from Crewe and was successful in establishing post-war car Rolls-Royce production with 5,201 examples built between 1946 and 1952, and a further 2,320 of the R-type which had a large boot. Increased power came in 1951 when the engine was bored out to 4,566cc. Just after the war the idea of a Continental Bentley along the lines of the Corniche was revived and was announced in 1952 on the R-type chassis. At about the same time automatic transmission, using the General Motors Hydra-matic gearbox manufactured under licence was offered on the R-type saloon. Ivan Evernden worked closely with coachbuilders H.J. Mulliner to produce a lightweight two-door body with lower frontal area and the completed car had a very attractive sloping fastback tail. With 120 mph performance it was the fastest production four-seater car in the world at the time and followed in the true Bentley tradition. Once again customers insisted on fitting heavier bodies and in 1954 the engine size of the R-type Continental was increased to 4,887cc by boring the unit out yet again.

In 1955 a completely new Bentley chassis was announced as the S-type with the 4.9-litre six-cylinder engine. It had a very attractive Pressed Steel body with a 123in wheelbase chassis compared with the 120in of previous post-war Bentleys. A Continental version with higher compression (7.25) engine was announced at the same time. Automatic transmission was now a standard feature, though Continental customers were able to specify the delightful manual gearbox up until 1957. The 4.9-litre engine was the ultimate stretch of the pre-war design and in the meantime Rolls-Royce had been working on an all new 90 degree V8 of 6,230cc. This alloy engine with hydraulically-operated tappets produced considerably more power and gave improved performance, even though it was not quite as quiet as the six. The S2 Bentley with this engine appeared with an unchanged external appearance in 1959. A further power increase in 1962 and revised frontal treatment with twin headlamp units turned the S2 into the S3. While up to this time the Bentley continued to outsell the Rolls-Royce versions of the model, the differences between the two marques were becoming fewer and fewer, and by the time the S3 arrived even the Continentals were little more than coachbuilt Bentleys with slightly improved performance.

The T-series Bentley announced at the 1965 London Motor Show retained only the 6,230cc V8 engine and automatic gearbox from the S3, in all other respects it was entirely new. It was the first monocoque construction Bentley and boasted

self-levelling all-independent suspension with high pressure hydraulics also operating the four-wheel disc brakes. It was a tremendous engineering advance but somehow along the way the sporting Bentley image had disappeared. There were no more Continentals, though coachbuilt two-door versions became available in 1967. In 1968 a revised cylinder head and three-speed automatic gearbox were incorporated and in 1969 a revised facia and interior to meet American Federal safety standards were standardized on all cars. The following year the V8 engine stroke was increased from 91 to 99mm, bringing an increase in capacity to 6,750cc. The financial troubles that beset Rolls-Royce Ltd in 1971 came just at the time when an improved performance model with 10 per cent more power and a coachbuilt body was being launched. Called the Corniche this was available as a two-door hardtop or convertible Rolls-Royce or Bentley. The only concession to a sporting image was the fitting of a rev counter.

Following the receivership and the subsequent flotation of the independent company Rolls-Royce Motors Ltd, the name of the Bentley subsidiary was changed to Bentley Motors Ltd in September 1973. Unfortunately for Bentley virtually all the effort of Rolls-Royce Motors was dedicated to re-establishing the Rolls-Royce car and so the Bentley name slipped into the background. By 1976 only 3.3 per cent of Crewe's production carried the Bentley badge.

That year the Corniche was the first Bentley model to benefit from the sophisticated fully-automatic bi-level air conditioning system developed by the engineers at Crewe. In 1977 the four-door cars received this air conditioning too along with other major engineering changes. Rack and pinion steering and revisions to the front suspension complemented a new facia, while externally the T2 model was identified by black polyurethane-faced bumpers and a front aim dam. With the arrival of the T2 the word 'Bentley' did not even appear on the rocker box covers – the boot badge, wheel trims and radiator were all that distinguished the Bentley from the similarly-priced Rolls-Royce Silver Shadow II. The Corniche was similarly affected, though it did continue as the model on which engineering improvements were introduced first, such as the mineral oil hydraulics and revised rear suspension in 1979.

The demise of Bentley nearly came with the replacement of the Rolls-Royce Silver Shadow by the new Silver Spirit in 1980. After all with so few people ordering Bentleys – only 58 four-door T2 Bentleys had been sold in three years compared with 10,566 Rolls-Royce Silver Shadow and Silver Wraith IIs – it hardly seemed worthwhile bothering with the different radiator and bumpers required. But there was a new Bentley saloon in 1980 and for the first time it bore a model name instead of a mark number or series letter. The Mulsanne was named after the long straight at Le Mans down which many of W.O's cars drove to fame in the 1920s. The Mulsanne was in essence a new

A Mulliner-bodied R-type Continental of 1953

A standard steel S3

A Continental with a rare and not wholly sympathetic Pininfarina body

A four-door T-series saloon of 1969

monocoque body with the revised rear suspension and mineral oil hydraulics already fitted to the Corniche. The Rolls-Royce 6,750cc V8 engine and GM400 automatic gearbox were carried over from the T2, and despite the new name the Bentley remained a Rolls-Royce clone. The soft ride and consequent body roll discouraged sporting driving, though the new style seats – sprung in a new way so that the occupants sat in, rather than on, them – helped. Safety regulations endowed the Mulsanne with a curved front bumper and made it 1.7 in longer than the Silver Spirit; they also spelled the end of the winged-B mascot on the top of the radiator.

With 134 cars sold in 1981, the Mulsanne marked a turning point in Bentley's fortunes. The arrival of the Mulsanne Turbo, available only as a Bentley, in 1982 set the marque on a new course from which it has not looked back. Performance was the *raison d'etre* of the Turbo and that was provided in abundance by the fitment of a Garrett AiResearch exhaust-driven turbocharger that boosted maximum power by 50 per cent to 298 bhp (DIN) and almost doubled the V8 engine's already massive torque. Maximum speed was governed to 135 mph, initially because of worries about tyres though such problems had been overcome by the time of announcement, while the 0-60 mph sprint took a mere 7 seconds. For a four-door saloon weighing nearly 2½ tons this performance was pretty impressive, especially since a higher final drive was fitted. Despite the power boost, Rolls-Royce levels of refinement were retained by matching the turbocharger down to 2,000 rpm so that turbo lag was barely noticeable. By the time production started six months after announcement all the first year's allocation had been sold.

Customers liked the performance but not the handling and body roll, because the Turbo was still a Rolls-Royce in suspension terms. While that was being tackled the range was broadened by the addition of Bentley Eight in 1984. This had stiffer front dampers, a bright mesh grille, straight grain veneers, cloth seats and some fittings deleted to sell at £49,497. This was the first step in marketing Bentley as a different marque and at the same time differential pricing of Bentley models, a change in marque colour from racing green to red and a name change for the Bentley Corniche to Continental were implemented. In the meantime the engineers had been working on a much stiffer suspension to complement the Mulsanne Turbo's performance. The result was the 1985 Turbo R (R for roadholding) which was also fitted with alloy wheels, ultra low profile tyres and a rev counter. In September 1986 a Turbo R put Bentley back in the record books with a new national one hour endurance record of 140.91 miles covered from a standing start and 15 other records.

The Turbo R and the styling exercise Project 90 were the talking point of the 1985 Geneva Show at which they were announced and reaction to the styling exercise confirmed that Bentley were going in the right direction. Project 90 was not intended for production though. For 1986 all Bentleys had a revised stiffer suspension compared with Rolls-Royce models and in 1987 all Bentleys had increased power from the fitment.

of Bosch fuel injection while safety was enhanced by anti-lock brakes. The Turbo R received a different interior with unique Bentley seats giving more lateral location at the same time. For the 1988 model year the Mulsanne S with different interior replaced the Mulsanne and provided a more sporting saloon that felt very different to drive from the Rolls-Royce Silver Spirit, and appealed to a different,younger owner. In 1987 almost 50 per cent of Rolls-Royce and Bentley sales in the UK were accounted for by Bentley – a situation inconceivable 10 years earlier.

The Mulsanne and the Mulsanne Turbo were important models in the 're-establishment' of the Bentley marque

Project 90 was one of the outstanding exhibits at the 1985 Geneva Motor Show

The New Three-litre Bentley.

Details of a High-speed Sporting Car, having an 80 mm. Four-cylinder Engine which will develop 65 h.p.

IN our issue of March 8th we announced that Capt. W. O. Bentley and Mr. F. T. Burgess were engaged in the design of a new car. We now are able to give a short description of the design, as the drawings have been finished and the machine is under construction.

The car is built primarily for speed, and is. intended for the enthusiastic sportsman of the motor world. Not only has it a most sporting appearance, but it is proposed that the peculiar feeling of absolute control obtainable with the genuine racing machine shall be experienced.

SPECIFICATION.

65 h.p., four cylinders, 80 × 149 mm. (2,994 c.c.) monobloc.

Four overhead valves per cylinder.

Ferodo cone clutch.

Four-speed gear box.

820 × 120 mm. tyres ; wire wheels.

Wheelbase, 9ft. 4in.   Track, 4ft. 8in.

Electric starting and lighting.

The engine has four cylinders, with a bore of 80 mm. and a stroke of 149 mm., giving a cubic capacity of 2,993.80 c.c. At 2,500 r.p.m. the engine is planned to develop 65 h.p., and the maximum r.p.m. will be 3,200. As the utmost efficiency is required from the engine a separate head is not used, but the cylinders are cast as one block with a considerable water space between each wall. Exceptionally large inspection plates are provided, both at the sides and at the ends of the casting, in order that the whole of the water system may be inspected before the engine is erected. There are four valves, each having two springs, located in the head of every cylinder, operated by rocking levers from the camshaft, which is placed on top of the cylinder block. A vertical shaft drives the camshaft through helical bevel gearing, and a cross-shaft, driven by similar means, operates the magneto at one side of the engine and a centrifugal water pump at the other.

There are two oil pumps, of which one drains the sump and delivers oil to a cooling tank placed below the radiator, while the other is fed from the cooling tank and forces oil to the crankshaft and connecting rod bearings. The position of the oil tank ensures that the lubricant will be cooled by the water in the lower part of the radiator.

The crankshaft is carried in five plain bearings, and has an oil retaining device on the tail journal. Aluminium pistons, of special design and unusual shape, are fitted. The engine is supported on the frame at three points, two at the rear of the crank case and one in the centre of the cross-member below the radiator. There is a cone Ferodo-lined clutch of large diameter fitted with a most ingenious balanced withdrawal gear.

In the gear box—which also is suspended at three points—are gears providing four speeds and a reverse. The propeller-shaft has one universal joint at the front, and a sliding universal joint at the rear, the latter being necessary as both torque and drive are taken through the semi-elliptic rear springs, and the axle therefore swings on the front shackle pin. To lubricate the rear sliding joint the propeller-shaft is

made hollow and filled with oil, which can reach the sliding surfaces through small holes drilled in the universal joint pins.

The car is driven by a helical bevel, and the bevel pinion shaft bearings have a special external adjustment. Two pressings welded together form the axle case, the construction being such that the differential can be removed from the back after a large cover plate has been detached and the driving shafts have been withdrawn. Both hand and foot brake shoes are of aluminium fabric-faced, and lie side by side within the rear wheel drums, the pull on the brake tension rods being equalised by a bevel balance gear.

Steering is effected by worm and worm wheel mounted throughout on ball journal and thrust bearings, and the steering column has an additional steady bearing halfway up. From the worm gear casing to this steady bearing, the column is enclosed in an aluminium stiffening tube, and the steering wheel is of racing type with a narrow rim of large diameter. Semi-elliptic springs are fitted to both the front and the rear axles. The wheelbase is 9ft. 4in., the track 4ft. 8in., and the racing-type detachable wire wheels carry 820 × 120 mm. tyres. It is anticipated that the chassis will weigh about 1,450 lb.

A two-seated, four-seated, or saloon body can be fitted to the chassis, but all will be on sporting lines, so as to be in keeping with the character of the car. With four passengers it is guaranteed that the machine will lap Brooklands track at 75 m.p.h. A lighting dynamo and starting motor will be fitted, and the chassis, with running boards, front mudguards, five lamps, five wheels and tyres, a revolution counter and speedometer, and tool kit, will be priced in the neighbourhood of £750.

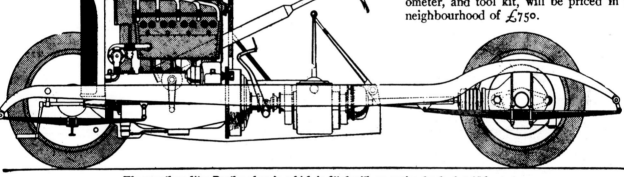

The new three-litre Bentley chassis, which is fitted with an engine developing 65 h.p.

A New British Sporting Car.

IT is but a few weeks since we urged the claims of the true sporting car and showed that, whereas the largest demand for sporting cars existed in this country, buyers were largely dependent upon foreign manufacturers to satisfy their particular needs. We are now able to announce that Captain W. O. Bentley, M.B.E., R.A.F., is engaged on the design of a new sporting model shortly to be placed on the market and intended to appeal to those enthusiastic motorists who desire a car which, practically speaking, is a true racing car with touring accessories, such as hood, wings, and dynamo lighting set. That it will have speed, power and efficiency seems beyond question

Capt. W. O. Bentley, M.B.E., R.A.F

from those details of the design which are already settled. During the war, it will be remembered, Captain Bentley designed the B.R.1 and B.R.2 aero engines as a result of previous experimental work with rotary engines, and it was due to Captain Bentley's enthusiasm and personal efforts that the engines put up such a splendid record under the R.N.A.S. and R.A.F on the Western front. Before this time Captain Bentley was identified with D.F.P. cars, and was a competitor in many races and trials both in the Isle of Man and at Brooklands. Associated with him is Mr. F. T. Burgess, who designed the Humber T.T. cars and drove one of them in the Island.

The Three-litre Bentley.

A British Super-efficient Sporting Car, the Engine of which is Designed to keep its "tune" in the Hands of the Average Owner.

This threequarter front view gives an admirable impression of the well-balanced appearance of the chassis. The effect is obtained largely by setting the radiator well behind the line of the front axle. Ball joints are fitted to the front axle to receive the shock absorbers.

THE Bentley chassis stands alone in its class as a car designed to give that peculiar and almost perfect combination of tractability and great speed usually to be found on machines built for racing and for racing only.

Essentially a light chassis with a very powerful engine, the car is nevertheless suitable for the average motorist who has not the time to maintain an engine in perfect tune, the whole point of the design being that the engine will do its work easily without the need of constant attention to tappet clearance or other minor adjustments. True, in the hands of the motoring e n t h u s i a s t who has mechanical ability and is able to obtain the last ounce of power from the engine, the car should well repay attention and care spent upon it, but the great majority prefer a car which will do its work year in and year out without trouble, and for such is the Bentley designed.

Aero Development.

An engine of this type would have had little chance of success prior to the war; it has been made possible, in fact, by dearly bought experience of multi-valve aero-

> ### SPECIFICATION.
> **Three-litre, four cylinders, 80 × 149 mm. bore and stroke (2,994 c.c.)**
> **Four valves to each cylinder, dry sump lubrication.**
> **Fabric cone clutch.**
> **Four-speed gear box.**
> **Semi-floating rear axle.**
> **Semi-elliptic springs.**
> **820 × 120 mm. tyres on detachable wire wheels.**
> **9ft. 4in. wheelbase. 4ft. 8in. track.**
> **Electric lighting and starting.**
> **Chassis weight, 14½ cwt.**

plane engines. Aeroplane engines now can perform reliably twice or three times the work that is required from a car engine of similar design, because the aeroplane engine is called upon to run at threequarter, full, or even full, power without variation for two or three hours at a time, whereas the car engine never is on full load even for an hour, since the throttle invariably is closed after a quite short burst of speed. The effect of this difference in treatment upon the reliability of the engine is obvious.

Designed for Efficiency.

That the Bentley car is easily able to realise the ambitions of its designer seems obvious after a close study of the chassis, every portion of which, down to the smallest detail, has received careful a n d mature consideration. Moreover, it is the intention of the manufacturers to test the car with more than usual thoroughness ere the first examples are allowed to reach the hands of private owners.

In order to obtain the utmost efficiency from the engine, a separate head is not provided, the cylinders being complete and placed upon an aluminium crank case, which is in two portions, the upper holding the five bearings of the crankshaft. Aluminium pistons of a special shape are used, with two narrow rings, and are held to the connecting rods by floating gudgeon pins, provided w i t h small buffers at either end to prevent the pins scoring the cylinder walls during running.

On the rear axle of the three-litre Bentley the sliding joint in the casing in front of the axle is lubricated by forcing oil through the hollow propeller-shaft by means of a pump provided in the tool kit. Observe also the flat underslung rear springs.

Above the cylinders is placed an aluminium casting to hold the bearings of the camshaft, which latter is driven by bevel gears and a vertical shaft from the forward end of the crankshaft, a splined joint on the shaft forming a universal joint, and allowing the overhead gear to be removed.

Valve Gear.

Four inclined valves are used in each cylinder, and are returned by concentric springs, those on one side being for the inlet, those on the other for the exhaust, all operated through rocking levers with adjustable tappet pieces. All the inlet passages are linked together by one large port running the length of the cylinder casting, and supplied with gas from a Claudel carburetter.

Water for cooling the cylinders is circulated by a large centrifugal pump driven from a cross-shaft, itself driven by helical toothed gears from the vertical shaft used for the camshaft drive. In the jackets themselves the water is distributed evenly by a rectangular copper pipe. At the other end of the cross-shaft is the magneto, which is bolted and spigoted to the shaft tunnel, but so arranged that it can be rotated slightly upon its axis to time the engine, the ignition advance when running being controlled from the steering wheel.

The lubrication system is a feature of the engine, since no oil is carried in the sump, there being

Gear box and clutch of the Bentley chassis. In front of the casing of the propeller-shaft joint is a pulley for the lighting dynamo belt. The beam shown on the cross-member in front of the gear box supports the nose of the box on the bolt in the centre.

Valve gear details of the Bentley. The hollow camshaft feeds oil to the bearings, and twin inlet and exhaust valves are fitted. Detachable hardened steel tappets are provided, and an oil way cut in the rockers.

two oil pumps in casings one above the other, driven by a continuation of the vertical shaft driving the camshaft. The scavenger pump takes all oil from the engine base and delivers it to an oil tank on the dashboard. The pressure pump draws from this tank and delivers, through a pressure-regulating valve, to all the crankshaft bearings and to the big ends, as well as to the rear overhead camshaft bush. Once oil has been forced to the latter, holes drilled in certain positions along the shaft and on the leading face of each cam supply the camshaft bushes and rocking lever gear, the surplus draining back *via* the breathers through short pipes provided both at the front and at the back of the engine. Continuing along the hollow camshaft, oil is led to the bushes and gears of the vertical driving shaft at the front of the engine.

An Unusual Breather.

No fewer than four breather pipes are fitted on the right-hand side of the crank case, these pipes being coupled together in pairs to form one outlet for each pair, whereby the air is in a state of balance at each outlet.

A starting motor has been considered as an actual portion of the engine itself, and is housed in a cylindrical case, forming part of the rear left-hand engine arm.

Left side of the Bentley three-litre engine. The exhaust pipe is of very large diameter, and is carried straight through the silencer and discharges directly to the open air unless the cut-in is used. In the latter case the gases emerge from the pipe into the silencer. The water pump delivers to the centre of the water jacket, and inside the jacket is a copper pipe which distributes the water evenly.

Sectional perspective view of the Three-litre Bentley chassis.

The Three-litre Bentley

Two brackets are riveted to the side members to receive the two rear engine supporting arms, the third point of the suspension being a flange on the nose of the crank case; thick fabric washers are interposed between the engine and the frame.

Clutch and Gear Box.

In the steel flywheel is a very light inverted bare cone clutch, for which the lining of fabric is secured in three sections in a special groove machined in the flywheel ring. Within the clutch centre is a long gunmetal spigot bush, supplied with oil under pressure from the tail bearing of the crank-shaft. Two ball bearings, actuated through a balanced beam, perform the actual work of clutch withdrawal, each ball race touching the clutch centre with equal pressure.

It may be mentioned that the holes for the engine and gear box holding-down bolts are drilled with one jig, so that the alignment is correct when the two units are bolted to the frame; but, to allow for distortion during running, the clutchshaft has a special universal splined joint at each end.

There are four speeds in the gear box, which has the gate quadrant carried free of the frame by an extension of the box itself, the whole unit being supported at three points in a somewhat unusual manner. At the forward end of the gear box there is a large cross-member having a U shaped recess in the centre to receive, but not touch, the end of the gear box, a steel beam bridging the U and taking the weight of the box on a bolt, of which the specially formed head is within the steel housing of the driving-shaft bearings. At the rear two arms on the gear box are bolted to another cross-member.

In the driving-shaft a floating gunmetal bush is employed as a spigot bearing; this is lubricated through holes drilled at the root of the teeth on the constant mesh gear, the action of the gearing forcing a small supply of oil to the bush as the teeth come into mesh. This method of lubrication is continuous, whether the direct drive is in use or not, but, as an additional safeguard, every time that the direct drive dogs are meshed, an extra supply of lubricant is forced through to the spigot bush. At the tail of the driven shaft is a large double-row thrust bearing, having between it and the centre boss of the propeller-shaft forward universal joint a rectangular section coil spring, which acts as an automatically self-adjusting distance piece; this is necessary, because the boss of the universal joint cannot always be in the same position on its taper on any two shafts.

Selected Mechanism.

All the striking rods are locked positively by a rocking fork, as well as by spring-operated balls, which limit the travel of each rod, it being impossible to move any striking rod other than the one

picked up by the selector arm, since the latter has fore and aft extensions, one or other of which always remains between the jaws of the locking fork. To allow the layshaft gears to be adjusted more or less deeply in mesh with the driven-shaft gears, the bearings of the layshaft are held in eccentric housings.

The casing of the large forward universal joint on the propeller-shaft forms an oil bath, the joint pins having cups which collect the lubricant and supply it to the bushes. At the tail of the propeller-shaft another universal joint is used to allow for endwise movement, owing to the fact that the axle swings upon the forward spring shackles of the rear springs.

Two steel pressings welded together form the axle casing, and take a portion of the weight of the car, the remainder being carried on the driving shafts connected to the differential. The bevel pinion casing is bolted to the front of the axle case, and the thrust bearings for this pinion have an adjustment which is accessible without dismantling any part of the axle gear, while the bevels and differential can be withdrawn through the back cover of the casing.

The overhead camshaft bevel-drive casing on the Bentley, showing inspection covers. The magneto bracket swings axially, giving easy timing setting. Observe the camshaft casing drain pipes leading to duplex breathers in crank case.

an angle to the circumference of the sleeve. In each slot is a stationary peg, and, as the sleeve is turned, the pegs cause it to move either upwards or downwards.

Chassis Lubrication.

It may be mentioned that on the water pump gland is the one grease cup on the car, all other portions of the chassis having been provided with oil wells to lubricate the various bearings. Each well can be filled up by the aid of a large pump—carried in the tool kit—and will supply its bearing for a considerable length of time. In the case of the shackles, self-lubricating bushes are fitted. Other points in connection with the Bentley chassis lubrication are that oil can be forced to both universal joints of the clutchshaft through a special orifice on the shaft. The brake pull equalising gear in its cross-tube can be supplied with oil from outside the frame; the rear universal joint is fed through the hollow propeller-shaft, and the steering tie-rod is filled with oil to supply the steering joints.

Thoroughness in Brake Detail.

Both expanding brakes operate in very large ribbed drums on the rear wheel hubs, and both have aluminium shoes in order to dissipate rapidly the heat set up by the friction of the fabric lining upon the drum. The detail work in connection with these brakes is exceptionally thorough, as it is possible to mount the pull-off spring slack, and to give them the required tension after they have been placed in the shoes. Moreover, both the lever and pedal are connected by tension rods to a tube held in self-centring bearings across the frame, and in this tube are two small differential gears, one set concentric with the other, which accurately distribute the load between the shoes in either drum. Self-centring bearings are used to prevent the cross-tube becoming jammed if the frame should distort over bad roads.

In future, front wheel brakes will be fitted to all standard Bentley cars. This system is undoubtedly ideal on a car with very marked acceleration abilities.

The steering gear consists of a worm and worm wheel mounted on duplex ball bearings, adjustment being provided for these bearings by placing in the steering wheel case a sleeve, concentric with the worm shaft, having in it two slots cut at

It is obvious that a great deal of thought has been bestowed upon the design of the chassis, particularly as concerns the detail, and it has been designed, not only with a view to speed—75 m.p.h. with four passengers being guaranteed—but also with due regard to tractability. Apart from excellence of design, the whole appearance of the chassis is very pleasing.

Bodywork.

Arrangements are being made to supply standard two-seater, four-seater, and light sporting saloon bodies. As examples of detail work, the scuttle between the dash and instrument boards opens like a bonnet, allowing access to all the terminals and connections behind the instrument board, while the revolution counter dial has three sets of figures, indicating the r.p.m. of the engine, and the road speed on top and on third gear which that engine speed represents.

Summed up, the Bentley is a car possessing an immense attraction for the many keenly enthusiastic people who desire to possess and use an automobile comparative to ordinary motors as a first-class hunter is to a cab horse. The compact suppleness and repressed fire are there as with the thoroughbred.

On the cross shaft over the propeller-shaft is a differential gear, through which the brakes are correctly compensated when in action. Observe the large drums.

TESTING THE THREE-LITRE BENTLEY.

A Car which Possesses Quite Unusual Characteristics, can Run Slowly on a High Top Gear, and is Very Fast on Full Throttle.

IF ever there was a paradox on four wheels it is the three-litre Bentley. Originally designed and subsequently described quite rightly as a sporting model, it has all the characteristics of that type of car, yet the effect of a trial run is to make one wonder what exactly is the definition of a sporting car.

Many years ago a car which travelled only with difficulty at under 30 m.p.h. on top gear, which was the proud possessor of an inordinately flat spot in the lower part of the carburetter range, which was exceptionally noisy and rather difficult to handle, was considered, when fitted with a light and speedy-looking body, to offer every possibility which the word sport might imply. There may be still cars which, to a lesser extent, are of this type, but t h e i r growing unpopularity is reflected in the sales records of their manufacturers. It is true that a really fast car may be termed a s p o r t i n g machine, and this defines the Bentley very well; but when one considers that it can be driven all day by the average motorist without anyone suspecting its latent speed, and without there being the slightest suggestion that the car is at all difficult to handle, the term "sporting car" becomes almost a misnomer. Indeed, this car can do many things which really are characteristic of the large six-cylinder.

A Trial with a Heavy All-weather Body.

In January, 1920, we described a run on one of the four-seater open cars. The latest car to be tried was greatly handicapped because it had a large and very heavy all-weather body, which, owing to the inclement weather, was closed for the greater part of the run. It was an old car also with many thousand miles to its credit, and one not too well looked after,

```
DATA FOR THE DRIVER.
15.9 h.p., four cylinders, 80 ×
  149 mm. (2,966 c.c.) Tax £16.
Sixteen overhead valves.
Tested weight of complete car
  less passengers 29 cwt. 2 qrs.
  19 lb.
Weight per c.c., 1.1 lb.
Gear ratios: 3.93, 5.3, 6.4 and
  10.4 to 1.
Spiral bevel final drive.
Semi-elliptic springs front and
  rear.
Tyres, 820 × 120 on detachable
  wire wheels.
Wheelbase, 9ft. 9½in.   Track,
  4ft. 4½in.
Fuel consumption, 20-25 m.p.g.
  Tank capacity, 11 gallons.
Chassis price, £1,050.
Chassis described in "The
  Autocar" August 27th, 1921.
```

the little details of the equipment being in that state to which the average motorist sooner or later seems to reduce such things. The body rattled somewhat, and, as a whole, the car was in a condition that one would least expect it to be in considering the character of the machine.

Thoroughly Docile in Thick Traffic.

Through thick traffic, and over wet, greasy roads, the Bentley was piloted out of London without the slightest evidence that it had any abnormal power, and for the most part with top gear in engagement, t h o u g h this gear is 3.93 to 1. Whether the car was moving slowly behind a horse-drawn waggon, threading its way between trams and other traffic, or accelerating, there was no trace of snatch or "judder," the engine picking up smoothly and well. It is possible to hear the v a l v e mechanism as a kind of minor accompaniment, and there was a suspicion that the exhaust was freer than is u s u a l; still the machine was behaving as an ordinary touring car.

Even at that, however, its brake power was brought out to the full, and, though the brakes act on the rear wheel drums only, their effect is very great. so great, in fact, that they are ample for the car's speed; further, there was not the slightest difficulty in stopping and holding the car on the Brooklands test hill at its steepest slope of 1 in 4 with either brake. A little of the car's power could be seen on Robin Hood Hill, where, in response to a movement of the throttle, the speedometer needle climbed rapidly and steadily, and was still moving upwards on the dial when the top of the hill was reached; this hill could be climbed at 40 m.p.h. if one required to do so. On the other hand, it could be climbed without trouble at 20 m.p.h.

Unfortunately a stiff cross-wind proved to be an obstacle at Brooklands, considerably increasing the resistance imposed by the body. This notwithstanding, the car was timed over a mile at a speed of 69.23 m.p.h., and obviously would have travelled at over 70 m.p.h. had the conditions been more favourable. The weight in conjunction with a comparatively high first gear ratio reduced the speed up the test-hill, the car averaging 13.35 m.p.h. thereon from a standing start.

Ultimate Speed on Indirect Gears.

Following these tests, the Bentley was taken to the straight to ascertain the time in which it was possible to accelerate from 10 to 30 m.p.h. on the various gears, and the result was extraordinarily interesting. On second, the change in speed was accomplished in 9s., on third in $11\frac{2}{5}$s., which, remembering the comparatively high gear ratio, is better than many cars for which accelera-

the gate, which possibly was due to the box being over-filled in the first instance. On the subsequent road run over our standard course, the car could be transformed into just what its driver chose to make it; at will it was a powerful, ordinary touring car, or very nearly a racing car, if the low gear was engaged early. Newlands Corner, for example, was climbed well on third. On White Downs, a nasty gradient

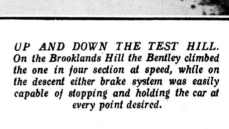

UP AND DOWN THE TEST HILL.
On the Brooklands Hill the Bentley climbed the one in four section at speed, while on the descent either brake system was easily capable of stopping and holding the car at every point desired.

on a lane really too narrow for so large a car, especially in bad weather, there happened a curious thing. The rear wheels, newly shod with a type of tyre which is not standard for the chassis, alternately slipped and gripped. In the process, a quite nasty " judder " was set up through the chassis, resulting in the machine losing almost all its way and making a slow climb on first. This same hill also brought out another point; that all cars of this type should have some form of water temperature control. As it was, the radiator was cowled with a special hood, and this hood, though efficient enough for ordinary running, was not suitable for fast hill-climbing, with the result that the water boiled ere the summit was reached. Had the hood been off, as it should have been, nothing untoward, as we subsequently proved on other steep hills, would have occurred.

tion is a claimed feature. It is possible to turn the car at full lock with the engine running slowly on top gear, which, by itself, is good evidence of flexibility. The ultimate speed of the car on each gear is further interesting evidence, as on first it is 34, on second 50, and on third 60 m.p.h., emphasising what a very useful second gear ratio this car possesses, and suggesting, as indeed it seems to be, that the third speed ratio is rather near to the top.

The only untoward matter in this series of exceptionally high engine speed tests was that the air release from the gear box allowed oil to be blown up through

A Fast Climb.

Box Hill brought out the sporting possibilities of the car, as it is perfectly within the driver's power to attain 40 m.p.h. over the straight stretches, and to take the car round corners quite smoothly with absolute certainty. For this special fast work, however, second speed must be engaged actually before the climb begins at all, with a touch of third and a brief use of first as occasion demands; in other words, the engine revolutions must be kept as high as possible. In such conditions the car seems to fly, developing a most astonishing amount of life and power. On this hill there was not the slightest trace of boiling, since the cowl had been removed, nor was there any during a later climb up Pebblecombe, which again was taken at high speed, partly on third, for the remainder of the hill on second, and with a little of the same curious wheel slip that had been noticed on White Downs.

At this point in the journey the all-weather body top was lowered, and the absence of the minor rattles, inseparable, it would seem, from an old body, greatly ennanced the attraction of the car. The steering is very nearly perfect, the more so in that this car is one of the very few having a thin-rimmed steering wheel of considerable diameter. The caster action of the stub axles straightens the car well after a corner, and this steering, combined with springs which become more comfortable with the increase in road speed,

materially assists in giving that feeling of the car being held fast to the road beyond possibility of deviation except at the driver's will.

So much for the Bentley as a sporting machine. On the run back to town it was tested as an ordinary car once more, and it was possible to drive from Kingston through Hammersmith Broadway to Hyde Park Corner, Marble Arch, down Oxford Street to Baker Street without using, or needing to use, any other gear than top. The car completely changes its character in these circumstances. It becomes quiet, with only a deep exhaust note just audible. There is no suggestion that the carburetter has an unusually large choke tube, and there is no difficulty in handling the machine. With a car so fascinating to drive as this, criticism is difficult, since minor defects pale to insignificance beside the many good points of the chassis. We would, however, suggest three things; that the brake pedal be allowed a greater range of motion, that thermostat control for the radiator is necessary, and that a clutch stop be fitted. The detail work is good, as indeed it should be, considering that the price of the chassis is £1,050.

AN UNUSUAL TEST BODY. It is somewhat rare to attempt fast climbs up the Brooklands Hill with a car fitted with a heavy all-weather body, but the added weight rendered the test the more interesting. Observe the ribbed oil sump on the Bentley, which is leaving the paddock at Brooklands to attack the hill.

THE AUTOCAR, November 10th, 1922.

Bentley.
Country of Origin: England.

BENTLEY MOTORS, LTD., 3, HANOVER COURT, W.1. (Stand 178, White City.)

Specification: 15.9 h.p., four cylinders, 80×149 mm. (2,996 c.c.), tax £16, pump and splash lubrication, inverted cone clutch, dual M-L magneto ignition, Smith carburetter, four speeds, separate gear box, spiral bevel drive, half-elliptic front and rear springs, 820×120 mm. tyres on wire wheels, Smith electric lighting and starting. Price: Chassis, £1,050; sporting four-seater, £1,295.

Features: This well-known chassis is made in three types, the "Tourist Trophy," the Standard, and the long wheel-base models. All are guaranteed to run 25 m.p.g. at 30 m.p.h., and their maximum speeds are 90 m.p.h., 80 m.p.h.,

and 75 m.p.h. respectively. Each chassis is designed on high efficiency lines, and embodies all the refinements found on racing cars. As well as being of sturdy construction, the chassis strikes a distinctly artistic note in all its details, and the Bentley is a very fine example of British automobile construction. Amongst the improvements found in the design is the new dynamo, which runs at camshaft speed and is connected to the overhead shaft by a double-fabric coupling. The position simplifies the wiring to the instrument board in a noticeable manner,

and the braking action of the dynamo helps to silence the valve gear. Dual magneto ignition is adopted, the magneto distributers being arranged accessibly in front of the engine. Great care has been paid to the question of lubrication, the engine being provided with a double sump, one portion of which acts as an air-cooled oil reservoir. There is only one lubricator on the whole chassis, all parts other than the water pump are lubricated internally through hollowed portions, which are so designed as to act as reservoirs.

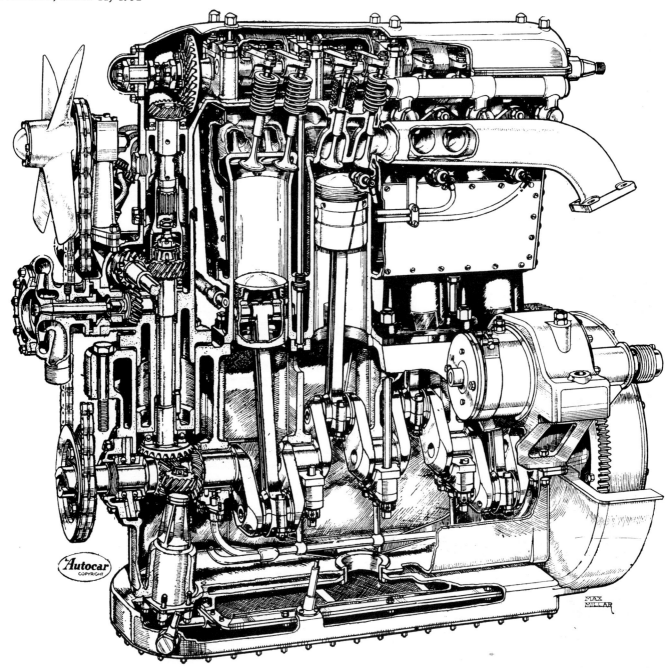

Four valves per cylinder, non-detachable cylinder heads, a fully machined five-bearing crankshaft, and shaft and gear drive to camshaft, magneto and water pump are features of the famous engine.

80 × 149 mm...

...BUT THE 3-LITRE FOUR-CYLINDER BENTLEY WAS FAMOUS FOR OTHER THINGS THAN ITS LENGTHY STROKE

by Max Millar

IN 1919, 33 years ago, first announcement appeared in *The Autocar* of a new 3-litre sports chassis designed by W. O. Bentley. This chassis, which was exhibited at Olympia and came into production in 1921, immediately created great interest on account of its qualities and general features, and because W. O. Bentley had announced that the car was built for speed combined with great reliability; and the Bentley did, in fact, achieve a supremacy in popularity in the fast car field after World War I in much the same way as one or two outstanding makes have done since the last war.

Without any question Bentley, with H. T. Burgess, chief designer, and H. Varley, chief of the drawing office, showed a mastery of form and detail, and his chassis are, to this day, outstanding examples of classic design. Many records stood to its credit, many of the 3-litre models (which, after all, went out of production in the late 'twenties) are in the hands of owners today, as can be verified by the records of the Bentley Drivers' Club.

The 3-litre Bentley power unit, an engine built for a thoroughbred sports chassis, has always been a favourite with me because of its clean proportions, handsome appearance, straightforward design and absence of complication. The unit was designed specifically to have the characteristics of a racing engine, but was detuned to give a high degree of reliability with economy in fuel consumption, yet there was no complication in the engine which would make maintenance difficult for ordinary owners.

Bore and stroke are 80 mm and 149 mm (capacity 2,966 c.c.), and in the earlier models the compression ratio was as low as 4.3 to 1; the power output was around 70 b.h.p. at 3,500 r.p.m.

In the various models, long- and short-chassis, from 1922 up to 1927-28, the compression ratios were gradually increased in stages up to 6.5 to 1, when 88 b.h.p. was developed at 3,500 r.p.m., while 100 b.h.p. was achieved in an experimental engine. From time to time modifications were made to pistons, connecting rods, water pumps, valve rockers and casings, oil pumps and sumps, but no radical change was made to the basic elements of the engine.

At the end of World War I, when the Bentley design team produced their first engine, the long-stroke, high-efficiency unit with multiple inlet and exhaust valves was the fashion in design, and the Bentley incorporated these features from the outset. The long stroke and a long connecting rod (295 mm, or approximately 11½in between centres) combined to produce an extraordinarily tall engine nearly three feet high, but beautifully proportioned. Those connecting rods,

Twin S.U. carburettors and the induction system on the 3-litre Bentley. The engine almost filled the bonnet of a Bentley chassis, and was superbly finished externally.

machined all over, each weighed 1lb 15oz complete, while the pistons varied from 1lb 1½oz (with rings and gudgeon pin) in the low-compression version to 1lb 7oz for the high-compression type. The slender rods stood up well to hard and sustained running, and such fractures as occurred were usually the result of overweight pistons being fitted.

The twin exhaust and twin inlet valves (37mm diameter) were adopted to enlarge the seating area and cooling surface of the valves and to increase power and reliability, with at least 20,000 miles between overhauls. The valves are set at an inclusive angle of 30 degrees, the inlet ports being siamesed and the exhausts each independently ported to the manifolds. Cylinder barrels, heads and ports are cast iron in one piece, but the casting is flanked on all four sides with detachable aluminium cover plates held by small screws. The jacketing is ample everywhere, and water flow past the cylinder heads and porting is accelerated vertically by positive flow streams in certain models from internal duct pipes in the cylinder jacket leading from the water pump. Out-take of water is from points opposite each pair of exhaust valves to an external gallery pipe and thence to the radiator.

Ahead of Their Time

The crankshaft is machined and polished all over and bored and drilled for normal pressure lubrication, the weight being 34lb. The five main bearings are normal in design, but the three centre bearing caps are anchored to the cylinder block by long bolts—this and other features in the engine, including the positive circulation of water in the cylinder jacket, mark the Bentley design team as being far ahead of contemporary design. There were several variations in the arrangement of the sump and oil pump, and that shown in my drawing and in other details such as valve rockers, pistons and water pump, makes a composite engine which may well differ from other examples.

A vertical drive with bevel gears at the front end of the power unit operates the overhead camshaft through a splined shaft and telescopic casing which permits the extension entailed by the upward expansion under heat of the cylinder block. Magnetos (for dual ignition) and water pump are operated by skew gears from the vertical drive. The camshaft has three cams for each set of valves, two operating the inlet valves through a pair of rockers, and the third opening and closing the exhaust valves through a

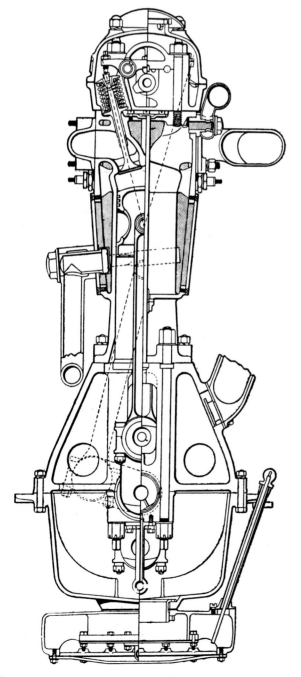

The tall power unit with its long stroke and multiple overhead valves is well demonstrated in this section. The detachable cylinder block and arrangement of the cylinder head were characteristic of racing engine design in the 1920 period. Out-take of water from the heads was through a duct close to each pair of exhaust ports.

The transversely mounted magnetos, driven by a cross shaft from the vertical shaft drive to the camshaft, are ideally accessible for maintenance, while on the crankcase are mounted the pressure oil filter, oil filler and starter motor in accessible positions.

single forked rocker. In the early models steel rockers were used, but later these were superseded by duralumin components. The dynamo, located on the bulkhead, is driven through fabric universal joints from the tail of the camshaft, while the starting motor is held in the exceptionally strong left-side engine supporting arm in an accessible position.

A single Smith five-jet carburettor was fitted to the early engines, later to be superseded by twin S.U.s. On the crankcase left side is the external high pressure oil filter, and an automatic belt tensioner is fitted when a fan is used on the engine for town work.

The success of the 3-litre in competition needs little comment, many of its exploits being classics in racing history. As early as 1922, only three years after W. O. Bentley's first inception of the car, the 3-litre covered 2,083 miles in the Double-Twelve-hour race at Brooklands at an average speed of 86.79 m.p.h.—a wonderful feat of endurance. Then, in 1926, at Montlhéry, the 24-hour record was broken at 95.03 m.p.h.—another feat of speed and reliability. In the same year, the world's record for 2,000 kilometres was taken at 100.23 m.p.h., and also the twelve-hour record at 100.96 m.p.h. "Sammy" Davis' and Dr. J. D. Benjafield's heroic performance in the 1927 Le Mans will also be remembered.

He Was Sure

Although "W. O." supplied his various standard chassis with definite limitations as to the all-up weight (bodywork and extras), he nevertheless had no hesitation in issuing a five-year guarantee with each chassis from 1921 onwards. The standard 3-litre speed model was capable of well over 85 m.p.h. and could be tuned to reach 100 m.p.h. The same car could crawl at 8 m.p.h. on top gear, and the advertised fuel consumption at 30 m.p.h. was 25 m.p.g.

As mentioned before, many of these fine cars are still regularly used and maintained by owners. One of which I have intimate knowledge, a 1924 short-chassis model, has covered over 100,000 miles and, although it has not been overhauled or tuned recently, it can reach 70 m.p.h. on third gear and do well in excess of 85 m.p.h. on top. The petrol consumption is 22 m.p.g. at 40 miles per hour and 17-18 for maximum performance, while oil consumption is virtually nil. These figures also approximate to those relating to another 3-litre owned by a friend and used regularly.

From figures supplied by the Bentley Drivers' Club, the 3-litre engine at 3,500 r.p.m. developed 70.72, 80.82 and 86.88 b.h.p. for the Standard, Speed and Le Mans models respectively.

I am indebted to W. O. Bentley, R. A. ("Nobby") Clarke and L. G. McKenzie for their assistance in gathering much interesting information about the engine.

Genesis

"S.C.H.D." writes: The beginnings of all this were fascinating. "W.O." and I were engaged with certain aircraft engines which functioned so oddly, being rotary, that they were a headache in themselves. When the war ended it was obvious that "W.O." was up to something, though what it was was difficult to determine, he being less talkative than a clam, while Burgess in the throes of design was security-minded to a degree never before equalled.

But when the scheme was fully disclosed, and the drawings were exhibited, what struck me most was that the pair had planned something as near a racing car as no matter; this was daring, to say the least of it, the market being what it was. Also, it seemed odd that Burgess, whose own idea of a new car I had seen, had been so completely converted to "W.O.'s" ideas.

When the moment came to test the new machine "W.O." and I had a great day, the car being photographed well on the right of the road in scenery as like that of France as possible because of the illegal speeds we wanted to mention. The impression then formed remains today. The car had unusual character. When you moved a control, whatever it was connected to moved at once, not as though there was a spring connection in between, and you could put the machine exactly where you wanted on corners. And when we came to race the first impression was abundantly confirmed, so much so that I can still vividly remember the *pleasure* of driving the 3-litre, and never felt quite the same regard for some of the later, larger engines—except perhaps the six. How to analyse the matter is difficult, but that engine seemed more human (or perhaps one should say more animal) than any other, more companionable on runs of hour after hour.

Since then there have been faster cars and fiercer cars, and very good they have been, but they do not supplant the engine I had seen created. And more of its success than most people believe was owed to the inborn stubborn determination of "W.O." to achieve what he thought was right.

F.C. Clement (Bentley)
effecting adjustments
at the pits.

Le Mans 1923

FINAL ORDER OF CARS, THE DRIVERS,

MILEAGE AND AVERAGE SPEEDS

		Miles.	Average in m.p.h.
1. Chenard-Walcker 3-litre (Lagache and Leonard)	....	1372.5	57.1
2. Chenard-Walcker 3-litre (Bachmann and Dauvergne)	....	1327	55.3
3. Bignan 2-litre (de Tornaco and Gros)	....	1284	53.5
4. Bentley 3-litre (Duff and Clement)	....	1198.5	49.9
4. Bignan 2-litre (de Marne and Martin)	....	1198.5	49.9
6. Excelsior (Dils and Caerels)	....	1188	49.5
7. Chenard-Walcker 3-litre (Bachmann and Glazmann)	....	1177	49.0
8. Lorraine-Dietrich (de Courcelles and Rossignol)	....	1157.6	48.2
9. Excelsior (Lecureuil and Flaud)	....	1134.5	47.3
10. Bugatti 1½-litre (de Pourtales and de la Rochefoucauld)	....	1113	46.3

THE AUTOCAR, September 21st, 1923.

FRONT WHEEL BRAKES FOR BENTLEY CARS.

Next Year's Models to Have all Four Brakes Actuated by the Pedal and Additional Shoes for the Lever.

IT is extremely significant that the Bentley car will in future have four-wheel brakes, because this chassis is provided already with rear brakes which are exceptionally powerful It will be remembered that when the Bentley car first was built a very great deal of time and attention was given to the brake gear, chiefly with the object of making sure that there should be no spring between the lever or pedal and the brake cam, so that the shoes moved at once, and were sensitive when applied.

Exactly the same scheme has been followed out for the front wheel brakes, which have now been added, and few mechanisms at present on the market afford such evidence of careful forethought. The brake pedal is of normal length, additional leverage not being required because mechanism has been adopted which ensures that the eight brake shoes are applied and withdrawn quite evenly, nor is there any servo mechanism, since none has been found necessary.

Method of Operation.

From the brake shoe a tension rod is taken to a long lever connected to a cross tube of substantial section and carried in spherical bearings so that it shall be freed from stresses caused by any slight frame distortion. This tension rod has on it the single adjustment which suffices for all four sets of shoes, a point of considerable benefit. The cross tube operates rods actuating the brake shoes through the medium of compensating bars which are encased and are backed by a friction grip, so that

Front wheel brakes are now standard on the Bentley. The rod from frame to brake cam has one sliding and one universal joint.

the bars only move to the extent necessary for compensation, but are solid when released, so that the brake shoes are positively withdrawn. Certain intermediary levers are necessary to convert a push into a pull on the rods connected to the cams, but the whole mechanism is perfectly simple and straightforward.

The small levers used in various parts of the actuation are of exceptionally strong section allowing no whip, and the rod that passes from the bracket on the frame to the cam on the front wheel drums has not only a sliding joint of substantial cross section, but a universal joint as well. Then the dust cover which takes the torque of the brake shoes is so designed that the fulcrum pin of the brake shoes is not overhung, and there is elaborate provision against the escape of oil either from the hubs or from the inclined pivots. Shock absorbers are part of the Bentley standard equipment, the front springs are unaltered, but the front axle section has been increased considerably in size in order to give it the necessary strength to withstand the strain.

Fabric Brake Linings Adopted.

It will be remembered that the Bentley brake shoes were of aluminium with detachable steel ends where the cam operates the shoe, and with cast iron lining. Fabric now has replaced the cast iron, and it may be mentioned that the pull off springs can be fitted slack and afterwards brought to the required tension, thus avoiding trouble in the fitting. An additional set of shoes is operated by the hand lever.

We were able to test these brakes, and can say that no better or more effective brakes have been tried on any of the cars which we have tested. Not only is their stopping power enormous if they are used purposely in a severe manner, but the car does not deviate from the straight line even when pulled up fiercely on loose road metal. On a slippery surface the car slides only for a very short distance when the brakes are applied with full power. In no case was the steering affected, and the brake power was as great when reversing as when going forward. Given normal handling, the mechanism is extremely efficient, and easily handled, and the brakes will last probably for a year without adjustment, or, at all events, with the very minimum of adjustment even if the mileage during that time is great.

A demonstration of stability and brake power. The Bentley with four-wheel brakes pulling up at speed on loose road metal.

THE AUTOCAR, November 16th, 1923.

BENTLEY FOUR-WHEEL BRAKES TESTED.

Instructive Demonstration of Stopping Power; Effect on Steering Negligible.

A FEW weeks ago we suggested that the R.A.C. should organise a test of vehicles fitted with four-wheel brakes, with a view to ascertaining the precise effect of such brakes in retarding the movement of the vehicle on which they are installed. It is satisfactory to observe that Mr. W. O. Bentley, the designer of the famous car which bears his name, recently submitted for test by the R.A.C. a three-litre Bentley of standard pattern.

The demonstration of the holding power of the brakes was held on Brooklands track, the concrete surface being dry at the time. The 820 × 120 mm. tyres had all-rubber treads, with an indented pattern. Not only was the demonstration designed to show the retarding effect of the brakes; it was also intended to prove whether or not the application of the front-wheel brakes had any appreciable effect on the steering.

A number of tests were carried out at various speeds, in the first instance with four passengers and in the second with two passengers in the car. In each case brakes on all four wheels were applied simultaneously, and the rear wheels were locked, but the front wheels continued to rotate. The following table shows the results obtained, but it would have been still more instructive had comparative figures been secured showing the stopping distances when only the rear-wheel brakes were used. We hope that in any further demonstration this point will be borne in mind. At the various speeds the results achieved were as tabulated below :—

Speed.	Stopping Distances.	
	With *four* passengers (laden weight, 4,036 lb.).	With *two* passengers (laden weight, 3,700 lb.).
10 m.p.h.	3 ft. 6 in.	4 ft. 3 in.
20 „	19 „ 9 „	22 „ 0 „
30 „	46 „ 0 „	42 „ 0 „
40 „	86 „ 6 „	91 „ 0 „*
50 „	144 „ 9 „	

The distance in this test could not be recorded, owing to the failure of the apparatus used to record the time of the application of the brakes.
The weight of the two extra passengers was almost wholly over the back axle.

A test was also conducted in which the brakes were applied when the car was being driven in a circle of 80ft. diameter at a speed of 19-20 m.p.h. and with four passengers on board. In this experiment the vehicle was brought to rest in 14ft., while with two passengers carried the distance was reduced to 12ft. 9in. The steering did not appear to be affected. Subsequently, the action of the brakes was demonstrated on the Brooklands test hill, and it was found that the vehicle could be brought to rest and so held in both directions on the 1 in 4 section.

It should be noted that throughout the tests only the pedal-applied brakes on all four wheels were brought into action, and no use was made of the separate rear wheel shoes applied by the hand lever.

Le Mans 1924

FINAL RESULTS OF THE 24-HOURS RACE.

Cars and Drivers.	Distance. Miles.
1. Bentley (2,995 c.c.), Duff, Clement	1,290¼
2. Lorraine-Dietrich (3,446 c.c.), Stoffel, Brisson	1,280
3. Lorraine-Dietrich (3,446 c.c.), De Courcelles, Rossignol	1,274
4. Chenard-Walcker (1,973 c.c.), Pisart, Chavée	1,192
5. Chenard-Walcker (1,973 c.c.), Dauvergne, Manso	1,165
6. Rolland-Pilain (1,992 c.c.), Delalande, Guignard	1,145
7. Brasier (2,092 c.c.), Verpault, Delabarre	1,138
8. Brasier (2,092 c.c.), Migeot, Jouguet	1,125
9. Rolland-Pilain (1,992 c.c.) Site, Tremel	1,11?
10. Bignan (1,979 c.c.), De Tornaco, Barthélémy	1,09?
11. Aries (1,085 c.c.), Gabriel, Lapierre	97?
12. S.A.R.A. (1,099 c.c.), Marandet, Piazzoli.............	958
13. Aries (1,085 c.c.), Louis Rigal, Delano	957
14. Amilcar (1,004 c.c.), Boutmy, Marcadanti............	937

The smile of victory. J. F. Duff and F. C. Clement at the conclusion of the long and arduous test through which they piloted the Bentley to victory.

BRITAIN WINS BY TEN MILES.

Magnificent Victory for the Solitary 3-Litre Bentley Over Forty French Rivals at Le Mans in the Rudge-Whitworth Twenty-four Hours Race.

Getting away at the commencement of the race. The massed start was employed, competitors being lined up in pairs.

F.C. Clement rounding the acute corner at Pontlieue during his spell of driving on the winning Bentley.

A NEW SIX-CYLINDER BENTLEY.

Chassis of Ingenious Design, with a Six-and-a-half Litre Engine, to be Manufactured in Addition to the Well-known Four-cylinder Model.

On the new six-cylinder Bentley, a radiator differing considerably from that on the four-cylinder model is adopted.

<table>
<tr><td colspan="2" align="center">SPECIFICATION.</td></tr>
<tr><td>ENGINE: Six cylinders, 100 × 140 mm. (6,597 c.c.). Twenty-four overhead valves, overhead camshaft with connecting rod drive, twin magneto ignition. Tax £38.
SPRINGING: Half-elliptic springs.</td><td>TRANSMISSION: Four-speed and reverse gear box, separate from engine.
WHEELS: Detachable wire wheels with 33 × 6·75in. tyres.
BRAKES: On all four wheels.</td></tr>
</table>

THE history of Bentley Motors, Ltd., is something of a triumph for the men responsible for the design and manufacture of the cars. Few firms have, in so short a time, achieved a fame not only national but international, and it is rare, indeed, that the first car built proves so eminently satisfactory and is subject to so little modification.

The four-cylinder three-litre was built primarily as a sports model. In course of time it has attained a considerable vogue as a fast and reliable touring car with an almost endless life, the original sports model being retained as a separate type of chassis, and it will interest all owners and prospective owners of the three-litre models to know that this chassis will be continued absolutely unaltered, and is not in any way superseded by the new six-cylinder.

The latter model, of which we are now able to give the first description, has been brought out because the firm has experienced a very great demand for a chassis which will take the heavy and luxurious type of closed body, and carry it in silence with a great degree of flexibility on top gear, and yet prove really fast when it is a question of maintaining a high average speed for long distances.

Such a demand has to be met by a larger engine, and obviously six cylinders are called for. Accordingly, it was decided finally that 6,597 c.c. would give ample reserve of power, the requisite speed, and would not prove too costly to run and maintain.

The new engine is extremely interesting. The crankshaft, which is remarkably sturdy, has eight bearings, a damper at the forward end, and the camshaft drive at the rear. It is the camshaft drive which at once attracts attention, not only because it is in a tunnel which materially increases the length of the engine, and therefore its imposing appearance, but because convention has been disregarded and the normal train of gears discarded in favour of three connecting rods. From the crankshaft a gear wheel drives another fabric gear which, in its turn, drives a small three-throw crankshaft, of which each crank pin is provided with the equivalent of a small big-end bearing. On the tail end of the camshaft is a similar three-throw crankshaft, also provided with three big-end bearings, and the two sets of bearings are each connected by a pair of stout tubes. The result is that the drive is transmitted regularly and evenly to the camshaft at half engine speed, and the only point where there might be noise is the reduction gearing.

The drive, however, is not so simple and easy to arrange as it sounds, and it took a long period of steady experiment before certain difficulties could be overcome. It is necessary, for example, to allow for any differences in the distance between the camshaft and crankshaft centres, to permit the gear wheels to be meshed more or less deeply and to allow for the expansion of the engine when heated. This

The overall length of the engine is appreciably increased by the vertical tunnel housing the camshaft drive.

has been done most ingeniously by holding the upper bearing for each of the pair of rods to the rods between powerful coil springs which balance each other. If the bearing on the camshaft has to move upwards slightly, it compresses two springs by the amount by which the other two springs are released. At the same time the springs allow a cushioning effect in the drive. Incidentally, the bearings for the rods are of aluminium, and the small crankshafts are hardened.

Damping Devices and Adjustments.

The camshaft itself drives the water pump at one end, the dynamo through fabric joints at the other, so that the irregularities set up by the action of the valves are damped out. Moreover, the cross-shaft driven from the camshaft and driving at each end a magneto, has a miniature plate clutch damping device as well. The cams can be set accurately by means of a vernier, which device also is employed for the two magnetos. Duralumin rocking levers, with hardened ends, actuate the valves from the cams with an interposed adjustment, there being two inlets and two exhaust valves to each cylinder, each valve having two springs.

Oil is supplied to all bearings under pressure from a gear pump, the lubricant passing through a filter on the delivery side, and the oil pipes leading to the underside of each main bearing, then travelling through the crank webs to the big end. Each crank pin being hollow, aluminium blocks are fixed within the crank pin to carry the oil passage, and avoid filling the entire crank pin with lubricant. Oil is forced also to the camshaft, whence it is sprayed on to the rocking levers, and finally fed through a pipe to small troughs on the top of the bearings for the connecting rods of the camshaft drive.

One of the three-throw crankshafts on which the connecting rods driving the camshaft are mounted.

Such oil as drains back to the crank case through the tunnel at the rear assists to lubricate the ball bearings on the two-to-one shaft, but, to avoid accumulation of lubricant in the valve chambers, drain pipes are led down at frequent intervals to the crank case.

Water Flow Proportioned.

Each cylinder is surrounded with water, and is in one piece with its head, while the water surrounds also the head and exhaust ports. Circulation is maintained by the centrifugal pump, and the cool water returning from the radiator is proportioned through the cylinder jackets by means of a copper tube with varying orifices which direct the water at the exhaust ports. A thermostat governs the water temperature by short-circuiting the

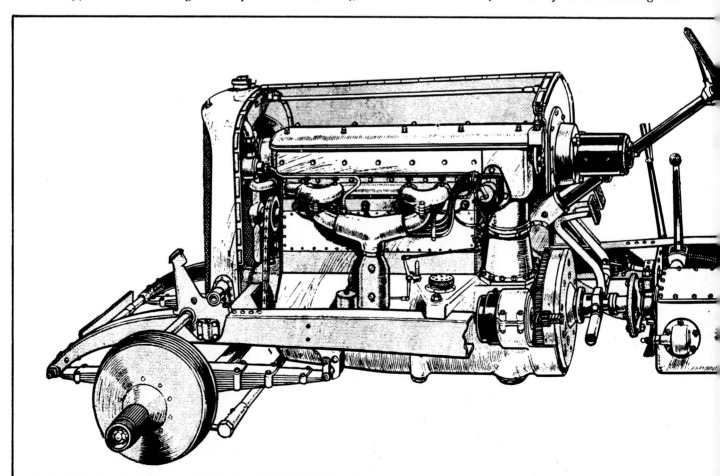

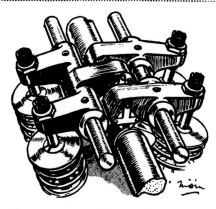

The arrangement of the duralumin rockers operating four valves per cylinder through three cams. Hardened steel cylinders, rigidly fixed in the rocker ends, are in direct contact with the cams.

Clutch plate and components of flexible mounting of clutch shaft.

The Bentley piston has a split skirt which is separated from the head below the ring slots by an annular slit, and is only attached to the crown by the gudgeon pin bosses.

radiator, but keeping the water flow speed and maintaining the supply to the jacket round the inlet pipe. B.H.B. pistons are used, the pistons having the head braced to the gudgeon pin bosses and the skirt divided from top to bottom.

Engine Insulated from Frame.

Steel connecting rods of H section having the white metal running direct in the big-ends, and floating gudgeon pins, are used. It is curious that the first inlet pipe of a series of experimental designs proved the most efficient with the employment of a single carburetter, a pipe of aluminium so contrived that the mixture passage to each port is of equal length. The exhaust manifolds are on the opposite side of the cylinder block.

Another interesting point is that the engine is mounted with its nose on a fabric pad, and, through the two rear arms, on stout blocks of rubber, and is, therefore, insulated from the frame entirely, as the rubber allows a slight vertical, as well as a horizontal, movement. As before, the plugs, of which there are twelve, all firing in pairs, are at the sides of the head. The magnetos can be advanced or retarded by being moved slightly on their spigot mountings.

Improved Clutch Mechanism.

An entirely new type of clutch has been adopted. The clutch fork has a beam equaliser as before, but, in place of rollers, two small links give a straight push at the clutch collar, which in turn operates long levers, withdrawing one of the driving discs from the fabric-faced driven disc. The levers can be adjusted so that each bears an equal amount of the load. The driven disc is

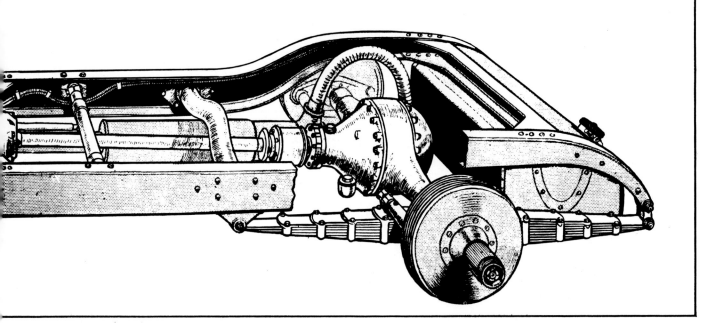

In this chassis drawing the disposition of the six-cylinder overhead valve engine, separate gear box, open propeller-shaft drive to the spiral bevel rear axle, and long, flat, semi-elliptic springs are plainly shown.

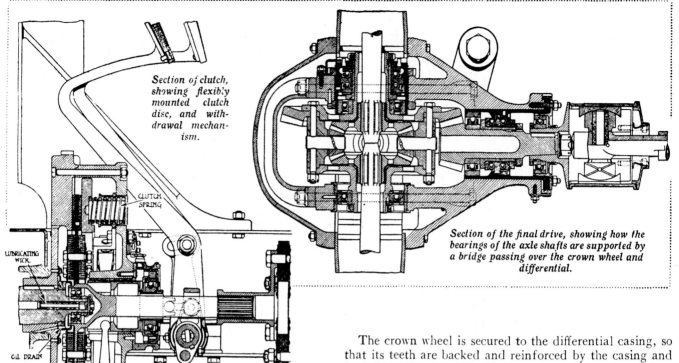

Section of clutch, showing flexibly mounted clutch disc, and withdrawal mechanism.

CLUTCH SPRING

LUBRICATING WICK

OIL DRAIN

FABRIC JOINTS

BALANCE GEAR

CLUTCH ADJUSTMENT

Section of the final drive, showing how the bearings of the axle shafts are supported by a bridge passing over the crown wheel and differential.

of duralumin with a fabric face each side to avoid over-heating the disc if the clutch slips. The duralumin is bolted to the clutch shaft through two fabric star-shaped pieces, the disc itself being centred on the clutch shaft in such a manner that part of the drive can be taken direct on the disc as well as through the fabric, and yet the disc allowed a certain freedom of movement. Six power-ful coil springs grip the discs. Even the self-aligning spigot ball race has a wick lubricator, and, should any oil escape into the clutch, it is caught in gutters and transferred outside.

Between clutch and gear box is a large fabric joint, the endwise movement of the clutch shaft being taken by splines. The gear box itself is slung from cross-members of the frame, and resembles that of the three-litre chassis, though it differs in detail. From the gear box the drive is transmitted through two universal joints, of which one is allowed to slide, to the rear axle, which is of entirely new design. The same double banjo casing is employed, but the bevel pinion journal ball bearings are backed by a double row ball thrust unit which can be ad-justed and then put into place very easily, so that it is impos-

The two-to-one reduction gear and triple connecting rod drive to the camshaft are located at the rear of the crank-shaft—a distinctly unusual feature of design

sible for anyone to loosen the adjustment too much, and therefore to allow the balls to damage the cage under the influence of centrifugal force. The bevel pinion bearings are, however, in a sleeve, so that the bevel pinion can be moved in a fore-and-aft direction by undoing the nuts on certain studs and turning one big nut one way or the other.

The crown wheel is secured to the differential casing, so that its teeth are backed and reinforced by the casing and its bolts. On each side are large ball races, the housings for which are part of the assembly which holds the bevel pinion. Here, also, is an ingenious point of design, as the two ball housings are stiffly braced together by an arched member passing from one to the other, and the bolts holding the housing caps pass right through, and so reinforce the housing. The same type of double ball thrust race is provided for the crown wheel, and a most ingenious form of ad-justment can be used to mesh the crown wheel more or less deeply with the pinion, the bearing on the side of the differential case which does not take the thrust being free to slide. Four differential pinions have been adopted, and the spider arms are held by bolts which pass right through the casing, each arm being hollow so that it may receive lubricant for the pinion bearings under centrifugal force, and a very clever floating bush, drilled to retain oil, is used for the bevels of the differential.

Direct Brake Operation.

As the axle is fully floating, the driv-ing shafts can be detached, and are made to butt against each other in the centre. The system of four wheel brake operation is practically the same as that of the three-litre, direct operated with no servo, but the extension shaft from the frame to the cams of the front wheels slides in a sub-stantial bearing on either side of the operating arm which is itself inside, not outside, the frame.

Finally, the steering gear has been redesigned purposely to take low pressure tyres, the worm having more than the usual number of teeth engaged with the segment of the worm wheel which, if complete, would be enormous, so that the tooth load is very low. The whole gear casing is oil-tight, as the gear itself is run in relatively thin oil which should be filled up to a certain level through a big filler. The sliding sleeve type of bearing adjustment is retained, and the column is braced by an external casing, the whole being secured to the frame of the car. A mixture control and a slightly different form of control housing with a horn switch in the middle have been adopted.

The frame is immense, deeper in section, and with much wider flanges, as well as with an additional tubular cross-member, while the rear springs have auxiliary upper leaves, each clipped at the end to the main leaves.

Altogether, a very clever design, and a car which should hold its own in any country, either as an example of British manufacture or on performance. Preliminary trials extending over many thousand miles in this country and in France have proved that the first cars of the type are satisfactory. Chassis of either 11ft. or 12ft. wheelbase will be available.

Le Mans 1925

Twenty Cars out of Forty-nine Starters Finish an Arduous Contest. Minor Troubles Dog British Competitors, but 3-litre Sunbeam Secures Second Place to the 3½-litre Lorraine-Dietrich.

Having relied upon the single-handed efforts of Duff and Clement in the 1923 and 1924 Le Mans races, in which they finished fourth and first respectively, the works entered two cars for the 1925 race for Duff and Clement, and for Kensington-Moir and Benjafield. During the opening laps, at first with the hoods up, Moir and Segrave's Sunbeam battled for the lead, Moir eventually taking it over on the fourteenth lap. At the end of the fifteenth, Moir failed to appear, eventually coming in to the pits to screw up the oil-filler cap through which oil was pouring. He rejoined the race in eighth place — stopping finally three laps later, having run out of fuel 15 miles before the first permitted fuel stop. Duff, too, had stopped at the same time, with a broken fuel pipe — running back from the far side of the circuit for a new one, and returning to refit it. Though the surviving car went well throughout the night, making up lost time, at 5 a.m. one of the "sloper" S.U. carburettor float chambers broke off and the car caught fire, being too badly damaged to continue. Both Bentleys were out of the race.

During the night. Davis (Sunbeam No. 16) and Duff (Bentley, No. 9) chasing two rivals.

DISTANCES COVERED IN THE RUDGE-WHITWORTH 24-HOUR RACE.

		Miles.
1.	Lorraine-Dietrich, 3,473 c.c., De Courcelles and Rossignol	1,388.1
2.	Sunbeam, 2,942 c.c., Chassagne and Davis	1,343.2
3.	Lorraine-Dietrich, 3,473 c.c., Stalter and Brisson	1,335.6
4.	O.M., 2,000 c.c., T. and M. Danielli	1,292.7
5.	O.M., 2,000 c.c., Foresti and Vassiaux	1,292.7
6.	Ariès, 2,957 c.c., Wagner and Flohot	1,277.2
7.	Chrysler, 3,310 c.c., Stoffel and Desvaux	1,262.5*
8.	Rolland-Pilain, 1,997 c.c., Sire and De Marguenat	1,255.3
9.	Diatto, 2,952 c.c., Rubietti and Vesprini	1,090.9*
10.	La Licorne, 1,493 c.c., Ballart and Doutrebende	1,185.6
11.	La Licorne, 1,493 c.c., W. and R. Lestiènne	1,173.8
12.	Chenard-Walcker, 1,095 c.c., Glaszmann and Hann de Zuniga	1,169.6
13.	Diatto, 1,996 c.c., Garcia and Botta	1,169.1
14.	Bignan, 1,979 c.c., Springuel and Clauze	1,166.8
15.	Chenard-Walcker, 1,095 c.c., Senechal and Lecoqueney	1,126.7
16.	Ravel, 2,492 c.c., Van den Bosch and Senet	1,118.2*
17.	E.H.P., 1,496 c.c., D'Aulan and Dely	1,110.5
18.	G.M., 1,496 c.c., Drance and Michelot	1,081.9
19.	Rolland-Pilain, 1,997 c.c., Delalande and Chalamel	1,064.6*
20.	S.A.R.A., 1,099 c.c., Erbe and Mottet	1,006.5

* Failed to cover minimum distance ; not qualified for final.

After putting up a magnificent performance on his Bentley, Kensington Moir was forced to abandon the race through running out of petrol 1½ laps short of his permitted stop.

CARE and MAINTENANCE of the 3-LITRE BENTLEY

How a High-grade British Car may be Kept in Perfect Condition to Give its Best Performance Over Many Years' Service.

Part I.

A series of Care and Maintenance articles dealing with well-known and popular cars has been for a considerable time an exclusive and widely appreciated feature of "The Autocar." The graphic illustrations which accompany the notes render the necessary adjustments easily understood by all owner-drivers. This is the twenty-fourth article of the series. Cars previously dealt with are as under :—

BEFORE discussing the adjustment of the components of the three-litre Bentley chassis, it is as well to mention that the manufacturers maintain an admirably organised service depot to relieve owners of Bentley cars from the need to effect anything more than the ordinary small adjustments of every day running. It may be argued that the owner of a car in, say, the north of England could not benefit from a depot near Hendon, N.W., and the answer to this is that the depot will come to him, as a member of the staff with the necessary tools and spares is often sent long distances immediately on receipt of a call for assistance.

So well has this system worked that the manufacturers now seal the engine and certain components so that the guarantee holds good only if these seals are broken at the service depot or by one of its representatives.

Overhead Valve Gear.

We will commence with the overhead-valve gear. Each cylinder has two inlet and two exhaust valves, and if an observer stands facing the radiator the nearest cylinder is No. 1, the exhaust valves are on the right, the inlet valves on the left. Separate cams and rocking levers operate each of the eight exhaust valves, a single cam and a twin rocking lever operating each of the inlet valves. When the engine is hot, and then only, the clearance between the adjustable end of the rocking lever and its valves should be 0.004in. for the inlet and 0.006in. for the exhaust.

The adjustment is plain, but it is well to remember that the clearance should be checked for a second time after the lock nut has been screwed home. This clearance

is for what is termed the long chassis, the valve clearance of the speed model is set at 0.015in. for both sets of rocking levers. Each rocking lever is stamped with an identification number, the exhaust for No. 1 cylinder 1 and 2, and so on up to 8.

The Rocking Levers.

It has been assumed that the cover plate for the whole of the valve gear has already been removed. If the rocking levers themselves have to be withdrawn, the aluminium bridge-piece is detached also. Note that at the forward end there is a recess to give clearance for the nuts holding the camshaft bevel to the camshaft, and that underneath the bridge-piece are holes which fit snugs on each bearing for the camshaft. This fact appreciated, it will be easy to replace the bridge-piece the correct way round. Once the bridge-piece has been

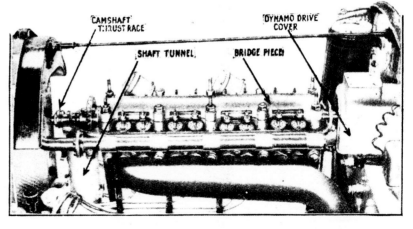

Overhead-valve mechanism of the speed model engine. It is important not to dismantle the camshaft thrust race when removing the camshaft.

removed, the long rods which act as axis pins for all the rocking levers can be raised from their bearings, at the same time bringing with them the whole of the mechanism connected with the rocking lever gear.

Removing the bridge-piece also releases the camshaft

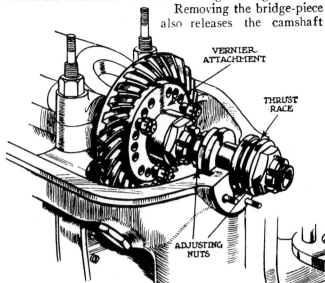

VERNIER ATTACHMENT

THRUST RACE

ADJUSTING NUTS

(Above) The camshaft bevel is attached to its shaft by a vernier and is adjusted by means of the two nuts shown. (Right) Timing marks on the upper bevel pinion of the vertical drive for the camshaft and on the casing.

bearings, of which the upper halves can be lifted out if the camshaft itself has to be removed, but in removing the camshaft *in no circumstances* must the large hexagon nuts locked by split pins be disturbed. These are shown in the sketch reproduced above, and are the adjustment nuts for the thrust bearing which locates the driving bevel of the camshaft exactly in position. It is important, also, that at the point shown in the drawing o.oo4in. clearance be allowed when the bevel is properly in mesh.

When the shaft is put back care must be taken to align the upper half of the camshaft bearing with the lower half so that the snugs are in the right position to enter the holes in the bridge-piece when the latter is replaced.

Reassembling the Valve Gear.

The camshaft comes away with its bevel and in the chamber at the forward end of the engine above the vertical drive tunnel is the driving pinion, the shaft of which has a splined joint in the centre. On the top of the bevel pinion one tooth is marked with a centre-punch and the casing has a corresponding centre-punch mark. When the flywheel has been turned until Nos. 1 and 4 cylinders are on top dead centre, the driving pinion centre-punch dot should coincide with that on the casing. Top dead centre is shown by a line scribed for the purpose on the flywheel, which is brought opposite to another line on a boss in the centre of the crank case behind No. 4 cylinder. After the mark on the driving bevel pinion has been made to coincide with the mark in the casing, the camshaft should be replaced so that its bevel meshes properly and the inlet and exhaust cams of No. 4 cylinder form a V with the apex downwards. This

is easier to effect than it seems, for if the camshaft is meshed one tooth too far in one direction or the other either the exhaust cam or inlet cams are horizontal.

The vernier by which the camshaft is attached to its driving bevel should not be disturbed in any circumstances. When the camshaft has been replaced in this manner and all the rocking levers are in position, the rocking lever adjustment, which in any case will have to be checked, should be slacked right back. If this is not done the bridge-piece may be kept off its seating because one valve is being depressed by a cam. After the bridge-piece is replaced the clearance of the valves should be checked in the ordinary way.

The Valves Themselves.

A special tool is used to lever down the valve springs and release the cotters. The valves themselves cannot be removed until the valve guides are withdrawn, for which it is necessary to clear away the camshaft, rocking levers, and the aluminium casing which is attached to the top of the cylinder by two small nuts in front and rear. Each guide can be prised out with a screwdriver and each is marked with an identification number.

MARK ON CASING

MARK ON GEAR WHEEL

Each valve is marked, the inlets with Nos. 1 and 2 for No. 1 cylinder, the exhausts 1X and 2X for No. 1 cylinder When the cover plate over the valve gear is replaced, the joint washer should not be forgotten. It is also important to remember the two steel caps, one round the driving shaft for the dynamo, and the other at the forward end. When the cover is lowered in position avoid damaging the washers behind the caps and tighten the caps themselves equally, taking particular care that the faces against which the forward cap rests are even.

Removing the Cylinders.

We will now assume that the cylinders have to be removed. The drain plug underneath the radiator on the near side should be undone to allow the water in the system, which totals 5½ gallons, to drain away. While this is happening, the radiator stay can be detached, the inlet pipe with the carburetter, the carrier for the ignition wires and the plugs should be removed, the

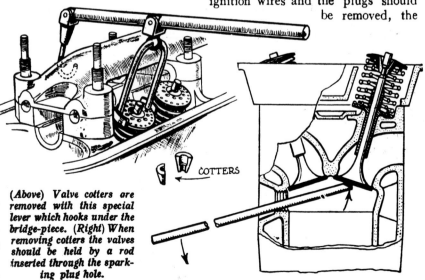

COTTERS

(Above) Valve cotters are removed with this special lever which hooks under the bridge-piece. (Right) When removing cotters the valves should be held by a rod inserted through the sparking plug hole.

33

exhaust branch uncoupled, and the camshaft and over-head gear removed, leaving the valves, valve springs and guides in position. Undo also the clip in the centre of the vertical shaft tunnel. The off-side water pipe can be unbolted where it is attached to the water jacket, the near-side water pipe either at the rubber joint near the radiator or the flange joint on the cylinder pipe. The pipe alongside the cylinders should not be detached, as it is not too easy to remake the joints.

The next component to be detached is the aluminium cover over the fabric joints for the dynamo. One fabric joint should then be uncoupled and the cylinder holding down nuts removed. If possible, a chain tackle hooked on to a bridge-piece on two of the bolts on the cylinder head should then be used to raise the block, the operation being carried out where there is plenty of light.

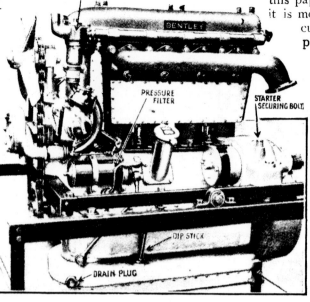

Decarbonisation.

It has been argued that the complete cylinder is more difficult to handle than the head. Possibly it may be, but the decarbonising of an engine of this type is an operation which is only undertaken after many thousand miles. The actual time taken by two mechanics to remove the block in ordinary circumstances was exactly 12 min. 6 sec., and obviously this time could be reduced to 10 min. on special occasions. On the particular engine on which the job was timed the cover for the dynamo fabric joints was not in position.

When the cylinder block has been lifted the valve guides should be levered out in the manner already described and the valves withdrawn, each being placed in a hole in a block of wood so that there is no doubt as to which valve is for which seating. Decarbonising can then proceed in the ordinary manner. The cylinders should be replaced carefully, one man lowering the block, the other guiding the pistons and rings into the corresponding cylinders. The holding down bolts should be tightened evenly, both for the cylinders and for the aluminium bridge-piece above the valve gear, and a supply of new joints, including rubber water pipes, should be available in case any of the old ones may have been damaged.

Gudgeon pins, which are a push fit, can be extracted easily. Each piston bears the number of its cylinder, which number is placed at the edge and not in the centre, so that in replacing the pistons in their correct cylinders the number should always be at the radiator side of the cylinder. The piston rings should have

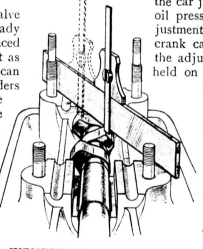

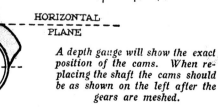

Three-litre Bentley engine with thermostat and the extra fan belt-driven from the crankshaft. The oil pressure filter, dip stick and draining point are also indicated.

A depth gauge will show the exact position of the cams. When replacing the shaft the cams should be as shown on the left after the gears are meshed.

0.006in. gap for the top ring, 0.004in. gap for the two other rings, and should be a good fit in the grooves of the piston. A spare piston should never be fitted unless it is carefully balanced to the remaining three.

The connecting rod small end bushes are of aluminium, the big end bushes are scraped to fit and are stamped with identification numbers, the same remark also applying to the crankshaft bearings.

Between the cylinder block and the crank case is a paper washer. If, for any reason, this paper washer has to be replaced, it is most important to remember to cut the necessary holes for the pipes which drain lubricant back to the crank case.

The marks on the dip stick on the left-hand side of the crank case indicate at the bottom the danger point and at the top a slight excess of oil. The exact contents of the sump can never be ascertained unless the car has been standing for at least an hour, as of the total of $2\frac{1}{2}$ gallons, $\frac{1}{2}$ gallon is carried in the working parts while running. The oil recommended is special Bentley oil or Price's Huile de Luxe.

Lubrication.

On the near side of the crank case is the pressure filter, which should be removed every 5,000 miles by undoing the nut holding the end plate nearest the radiator, taking out the gauze and swilling it in clean petrol. Never wipe the gauze with a rag, and when replacing it see that the gauze cylinder fits into the spigots on the filter chamber lids. If the sump has to be drained, the large hexagon cap nut, low down on the near side and close to the forward end of the sump, should be removed and then the car jacked up at the back. If the oil pressure needs adjusting, the adjustment is on the off side of the crank case at the forward end, and the adjusting valve consists of a ball held on its seat by a spring backed by a screwed plug. If the lock nut is undone, screwing the plug further in increases the oil pressure, which should be about 12-15 lb. at 40 m.p.h. in ordinary weather. It is most important to lock the adjustment nut tight home.

If it is suspected that one of the two magnetos is not functioning properly—this will be shown at once by a drop in power and speed—one magneto should be switched off, and if No. 2 magneto is functioning correctly the first magneto should be switched on again before the second is in its turn switched off. If No. 2 is switched off before No. 1 is switched on again, the silencer will fill with unexploded gas, which being afterwards ignited, may burst the silencer.

Very great care should be taken with the adjustment of the platinum points, for power will be lost if the gap becomes greater than 0.012in., while it goes without saying that both magnetos should fire at exactly the same moment. On the flywheel is scribed a line which is marked with the firing point of the cylinders at a full advance of 40°. The proper moment for the magneto break when the engine is at its best is 45°, which means that the line should be disregarded for the moment, but that the nut on the clutch cover just in front of this line should be brought in line with the mark on the crank case, in which position the contact makers should break, thus giving 45° advance.

To synchronise the break the contact maker should be advanced full upwards, a piece of cigarette paper should be placed between the platinum points of each magneto, then the flywheel moved in the normal direction, whoever moves the flywheel watching the position of the timing mark and the second man noting the exact moment when the cigarette papers are released. A more accurate method is to rig up in advance the electrical device illustrated. If the centre bolt which holds the contact maker is removed and the point on one wire held to the contact maker arm while the other is pressed against the boss holding the stationary platinum point, the electric lamp will light up as long as the platinum points are in contact and will go out exactly at the moment they separate. Looking from the radiator end the right-hand magneto runs clockwise, the left-hand magneto anti-clockwise.

Replacing the Magneto.

Imagine that a magneto has to be replaced by a new one; it will not have the special jaws through which it is driven from the cross-shaft, but the jaws from the previous instrument will be used. Each magneto is held in position by three bolts. The magneto cannot be removed until Nos. 1 and 4 cylinders are on top dead centre. The importance of this will be realised when it is stated that on the cross-shaft casing is a castellated and split-pinned nut which looks very much as though it holds the magneto, whereas it actually holds the cross-shaft bearings. If the three nuts holding the magneto in position have been undone and the magneto will not come away because 1 and 4 are not on top dead centre, it is possible that the castellated nut should be undone also, which would derange the whole cross-shaft drive.

Assuming the magneto to have been successfully removed and replaced on the bench, the first thing to do

Timing diagrams of the three-litre Bentley. It will be seen that the speed model is given a 15° lead on the exhaust valve over the standard engine.

after this is to put the driving jaw on the armature spindle, noting that though there is a key-way on the armature spindle, no key is used. The driving jaw should be put on only just tight enough to prevent it moving accidentally. The flywheel should then be turned until the 45° advance point is reached, and the magneto should afterwards be put back on the engine and bolted up in position with the bolts in the centre of their slots, the contact breaker and distributor covers removed, and the contact breaker at full advance. Then by means of a spanner on the centre bolt of the contact breaker, the whole armature should be turned until the contact points break, care being taken that the break is for No. 1 cylinder, as shown by the position of the distributor arm, which should point outside front. Then the magneto should be very cautiously withdrawn, and with the utmost care the jaw on the armature should be tightened home firmly. The magneto should then be put back, and if the contact maker has not moved the setting is all right.

Further Points to be Noted.

Any more delicate adjustment should be made by rotating the magneto on its spigot. Exactly the same process as that already described is then followed out for the second magneto.

Never run the car with one magneto switched off: it is very bad for the magneto, and remember that each distributor has a grease cup which must be filled at intervals. Furthermore, before deciding that a magneto is at fault, disconnect the switch wire from the contact maker cover, as the trouble may be in this wire and not in the magneto. The plugs recommended are K.L.G. type J1 for the standard cars, and K.L.G. type F12 for the latest speed model.

Concerning the water circulation, the pump gland is at first something of a mystery, but the pump is detached bodily by undoing four nuts, leaving the two shown in the sketch alone. These two nuts hold the pump gland flange and should be given not more than a quarter of a turn if the pump leaks, which will be noticed when water trickles through a drain provided in the front of the crank case for the purpose. Giving the nuts more than a quarter of a turn may jam the pump spindle, and both should be just tight—no more in ordinary circumstances. When the pump has been detached bodily these two nuts are undone, the gunmetal flange is withdrawn, and the packing, which is Palmetto, can be replaced.

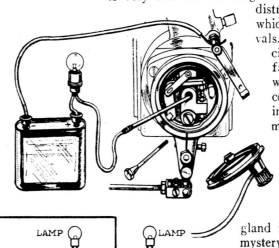

The exact moment the contact points separate can be checked with the aid of a small battery and two lamps wired to the contact maker centre and to earth.

Care and Maintenance of the 3-Litre Bentley.

Sometimes a pump leak can be stopped by screwing down the grease cup, which, by the way, should always be kept full of thick grease.

Sometimes the pump spindle will bring away with it the shaft connection from the cross-shaft skew gear. In that case it will be noticed that the hollow spindle has a square orifice at one end. This square orifice fits the pump spindle, the other end does not, and, moreover, two faces, one on the pump spindle, the other on the shaft, are marked to show which faces must be fitted together. The gland washer must be put back with the mark o in the right position when the operation is completed.

THE AUTOCAR, May 28th, 1926.

Care and Maintenance of the 3-Litre Bentley

How a High-grade British Car may be Kept in Perfect Condition to Give its Best Performance Over Many Years' Service.

Part II.

THE thermostat should be adjusted only if the car suffers from overheating. To adjust the disc valve the thermostat cover is unscrewed, the split pin which fastens the bronze valve head to its spindle withdrawn, and the valve unscrewed a very slight amount to increase the flow.

A special Bentley-Smith carburetter for the standard cars, differing in many respects from the ordinary Smith, is used. In this the control to make starting easier in cold weather and also admit extra air does not block up two of the choke tubes as is usual, but raises a sleeve, entirely cutting off the air from the slow-running jet. To start, therefore, it is important to close the hand throttle completely and then cut off the air for the slow-running jet. When the engine has started the control must, of course, be returned to normal position; the extra air, on the other hand, should not be kept open the whole time if the car is on full throttle and maximum power is required.

The Supply of Gas.

In starting engines on a very cold morning, it is a good plan to declutch, as this allows the starting motor to spin the engine more rapidly, and at the same time to snap the throttle pedal open and shut once or twice while the engine is being driven. The normal carburetter setting is 40 slow runner, followed by the jets in succession of 45, 75, 50, and 35. If economy only is desired, or if the weather is very hot, the jets can be altered to 35 slow runner, followed by 42, 70, 50, and 35. If a jet is choked that fact can be ascertained quite readily by detaching the float chamber with the jets, then tilting the float chamber so that petrol flows out of all the clear jets but

not out of the one which is blocked. The full open position of the throttle is shown by a mark filed in the end of the throttle spindle, which should be vertical when the throttle lever is against its stop. The slow-running position is set by the opposite stop.

Sometimes dirt may get under the seating of the suction valve, which is in the top of the vacuum tank at the point where the tube from the inlet pipe joins the tank. This valve should be taken out and cleaned, or petrol may run down into the inlet pipe. The main reservoir holds nine gallons, with an additional two gallons trapped as a reserve and brought into use by turning a small tap handle.

For the speed model two S.U. carburetters have been adopted. For these slow running is controlled by a small needle valve in the inlet pipe close to the carburetter

Speed model carburetters, showing the slow-running adjustment on the inlet pipe and the lubricator for the dashpot.

36

flange. To obtain access to the needle valve unscrew the knurled head, remove the coil spring, and the screw-driver head of the valve will be disclosed. Screwing in the valve decreases the amount of petrol. Air for this auxiliary jet enters through the main air intake. Owing to the position of the carburetters the float chamber should never be flooded nor the intake blocked with a rag, as this will cause liquid petrol to enter the engine. Naturally it is important to see that the two throttles open to the full and at the same time. For a power setting the needle should project from its piston for a distance of from 1 to 1.25 mm.

Gear box of the three-litre Bentley, showing the bridge piece at the front and the speedometer drive in a casing at one side. The large nut in the centre of the bridge piece should not be undone when removing the box.

One engine detail remains to be mentioned which might easily escape observation. The jaw attached to the front end of the crankshaft for the starting handle projects through a flange, the flange being bolted to the face of the crank case. As this flange holds the thrust bearing of the crankshaft in position, it should never be allowed to become slack.

How to Remove the Auxiliaries.

As regards auxiliaries, the dynamo can be detached by undoing the bolts round the securing flange, two persons being necessary for this purpose, then the fabric joint is uncoupled and the small pipe from the greaser for the dynamo bearings pulled out. If this pipe is not removed the dynamo cannot be withdrawn. Dynamos should cut in at approximately 20 m.p.h. on the speedometer and should charge at the rate of 9 amps. The accumulator should frequently be inspected and distilled, not ordinary, water added as needful to bring the liquid to a level just above the plates.

The starting motor is held in position by one long bolt which passes through the cylindrical housing and engages with a notch on the side of the dynamo. The lock nuts on this bolt must be undone and the bolt driven through downwards. It is convenient, also, to remove the oil filler.

No adjustment is required for the clutch spring. A minimum of a quarter of an inch play in the floorboards should be allowed for the pedal, measuring from the moment when the rollers attached to the clutch fork touch the clutch withdrawal mechanism, backwards until the pedal touches the floorboards, and the driver should not rest his foot on the clutch pedal itself. If a slight squeak develops in the clutch-operating mechanism, the two rollers on the end of the clutch fork should be lubricated, and it will be noticed that each roller is mounted on an eccentric for adjustment.

In the gear box a mixture of two quarts of engine oil and one quart of amber oil should be used. The assembly of the parts is quite straightforward, the idle gears being locked by a fork moved by the selector finger, while the gears which are in mesh are locked by spring-loaded balls housed in part of the withdrawal forks, the ball being got at by removing a split pin and unscrewing a cap with a screwdriver. If, for any purpose, the driving and driven shafts are withdrawn, one of the bearings will be found inside what is termed the rear nose piece and held in that position by a threaded ring notched for a special spanner. Do not attempt to remove this ring, as it is locked by a one-eighth grub screw filed off flush with the casing and very difficult to find.

Adjustments to the Transmission.

The layshaft is mounted in bearings held by eccentrics. The cap on the outside of the box has a ring of bolt holes. By slacking off the bolts and moving this cap in a clockwise direction the gears are meshed more deeply, but no adjustment of any sort should be effected without marking the position from which the adjustment started. From one side of the box the speedometer gears can be withdrawn bodily in a gunmetal casing. If the gear box has to be removed from the chassis, do not undo the centre bolt of the front mounting, but undo the entire steel bridge-piece from the cross-member. If the centre bolt is removed, the alignment of the gear box with the engine is altered. At the rear of the box the whole of the universal joint can be dismantled easily, and oversize slippers for the spider are available. The spider, incidentally, can be taken apart when one bolt is undone. The same applies to the rear universal joint.

In the back axle, lubricant should be put in only after the car has been running, and should be allowed to reach a level one inch below the mouth of the filler cap. The differential mounting and bevel adjustment are essentially a matter for the service depot.

As regards brakes, the car should first be placed on four secure jacks, each wheel free from the ground, and two persons should effect the adjustment. On the brake cross-rod, where the compensating mechanism is located, will be found three groups of levers as shown in the sketch. Groups A and B operate

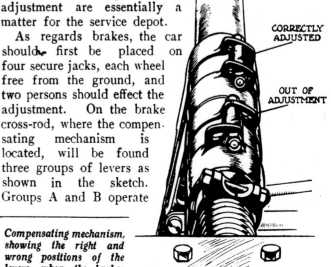

Compensating mechanism, showing the right and wrong positions of the levers when the brakes have been adjusted.

CORRECTLY ADJUSTED

OUT OF ADJUSTMENT

the front and rear brakes for their particular side of the car. On top of each group is a bolt in two slots. Close to A group is a third set of levers, C, almost exactly the same to look at and connected to the pedal by a rod which is adjustable.

First of all, the rods for the rear brakes, which, by the way, are the rods nearest to the centre of the chassis, and the front brakes should be very carefully adjusted so that the bolts marked in groups A and B are in the centre of their grooves. Then the brake should be applied. If the bolt in group C is then found to be not in

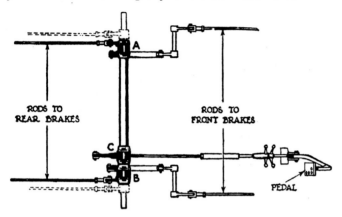

Simple diagram showing the method of four-wheel brake operation. The groups of levers are lettered for reference with the text.

the centre of its slot, the rear brakes should be slacked off equally and the front brakes tightened equally, or *vice versa*. In other words, A and B are the individual adjustment, and the position of C shows the exact relation between the front and rear sets of brakes. When bolt C is at the centre of its slot all further adjustment is effected with the rod between the pedal and the brake mechanism, which adjustment can be got at when the floorboards of the driving compartment are lifted.

Halo lining is used and is recommended, segments of the correct radius being available from the service depôt and sent out undrilled, together with a quantity of aluminium rivets, so that the linings can be drilled carefully and riveted to the brake shoes. When this is done, one inch of the lining for the front brakes should be backed off at the top of the rear shoe and at the bottom of the front shoe, while the rear brake linings should be backed off equally on both sides to not quite the same extent.

This will stop the brake shoes snatching when the brakes are applied while the car is travelling backwards.

Care of the Brakes and Steering.

The rear hubs, together with the brake drums, can be detached after the Rudge-Whitworth wheels have been withdrawn by undoing the centre nut on the driving shaft and using a special hub drawer, of which two are supplied with the kit, one for the right- and one for the left-hand wheels. The driving shaft itself can be pulled out, and great care should be taken to put each driving shaft back on its original side, as one has a left-hand and the other a right-hand oil-retaining groove.

The brake shoes themselves have springs so mounted that each spring can be fitted quite slack and afterwards set to the right tension, it being important to ensure that the brake spring tensions of all shoes are equal. The shoes are stamped for identification to ensure their being put back in the same position. The hardened end piece near the cam can be driven off sideways. The ball bearing in the rear hub is housed in a chamber behind a special

nut, on which nut is a flange drilled with many holes for the locking mechanism, a bolt being put through from the back of the drum and meshed in one of these holes.

Worm and worm wheel steering gear is employed, and it is best to leave the adjustment of the worm and worm wheel to the service depôt, as there is a possibility of jamming the steering gear in certain circumstances. If, however, the steering column is adjusted for rake, it is well to remember that the ignition advance lever is altered also, and the ignition must be reset accordingly. Amber B oil should be used for the steering gear itself, and the adjusting sleeve, which is visible when the filler cap is unscrewed, should not be touched. Timken bearings are provided in the front hubs, and the hub itself is not difficult to withdraw.

The stub axle fork has a bushed top, and the axle pin is held by a taper to the boss in the end of the axle itself. The cap on top of the stub axle covers the ball thrust bearing and its adjustment, and the cap cannot be removed without first withdrawing the brake drum dust cover. The clearance between stub axle and axle should be 0.030in., the pivot angle 2.5°. Each joint in the steering consists of a ball held between two caps backed by strong springs. Wear, therefore, is automatically taken up, but a damaged spring can be withdrawn by unscrewing the end cap, remembering to lock it when it is replaced.

Correct Front Wheel Track.

The tie-rod can be adjusted by undoing the two hexagon lock nuts provided for the purpose, and turning the rod by means of the spanner, the rod having a right-hand thread at one end and a left-hand thread at the other. When the car is new the wheels, measuring from rim to rim—not from tyre to tyre—should converge towards the front of the car $\frac{3}{16}$in. It is worth while to check the front wheel alignment at regular intervals. Bushes are provided in the eyes of each spring, which, with the shackle bolts, can be replaced without much trouble when wear takes place.

There remain one or two hints which may be of service. The engine should not be raced when the gear lever is in neutral, nor immediately after the engine has started from cold, a point which particularly applies if a car has been left in the garage for a day or two. No grease

Rear brakes for the Bentley with the pull-off springs which can be tensioned after they have been attached to the brakes. The circular casing round the driving shaft can be unscrewed, but is locked by a single bolt placed through one of the holes in the flange.

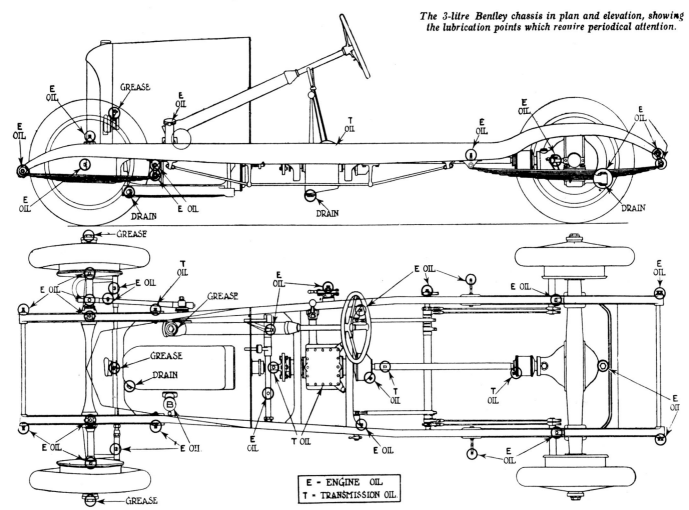

The 3-litre Bentley chassis in plan and elevation, showing
the lubrication points which require periodical attention.

E - ENGINE OIL
T - TRANSMISSION OIL

should be put in the rear, and only a little in the front, hub caps, otherwise lubricant will work into the brakes. The rear axle should not be overfilled, and the Rudge locking rings for the wheels should be moved only with a copper or hide hammer, remembering that the nut is undone by turning it in the direction in which the wheel turns when the car is going forward. Lastly, the starting handle should not be left hanging down. It has a clip to hold it upright, and if this is not used the dogs may engage with those on the crankshaft, and the subsequent noise will cause the owner apprehension as to what is happening. The information given will assist owners to get the best results from a fine car possessed of a remarkable all-round performance.

The Olympia Show.

Fast, effortless travel is assured with the renowned 15.9 h.p. three-litre Bentley chassis, fitted with a threequarter coupé-cabriolet body on particularly graceful lines.

BENTLEY. (155.)

Country of Origin: England.

BENTLEY MOTORS, LTD., POLLEN HOUSE, CORK STREET, W.1.

37.2 h.p., 6 cy's., 100×140 mm. (6,597 c.c.), tax £38, mag. ignition, pump cooling, single disc cl., 4-sp. separate gear box, spiral bevel. ¼-E. front and rear springs, 33×6.75in. tyres on wire wheels. Price: Chassis, £1,450; 7-seater saloon, £2,600.

PRIDE of place is taken by a six-cylinder model on which is mounted a Barker "Sedanca" seven-seater convertible body. This car is either an interior drive limousine (with or without partition behind the driving seat) or, by removing the front part of the head and the front windows, it becomes a *coupé de ville*, with the driver outside. The interior appointments of this car are superb; the entire upholstery is in fawn cloth, with beautifully inlaid woodwork, although restraint has been shown in the amount of this. Two disappearing extra seats are fitted, and between them is a companion which is wonderfully stocked with travel accessories, in view of its small compass. Alongside this car is shown, on a separate stand, the six-cylinder engine, an attractive exhibit to students of power unit design.

15.9 h.p., 4 cyls., 80×149 mm. (2,996 c.c.), tax £16, mag. ignition, cone cl., 820×120 mm. tyres. Price: Chassis, £925; 4-seater touring car, £1,125.

Le Mans 1926

FINAL PLACINGS IN THE THIRD AND SECOND BIENNIAL RACES.

Miles.
1. Lorraine-Dietrich, 3,447 c.c. (Bloch and Rossignol) 1585.99
2. Lorraine-Dietrich, 3,447 c.c. (De Courcelles and Mongin) ... 1574.2
3. Lorraine Dietrich, 3,447 c.c. (Stalter and Brisson) 1493.4
4. O.M., 1,990 c.c. (Minoia and Foresti) 1446.4
5. O.M., 1,990 c.c. (M. Danieli and T. Danieli) 1405.92
6. Bentley, 2,998 c.c. (Davis and Benjafield) 1284.6
7. Th. Schneider, 1,954 c.c. (Tabourin and Lefrancq).......... 1265.5
8. Rolland-Pilain, 1,998 c.c. (Chalamel and Stremler)......... 1259.9
9. E.H.P., 1,203 c.c. (Bussienne and Decostier) 1194.5
10. Salmson, 1,094 c.c. (Casse and Rousseau) 1189.4
11. Corre-la-Licorne, 1,481 c.c. (Ericalde and Galoisy) 1173.5
12. S.A.R.A., 1,099 c.c. (Lecureul and Marandet) 1167.8
13. S.A.R.A., 1,099 c.c. (Duval and Armand) 1117.7
14. Aries, 1,098 c.c. (Gabriel and Paris) 1092.9

Right: Clive Gallop and Thistlethwayte drove one of the brand new Super Sports models with 9ft wheelbase and new radiator that tapered towards the base - the cars subseqently being referred to as the "100 m.p.h. Model". Sadly, at 9 a.m. on the Sunday, this car – lying fifth – retired with a broken rocker.

Left and below: Two of the three works entries were standard Speed Models on the 9ft 9½in. chassis, driven by Sammy Davis and Dr. Benjafield, and by Frank Clement and George Duller. The Davis-Benjafield car, subsequently forever known as "Old Number 7" finished sixth, having snatched second place from one of the leading Lorraines during the last hour – and then, with brake failure, run into the sand at Mulsanne, 20 minutes before the end. The third car (Clement and Duller), having climbed from seventh on lap 21 to second on lap 25, ran wide at Arnage into the sand – losing two hours and third gear.

A young Sammy Davis (in overalls to the right of the picture) stands by the car he shared with Benjafield, at the pits during practice – "Old Number 7" as it became known, and winner of the race the following year.

Dr. J.D. Benjafield, during one of his spells at the wheel, takes No. 7 Bentley through Arnage.

Grand Prix d'Endurance

F. C. Clement, on No. 1 Bentley—the 4½-litre—getting away first at the start of the 24-hour race, followed by Dr. Benjafield on No. 3.

Bentley Three-litre, Driven by Dr. J. D. Benjafield and S. C. H. Davis, bears British Colours to Victory with 1,472.66 Miles, after being Involved in a Sensational Smash. Salmson Wins Third Biennial Rudge-Whitworth Cup with 1,244 miles.

FINAL PLACINGS AND DISTANCES IN THE GRAND PRIX D'ENDURANCE.

Bentley, No. 3, 2,989 c.c., Benjafield and Davis	.. ..	1,472·6 Miles
Salmson, No. 25, 1,094 c.c., De Victor and Hasley	.. ..	1,254·8 ,,
S.C.A.P., No. 15, 1,493 c.c., Desvaux and Vallon	.. ..	1,190·1 ,,
E.H.P., No. 26, 1,094 c.c., Bouriat and Bussienne	.. ..	1,167·7 ,,
S.A.R.A., No. 21, 1,099 c.c., Marandet and Lecureul	.. ..	1,146·07 ,,
Tracta, No. 20, 1,099 c.c., Gregoire and Lemesle	.. ..	1,048·5 ,,

FINAL OF THIRD BIENNIAL CUP.

1. Salmson, No. 23, 1,094 c.c., Casse and Rousseau	.. ..	1·239 Points
2. E.H.P., No. 26, 1,094 c.c., Bouriat and Bussienne	.. ..	1·159 ,,
3. S.A.R.A., No. 21, 1,099 c.c., Marandet and Lecureul	.. ..	1·139 ,,

Sammy Davis, at the wheel of the badly damaged No. 3, 3-litre Bentley, on his way through Arnage, and to outright victory. It was in this same car that he had crashed the previous year, 20 minutes from the finish and when lying second, due to brake failure at Mulsanne Corner.

HOW No. 7 BECAME No. I.

Impressions of the Epic Struggle on the Winning Bentley in Le Grand Prix d'Endurance.

By S. C. H. Davis, of *The Autocar*

REFLECTING upon the 24-hour gruelling at Le Mans, the most gratifying feature of the whole affair is the fact that we brought old " No. 7 " Bentley into the place that she deserved.

It is perfectly true, of course, that programme order gave the old car this year " No. 3," but as far as " Benjy " and myself are concerned, she will always be affectionately recalled as No. 7, the number she carried last year in the same race. We rather felt that No. 7's own opinion of matters ran rather like this :—

" One of you two has been over a bank with me when we could have got a place, and the other has been up a tree when, again, we would have had a place. Now, if you two drivers behave yourselves this year, we will really show them what we can do."

Results of the Crash.

And the extraordinary part of it all is that No. 7 did show, in no uncertain manner, what she could do. The crash could not possibly have been avoided ; the result of the crash almost flattened the right-hand head light, broke the right-hand side light, buckled up the front wing, loosened the running board and rear wing, loosened the accumulator box, bent the right-hand dumbiron, which put the axle slightly out of parallel, and dented a wheel. We had to change the wheel, rig up an emergency lamp on the right-hand side, and tie up everything else with cord and straps as best we could.

That done, nothing whatever was required for the car. The bonnet was never lifted, all eight plugs were firing at the end, the dynamo charged full, the S.U. carburetter pistons did not stick, the tyres gave no trouble, and the engine was every bit as lively when the old car finished as it was at the commencement.

The new brake adjustment was absolutely perfect and was used to the full before the race ended, and after two years' running that was a pretty good testimonial to a rather wonderful car.

I would also like here to withdraw my opinion about the Bentley duralumin rockers. I did not believe in them, even though it was proved that the rockers for the Six Hours Race were definitely not the size called for by the drawing, but there is not so much as the least thing the matter with any of the rockers of this car.

As regards technical details, the maximum speed which the car could attain was 90 m.p.h., though this maximum was not used during the race itself for obvious reasons, and the limit of revs., unless an all-out signal had been shown, was 3,500, though, for most of the circuit, it was thought wise to keep to 3,000 or 3,200 r.p.m. The brakes this year were so much more powerful than last year that the car could be taken at full speed a hundred yards nearer to every corner in perfect safety, and the smaller wheels made the machine much easier to hold

As to speed on corners, Mulsanne was taken at from 27 to 30 m.p.h.,

Arnage's final bend probably at 27 m.p.h., and Pontlieue hairpin, as a precaution, somewhere about 15-20 m.p.h. White House corner, on which the collision occurred, could be taken at full throttle and was approached downhill. The fastest parts of the circuit were downhill to Pontlieue and then on the gradient between the two all-out corners which preceded the long straight. The top gear ratio was 3.53 to 1 with 31 × 5.35in. tyres, so that 3,200 r.p.m. gave approximately 85 m.p.h.

A Crippled Car that Won.

Several people have asked how much practising was done. In all, about 220 miles, the car being run as little as possible with the idea of getting it into perfect condition about one-third of the way through the race. The petrol consumption was roughly 10 m.p.g., the oil consumption roughly a gallon to 200 miles.

In the matter of the race itself, " Benjy " and I think that it was the most dramatic affair that has ever happened. Not only was there a record crash, but it was a crippled car that won, and, at the end of twenty-two hours' hard fight, there were only two minutes between the two principal rivals. Moreover, there have been few races run with such appalling weather conditions, for, during part of the night, streams of solid water came down from the skies as though there had been a cloudburst, which, on top of the fact that we only had one head lamp, and that one on the wrong side, made the

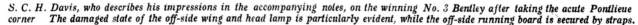

S. C. H. Davis, who describes his impressions in the accompanying notes, on the winning No. 3 Bentley after taking the acute Pontlieue corner   The damaged state of the off-side wing and head lamp is particularly evident, while the off-side running board is secured by straps.

In the yard at the Hotel Moderne, Le Mans, headquarters of the Bentley team through the years, and headquarters of a great many Le Mans teams up to the present time. The three 1927 team cars are shown under preparation – in the foreground No. 1 4½-litre (YH 3169; Clement and Callingham); No. 2 3-litre (MK 5205; Duller and d'Erlanger); and No. 3 3-litre (MK 5206; Benjafield and Davis). No. 1 was the first production 4½-litre, which retired after the White House crash, having completed 35 laps and in the lead; it also set up a new lap record of 73.4 m.p.h. No. 2, also involved in the White House crash, retired having completed 34 laps. No. 3, also in the White House crash – won the race.

night run particularly trying for us. The crash it is difficult to talk about. One's mind refuses to remember, with any accuracy, anything more than minor detail. The only warning that anything was wrong was dirt and mess on the road before the corner, and round the corner the rays of the head lights, which had just been lit, disclosed a most extraordinary sight. Piled in a mass across the road there seemed to be at least four cars, one lying on its side, another banked steeply up on top of it; passage through between them all there seemed to be none, with the result that after standing on the brakes, our car skidded violently into the wreck of No. 1, and hit it with a sickening noise of rending metal. How anybody got out of the affair alive, much less without serious hurt, was a miracle.

Since, however, the car could still be driven, driven it was, and, considering the damage, it was not as hard to handle as one would imagine; but "Benjy" does deserve full marks for not only taking over the car in its crippled condition without

knowing, as I did, the full extent of the damage, but also for putting up an extraordinary performance at night with one head lamp only, more especially as he is not fond of night driving and does not see as well as some other people do in the circumstances.

The French officials did every possible thing that could be thought of to help. They granted the car another spare wheel in place of the damaged wheel because the damage had not been our fault. They did everything to help, and—that brings up another point—the drivers of the smaller French cars got out of the way without the slightest hesitation whenever we wanted to pass.

Another thrilling incident was the battle with the Aries, a struggle the more intense because Chassagne is a personal friend of mine, and is one of the finest of the old-time drivers, having the very essence of the sporting spirit. Even at the height of the battle, when every second was of the utmost value to his car, Chassagne actually cut off and went right down to the side of the road to give the Bentley an absolutely free passage.

Moreover, at the end of the race, the whole Aries team cheered the victor across the line, despite their having suffered one of the most bitter disappointments that was ever in the lot of a racing *équipe*. As a personal matter I would have preferred by far that Chassagne had finished second.

Some mention has been made of the difficulties of the night run. It will give, perhaps, a better idea of " Benjy's " performance if I say that the downpour was so heavy that the water actually filled one's goggles, washing the accumulation of dirt therein into one's eyes until the pain became almost beyond bearing.

Finally, I think that the finest action one man has ever done to another occurred when " Benjy " stopped at the pits on purpose to give me the honour, and remember that it was an honour one will bear all one's life, of taking old No. 7 for those last two triumphal laps to see the greatest sight in motor racing, the big yellow flag, which shows that victory is complete. Deliberately to deny oneself this is almost superhuman, and to me the act will be indelible.

The Autocar

June 22nd, 1928.

THE 24-HOUR

W. Barnato and B. Rubin (4½-Litre
durance at 69·11 m.p.h. Casse and
the Fourth Bi-Annual

Below: The three 4½-litre works entries, with
Sir Henry Birkin and Frank Clement. The
centre car was the famous Number 1 of the
previous year's Le Mans 24 Hours.

24 Hours.	Miles Covered.	Avera Speed.
		m.p.h.
Bentley 4 .... (155)	**1658.6**	**69.11**
Stutz 1 ...... (149)	1504.1	60.42
Chrysler 8 ... (145)	1549.4	64.56
Chrysler 7 ... (139)	1498.8	62.45
Bentley 3 .... (136)	1451.2	60.46
Alvis 27 ..... (133)	1420.6	59.19
B.N.C. 32 ... (131)	1410.1	58.75
Itala 12 ..... (131)	1403.1	58.46
Alvis 28 ..... (131)	1396.8	58.20
Salmson 35 .. (128)	1372.2	57.17
Lagonda 16 .. (126)	1353.8	56.39
Tracta 29 .... (120)	1282.2	53.42
Lombard 37.. (117)	1253.0	52.21
E.H.P 36 ... (116)	1240.0	51.67
Sara 19 ...... (114)	1226.6	51.11
Tracta 31 .... (111)	1183.7	49.32
Tracta 42 .... (110)	1162.3	48.43

Left: Bernard Rubin refuels
No. 4, 4½-litre which, shared
with Woolf Barnato, won the
race at 69.11 m.p.h.

RACE AT LE MANS

B. RUBIN

Bentley) Win Grand Prix d'En-Rousseau (1,100 c.c. Salmson) Secure Rudge-Whitworth Cup.

Below: Streaming away from tne start – Birkin's 4½-litre is nearest to the camera, followed by Clement's 4½-litre, Chiron's Chrysler and Barnato's 4½ – the eventual winner. This was Bentley's third Le Mans win.

The two most successful cars at the pits togetner – Rubin on No. 4 Bentley moves off after taking over from Barnato, while Salmson No. 35, winner of the fourth Rudge-Witworth Cup refuels its tank.

Barnato's Bentley regains the lead from the Stutz on the fast run down to Mulsanne corner.

Birkin, after cutting away the ruined tyre, drives his Bentley very fast up to the Arnage S-turn on the bare rim.

"THE AUTOCAR" ROAD TESTS

4½-LITRE BENTLEY

FEW cars have provided quite such a puzzle as the 4½-litre Bentley, for if its specification be put down coldly on paper, and without comment, it suggests at once a machine which is not of the most modern type. The big four-cylinder engine should, one would imagine at first, be at least a six-cylinder to hold its place against all rivals. Yet this car became famous almost as soon as it was produced, and is particularly popular at the moment.

This really means that the car cannot be criticised simply in terms of its specification, and that is a point which strikes one most forcibly after a long trial run. It

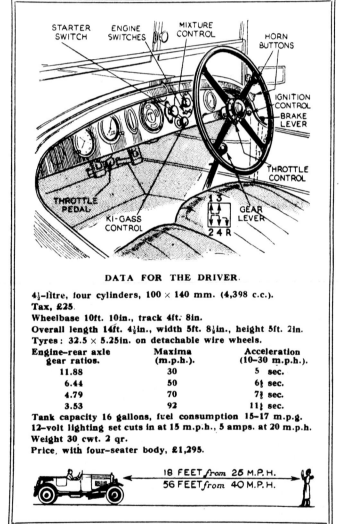

DATA FOR THE DRIVER.

4½-litre, four cylinders, 100 × 140 mm. (4,398 c.c.).
Tax, £25.
Wheelbase 10ft. 10in., track 4ft. 8in.
Overall length 14ft. 4½in., width 5ft. 8½in., height 5ft. 2in.
Tyres: 32.5 × 5.25in. on detachable wire wheels.

Engine-rear axle gear ratios.	Maxima (m.p.h.).	Acceleration (10-30 m.p.h.).
11.88	30	5 sec.
6.44	50	6½ sec.
4.79	70	7⅜ sec.
3.53	92	11⅛ sec.

Tank capacity 16 gallons, fuel consumption 15-17 m.p.g.
12-volt lighting set cuts in at 15 m.p.h., 5 amps. at 20 m.p.h.
Weight 30 cwt. 2 qr.
Price, with four-seater body, £1,295.

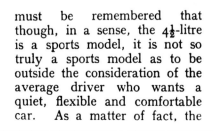

18 FEET from 25 M.P.H.
56 FEET from 40 M.P.H.

machine is two cars in one, according to the type of driver at the wheel. Given an enthusiast as pilot, then the power, speed and, what can only be called the tractability, of the big machine are simply wonderful. It has a feeling of tremendous power that, say what one may, is extremely pleasant. It makes one think that, after all, there is more in the four-cylinder engine than one would imagine; that, indeed, the suggestion of power given by the engine when pulling at low speed on a high gear is by no means unpleasant.

And withal there is no suggestion of undue noise. The exhaust, it is true, has a drone with the throttle open, and a rather fascinating burbling noise at very low engine speed, but one is not conscious that the engine, or the car as a whole, is noisy. Particularly does this apply to the indirect gears, for third and second are extraordinarily quiet, and third and second are gears meant to be used if the full performance of the machine is to be realised.

To obtain the car's full maximum the shock absorbers have to be kept tight—tighter, that is, than they should be for comfortable town work or for ordinary touring. With the shock absorbers tight the car holds the road as though glued to it, while the steering is light, direct, and very certain. That is another great point. It is one of the most pleasant existing cars to drive, and a driver in tune with it knows that he has full control, that the car will do everything he wills from the very moment it moves off from a standstill.

The gear change could not possibly be better or more delicate. The gears can easily be changed with a thumb and finger of one hand, and changes from top to second or from second to top are equally easy and entirely noiseless.

Further, the brakes are very powerful indeed, as the stopping distances show, added to which they are sensi-

must be remembered that though, in a sense, the 4½-litre is a sports model, it is not so truly a sports model as to be outside the consideration of the average driver who wants a quiet, flexible and comfortable car. As a matter of fact, the

tive and, however violently applied, are not uneven. The wheel, controls, throttle, ignition, gear and brake levers are in their natural places in respect to the driving seat, the pedals are sufficiently wide apart that one does not interfere with another.

Thus much for what may be termed the fiercer mood of the car; but supposing it is needed for town work and the driver does not feel that much gear changing is desirable, then the extraordinary feature is that the big four-cylinder will run on top gear as though it were a six, with only the curious and not unpleasant torque effort to show that there are but four cylinders in the power unit. It is an exceptional car to handle on top, and it is remarkably smooth and quiet for town work. That is why there are two totally different characters contained in the same car, and why it is useless to go into details of equipment or of specification, since it is as a whole, and very much as a whole, that the 4½-litre Bentley appeals. In that appeal there is something more of the living animal than in most cars.

the front......

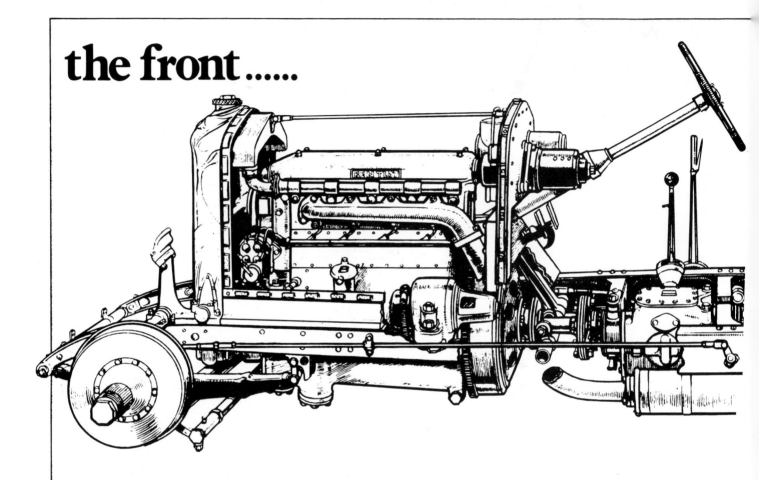

......and rear

THE 4½-LITRE CHASSIS, the prototype of which was based on a 10ft. 10in. wheelbase 3-litre chassis with a larger engine of bore and stroke 100 × 140 mm. This first example made its debut at Le Mans in 1927, and was wrecked in the famous White House crash when leading the race (Clement and Callingham). On its second appearance, two months later, in the 24-hour Grand Prix of Paris, at Montlhéry, it won by 11 laps, at 51.99 m.p.h. (Clement and Duller).

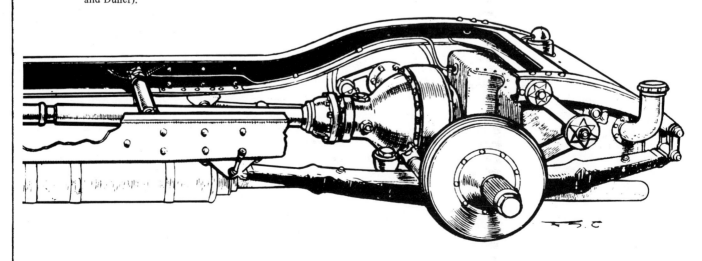

Brooklands Double-Twelve

Britain's first 24 hour race

THE FINEST ENGLISH RACE

A Personal Story of the Dramatic Struggle Between Bentley No. 6 and Ramponi's Alfa Romeo in the Brooklands Double-Twelve Race.

By S. C. H. DAVIS.

A DRIVER'S narrative of a race is, and can only be, personal, just one man's experience out of many, and by no means necessarily the most exciting at that. Without the slightest wish to suggest that the methods adopted are necessarily the best, it is exceedingly difficult to avoid a tinge of the pedagogic. But, as comparisons are always interesting, it is difficult to leave out one's method of doing things, if only just for the amusement of other drivers.

First of all, I think it was in every possible way a magnificent race, not because Brooklands track is an interesting place to drive on, but just because of the intense excitement of the battle between my team and the Alfa Romeos, and the particular fight between that splendid sportsman Ramponi and myself.

The Friday's show was interesting only in a minor way, because team tactics made those twelve hours just a succession of sparrings for position. But at the end of them our strategical plan was proved sound, for the real danger then lay with Ramponi and Ivanowski, or with the Salmson; the Rileys had been dangerous, and

would be more so in their next race; so far our (the Bentley) charts were accurate. Moreover, No. 6 was in capital condition, just about ripe, that is, good for 4,000 r.p.m. at need, and with heaps of brake adjustment in hand. It had run extraordinarily well. It consumed rather more tyres than we had anticipated, but it was as steady as a rock at 104-105 m.p.h., and one cautious experiment showed that it would go up to 107 m.p.h., and even more, if required by the signals from the pit.

The start on the Saturday was beautifully exact. We had arranged beforehand certain things which helped the engine enormously, and the car was ambled round at 2,000 revs. on top, until my mechanic Head's signals to the pit showed them that the temperature and oil pressure were right and the pit signal told us to get on with the job. Thereafter we could open up and the car really began to move, everything running like a clockwork mouse, and the revs., cut-off point, and change up varying exactly in response to pit signals.

Then it began to rain. There is nothing I loathe more

than rain, and what had been a quite comfortable and enjoyable ride became depressingly exciting. The first intimation of this excitement was a front and rear wheel skid which ended with a wump into the sandbank, shot a huge cloud of sand into the air and into the car—I swallowed a lot—but did no damage other than to remove our starboard accumulator box lid, which was already loose. The trouble was that the Byfleet banking was much drier than the turn, and I hadn't realised how hard it was raining, so, rather stupidly, was caught napping.

From then onwards we seemed to have skids all over the place, and, as all the small cars promptly came up the banking for safety, matters became unpleasantly congested, and I had to cut out at the end of the pits instead of under the bridge across the finishing straight. This was annoying, as, relatively, the Alfas were not so much affected.

Fortunately, the rain gave up its fell work just when I was wondering how the deuce one could drive without being able to see through the windscreen or round it, and when every other car had such a backwash of spray that all you could see of it were the crew's heads. Anyhow, we had lost a lot of valuable time, but we made up some of it on refilling at the pit, and went up a little in revs. as well.

Curiously, it was not as fast a day as the Friday, for the wind had shifted, and, whereas we got 3,500 r.p.m. at the end of the mile timing box on Friday, we could only get up to that near the end of the Byfleet banking on Saturday.

Then there was another joke. For tactical reasons I took on an eight-hour spell, after six hours of which Head and I felt

desperately hungry, but had nothing to eat on board except throat lozenges, which are unsatisfactory as food, though good enough for the arid dryness which afflicts every driver after a time. Naturally, when we stopped at the pit the second time a drink was worth a king's ransom, but, due to my having no voice left, nobody could understand what I wanted. Eventually I croaked " Water," and was instantly handed the disgusting jug which we used for refilling the radiator ; thereafter I gave it up as hopeless.

Meantime we were getting where we wanted, save that at eighteen hours we had not got the lead as we had hoped to have, and we only headed Ramponi at nineteen hours, but that seemed satisfactory, and the run so far had been good, hard driving, really worth while.

Ramponi passes a Frazer Nash.

A little after the twentieth hour we were called in and relieved, and were not as pleased about it as a well-disciplined crew should be, because I was just feeling comfortable, and Head, though hungry, would go on for ever. In any case, it would not have been fair to Gunter, whom I had already robbed of most of his legitimate share of enjoyment, and who was driving a capital first race and taking things seriously, exactly as ninety-nine drivers out of a hundred do not. And he had a rotten spell, for a tyre collapsed on the turn. That was an awful moment, since the machine was much overdue, and most of us in the pit were nearly sick with apprehension before it limped in slowly with a hairy caterpillar of loose cord on the near rear wheel rim.

In the meantime, Ramponi had been going well, and was quite a way ahead on formula with less than two hours to go. Then I received orders which resulted in the finest battle I have ever had bar none as we took over for the last exciting spell.

Changing over—two hours to go.

Worthily did No. 6 respond. On the Byfleet banking the needle went up steadily, 3,200, 3,400, 3,500, then off the banking at 3,750, 3,800 (about 107 or 108 m.p.h.). Down the finishing straight to the bridge the great car was alive.

Just beyond the bridge I cut out, braked heavily, turned a little, accelerated, changed to third, then, gradually opening the throttle, went straight through at 2,800, about 60 m.p.h., to complete the turn high on the banking, gathering speed by driving down the slope at once. It was like a climbing turn on a fast 'plane.

Thus we continued round after round, and as the car settled down to real speed we watched out for the little red Alfa, and, with lap scorer and watch, estimated our gain as we ran. It really was rather wonderful. Head signalled the oil pressure regularly to the pit, we crouched as low in the car as we could, tilted the two little screens to an acute angle, and the turn on to the home banking became sheer joy.

Critical Moments.

There was no time now to be extra cautious in passing people ; we *had* to get through, whether things were close or not. How I wished that mechanics would look back as the Bentley came down the straight at 108 m.p.h. between other cars and the railings. One just hoped these other cars would not swerve!

Ramponi was going great guns, too, for the signal at his pit stood in the faster position round after round with his initial " R " below it. It was fine to see him use his head to take every advantage. Never for a second did the red Alfa get in the way ; always he or his mechanic signalled us to pass, and, as we passed, desperately he tried to tuck in behind to get our slip stream and be " towed." If I passed just after the turn he could do this all the way to the Byfleet banking and drop off exactly as we reached 102.

On my part I tried, sometimes successfully, to go to the very top of the banking and shake him off in that way. On the sandbanked curve we really did—it is the first time I have seen this—corner as they do in pictures, all four of us in the two cars leaning right out and taking it all we knew. Gradually we overtook the Alfa the right number of times, and matters were looking hopeful when some confounded person— quite rightly from his point of view—sig- nalled us in because our loose bonnet clip allowed the side of the bonnet to lift a little, though, lift- ing, it was fully se- cured by the strap, and there is no regu- lation requiring bon- net clips. That en- tailed one slow lap, a stop to refix the bonnet clip, one standing-start lap, a beastly waste of time at such a crisis.

But Ramponi had his troubles, too, for the Alfa Romeo's accumulator box broke loose, and for two rounds we passed the little car stationary at its pit. The sight wound one up to such extent that I took the corner at 3,000 on third and nearly scared myself into a fit while a photographer leaned calmly over the banking top and fired a camera within what seemed two feet of my face.

Then came another bother. With an hour more to go I discovered a white strip on the tread of the star- board rear tyre, which one could see clearly by looking back as we accelerated after the turn. It was not a nice sight. But anyhow, we couldn't possibly stop or slow if all the tyres had gone funny ; and I had an odd feeling that it would last.

I hoped " W.O.," the team *Patron*, wouldn't see it, and wished like blazes the pit would show the " all out " signal. It would make no difference to the tyre, anyway, and the constant repetition of " O.K." didn't seem to meet the situation, as we calculated things from the car while Head fed me with bull's-eyes of a particu- larly vicious brand. We even got to 3,900 down the straight, which is most inspiring, but orders are orders, and 4,000 was left alone.

The Finish.

Half an hour from the finish—it seemed an impossible time—the oil pressure gauge went to zero on the bank- ing, flickered, went to 20 at 3,700, flickered again. Five rounds later its maximum was ten—we were running out of oil, and Head had already let in the reserve supply. Well, if we burst, we burst, but at all events we would burst in style. The engine never faltered.

Ten minutes from the end we did not know whether we had caught the Alfa enough times or not, the tyre looked bad, and the oil gauge reading was intensely depressing. Five minutes from the end—and each second seemed an hour—I thought it would be just racing luck if we cracked up then, had another bull's-eye, and wondered whether I should ever be able to sit down again.

Then, at last, the chequered flag, a puff of smoke on the right, and, as we throttled down, the bang of a maroon high up. We had finished ; it was a great moment. When we reached the pit I had a look at the tyre, and it didn't seem so good ; then, after the usual photo- graphic stunts, went off to see Ramponi just in time to hear that he had won and we had lost by no more than 200 yards each hour.

He thoroughly de- served it, and we had a most interest- ing talk over things that only he and I know in all the world about those last two rounds.

No. 6 in the lead with only four more hours to go. The scoreboard also shows the class leaders at three-quarter distance.

Brooklands six-hours 1929

POSITIONS OF CARS WHICH COMPLETED THE DISTANCE.

Driver.	Car.	Capacity c.c.	Miles to Run.	Schedule Average (m.p.h.)	Actual Average (m.p.h.)	Remarks.
1. W. Barnato J. Dunfee	Bentley	6,597	439.49	73.25	75.88 h. m. s. 5 47 30 m.p.h.	1st in race. 1st in 8-litre class.
2. L. Headlam W. Headlam	Alfa Romeo (S.)	1,750	418.56	69.76	70.22 h. m. s. 5 57 35 m.p.h.	2nd in race. 1st in 2-litre class.
3. H. W. Cook	Bentley	4,398	436.87	72.81	72.94 h. m. s. 5 59 25 m.p.h.	3rd in race. 1st in 5-litre class.
4. J. D. Benjafield	Alfa Romeo (S.)	1,750	418.56	69.76	69.57	4th in race. 2nd in 2-litre class.
5. R. F. Oats	O.M.	1,991	402.86	67.14	66.22	5th in race. 3rd in 2-litre class.
6. G. E. T. Eyston G. Ramponi	Alfa Romeo (S.)	1,494	415.94	69.32	67.90	6th in race. 1st in 1½-litre class.
7. F. S. Barnes J. D. Barnes	Austin	747	313.92	52.32	50.72	7th in race. 1st in 750 c.c. class.
8. W. B. Scott	Bentley	4,398	436.87	72.81	69.91	8th in race. 2nd in 5-litre class.
9. T. E. Rose-Richards	Lagonda	1,954	402.86	67.14	63.08	9th in race. 4th in 2-litre class.

Both works Bentleys entered for this race ("Old No. 1" Speed Six – Barnato and Jack Dunfee: and Cook's and Callingham's 4½-litre) had run at Le Mans a fortnight before; two 4½-litre cars were privately entered (Holder and Scott); and Birkin ran the prototype Blower 4½-litre, the car which subsequently became the famous single-seater, now owned by Russ-Turner. Of the 38 starters, only nine cars completed their minimum required distances, three of these being Bentleys – the winning Barnato/Dunfee Speed Six, the Cook/Callingham 4½-litre (third), and the Scott/Patterson 4½-litre (eighth). Right: Barnato helps Dunfee out of his helmet after the race, and, below – the winning Speed Six at the end of the Finishing Straight.

October 18th, 1929.

Brooklands 500 miles 1929

Fastest Event of its Type Ever Run at Brooklands Won by 4½-litre Bentley Driven by Clement and Barclay: Speed Six Bentley Second, and 4-litre Sunbeam, in Spite of Serious Trouble, Third.

Left: "Old No. 1" Speed Six, with Sammy Davis at the wheel, at over 125 mph on the banking; it put up fastest race lap at 126.09 mph. Below: Frank Clement and Jack Barclay, drivers of the winning 4½-litre which, unsupercharged, averaged 107.32 mph for the 500 miles.

A SUPERCHARGED BENTLEY

Installation of Twin-rotor Blower Increases Already Excellent Performance of the 4½-Litre.

ONE by one the well-known sports cars are being provided with superchargers. That the additional unit must enhance the performance is obvious, and as long as performance is judged by competition within certain classes rated by engine capacity anything which will secure more power from a given engine clearly has its advantages.

What is not so obvious is that experiments with a supercharger prove it to be a quite good carburetter, in that it makes an engine which is normally on the rough side considerably smoother, and enables the carburetter of to-day to adapt itself more easily to the wide range of engine speed which is required.

It is additionally interesting that so big a machine as the 4½-litre Bentley, already capable of a high performance, should be provided with even more performance by supercharging. It is obvious, of course, that the demand for these cars lies at present more in the sports world than with the average motorist, which is not to say that future experiments will not disclose the value of the supercharger in some form or another for the needs of everyday motorists. It is no secret that experiments have been carried out for a very long time with 4½-litre Bentleys and a supercharger, and it is no new and untested machine, therefore, which is taking its place in the range of models.

As far as the engine goes there has not been much alteration, but a drive is taken from the front of the crankshaft through fabric joints to one shaft of a twin-rotor Roots-type blower designed by Mr. Amherst Villiers and carried in an aluminium casing between the front dumb-irons of the frame and below the radiator, which is altered to receive it. The supercharger is arranged so that the engine's lubrication system feeds the gear wheels which drive one rotor shaft from the other,

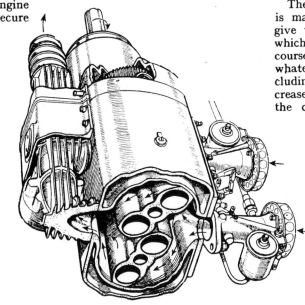

The Twin-rotor blower and two carburetters.

supplying enough also for the rotor blades themselves.

On one side of the aluminium casing are, curiously enough, two carburetters through which the supercharger sucks mixture, expelling it on the far side under pressure to a pipe carried right up to the intake ports on the cylinder block. The better to safeguard both pipe and supercharger should an explosion occur in the inlet pipe there are a series of spring-loaded safety valves along the pipe itself.

The appearance of the supercharger is massive, and at first it seems to give the car an odd appearance, to which one becomes accustomed in course of time. There is no doubt whatever that the performance, including the acceleration, has been increased remarkably without making the car difficult to handle on the road in ordinary circumstances.

The price of the new chassis will probably be round about £1,500, and the type is now in production.

It is expected that the first batch of examples of this new model will be brought through the works before long, and some fifty will be built before the end of the year. The original 4½-litre car will remain, of course, in the range of standard models. It is not really intended that the supercharged machine shall supersede the earlier model in any way whatever, nor, incidentally, is it meant that the new chassis shall be suitable solely for competition work or for racing generally.

So far the first of the new cars has run only in one race, and during that event was held back, since the affair was rightly regarded as a test, as, in fact, the *only* real test, to prove the capabilities of the mechanism before the machine shows its real form against antagonists. It was originally destined that this first trial should be the much more severe race at Le Mans, but, as always happens with a new model, certain difficulties of an unexpected nature had to be overcome, and before they were overcome the machine had no reasonable chance of success in the face of active opposition.

That the new Bentley will prove a worthy member of its family is certain, and that it will enhance their reputation is not improbable.

The supercharger is mounted between the front dumb-irons.

Le Mans 1929

BRITAIN'S VICTO

**GRAND PRIX D'ENDURANCE.
24-HOUR RACE.**

	Miles.
Bentley (Capt. Birkin and Woolf Barnato)	1,767.25
Average : 73.027 m.p.h.	
Bentley (Glen Kidston and J. Dunfee)	1,695.95
Bentley (J. D. Benjafield and Baron E. D. d'Erlanger)	1,614.57
Bentley (F. C. Clement and J. Chassagne)	1,592.8
Stutz (Bouriat and Philippe)	1,556.26
Chrysler (H. Stoffel and R. Benoist)	1,544.03
Chrysler (Cyril De Vere and Mongin)	1,512.95
Lea-Francis (K. S. Peacock and S. H. Newsome)	1,380.63
Tracta (Balart and Debeugny)	1,290.7
Tracta (Gregoire and Valon)	1,280.13

Below: Barnato and Birkin (top row), who scored the first Speed Six victory. Kidston and Jack Dunfee (lower) second in an unblown 4½-litre.

Baron d'Erlanger, under Kensington Moir's pungent instruction, fills the sump of the third-placed 4½ while a mechanic inspects the rear tyre treads.

RY AT LE MANS

About the Bentleys :

As to this year's race, I cannot help wishing that there had been some real opposition, magnificent as it is to find a time when the Bentleys were so superior to everybody else that they could just do what they pleased, and pleasing as that undoubtedly is to anybody who remembers the early struggles of the *marque* in the same race.

* * *

By the way, the histories of some of the cars are interesting. No. 1 is new, but ran in the " Double-Twelve." No. 9 was the original 4½-litre which first ran at Le Mans and crashed, then won the Montlhéry 24-hour race, then won last year's Le Mans race. No. 10 ran in last year's event and was second in the " Double-Twelve." No. 11 ran last year, took part in the " Double-Twelve " as No. 5, was driven by Mrs. Bruce single-handed for the record at Montlhéry, and was put almost straight into the Le Mans race to replace one of the supercharged cars which did not start.   S.C.H.D.

Left: The start — No. 1 Speed Six gets away first with H.R.S. Birkin at the wheel — the car that finished first, covering 1,767 miles in the 24 hours.

The finish: Birkin crosses the finishing line with the victorious Speed Six, followed by the remaining three team cars in second, third and fourth positions.

"THE AUTOCAR" ROAD TESTS

No. 72.—BENTLEY SPEED SIX WEYMANN SALOON

Immense Fascination of a Fast, yet Really Tractable, Car not Easy to Analyse.

I1 is extraordinarily difficult to explain in words or writing the exact fascination of a big, fast car of the type so ably represented by the big Bentley speed model, and it is very doubtful whether anybody who has not driven a car in this class would ever be able to analyse, much less understand, the curious fascination which such a car undoubtedly possesses, albeit many smaller machines seem to be capable of giving every bit as much satisfaction to their proud owners.

Possibly the sheer insolence—for insolence is the only word—with which this big car does its work, and the lordly suggestion of great superiority—which may, of course, exist only in the imagination of its drivers, but is none the less real for that—has much to do with the question.

Certainly an ability to maintain either a high or a low average with practically no throttle opening and a big engine apparently doing nothing is three-quarters of the secret of the success of such a type of car, and, as a matter of fact, the

Bentley is not really a "speed model" in what is nowadays the accepted sense of the word, despite its performance. It is genuinely a fast and to many people a very fast, touring car, developed directly from the ordinary model, and differing from that model scarcely at all as far as the external appearance and external details are concerned.

There is absolutely nothing that is fierce or even suggests fierceness; the car is absolutely tractable, and can be handled on top gear in the conventional way in which all these big sixes are handled. Nor will the car, so driven, give any idea of its real power. Naturally, it is a machine which can be driven most comfortably in the ordinary way on two gears only, second, or if you prefer it, first, for starting from rest, and top just as soon as the car has started.

And there is undoubtedly charm in the way in which the big car answers immediately to its driver's control with more than a little that suggests the intelligence of an animal, and giving just as much response to good treatment. Obviously, also, much depends on the adjustment of the shock absorbers, which, for a machine possessing such a range of speed, give better results when comparatively slack for what may be called town work, and then should be run with increased pressure when any matter of speed on the open road is in question.

And the speed of the car should satisfy anybody, just as much as the way in which the car does its work is something eminently satisfactory. It can go much faster if required and sacrifice but little of its flexibility, but the performance it possesses in the normal way is more than sufficient even for an enthusiast.

Undoubtedly this type of car shows to best advantage on a really long run, because then, and only then, does the driver realise that the great characteristic of the machine is its power to continue at a high average without reaching at any time an abnormally high maximum, and without being at all tiring however many hours one may spend at the wheel. Moreover, there is something, which is sensed rather than anything else, which makes the Bentley feel that it is absolutely, entirely and accurately under its driver's control with the minimum of effort whatever the speed and however the road may twist or curve.

No car of this type is expected to give any idea that there is a big power unit doing anything at all under the bonnet, and that is certainly a point in favour of this particular machine all through its speed range. The indirect gears are rather noisy by contrast with gears which are being produced and have been standardised recently—but any noise there is would probably have been taken for granted not much more than a year ago.

The brakes are really good and, curiously enough, the use of the vacuum servo motor does not lessen the sensitiveness

ot the mechanism, or seem to give that curious feeling that the control is indirect, as is often the case.

The gear change is characteristic of the car in that it responds admirably to any driver who prefers to feel for the gear teeth or dogs rather than to effect the change by just judging the length of the delay in the lever's movement, and at no time is the locking mechanism for the various striking rods in any way obtrusive.

Over and above all this, the power unit under the bonnet is well finished, even to the aluminium casting of the crank case and the valve cover, and though that finish may not contribute one iota to the reliability or performance of the machine, it none the less makes it a more satisfactory possession, and there is more in that fact than many people having the entirely commercial view would ever understand.

All the instruments are well grouped and well lighted, the head lamps are excellent, and the car as a whole is very comfortable. A closed body is, of course, what one would expect in days when the greater percentage of the cars on the road carry this type of coachwork, and yet, despite its undoubted advantages in the eyes of most motorists, it is hardly of the type which really allows one to enjoy a chassis of this kind to the full.

Finally, one may discuss this or that point in the general detail or main design, attributing advantages to some things, and the inevitable disadvantages as well, but the real point that has made the Bentley car one of the most successful machines that has been built is simply that it *is* a Bentley; that despite all questions of design, the complete car has truly that mysterious quality which makes one forget it is a machine at all. To say that a car possesses that quality is to pay it the highest—and in the case of the Speed Six Bentley a thoroughly deserved—compliment in one's power.

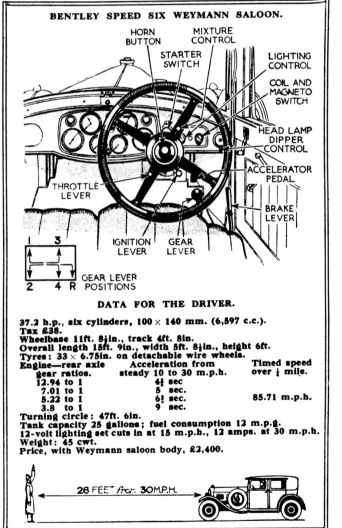

BENTLEY SPEED SIX WEYMANN SALOON.

HORN BUTTON
MIXTURE CONTROL
STARTER SWITCH
LIGHTING CONTROL
COIL AND MAGNETO SWITCH
HEAD LAMP DIPPER CONTROL
ACCELERATOR PEDAL
BRAKE LEVER
THROTTLE LEVER
IGNITION LEVER
GEAR LEVER
GEAR LEVER POSITIONS

DATA FOR THE DRIVER.

37.2 h.p., six cylinders, 100 × 140 mm. (6,597 c.c.). Tax £38.
Wheelbase 11ft. 8½in., track 4ft. 8in.
Overall length 15ft. 9in., width 5ft. 8½in., height 6ft.
Tyres: 33 × 6.75in. on detachable wire wheels.

Engine—rear axle gear ratios.	Acceleration from steady 10 to 30 m.p.h.	Timed speed over ¼ mile.
12.94 to 1	4½ sec	
7.01 to 1	5 sec.	
5.22 to 1	6½ sec.	85.71 m.p.h.
3.8 to 1	9 sec.	

Turning circle: 47ft. 6in.
Tank capacity 25 gallons; fuel consumption 12 m.p.g.
12-volt lighting set cuts in at 15 m.p.h., 12 amps. at 30 m.p.h.
Weight: 45 cwt.
Price, with Weymann saloon body, £2,400.

26 FEET from 30 M.P.H.

"THE AUTOCAR" ROAD TESTS

No. 76.—SUPERCHARGED 4½-LITRE BENTLEY
The Appeal of Immense Power, Linked with Great Docility.

The illustration above indicates the size of the Supercharged 4½-litre Bentley compared with a 40-50 h.p. Rolls-Royce.

A GREAT deal is expected of any Bentley, simply and wholly because of the name and because of the manner in which that name has been gained. But it is interesting for a moment, in dealing with the supercharged 4½-litre, to regard the car from an angle quite apart from the speed, and see what its advantages are in other directions.

For instance—and this the driver who comes under that popular heading of the average motorist may be disinclined at first to believe—the big car can be throttled down to 8 or 9 m.p.h. on top gear, and can be driven in traffic almost entirely on top and third, and then there is practically nothing which makes the car any different to handle from any other machine. Certainly there is no suggestion then of fierceness, nor is there any such suggestion when, with the throttle right back, the car is cruising normally and quietly along a busy main road at the general speed of the line of traffic. This ability of the car to potter so docilely is, in fact, one of the greatest charms in a sense, remembering what is being held in reserve all the time; and whatever the need of the moment may be — extremely rapid acceleration or

fast work on a suitable road—the driver knows full well that the car will respond instantly to the controls.

Certainly, too, the acceleration is remarkable, and although the utmost can be obtained from a machine of this type only by intelligent use of the indirects, there is so much power that even on the high top ratio the majority of hills can be taken fast, if the owner wishes, while, of course, for the enthusiast there are few things more fascinating than the proper use of a close-ratio gear box. Acceleration is becoming one of the most vital factors of all under present-day road conditions, and, as a general rule, a car with really brilliant acceleration is a safe car—that is, in the right hands, of course.

As to actual maximum, quite obviously it is of the order that is adequate for all tastes outside a race proper, and there is no doubt the production machine lives up to the elusive phrase in being "a hundred mile an hour car." In point of fact, the machine tested was all but brand new, in spite of which the speedometer reading during the timed test on the track was 101 m.p.h., comfortable readings on the indirect ratios being, by the way, 38, 58 and 70 m.p.h. on first, second and third.

But for practical, everyday purposes in this country what really matters is the ability of the car to get quickly to a fast cruising speed and to stay there with no suggestion of effort of any kind for as long as conditions allow. It is interesting, incidentally, that from inside the car the sound of the supercharger itself is scarcely audible.

The machine controls exactly as it should in every respect, wherein lies one of the greatest differences between a car of this calibre and another of more ordinary type, though some drivers might prefer a slightly longer gear lever; the brake operation is light and the brakes are properly decisive and smooth, while the hand brake, controlled by the outside lever, is powerful, too.

The independent bucket seats in the front are easily adjustable and very comfortable indeed, the back seats are adequate, there being two doors to the back compartment, the upholstery is admirable, there is provision for side screens, and the tonneau cover is neat and most effective. The main windscreen is excellent, h a v i n g a single panel which can be opened fully by means of outriggers, there are ventilators in the scuttle sides, and the screen wiper is of the type driven in conjunction with the speedometer, which, of course, does not cease to function when the throttle is opened suddenly.

The hood is held securely, without rattle, and has a neat cover—things which, in conjunction with a good tonneau cover, a r e practically essential for a fast, open four-seater that may be used for a considerable part of the time with only the front seats occupied. It often happens with a sports car travelling fairly quickly, the windscreen being relatively close to the driver, that short of a downpour the hood need not be raised, the rain mostly passing over and beyond the crew in the front; which is all right provided there is protec-

tion for the back compartment to prevent puddles of water collecting.

The instruments are mounted individually, but are neat, and an external lamp gives a soft, green-tinted light; the instruments include a revolution counter, a clock, and a good fuel tank gauge, an engine thermometer not being a standard fitting. The bezel-type control on the instrument board for the lights is good, though there is no dimming device, and, with all lights on, including the instrument illumination, the current output at 40 m.p.h. just failed to balance the consumption.

Concerning general detail and equipment, the supercharger gear at the front is enclosed particularly neatly, the engine as a whole is beautifully finished, both sets of plugs are accessible, as also both magnetos, the quick-action oil filler is big, as well as excellently placed, and the oil level indicator, giving a permanent visible reading, is good.

The tools are carried in a container, of which the lid forms part of the running board, and which can be locked

There is provision for changing the tail lamp from the right to the left-hand side when the car is taken abroad; and t h e finish everywhere, with chromium plating for the bright parts, is w h a t o n e expects to find.

There is something unusually impressive about the B e n t l e y radiator, especially from the dead-front view, and, somewhat curiously perhaps, those exposed details such as the hand-brake gear help to give the idea of an engineering job, which, apart from a few English exceptions, is as a rule suggested chiefly by the bigger and more expensive cars which are the product of Continental manufacturers.

A car with the strongest possible individuality, and it is certain that it is immensely l i k e a b l e no matter from what angle one may regard it.

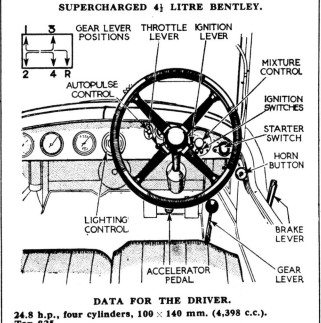

SUPERCHARGED 4½ LITRE BENTLEY.

GEAR LEVER POSITIONS — THROTTLE LEVER — IGNITION LEVER — MIXTURE CONTROL — AUTOPULSE CONTROL — IGNITION SWITCHES — STARTER SWITCH — HORN BUTTON — LIGHTING CONTROL — BRAKE LEVER — ACCELERATOR PEDAL — GEAR LEVER

DATA FOR THE DRIVER.

24.8 h.p., four cylinders, 100 × 140 mm. (4,398 c.c.).
Tax £25.
Wheelbase 10ft. 10in., track 4ft. 8in.
Overall length 15ft. 4½in., width 5ft. 8½in., height 4ft. 8in.
Tyres: 33 × 6in. on detachable wire wheels.

Engine—rear axle gear ratios.	Acceleration from steady 10 to 30 m.p.h.	Timed speed over ¼ mile.
9.3 to 1	4⅘ sec.	
5.7 to 1	6⅘ sec.	
4.7 to 1	7¼ sec.	
3.53 to 1	11½ sec.	97.82 m.p.h.

Turning circle: 49ft.
Tank capacity 16 gallons, fuel consumption 11 m.p.g.
12-volt lighting set cuts in at 20 m.p.h., 7 amps. at 40 m.p.h.
Weight: 37 cwt.
Price, with open four-seater body, £1,720.

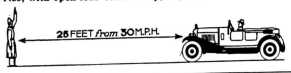

25 FEET from 30 M.P.H.

Le Mans 1930

The victors—Woolf Barnato and Glen Kidston.

LE MANS

Britain's Success in the Twenty-four-hour Grand Prix d'Endurance. Bentley First and Second. All Records Broken. New Talbots finish Third and Fourth. Germany's Valiant Effort with one Mercedes Fails after Eleven Hours. Nine out of Eighteen Finish.

A few seconds after the flag fell. The ultimate winner, followed by Davis and the rest of the field.

Above: Watney's and Clement's Speed Six, which finished second, makes a night-time pit stop. **Below:** The same car at Arnage. **Right:** The victors: Kidston and Barnato in the winning Speed Six, with Watney (left) and Clement standing alongside (Speed Six; second place). **Below, right:** Benjafield (bare-headed) takes the blown 4½-litre through Pontlieue; the car retired with a collapsed piston when lying third. **Bottom:** The Davis/Clive Dunfee Speed Six (which crashed after 21 laps) leads an M.G. Midget and Kidston's Speed Six into Arnage. This was Bentley's fifth Le Mans win and last appearance as a works team.

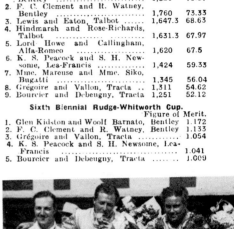

A STILL BIGGER

Eight-litre Six-cylinder which, as a Whole, Forms a Magnificent Piece of Engineering Work.

LYING behind the new eight-litre Bentley 110 × 140 mm. six-cylinder chassis is the endeavour to provide the ultimate expression of motoring as an ideal. Price is, naturally, not the ruling factor it has become in so many chassis to-day, even though that price is not high as machines of the type go. And, although no car, large or small, can be designed unhindered by the question of cost, yet motoring is at its highest level when a big engine forms the power unit and nine-tenths of the machine's work is accomplished with the throttle only just open.

There results something which, if its body, chassis and other details are as they should be, has that sense of great latent power which alone gives propulsion without effort in the maximum of comfort and speed that does not tire however long the distance.

The new eight-litre is the result of a long experience with the famous Big Six, and, though it is not intended to be a sports model in any shape or form, results from an experience with racing machines that is second to none. There are few drastic alterations, therefore, the design following

BRITAIN'S LARGEST CAR.—The new 8-litre Bentley follows closely the well-known Big Six in general layout. The frame, being upswept at both ends, the whole car is brought lower.

BENTLEY

logically from what has gone before, and the alterations all showing how this or that problem occurring in the older car is solved in the new. For one thing, the cylinder block, almost exactly like that of the 6½-litre, has its ports reversed, for the reason that, the controls for the two big S.U. carburetters being now wholly on the right side, instead of crossing to the left, can be simpler and more direct, a thing assisted by the improved eccentric-operated mixture control of the new instrument.

Then the exhaust branches, neatly sheathed in aluminium sheet, seem to fall more naturally on the left side, the total result being that the whole power unit is cleaner. That has entailed placing the Delco distributor on the left, since it can easily stand what exhaust heat there is, and replacing it on the right-hand side by a Bosch magneto, both coil and magneto operating together and feeding each its own row of plugs, so that the compressed gas is fired from both sides of the combustion chamber.

The head, by the way, is still part of the cylinders, not detachable, and on it a single camshaft operates the

Left side of the engine, which is now the exhaust side. The camshaft eccentric drive is within the tunnel behind the cylinders.

twenty-four valves through duralumin rockers, each set of rockers being supplied with oil as before. The interesting camshaft drive, a set of eccentrics driving another set on the camshaft through connecting rods, and itself driven by one steel and one fabric gear, is retained as being quiet and easily looked after, since otherwise two pairs of gears would have to be used instead of one. Crankshaft, connecting rods, pistons, and lubrication are all similar to those of the 6½-litre in all but size, and the damper,

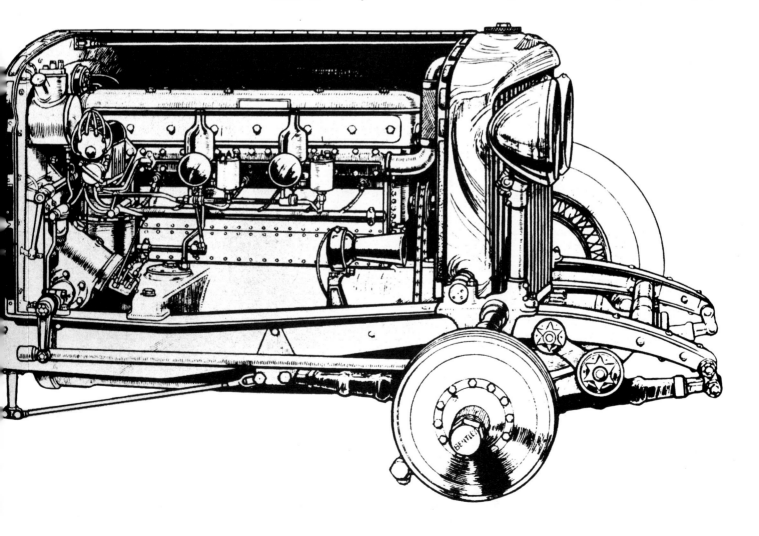

A Still Bigger Bentley.

a slipping flywheel at the forward and of the crank, has been modified from racing experience, which shows how extensive is the scope of racing to cover what would be thought a purely touring auxiliary.

The carburetters are fed from a big vacuum tank through an accessible filter with a metal bowl, and each instrument has the separate slow runner fixed especially for Bentleys, the main fuel tank at the rear being now of 26 gallons' capacity and slung on one central cross tube and one forward bracket to relieve the tank from stress.

A new, characteristically magnificent, radiator, this time an internal block bolted to a separate shell, looks unusual, because it has big thermostatically operated shutters in front, the thermostat, encased in the top tank, closing the shutters until the water is sufficiently warm. This is a departure, for previously the instrument controlled water flow direct, but the new scheme gives a bigger outlet for the water from jackets to radiator, and, since the radiator water is always circulating, makes it unlikely that the radiator contents might freeze on a very vold day. Two drain plugs make certain the tubes will empty completely, and a steam valve prevents water escaping down the vent tube, which is sealed unless steam generates.

Direct–driven Dynamo.

The dynamo lies under the radiator and is driven direct from the crankshaft, all the electrical components having separate fuses, while the wiring along the chassis consists of stout, insulated cables held in rubber bushes. That irritating noise which is caused by the shock engagement of most starting motor pinions is avoided on the Bosch starter by a solenoid control sliding the pinion gently into engagement with the flywheel teeth before the turning effort commences. Big Zeiss head lamps are mounted on pedestal brackets which have separate adjustments for moving the lamp up or down, to one side or the other, so that the correct setting one way is not altered when the other adjustment is used.

A rubber mounting takes the weight of the engine at the rear; the clutch is a larger version of that on the 6½-litre with a big adjustable clutch stop; and the gear box is entirely new, as a glance at its shape reveals. To-day, a big car must have quiet gears; the wailing of an indirect is anathema; but, as a rule, only top and third are really

quiet, first and second remaining unchanged. In the new Bentley box all the gears should be quiet, the main change being to stiffen everything considerably, and to add bearings, apart from the effect of the additional surface of the gears to lighten their load. Rubber mounting is employed for this component, also it is separate from the engine—an unusual point these days—and the gate, with its lever, has been modified a little. Actually, full justice can only be done to this box by a very long description, but the main point is its practical effect.

Aft of the gear box runs a huge tubular propeller-shaft with two Hardy Spicer joints, the axle torque being taken by the rear springs. Another change brought about by the urgent need for bringing down the height of the chassis is the adoption of a hypoid gear—that is, a bevel couple of which the pinion is engaged with

A semi-plan view of the chassis showing how stiffly the side members are braced together by numerous tubular cross-members.

the crown wheel, not on the fore and aft centre line, but below that point, which results in the pinion having an action that is a little like that of a worm gear, as it were, a compromise between that and a bevel. The gear is massive, since rigidity and accuracy of adjustment are essential, but, because of the lower bevel pinion, the whole of the chassis can come down. This is effected by curving the frame, a much deeper and stiffer frame, downwards behind the radiator so that the forward engine mounting is a little, and the rear mounting a good deal, lower than that of the 6½-litre the power unit sloping backwards, which arrangement brings the gear box lower as well.

Stiff Side Members.

Just where the rear axle side sleeves extend the frame runs sharply upwards to give the maximum flat surface for the body, then curves gently to the rear dumb irons, and a number of really big tubular cross-members tir the two side members stiffly together in one rigid whole. So big is this frame that it forms an interesting contrast to those of other models.

By one or two modifications the vacuum servo motor controlling the brake is smoother in action, the brake gear has the characteristic controlled compensation—the balancer moving when required, not each time—and large tubes running forward to the front brakes, but there are eight shoes, two to each drum, not twelve in all, the rear shoes being operated by the lever through a separate control, and the rear brakes have cables instead of rods. The cam also has been considerably modified.

The steering gear is as before, but the column is supported closer to the wheel; the steering arm on the stub axle is brought nearer to the centre of the spring; and, a big change, the front springs have forward shackles. The whole suspension has been redesigned; the rear springs are alongside the frame instead of beneath it, and nearer, therefore, to the hubs; each spring eye is covered by an aluminium housing which takes in part of the spring leaf, acts as an oil retainer, and is an anchorage for the gaiter as well, oil being retained because cork washers take up the clearance from the shackles.

In front are mounted B and D friction shock absorbers, but the rear axle has the hydraulic double-acting B and D's with additional damping chambers that made such a remarkable difference to the racing machine.

The Autocar Road Tests

8-LITRE BENTLEY SALOON

Motoring in its Very Highest Form: The Tremendous Performance.

IT may seem slightly unusual to commence a description of a car's test by disagreeing quite thoroughly with a statement made by a representative of the manufacturer when introducing the model at one of the firm's functions, but so great appears to be the discrepancy between what one would naturally expect and what is actually provided that a word or two of argument is essential.

At the time of the Olympia Show the 8-litre Bentley was introduced in such a way as to stress to the full the fact that it was designed to be that rather mysterious type of vehicle which is generally known as a town carriage; and undoubtedly a great many people who listened to that announcement went away under the impression that performance was the very last thing on which the car based its claim to consideration—so much so that certain people undoubtedly believed that the performance was sacrificed to obtain other possibilities.

Now, in the first place, although everybody knows what is meant by a town carriage, and, further, can realise the distinction between that and a sports car, it is not, in fact, easy to see where one type stops and the other begins. Quite apart from that, the one thing, the dominant note, of the new Bentley is its tremendous performance, and on that performance alone it stands right in the forefront as an equal, at least, of any other car in existence. One glance at the figures in the table overleaf shows, as no sentences or phrasing can, that the big 8-litre is something quite out of the common run of cars, even when allowances are made for the increase in engine capacity as compared with the $6\frac{1}{2}$ litres of the earlier six-cylinder model.

Therefore, it is impossible to allow that the car can be described, or in any way regarded, as just a town carriage and nothing more; and to remain silent concerning, or in any way belittle, the performance factor is, from the sales point of view, to disregard the principal reason why this splendid car should succeeed.

Had it been that the performance made the car difficult to handle on top gear at low speed, heavy to manoeuvre in traffic or in a confined space, harsh or noisy, then the performance by itself might justly be regarded as simply that of a sports car, though few of these features are easily noticeable even in the modern sports car, unless it has been tuned for racing.

Quite on the contrary, this car can be driven really

softly on its high top gear as slowly as a man walks, and can accelerate from that without snatch and without difficulty, and the whole time the engine, being well within its power, is silent and smooth; in fact, it is only really apparent that there is a big engine working under the bonnet at all, and that so high a top ratio is used, when the machine is accelerated from a crawl. For all practical purposes, therefore, the machine does its work on the one gear, in town or out of it, and it is with that one gear that it best suits the average driver.

The new gear box is interesting, the longer movement of the lever from one slot to another being a little puzzling at first to anyone who is accustomed to the earlier models, a point emphasised because to start on second and then change at once to top is the obvious way of handling the machine. The gears are quieter than before, and will be quieter still when there has been opportunity to obtain more experience with this type of box.

The use of two broad shoes in each of the rear wheel brake drums, instead of four relatively narrow shoes, has certainly improved the brake power, and certain alterations have made the vacuum servo motor seem more definite and more positive, so that to the driver it really appears as though he can feel the shoes touch the drums and thus command a more delicate control. But the great change in the machine, apart from its engine, is the way in which the car, travelling fast and with a saloon body, can be taken round curves and corners with its shock absorbers adjusted as for town work. It is true that when once one was accustomed to the earlier 6½-litre that model seemed as steady as could be wished —provided the shock absorbers were really tight— yet the new car is steady with easy riding springs and so puts the earlier model entirely in the shade, a thing due in great

part to the big, stiff frame, though the fact that the springs are farther apart and the chassis lower may have a great deal to do with it as well : and this rigidity makes the big car almost as tractable as one of the smallest machines on the road, while it seems to have no side sway whatsoever on a fast corner.

It is possible, of course, to go right over the chassis, pointing out here and there where improvement is apparent, but, when all is said, it is not a matter of detail improvement that makes the 8-litre Bentley what it is, for the thing that counts above everything else is the way in which the big machine does its work, and its sense of great latent power. Exactly this and nothing else is the real reason why so big a machine has a future.

Putting it another way, one can breakfast comfortably in London yet lunch at Catterick Bridge, and during the whole of a run of this type there was none of the intenseness that usually comes into fast driving; indeed, it was practically impossible to believe that the car was travelling at anything like the pace the speedometer showed, though subsequent tests proved that speedometer to be reasonably accurate. In spite of the average, not a single village or town was traversed at anything like the pace that is maintained by the driver of an ordinary car, and in most cases it seemed much more pleasant to go through at a genuine 11 to 15 m.p.h.

Apart from that, the best testimonial to the ease with which the car did its work lay in the fact that the occupants of the two front seats were conversing naturally during the whole of the run.

In France the Bentley has kept up a cruising speed of 70 m.p.h. without the engine seeming to do anything at all, and, if the long northern roads offer, can go right up to 100 m.p.h. on the flat with surprisingly little apparent effort.

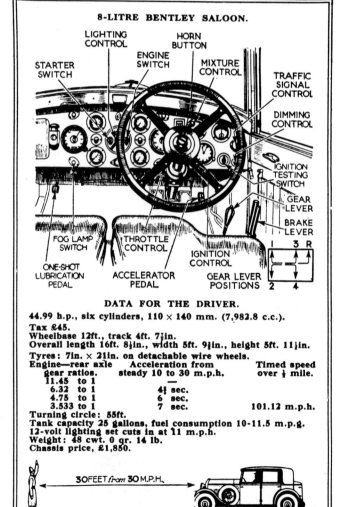

8-LITRE BENTLEY SALOON.

LIGHTING CONTROL — HORN BUTTON — ENGINE SWITCH — STARTER SWITCH — MIXTURE CONTROL — TRAFFIC SIGNAL CONTROL — DIMMING CONTROL — IGNITION TESTING SWITCH — GEAR LEVER — BRAKE LEVER — FOG LAMP SWITCH — THROTTLE CONTROL — ONE-SHOT LUBRICATION PEDAL — ACCELERATOR PEDAL — IGNITION CONTROL — GEAR LEVER POSITIONS

DATA FOR THE DRIVER.

44.99 h.p., six cylinders, 110 × 140 mm. (7,982.8 c.c.).
Tax £45.
Wheelbase 12ft., track 4ft. 7½in.
Overall length 16ft. 8½in., width 5ft. 9½in., height 5ft. 11½in.
Tyres : 7in. × 21in. on detachable wire wheels.

Engine—rear axle gear ratios.	Acceleration from steady 10 to 30 m.p.h.	Timed speed over ¼ mile.
11.45 to 1	—	
6.32 to 1	4½ sec.	
4.75 to 1	6 sec.	
3.533 to 1	7 sec.	101.12 m.p.h.

Turning circle: 55ft.
Tank capacity 25 gallons, fuel consumption 10-11.5 m.p.g.
12-volt lighting set cuts in at 11 m.p.h.
Weight: 48 cwt. 0 qr. 14 lb.
Chassis price, £1,850.

30 FEET *from* 30 M.P.H.

Coachwork 1930

Right: A four-door four-light fabric saloon by the Hoyal Body Corporation (1928) Ltd. on a 6½-litre chassis.

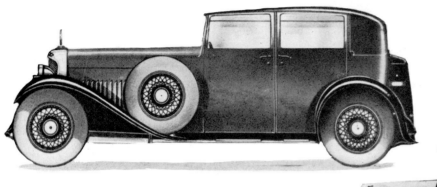

Left: Martin Walter's "Sarre" Weyman saloon on a 4½-litre chassis.

Right: Open 4-seater sporting coachwork by Van den Plas on a 6½-litre chassis.

Left: Woolf Barnato with his special-bodied Speed Six by Gurney Nutting – now owned by Hugh Harben (see page 121).

Right: A sportsman's coupe 6½-litre with fixed head. (J. Gurney Nutting & Co., Ltd.).

VINTAGE

THE 8-LITRE

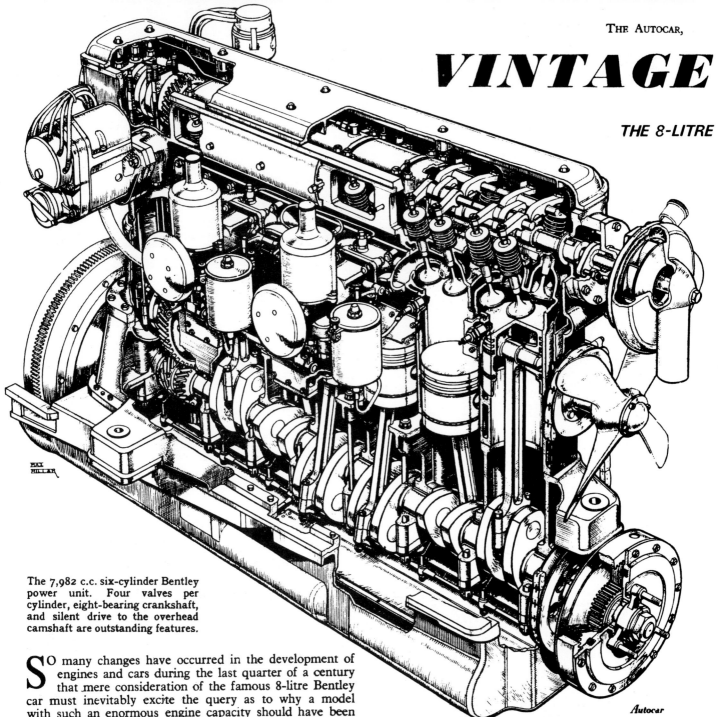

The 7,982 c.c. six-cylinder Bentley power unit. Four valves per cylinder, eight-bearing crankshaft, and silent drive to the overhead camshaft are outstanding features.

Autocar

So many changes have occurred in the development of engines and cars during the last quarter of a century that mere consideration of the famous 8-litre Bentley car must inevitably excite the query as to why a model with such an enormous engine capacity should have been designed for sale as a standard product.

During those years, and especially since the last war, the drive with British manufacturers has been steadily towards smaller engine capacities, higher power and torque, lower fuel consumption and general all-round economy; engine capacities now are seldom more than 4½ litres in the larger cars, while 3,000 c.c. or much less has been ample for many high-performance cars.

Although engine capacities have tended to become very much smaller over the years, the outstanding feature in car design has been, nevertheless, the virtual abandonment by the majority of manufacturers of the production and sale of separate chassis in favour of the integral construction vehicle, enabling the makers to retain full control of the design of the car and engine and its ultimate performance, with cost-cutting applied in every possible direction.

In the 1930 period, when there was a much larger number of big cars on the market, chassis were built, as a matter of course, to be fitted with standard bodywork by the manufacturers, or with coachwork produced by specialized firms. Within the performance requirement of the average buyer, this system of chassis-plus-bodywork was perfectly satisfactory, but when one came to a luxury car such as the Bentley, the situation was markedly different; to produce the best results, the *tout ensemble*

Though none of the 8-litre cars produced by the old Bentley company bore this type of coachwork, there are one or two specialist-built examples still about (this is Forrest Lycett's). Their big radiators and entirely purposeful appearance make them among the most impressive cars ever built.

LEVIATHAN

BENTLEY ENGINE · GREATEST OF THEM ALL

By MAX MILLAR

in excellence had to be matched to a much closer degree, especially with closed bodywork.

The 8-litre, six-cylinder Bentley chassis was the last of a series to be produced by W. O. Bentley before the re-organization into the present company, and it was designed to take almost any type of passenger bodywork that could be fitted to the chassis, irrespective of its bulk, height and weight, and to maintain a speed of a genuine 100 m.p.h. with the maximum of reliability and roadworthiness and at the same time the manners of a good town carriage. Whereas, with other Bentley chassis, there were always some limitations as to bodywork weight and so on, none applied to the 8-litre model, such was the capacity of this giant.

Specification

To cater for what might occur in the matter of all-up weight, air drag, passenger and luggage weight, fuel for long-distance travel and other imponderables, W. O. Bentley designed a big engine on very much the same lines as the previous 6½-litre six-cylinder, but with a capacity increased from 6,597 c.c. to 7,982 c.c., and fitted it into a long wheelbase chassis. The prime characteristics of engine behaviour had to be: Maximum r.p.m. not much higher than 3,000, sustained and smooth pulling power over a wide speed range, freedom from major servicing over long periods and complete reliability for high-speed motoring. Petrol in those days varied from 1s 2½d to 1s 4½d a gallon, so that fuel consumption at 10-15 miles per gallon represented a total cost no higher than would be the case with a much smaller car at the present time.

In the range of Bentley engines, from the early 3-litre four-cylinder unit to the big 8-litre six-cylinder, W. O. Bentley had always shown a strong individuality and taste in design. This was exemplified in the adoption of four valves per cylinder to obtain ample cooling of valve seats and other locally hot areas; non-detachable cylinder heads; built-up cylinder water jackets for internal access to cylinder and head castings; lightweight connecting rods and crankshaft; multiple crankshaft bearings; neatly arranged and very accessible auxiliaries; and a superb finish inside and outside the engine. Externally, every Bentley engine had to be faultless to the connoisseur—none more so than the vast 8-litre.

With a bore and stroke of 110 by 140 mm, the 8-litre engine pulls standard top gear ratios of 3.533, 3.785 or 4.071 to 1, according to the rear axle chosen; on seven special chassis a ratio as high as 3.3 to 1 was fitted. This, with a tyre size of 7.00 × 21in, resulted in a speed of 32 m.p.h. per 1,000 r.p.m. in top gear. At 5.3 to 1 compression ratio, 225 b.h.p. was developed at 3,500 r.p.m.; at 6.1 to 1, 230 b.h.p. at 3,300 r.p.m.

Getting Inside

The cast-iron cylinder block has side plates of stainless steel secured by a multitude of 2 B.A. studs and nuts, to facilitate full inspection and cleaning of the jacketing and also the cylinder casting generally. A detachable plate on top also enables the interior of the cylinder head to be examined when necessary. The block is secured to the Elektron crankcase by pairs of long bolts extending to the main crankshaft bearing caps, the upper nuts of which are concealed behind the lower extension of the water jacket plates.

As was common in the days when it was designed, the crankshaft, of marine design, has no balance weights, but is supported by seven main bearings, and has, at the front, a large multi-plate friction damper, which is assisted in its work by the driving of a large dynamo. An eighth main

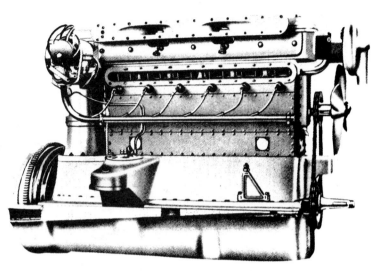

Carburettors and induction casing .emoved to show the main manifold leading to the twelve inlet valves.

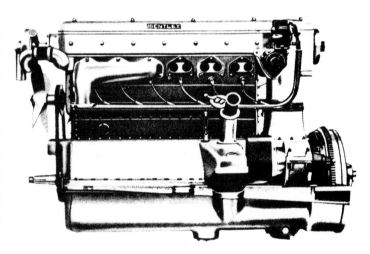

Left side of the 8-litre engine with one exhaust manifold removed to reveal twin exhaust ports in each cylinder.

bearing, just ahead of the flywheel, acts as a rear support for the shaft. The connecting rods, which are machined all over, are light in weight and small of mass, and both crankshaft and rod bearings are of white metal and steel backed. The alloy split skirt pistons, each with two compression and two scraper rings, have fully floating gudgeon pins provided with soft metal end caps. Lubrication of the main and other bearings is effected in the normal manner from an oil pump in the rear part of the Elektron five-gallon sump, the drilled crankshaft being fed from a fore and aft gallery pipe below the main bearing caps.

An outstanding attraction of this great engine is the layout of the drives to the overhead camshaft and auxiliaries, there being possibly no other engine in the world which could provoke such interest in these respects. In his early days, W. O. Bentley was a locomotive engineer apprentice in the old G.N.R. shops at Doncaster, and readers who may be conversant with earlier G.N.R. designs will recall the classic beauty and neatness of the locomotives built in these works. Something of this same regard for design was exhibited when W. O. Bentley produced the 8-litre engine, with a predilection for finely finished parts and excellence of detail arrangement.

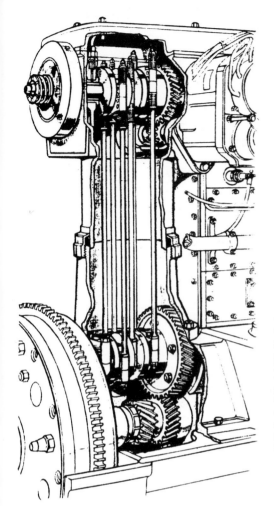

the system of drive to the camshaft requires no periodical attention or adjustment whatever, over mileages of as much as 50,000 to 70,000 miles, while, of course, the take-off point for the drive from the rear end of the crankshaft is ideal. A disadvantage of the system, seen through modern eyes, is the substantial addition to the overall length of the engine, which now could no doubt be materially reduced by suitable design and manufacturing methods.

As was standard on all previous Bentley engines, the main casing above the cylinder block of the 8-litre contains an internal casing carrying the camshaft and rocker assembly, from which one cam operates a pair of inlet valves, while two cams are used for the two exhaust valves for each cylinder. Long detachable side plates permit feeler adjustment of the

8-LITRE BENTLEY

rockers and valve stems, but adjustment is seldom needed in view of the size and reliability of the engine.

With such a large capacity, the fitting of two sparking plugs per cylinder was considered a necessity, the plugs on the exhaust side of the engine being energized by a coil, while the others (on the induction side) are operated by a magneto. A cross shaft, skew gear driven from the camshaft and mounted in the rear of the camshaft outer casing, drives the distributor and contact breaker on the left side, and also the magneto on the right side, giving perfect accessibility to these electrical components and their wiring and controls.

The setting of the camshaft is distinguished by the unusual location of two units; a friction damper at the rear end and the centrifugal water pump at the front end, the latter delivering water by a short, curved pipe into the front end of the cylinder jacket and thence to an internal gallery pipe and jets which direct the coolant to the exhaust ports. The only auxiliary not operated from the camshaft is the fan, which is belt driven from the front end of the crank-

The coupled rod drive between the lower, subsidiary crankshaft and the overhead camshaft. The three vertical reciprocating rods and the pair of miniature crankshafts provide a smooth, uninterrupted rotational movement to the camshaft.

To ensure a sweet, smooth and completely silent drive to the overhead camshaft, Bentley introduced a coupled rod mechanism which was a counterpart of the driving wheel side rods on a locomotive, except that three coupling rods were used instead of two.

In the Bentley, a miniature three-throw crankshaft located in bearings in the after part of the crankcase is driven by helical gearwheels at a 2 to 1 ratio from the main crankshaft, the throws being set at 120 deg to each other. At the rear end of the overhead camshaft is a duplicate of the three-throw crankshaft in the crankcase, and the pair of shafts are coupled together by three vertical rods, each having bearings at top and bottom.

Locomotive-type

A pair of shafts, each with two throws set at 90 deg (as the driving wheel crankpins are set on a locomotive), would transmit the drive to the camshaft perfectly well, but owing to the fact that the crankpins on the three-throw shafts of the Bentley engine are so large in relation to their throw that they are, in effect, eccentrics, a triple rod drive to the camshaft was substituted to ensure a very low-friction transmissions, with a completely even torque, combined with almost perfect silence in running.

The large bearings at the upper and lower ends of the coupling rods are split for assembly with the one-piece crankshafts, but in order to compensate for slight variations of the cylinder block height under temperature variation, a series of ground washers are fitted on the shafts of the coupling rods, above and below the halves of the upper bearings, the fractionally small clearances between the washers being filled with oil from the engine lubrication system. In effect, the washers can breathe oil and pulsate to allow the upper bearing to move vertically in sympathy with the upward expansion of the cylinder block, with no appreciable play in the bearing itself. In normal practice,

The small, three-throw crankshaft attached to the rear end of the camshaft for the reciprocating drive to the latter.

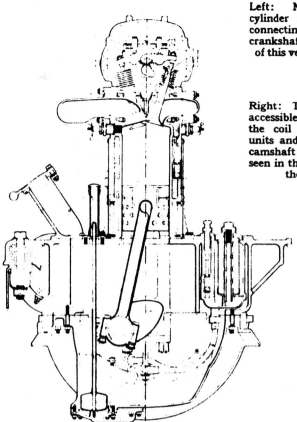

Left: Non-detachable cylinder heads, slender connecting rods and crankshaft were features of this very big engine.

Right: The high and accessible mounting of the coil and magneto units and the overhead camshaft damper are seen in this rear view of the engine.

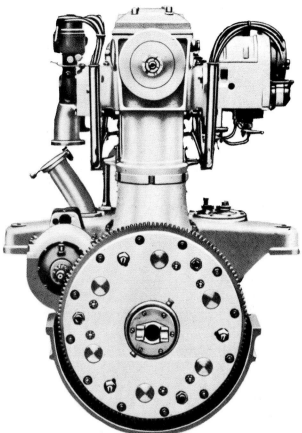

shaft. The whole setting of the auxiliaries and their method of drive is a masterly piece of design, enabling the engine to have an exceptionally clean and orderly appearance seldom seen on modern power units.

The carburation system comprises two very large bore S.U. carburettors, connected to a common induction manifold and leading to the twelve inlet valves, and a miniature idling carburettor mounted midway between the two main instruments and feeding mixture through small bore pipes to a point near each main throttle. This small carburettor, which draws fuel from one of the main float chambers, was fitted to obtain an economical mixture for slow idling, which is essential for a big engine used for town work.

Two other prominent features of the 8-litre unit, which put W. O. Bentley far ahead of his time, are the three-point rubber suspension of the engine, and the positive engagement of the starter pinion before the motor is energized. The separately located gear box, it may be noted, is also mounted on rubber, again at three points.

Much has been written on the general performance of the 8-litre model and of its capacity to eat up the miles, but unquestionably its appeal to the present-day motorist would be its very size and capacity to pull like a giant with just a whiff

The outer casing of the induction manifold, with idling carburettor located between the bolting-up faces of the two main carburettors.

of throttle, if only one could afford nowadays to motor with such a car. W. O. Bentley has said that he used regularly to leave his London office at 9 a.m. in his 8-litre, have an early lunch at Catterick, visit Carlisle, and then be back in London the same evening—some 600 miles in not much more than twelve hours. Then there was W. O.'s famous run between Dieppe and Cannes during daylight hours, among other feats of very fast touring in the 'thirties, while an

8-litre Bentley was the first to lap Brooklands at over 100 m.p.h. with closed bodywork.

The average weight of an 8-litre saloon is 48 to 50 cwt, the chassis being very strongly built to cope with high speeds. A number of the cars are still in very good running condition, and certain engines have been converted to three carburettors, still further to increase performance, the maximum horsepower being raised in one case to 268.

The very neatly arranged contact breaker and distributor unit, and other accessories at the rear of the engine.

Talking of Sports Cars
HUGH HARBEN'S SPEED SIX BENTLEY

By RONALD BARKER

'Babe' Barnato in his heyday, as one of the famous Bentley Boys

Left: This is what Hugh Harben bought little more than a year ago

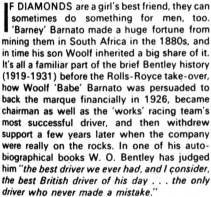

Two facing forward and one side-saddle, by Gurney Nutting

Without the winged 'B', would you have guessed the identity?

IF DIAMONDS are a girl's best friend, they can sometimes do something for men, too. 'Barney' Barnato made a huge fortune from mining them in South Africa in the 1880s, and in time his son Woolf inherited a big share of it. It's all a familiar part of the brief Bentley history (1919-1931) before the Rolls-Royce take-over, how Woolf 'Babe' Barnato was persuaded to back the marque financially in 1926, became chairman as well as the 'works' racing team's most successful driver, and then withdrew support a few years later when the company were really on the rocks. In one of his autobiographical books W. O. Bentley has judged him *"the best driver we ever had, and I consider, the best British driver of his day . . . the only driver who never made a mistake."*

So the odds are that without the Kimberley diamonds we might never have heard of 'Babe' Barnato or the Speed Six Bentley, although this model was developed from the Standard 6½-litre which came on the scene before Barnato, in late 1925. According to Bentley historian Darell Berthon, 368 Standard 6½s were made during 1926-30, and only 177 Speed Sixes during 1929-30.

Hugh Harben's example has the special distinction that it was chairman Barnato's own car, and much photographed when delivered to him in June 1930. He is said to have sketched an outline of its closed body on the back of an envelope and told Gurney Nutting to get on with it. They in turn told him it couldn't be a four-seater with that tumbling roof of his, but they could compromise with a seat for one set cross-wise in the back; better sacrifice a passenger than an inspired design, so that's the way it was agreed.

Beyond this seat is a sort of carpeted patio for picnic hampers or luggage, between two large cocktail cabinets which were certainly not put there for decoration. A detachable panel

enabled him to reach goodies in the boot without getting out of the car. All in all, it was a pioneer G.T. coupé in the true sense. Probably it was with this car that Barnato won a wager in 1930; setting off from Cannes by road at the same time as a friend left in the Blue Train, Barnato arrived in London with four hours to spare before meeting his friend at Victoria.

Woolf Barnato died in 1948, but had parted with this car many years before. For a time it belonged to Charles Mortimer, who sold it to Reg Potter in 1941, and it was from him that Harben managed to prise it last year after somewhat protracted negotiations. By this time it was in a very rough state, and what Harben really wanted was a touring Speed Six. Mercifully he was persuaded to preserve the unique body. *"Restore it as it is,"* his friends suggested, *"and if you don't like it you can then swop it for an open car."*

Being the sort of man who, when he wanted a new house, designed and built it himself (with his wife's active help), and having the facilities of a precision engineering business at his disposal (primarily engaged on research and development for aircraft braking systems) he made very rapid progress, completing the job just in time to drive the Bentley to London for display in the ballroom of the Dorchester during the Bentley Drivers' Club Annual Dinner-Dance last October.

It's not exactly as the 'Babe' had it; originally the bonnet top and sides were fabric-covered like the rest of the body, and it was all black. Now it's only black above the waistline, deep green below it, and the bonnet has been uncovered, as the Harbens prefer it that way. Weathershields have installed a Webasto sun roof, so neatly that it escapes notice until pointed out. The screen is now fixed instead of hinged, and the back window, once barely

Fast-back design of 38 years ago—a real pioneer among GT coupés. Note the neat installation of the Webasto sun roof

All the original instruments, including a Hobson Telegauge for fuel contents (top centre), plus a brake vacuum gauge to the right of the steering column. Levers on the wheel hub are for ignition timing, mixture and throttle

Triple eccentrics behind the block drive a single overhead camshaft, operating four valves per cylinder in a non-detachable head

more than a 2 in. slot, has been deepened slightly in the interests of safety. Otherwise it's just as it began over 38 years ago, even to the Bosch electrics but Zeiss headlamps with glass mirror reflectors, as specified by Barnato, and his choice of fatter section tyres for the back wheels—7.00 X 21 in., whereas the fronts are 6 in.

A very professional trimming job in beige leather, with cloth roof lining and thick carpeting to match, was entrusted to Meynell and Phillips of Burton-on-Trent; the instrument panel, incidentally, is also faced with leather. Coffin manufacturers in Tipton made a beautiful job of all the decorative woodwork—it must have been rewarding for them to have some of their handiwork neither buried 6 ft. nor committed to an incinerator.

Somehow this body seems to change character as you walk round it; most imposing is the three-quarter front, emphasizing the great length and depth of the bonnet—the filler cap stands an inch or two above a Mini roof!—in relation to the compact passenger-carrying section, putting one in mind of the *Flying Scotsman*; a reminder of 'W.O.'s' pre-World War I apprenticeship with steam locos.

From three-quarter rear, though, the true originality of the design is very striking, pleasingly unconventional without being freakish. But it is the dead rear view that's the big surprise; it looks such a squat little package that you would never take it for a big Bentley without the winged 'B' on the boot to identify it. The saucy upsweep of the mudguards, perhaps inspired by the Windmill ladies (Barnato was not averse to night-clubs, they say) leaves the wheels and tyres completely naked from this angle, and draws attention to a rather narrow track of 4ft. 8in. Indeed, two of those great tyres laid together flat on the deck would exceed the track by 14in.

We went for a brief run, but taking things rather easily because less than 1,000 miles had been covered since the complete rebuild. Like all sporting bodies of the times it seems extra-ordinarily small and narrow, though not restrictive or claustrophobic inside—cosy might be the word; it gives the passengers a sense of closer involvement in a journey which isn't there with current flush-sided bodies, especially those divided up the middle by a deep transmission tunnel and console (that dreadful word!).

W.O.'s links with the railway come to mind again when you look forward over that great bonnet, half expecting to see the twin tracks of the Iron Road converging into infinity; but the turning circle is less than a loco's, even if you would measure it in yards rather than feet. At present the steering is heavier than it should be, a problem that may have been solved by the time you read this.

I was warned that the C-type gearbox is none too easy, but it's only a bit unforgiving until one gets to know the ratio spacings. What is it, I wonder, about the pinion tooth profiles that decides whether a gear whine is to be melodious and agreeable—aristocratic even—or plaintively discordant? The engine is obviously in perfect order, being mechanically very quiet (assisted by those locomotive-style triple eccentrics driving the overhead camshaft), responsive and torque-active right down to 400 rpm in top gear. The sheer flexibility of very large engines with low compression ratios is always a delight. At the top end there should be about 180 bhp at 3,500 rpm and a maximum of over 100 mph. The 6½-litre Bentley was renowned for very powerful braking with vacuum servo assistance, which it needs with something approaching 2½ tons to stop from 100, but Hugh Harben has wisely added a reservoir and vacuum gauge to keep them operative for several applications with a 'dead' engine. Firm, vintage suspension, of course, completely in character with the car.

Next September there's to be a Bentley pilgrimage to Le Mans, and the Harbens plan to join the Faithful in the Chairman's Speed Six. If he has retained any influence in the super-natural world, I'm sure he will try to go with them—at least in spirit.

A BENTLEY 4-LITRE SIX

An Interesting New Model with Several Original Features. Great Strength Apparent in the Frame Design

WHEN a concern of the standing of Bentley Motors, Ltd., produces a new model, it is something of an event. It is, moreover, an event which indirectly interests all motorists, for although the new chassis falls in a price class which is primarily of direct interest to comparatively only a few, nevertheless it embodies all that is latest in design, all that is modern in construction, and, as such, it introduces features which may be widely followed in later years, even on quantity-production cars selling at a tenth of the price.

This is not to suggest that the new Bentley is in any way too advanced. It is on well-tried lines, but it incorporates many novel features, such as :

(1) a six-cylinder engine with an unusual design of combustion-chamber and valve arrangement.

(2) a four-speed gear box, separately mounted, with constant-mesh third-speed wheels and a multiplicity of bearings for the shafts,

(3) a double-dropped frame of great strength, united by no fewer than seven tubular cross-members,

(4) an unusually accessible single-point adjustment for the four wheel brakes, and

(5) the use of Elektron—a magnesium alloy—in place of the more usual aluminium alloys, thus effecting a considerable saving in weight.

New Engine Design

Otherwise the chassis follows previous Bentley practice very closely, being similar, in particular, to the eight-litre chassis, especially in matters of detail. Its main dimensions are : Wheelbase 11ft. 2in., or 11ft. 8in., for the short and long chassis, track 4ft. 8in., overall length 15ft. 10¾in., or 16ft. 4¼in., overall width 5ft. 8½in., and ground clearance 7in.

Naturally, the greatest interest lies in the engine, since this is such a distinct departure from previous Bentley designs. The cylinders are formed in a single casting of iron, and have a bore and stroke of 85 × 115 mm. (3,915 c.c.), giving an R.A.C. rating of 26.8 h.p., and, therefore, calling for an annual tax of £27.

Even at first sight, the cylinder block apprises one of the unusual, for on the near side the cylinders have each a single large valve, slightly inclined to the vertical and set some distance from the cylinder bore and at

---

SPECIFICATION

ENGINE.—26.8 h.p. six cylinders, 85 × 115 mm. (3,915 c.c.), tax £27. Detachable head, overhead inlet valves, side exhaust valves, two carburetters, coil ignition.

TRANSMISSION.—Dry single-plate clutch, separate four-speed gear box with constant-mesh third. Ratios: 14.85, 7.81, 6.16, and 4.58 to 1; open propeller-shaft, spiral bevel final drive.

SUSPENSION.—Half-elliptic springs back and front, with friction front and hydraulic rear shock absorbers.

BRAKES.—Internal expanding two-shoe brakes on four wheels, self-servo front brakes, direct mechanical operation.

MAIN DIMENSIONS.—Track 4ft. 8in. Wheelbase 11ft. 2in. or 11ft. 8in. Overall width 5ft. 8½in., length 15ft. 10¾in. or 16ft. 4¼in. Ground clearance 7in. Turning circle, right 47ft., left 46ft. Tyres 20 × 6.5in., pressure 37 lb. per sq. in. Approximate chassis weight 32 cwt. Petrol tank capacity 20 gallons; consumption 14—15 m.p.g. Oil consumption 1,500 m.p.g.

---

an angle to its transverse diameter. These are the exhaust valves, for the inlet valves are arranged in the detachable cast-iron head, and they are so set in order that the valve ports may be thoroughly water-jacketed, and thus any possibility of local hot-pockets be eliminated.

The inlet valves are also large ; they, too, are slightly inclined to the vertical, and are set well over to the off side of the head, opposite to the exhaust valves. The inlets are masked, while the combustion-chamber is of Ricardo type, with only just the necessary clearance over the piston crown, and a decided pocket over the exhaust valve. Each sparking plug is located in the centre of this combustion space, being set at a slight angle to the vertical. The design of the combustion-chamber and the arrangement of valves and sparking plug are such that the utmost possible use may be made of the fuel taken into the cylinders, and, with a compression ratio of 5.5 to 1, by no means high for these days, the power output at 4,000 r.p.m. is 120 b.h.p.

A Rigid Crankshaft

Mixture is supplied by two S.U. carburetters feeding into a single induction manifold running along the off side of the engine, and it has been found that the insertion of baffles in the manifold improves the distribution of the mixture. The exhaust manifold is of large size, and is on the near side of the engine, as also are the sparking plugs, which are very accessible.

The crank case is of Elektron and is obviously designed for great rigidity, the supports for the bearings being particularly massive. Great rigidity has also been secured in the crankshaft, which is carried in seven bearings of large diameter. The crankpins are also of large diameter ; in fact, the circumferences of the main journals and crankpins overlap, the result being a shaft which is so rigid that the vibration damper usually associated with six-cylinder engines is omitted. Owing to the diameter of the crankshaft bearings it is possible to reduce their length, and this also applies to the big-end bearings.

The main bearings have bronze shells lined with white metal, while the connecting rods have thin mild steel shells, also white-metal lined, and the caps of the rods are strengthened by two ribs and are secured by a single bolt on each side. The rods are steel, of H section, with bronze bushes in the little ends for the floating gudgeon pins, while the aluminium pistons carry three compression rings and a scraper ring above the gudgeon pin, with a second scraper ring in the skirt, and are notable for the unusual shape of the crown, which is necessitated by the combustion-chamber design.

Seven large bearings are also provided for the camshaft, which is housed in the crank case. It operates the exhaust valves through tappets in the ordinary way, and the overhead inlet valves through push-rods and rockers, the push-rods being concealed in the cylinder casting. The tappets have the usual form of adjustment.

At the front of the engine are the helical-toothed pinions which drive the camshaft and auxiliaries, and at the rear end of the camshaft there are two bronze skew gears which drive similar gears on the vertical shafts operating the oil pump and the distributor of the Bosch coil-ignition system. The oil pump is of gear type and is sub-

Off side of the engine showing the oil filler, oil gauge, starting motor and two carburetters.

merged; it supplies the main bearings direct, and the crankshaft is drilled to carry oil to the big-end bearings, oil being supplied at a pressure of 40 lb. per sq. in. A suction filter surrounds the pump, and a pressure filter is fitted in a chamber in the off side of the crank case. A large oil filler is located on the off side, towards the front, and near it are a gauge to show the depth of oil in the sump and the handle which operates the drain tap.

The ignition distributor is very accessible, and it stands up at the rear of the cylinder block, on the near side,

and just above it on the aluminium dash are mounted two coils, one of which is a spare. This is an excellent arrangement as, in the unlikely event of a coil failing, it does not require a skilled electrician to change over the wiring to the spare coil, since the various connections are, of course, the same on both. The dynamo is also on the near side, towards the front of the engine, being driven from the distribution gear. The water pump is driven in tandem with it, and is situated to the rear of it, being so mounted that the gland is accessible for attention when necessary, while the complete pump could be easily dismantled without interfering with any other component. The radiator of the new car follows the imposing Bentley lines, and has shutters operated automatically by a thermostat in the header tank. The capacity of the cooling system is six gallons.

The Bosch starting motor is mounted on the off side, and this instrument has the advantage that its pinion is brought gently into engagement with the flywheel teeth by a solenoid control, so that the engagement is quiet and devoid of shock.

This interesting power unit is carried in the frame on two longitudinal tubular members, there being three substantial mountings on each side of the crank case, beneath the wide ribs which stand out along each side of the case, and the tubular supports are carried on large rubber mountings on a frame cross-member at the front and on brackets on the main frame members at the rear.

Power is transmitted by a dry single-plate clutch with an adjustable clutch stop, and the short clutch shaft has a

On the near side, beneath the exhaust manifold, is the detachable plate which covers the tappets. Dynamo and water pump are very accessible.

A Bentley 4-litre Six

fabric joint at each end. The gear box is similar to that introduced on the 8-litre model, and great care has been taken to obtain silent operation on all speeds. The case is of Elektron and is split vertically, while it is stiffened up by the large number of bearings provided for the shafts. The constant-mesh gears and the third-speed gears each have a bearing on either side, there being thus eight bearings in this front portion of the box. The main shaft has also two bearings and the layshaft another, while there is a bearing also at the front of the driving shaft, so that there are thus twelve bearings in all in addition to the spigot bearing. In particular the third-speed driven wheel is very rigidly mounted ; it is not carried by the shaft, which has a clearance through it, the driving connection being through the dog clutch, which slides on splines. This clever design gives a third speed which should be, and remain, silent.

Constant-mesh straight-tooth gears are used for third speed, and the en-

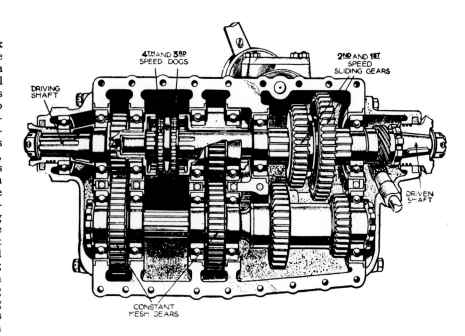

The cleverly designed gear box in section, showing the massive bearings of the constant mesh and third-speed gears. There are twelve bearings in all.

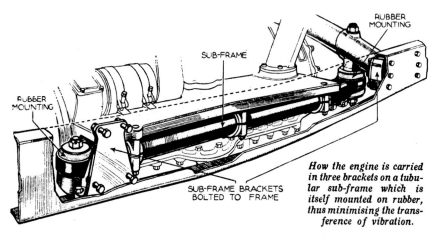

How the engine is carried in three brackets on a tubular sub-frame which is itself mounted on rubber, thus minimising the transference of vibration.

gagement of top and third gears is by dog clutches. In the interest of quiet running all gears are ground. The box is suspended on rubber mountings from frame cross-members, and the gate and gear lever are carried by a side extension for operation by the driver's right hand. Behind the gear box is a tubular propeller-shaft of large diameter, with a Hardy Spicer joint at each end, and a spiral bevel final drive

is fitted in the rear axle, which follows usual Bentley practice.

The front axle also is of orthodox design, but a new steering gear with a

worm and wheel mechanism on ball bearings is used, ample adjustment for rake being provided. Both front and rear axles have long half-elliptic springs, and the suspension system generally is modelled on that of the 8-litre chassis, since it has proved so satisfactory. The front springs are, however, shackled at the rear ends and not at the front; they are controlled by B. and D. friction-type shock absorbers, while the B. and D. hydraulic type is used for the rear springs.

The brakes are designed for direct mechanical operation, without the use of a servo motor as on the biggest chassis; the drums are of large diameter, and the front shoes are arranged to provide their own servo action. The shoes are of Elektron and are lined with Ferodo. The brake gear incorporates the controlled compensation which has been well proved on previous models, and a very accessible single-point adjustment takes the form of a large wing nut on the main frame

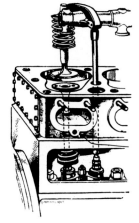

A spare coil is mounted ready for use.

In front view the new chassis is most imposing, the radiator being set between the frame members.

Details of the valve gear and tappets.

member on the off side. The handbrake lever operates the shoes in the rear wheel drums through a separate control. Rods operate the front brakes, but cables are used for the rear brakes. Rudge - Whitworth wire wheels are shod with 20×6.5in. Goodrich tyres.

A feature of the new chassis is the very strong, rigid frame modelled on the lines of that of the 8-litre. The side members are not only deep and of stout material, but they are united by no fewer than seven large-diameter tubular cross-members disposed one between the front dumb-irons, one behind the radiator and carrying the front ends of the engine bearers, two amidships carrying the gear box, one at the point of attachment of the front ends of the rear springs, one rather to the rear of the back axle, and one between the rear dumb-irons.

The double-dropped side-members run parallel from the rear to the cross-member supporting the back of the gear box, where they taper slightly to the points of attachment of the rear ends of the front springs, and then are parallel to the front dumb-irons. The fuel tank is slung at the rear of the frame, and has a capacity of 20 gallons; petrol is supplied to the carburetters by a large Autovac tank on the dash.

It will be apparent from the description that great sturdiness of construction is a feature of the new model, but apart from that there is abundant evidence of careful attention to all the minute details. Thus the Tecalemit system of central chassis lubrication

The gear box is carried on rubber mountings by two of the strong tubular cross-members of the frame, and has right-hand control.

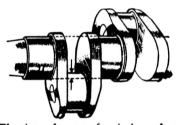

The circumferences of main journals and crankpins overlap, giving a very rigid crankshaft.

is fitted, ensuring that springs and other moving parts are kept in the best condition to fulfil their tasks, and taking from the shoulders of the owner-driver much of the responsibility of maintenance.

Again, not only is the electrical equipment very carefully chosen for its suitability, but the wiring is neatly disposed and the various circuits have their own individual fuses neatly mounted in cases on the engine side of the dash. Each of the Bosch head lamps, for example, has its own fuse in its circuit, so that the risk of a sudden black-out when driving at night is reduced to the absolute minimum.

From the general specification of the chassis and from the various details of design and construction it will be apparent that this new production is of a very high quality, and that the price of £1,225, which has been fixed for both the long and the short wheel-base chassis, is not high. The prices of the complete cars which will be offered have not been settled at the time of going to press, but the range will be very complete, and will include two open four-seater tourers, one having two doors and one four doors; a six-light limousine, a four-door four-light saloon, a two-door two-light close-coupled saloon, and a four-door sportsman's saloon with sliding windows, these four being of semi-panelled Weymann construction; and a six-light limousine, a limousine de ville, and a sedanca, these three being of coachbuilt type. The new Bentley will thus cater, with a wide range of models, for those who require a car of quality.

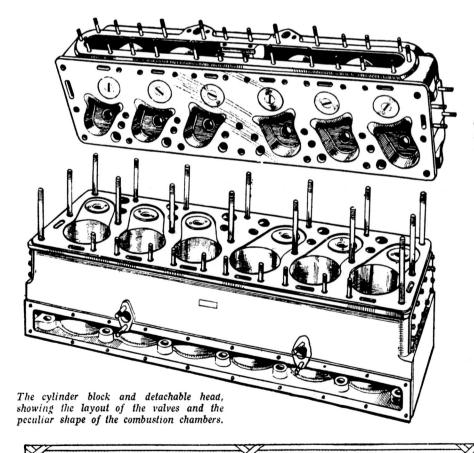

The cylinder block and detachable head, showing the layout of the valves and the peculiar shape of the combustion chambers.

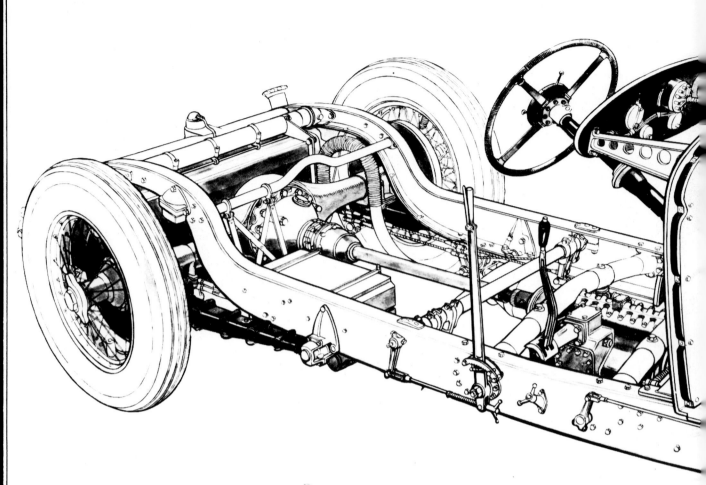

ENGINE.
Six cylinders.
85mm. bore.
115mm. stroke.
3915 c.c. capacity.
R.A.C. Rating,
26·84 h.p.

VALVES.
Overhead inlets.
Side by side exhausts

CHASSIS.
Wheel base:
long, 11 ft. 8 in.;
short, 11 ft. 2 in.
Track, 4 ft. 4½ in.

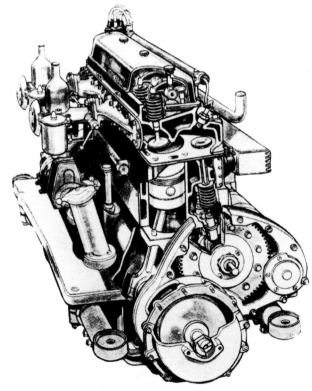

GEAR RATIOS.
1st	3·242 : 1
2nd	1·792 : 1
3rd	1·345 : 1
4th	1·000 : 1
Reverse	2·926 : 1
Back axle ratio	4·58 : 1

NEW 4-LITRE BENTLEY SIX

THE NEW CHASSIS, WHICH IS PRICED AT £1,225.

Drawn by Max Millar.

Bentley goes broke

and causes the motoring sensation of 1931

By Graham Robson

FIFTY YEARS ago, on 10 July, 1931, the world of motoring was shocked by the dramatic news that Bentley, had called in the Receiver! In many ways, this signalled the depth of the British Depression – for that most famous of car manufacturers, the five-times winners at Le Mans, were insolvent. Four months later, Rolls-Royce Ltd bought the assets, and the name of Bentley was saved from extinction. A simple story of misfortune – or was it? It took many years for the real truth to unfold.

The British public in general, and motoring writers in particular, were not as cynical in those days. In 1931, somehow, it seemed unthinkable that Bentley should go bankrupt; in the 1970s and 1980s it wouldn't cause the same sensation. Aston Martin, Lamborghini, Jensen, Maserati – even Rolls-Royce – all went broke at one time or another in the 1970s, and the fabric of society still exists. So what happened in 1931, and why? Could it, indeed, have been avoided?

Because Bentley Motors were not a public company, few knew much about its profit and loss figures. Almost everyone assumed that a firm which built such splendid cars, and which won so many races, had to be profitable. In any case, didn't they have the fabulously rich Woolf Barnato as chairman, and wasn't W. O. Bentley still churning out better and even faster cars every year?

It was only partly true. If the Vintage enthusiasts would ever admit it, there was really only one basic Bentley design, and that had been schemed in 1919, drawing heavily on 1913-1914 design standards. The cars were getting bigger, heavier, and faster, but they were also getting more expensive. Bentley had always been underfinanced; worse (and this was what very, very few people knew) was in fact that in 12 years it had gone through three

jected £65,000 of capital since 1927), who applied for the Receiver to be appointed.

There was general astonishment that Bentley Motors should be adjudged insolvent, especially as the chairman, Woolf Barnato, was thought to be a very rich man to whom his Bentley investment was an easy-to-bear indulgence. It might be significant that when Barnato heard about the London Life application, he was in New York, esconced with his financial advisers in that troubled continent. Whatever, he let it be known that he was "unable to meet these debts" and allowed the company to collapse; after five years of fruitless endeavour, no doubt he had decided that enough was enough.

Perhaps the public should have recognised the portents in 1930, when Bentley abruptly withdrew from motor racing immediately after that fifth Le Mans victory. It was all very well for our revered Sports Editor, S. C. H. "Sammy" Davis, to write that: "It is obviously and exactly the right moment for the big cars to stop when their record is really rather wonderful . . .", and " . . .The Speed Six team had reached a point where, if they did win a race, they got no credit because everybody said they

the case been put to the court than a completely unknown organization, the British Central Equitable Trust Ltd., put in a counter offer larger than that made by Napier. Everything looked set for a courtroom auction until the judge pointed out that such proceedings were below the dignity of a court of law, and demanded sealed bids at the end of the afternoon. Napier upped their bid by a mere £1,100, but the shadowy Trust increased theirs quite massively. Far from the margin being "a matter of a few hundred pounds", as W.O.'s "ghosted" book states, the winning bid was for £125,256 – no less than £20,481 more than Napier's final evaluation.

That was shattering enough – especially to W.O. himself, who had been so convinced that Napier would be his new bosses that he had been working on a new short-stroke engine design for them for several weeks – but there was an even bigger sensation when the British Central Equitable Trust Ltd. immediately sold their prize to Rolls-Royce Ltd. The move came at once – The Autocar reported the Trust's purchase in the 20 November, 1931, issue, and the resale to Rolls-Royce Ltd. the following week.

It looked like a put-up job at the time, and we now know that this was so. Well before the court case was to be heard, Rolls-Royce had done the deal with the Trust, and when Sir Arthur Sidgreaves (managing director of Rolls-Royce) reported back afterwards it was made perfectly clear that it was Rolls-Royce's, not an independent concern's, money which had been involved.

W. O. Bentley, who, if not naive, like to think the very best of everyone, did not know what to make of all this. At first he thought that he could continue to work with Napier, but he soon found out that his

different lots of capital, and had only recorded one annual profit since the last reconstruction of 1926.

Marketing policy, too, between 1929 and 1931 had been of the head-in-the-sand variety. At a time when the whole world, *not* merely the United States, was heading for economic disaster at a terrifying rate, Bentley Motors first introduced an esoteric 4½-litre supercharged model, and followed that up with the huge and magnificent, but incredibly costly, 8-litre design. The fact that panic then set in among the directors didn't help, for they then commissioned the design of an all-new 4-litre engine (which cost a great deal of money in tooling), and lumbered it with the job of hauling around a slightly shortened version of the 8-litre's chassis, transmission and suspension.

Not only was demand for the famous Bentleys falling, therefore, but there was still less demand for the new models. The Blower model was unreliable, having proved this publicly on the race tracks, the 8-litre was for plutocrats only, and the 4-litre didn't seem to appeal to anyone. The classic cash flow crisis developed during 1931, and it was a major creditor, the London Life Association Ltd. (which had in-

ought to have won, and if they didn't win every ill-wisher in the place made as much capital of it as possible . . .", but the fact was that they could no longer afford to go racing any more. (In later years, incidentally, a book "ghosted" for W. O. Bentley gave annual racing costs which were quite ludicrously under-stated, and have since been treated with disdain.)

Even so, it was not the collapse itself, but what happened in the next few months, which really lends spice to the affair. Patrick Raper Frere was appointed Receiver by the Chancery Division of the High Court, and immediately set about finding a buyer for Bentley Motors as a going concern. Within weeks he had attracted the attention of Napier (As *The Autocar*'s news pages of 14 August, 1931, confirmed), and by September he was convinced that such a fusion was the best solution to the impasse. He had even convinced H. T. Vane, managing director of D. Napier and Son Ltd., that Bentley Motors were worth £103,675, and all that remained was to convince the courts that this was acceptable.

What followed could have been written by Gilbert and Sullivan, or more likely by Sir Arthur Conan Doyle. No sooner had

life-long binding service agreement with Bentley Motors now meant that he "belonged" to Rolls-Royce. The result was that he was obliged to take a somewhat nebulous job with Rolls-Royce, although he had nothing to do with the design of the first of the Rolls-Bentleys.

So, why did Rolls-Royce take over Bentley at all, and why did they choose such a secretive way of doing it?

The under-cover method was almost certainly chosen to minimize any commercial embarrassment which would have followed if the court-room bargaining process had finally gone against them. They wanted the assets of Bentley Motors for one very simple reason – to stifle the competition to their own products. Not only was the latest 8-litre Bentley equally as well-engineered as the current 40/50 hp Phantom II Rolls-Royce, but was considerably faster *and* possessed a race-winning reputation. Of equal importance was the likelihood that a Napier-Bentley fusion would eventually have resulted in a new car equally as outstanding as the 8-litre Bentley, or the massive Napiers built immediately after the 1914-1918 war.

It was, without any doubt, *the* motoring sensation of 1931.

THE 3½-LITRE BENTLEY

Long-awaited Model Makes its Début. New Thoroughbred Amongst 1934 Cars With 90 m.p.h. Performance, Combined With Extremely Easy Action and Control, to be at Olympia. Full Particulars, Prices, and Road Impressions

Photogravure Illustration of the Chassis by F. Gordon-Crosby appears on pages 626-627

ONE of the most interesting and at the same time most curious things in connection with motoring is the way in which certain cars acquire what can only be termed a personality, odd though that term may seem in connection with machinery. Once achieve this point and a firm has every prospect of success, since the owners of the car in question hold stoutly the opinion that there is no better machine to be had, and take, as it were, a personal pride in any success the *marque* may attain.

So it is with the Bentley. From the day that car made its first appearance as a three-litre, onwards to the time when it upheld the English colours so stoutly in race after race, the Bentley became something more than machinery to all who were interested in cars. Consequently, when difficulties not connected with the car itself overcame the company, the effect was definitely dismal and was felt in a very much wider circle than that which included only those personally or practically concerned with the cars. Even now, to a certain extent, the exploits of the earlier Bentleys have become in some kind a tradition, and whatever may be said for and against racing this aftermath is, without doubt, of great value.

When it became known that the firm of Rolls-Royce were interested in the Bentley, the motoring world in general

was at once intrigued, for a car of Bentley type manufactured with the organisation Rolls-Royce possess seemed likely to be something altogether out of the common, and if that car remained of the same type it would be more interesting still. People remembered that once upon a time Rolls-Royce had taken part in competition, inevitably doing well.

Excellent Auguries

The great success of the racing Schneider Trophy engines seemed a good augury; there remained no doubt that the technical department and works at Derby could, if given time, produce an exceedingly good sports car. There followed rumours. Inevitably it was suggested that the new car would be the direct rival of the Italian racing machines; people even swore that they had seen such a car which in every way resembled the Italian Grand Prix machines, but the type, fascinating as it may be, appeals to too small a section of the community to be a practical proposition with which to restart business with a famous firm, and after due experiment with various types, the chassis decided upon was a 3½-litre six-cylinder.

That 3½ litres was chosen is interesting, because the original Bentley three-litre still sells well, and the gap left when its manufacture ceased has never been properly filled.

The new car, of course, differs radically from the last machines of the direct line, but, then, a 1934 Bentley would have differed just as much had manufacture never been interrupted. The chassis is much lower, looks longer, and is slimmer than hitherto; the engine, which has a bore of 82.5 and a stroke of 114 mm., gives a taxable rating of 25.3 h.p., and a swept capacity of 3,669 c.c. The engine is flexibly mounted in the chassis at the rear on rubber pads, and at the front on a flexible beam incorporating a shock-absorbing device. The head is detachable and carries two valves for each cylinder, operated by push-rods and rocking levers from a camshaft carried in bearings in the side of an aluminium crank case.

Seven bearings are provided for the massive crankshaft; there are two S.U. carburetters connected by a balance pipe, and the lower part of the crank case is a sump from which a single-gear pump delivers oil under pressure to the main bearings, the valve gear being fed by the quantity passing the ordinary spring-loaded pressure-control valve. Water is circulated by a pump, the radiator temperature being governed by shutters operated from a thermostat, and a four-blade fan is provided. A double S.U. electric pump feeds fuel from an eighteen-gallon tank at the rear to the carburetter float chambers, the tank being arranged

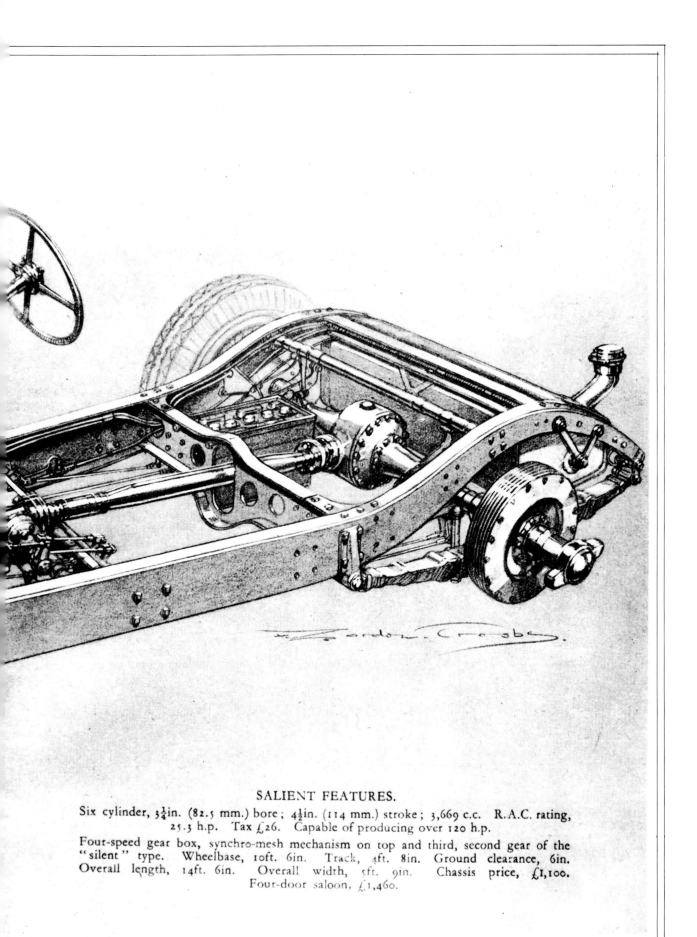

SALIENT FEATURES.

Six cylinder, 3¼in. (82.5 mm.) bore; 4½in. (114 mm.) stroke; 3,669 c.c. R.A.C. rating, 25.3 h.p. Tax £26. Capable of producing over 120 h.p.

Four-speed gear box, synchro-mesh mechanism on top and third, second gear of the "silent" type. Wheelbase, 10ft. 6in. Track, 4ft. 8in. Ground clearance, 6in. Overall length, 14ft. 6in. Overall width, 5ft. 9in. Chassis price, £1,100. Four-door saloon, £1,460.

How the instruments are grouped. A large speedometer and a revolution counter are on the right.

closed in leather gaiters, and have hydraulic shock absorbers. The four wheel brakes are operated through rods by a disc-clutch type mechanical servo motor mounted on the gear box, the front shoes being compensated relative to the rear and the brakes on each axle relative to each other. A hand adjustment is provided for the foot brake. Worm and nut steering gear, which is light and not too low geared, has been adopted. A large spring steering wheel is used with four short control levers arranged around the centre.

All the minor portions of the chassis are fed with oil by a foot pump permanently installed on the chassis feeding these bearings through pipes. A revolution counter is part of the dashboard equipment, the wheels are wire, the tyres—a new India pattern called the "Speed Special"—are 18×5.50in., while the wheelbase is 10ft. 6in., the track 4ft. 8in., the overall length 14ft. 6in., minimum clearance 6in., and the overall width 5ft. 9in., the chassis complete being priced at £1,100, the open four-seater £1,380, and the saloon £1,460. The chassis generally is of sturdy construction, with very long springs, and scales with petrol, oil, water and battery 22 cwt. 1 qr.

Cars of this type have been tested thoroughly both at Brooklands and at Montlhery, and on long-distance continental work, a photograph of one of them being published in *The Autocar* some time ago while it was engaged in trials on the road.

The Bentley radiator shape has been adapted to the new lines with success, and the famous winged B badge is retained. Several chassis with varying types of coachwork will be exhibited at Olympia next week.

to reserve two gallons for an emergency, and its contents, of course, being shown on an instrument board dial.

Battery and coil ignition has been adopted (there is a spare coil and make-and-break mechanism mounted conveniently on the dash), with one plug for each cylinder and a governor controlling the ignition point under correction from a lever on the steering wheel. The dynamo varies its charging rate according to the state of the battery, and the starting

motor pinion commences its work gently so that noise is avoided.

A disc clutch transmits power to a four-speed gear box with right-hand control, and synchromesh mechanism for top and third gear with a "silent" second speed, power being transmitted from the box to the rear axle through an open propeller-shaft, the torque of the spiral bevel being taken by the rear springs, while the rear axle itself is very light. All four springs are half-elliptic and en-

THE BENTLEY ON THE ROAD

Remarkable Road Holding and Docility Features of High Performance Car

ON the road the new 3½-litre Bentley proved a most satisfying vehicle. When I took over the car in London and threaded my way through the thick traffic, there was nothing about its action which suggested its latent capabilities, save for nippy acceleration. Its general behaviour, its docility, its comparative silence and ready pick-up on top gear with no suggestion of pinking, were more in keeping with a normal well-behaved touring car. Once the open road had been gained and some of the power which the engine develops unleashed—120 b.h.p., by the way—the true appeal of this newcomer under a famous name became apparent. On its 4.1 to 1 top gear, it would skim the ground as only a high-spirited car can do, scurrying up hills with ever-increasing speed and sweeping round open bends with a safety and assurance allied only to low-built cars with perfect weight distribution.

The equipment includes a large-sized speedometer registering 110 m.p.h. and a large revolution counter scaled up to 5,000 r.p.m., mounted side by side in front of the driver, and a central illuminated instrument panel with the usual indicators. At 3,000 r.p.m. the speed recorded is 72 m.p.h. on top, and at

3,500 r.p.m. 82 m.p.h. A red mark has been introduced at 4,500 r.p.m., which is the desirable limit speed of the engine,

and gives a road speed of 94 m.p.h. On the third gear of 5.1 at maximum engine revolutions the speed is 75 m.p.h.;

On Ivinghoe Heights, incidentally showing the treatment of the tail in this open model.

on second gear, 7.08 to 1, it is 54.25 m.p.h., and on first gear of 11.3 to 1 the speed is 34 m.p.h. But the new Bentley will not appeal solely on account of its maximum speed capabilities. As every sports car owner appreciates, liveliness and nippy acceleration belong mainly to cars having a high power-weight ratio and a high ultimate speed; therein the Bentley scores, since the weight of the open four-seater car I tried in three counties was no more than 28 cwt. 2 qr. complete for the road. Hills which in their day were used as test climbs seemed quite incapable of showing off the true performance of the new car. Aston Hill, near Tring, for instance, once a famous trials ground,

is simply as naught to the car—the speed is too great to enable the bends to be taken without easing down considerably. The neighbouring ascents on this range and again round about Ivinghoe only served to demonstrate remarkable road-holding on the bends and the absolute silence of the synchromesh third speed.

Among the by-lanes of Hertfordshire the car exhibited no trait of super-sensitiveness save when demanded by the accelerator pedal, but would amble along in the most docile manner on top gear without fuss or rattle. From slow speeds on top gear, the accelerator pedal governing the two S.U. carburetters was suddenly depressed, and after slight hesitancy

the speed goes up in a veritable crescendo. There is a complete absence of hissing from the carburetters, a large air cleaner being provided. On the lower gears the pick-up is, to say the least, thrilling.

In effect, the new 3½-litre Bentley is a wonderful blend of a reasonably quiet car with all the attributes of a docile well-mannered touring vehicle, but possessed of remarkable liveliness and the fierce acceleration associated with a high-spirited sporting car when occasion demands. It has finger-light steering, an exceptionally flexible engine, smooth throughout the wide range of action, a springing system which is remarkably effective in conjunction with hydraulic shock absorbers, and servo brakes quite exceptional not only in their retarding effect, but in the light pressure needed to check speed.

"At Home" Immediately

It is a car with which a driver immediately feels "at home," which is the concomitant of a feeling of safety. The hand controls embodied within the spring steering wheel are four in number: (*a*) throttle closed and open; (*b*) mixture, run and start; (*c*) ignition advance and retard; and (*d*) head lamps dipped and normal. Although a cut-out is provided for Continental use, it was found that when open the noise created was no more than that of the average sports car. When closed the engine is much quieter than normal sports cars, a mere exhaust rumble being audible to the passengers. Ninety-three m.p.h. was the best speed recorded with three passengers, and that with the cut-out closed, so that the makers' claim of an honest 90 m.p.h. is well substantiated. The 3½-litre Bentley will be hailed as a notable new thoroughbred among the 1934 range of cars, and one which will attract a great deal of attention. G. S.

BENTLEY COACHWORK

Intriguing Up-to-date Designs for a Speedy Modern Chassis

NATURALLY enough, for the new Bentley chassis some very fine examples of coachwork are being produced by the specialist coachbuilders. In these long, low sweeping lines, which are now so popular for sports cars of all sizes, are seen in their best form, for the chassis is one which lends itself admirably to the purpose.

Amongst the most interesting so far seen are two designs by Park Ward and Company, Ltd., one of these being a two-door all-weather four-seater and the other a four-door close-coupled sports saloon.

The all-weather model, by its nature, seems particularly suited to the chassis, for, owing to the careful design of the head fitting, the car, when open, forms a typical sports four-seater, the head folding perfectly flat to lie level with the top of the body sides and being neatly hidden by an envelope. At the same time, when the car is closed, it has all the comfort and weather protection of a drop-head foursome coupé, the doors carrying metal-framed glass windows, useful for protection when the head is down.

The lines of this model are decidedly

sleek, and the falling waistline, which is becoming so popular, adds to the suggestion of speed. The spare wheel is carried at the rear of the commodious luggage compartment. The lines of the swept wings and running boards also blend well with the general design, and the side valancing of the wings should ensure their efficiency from a protection point of view.

The four-door sports saloon is also a most attractive car with a horizontal waist moulding running from radiator to stern, broadening over the doors, and

dividing over the rear wings to pass across the back panel, and down the tail. The doors are hinged on a narrow central pillar with concealed hinges, and flush-fitting traffic indicators are let into the pillars. Swept wings and running boards are employed in this design also, and the lower edges of the bonnet, scuttle, and doors are correspondingly swept too. On both designs long bonnets have inclined rear edges and inclined louvres. The swept tail of the saloon forms a large luggage compartment, on the lid of which a spare wheel is mounted.

Park Ward four-door close-coupled saloon.

For the new chassis a very handsome foursome coupé has been built by Barker and Co. (Coachbuilders), Ltd., and in this design also the falling waistline is seen, it having a particularly graceful sweep. This body can also be described as a cabriolet de ville, for the front part of the head can be folded up in the manner of a de ville extension, so that the front seats are uncovered, while the rear seats have the protection of the head.

A feature of the design is the large boot, giving ample accommodation for luggage and tools, the spare wheel being carried at the rear with a slight inclination. In order that the head may lie flat when folded a recessed portion is formed between the back rail of the body and the boot. Graceful swept lines merge into a slightly swept running board, and traffic indicators are, in this case, let into the scuttle.

Three-position Head

A four-seater drop-head coupé has been produced, also, by Thrupp and Maberly, Ltd., and in this case the head can be completely opened, or the front portion may be folded back. The falling waistline is again seen and is emphasised by a broad moulding with a super-imposed bright strip as a relief. The swept wings are well balanced at the sides, and a large panelled luggage container at the rear is fitted with suitcases, with the

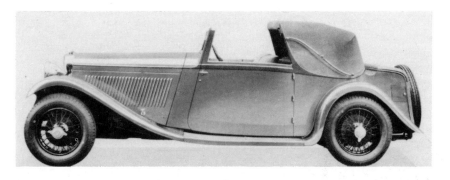

Barker foursome cabriolet de ville.

Owen sedanca coupé.

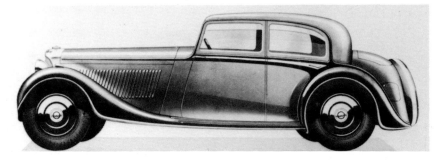

A Thrupp and Maberly four-door four-light design.

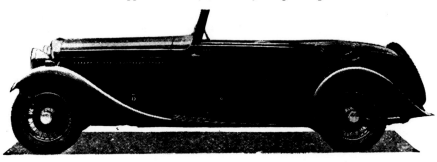

Park Ward all-weather body.

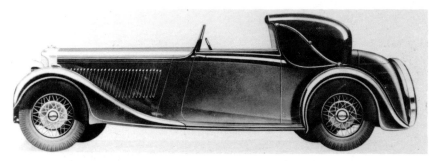

Thrupp and Maberly two-door four-seater drop-head coupé.

tools mounted in the lid. The spare wheel is carried at the back of the luggage boot, and has a metal cover.

The Owen sedanca coupé, a registered design built by H. J. Mulliner and Co., Ltd., for H. R. Owen, Ltd., is designed to give full accommodation for four passengers and plenty of luggage space. Graceful sweeping lines, good proportions, and the neat manner in which the head is folded are features of this handsome body, and it should be noted that in this case also the front portion of the head can be folded back if desired. The price of the complete car is £1,350.

Fixed Head Coupés

A two-door close-coupled fixed-head coupé is being produced by J. Gurney Nutting and Co., Ltd. This is a four-light body, and it is fitted with a sliding sunshine roof. A large luggage container at the rear has the rear wings panelled integrally with it, and in the lid of the trunk the tools are accommodated. The swept wings and running boards and the slight fall given to the waistline combine with the good proportions to make an attractive vehicle which will appeal to many.

Those to whom the fixed-head coupé makes a particular appeal will be interested in a close-coupled design on sporting lines by Freestone and Webb, Ltd. The proportions and lines are such as to give the car a well-balanced appearance.

Jack Barclay, Ltd., is also offering a number of special bodies on the new chassis, and, in particular, an all-weather model, which can be used completely open or closed, or with the de ville extension rolled back. This is a sporting-looking vehicle with long graceful lines and swept wings incorporating the running boards.

A Streamlined Bentley

Details of an Outstanding Example of Aerodynamic or Airline Design

By A. G. DOUGLAS CLEASE, B.Sc.

AT the moment there is considerable interest amongst coachbuilders and their clients in streamlining, or aerodynamic design. Opinions are divided as to how far streamlining should be carried out, for if an attempt is made to give a true streamline form to the front of the car, the result is so unorthodox as to meet with criticism, admirable though it may be technically.

In course of time it may be that such designs will be accepted without comment as one becomes accustomed to them, but at the moment, in this country, the preference seems to be for a streamlined body only, the front of the car presenting an orthodox appearance. An outstanding example of this type is shown in the accompanying illustrations, and it has recently been completed by Thrupp and Maberly, Ltd., for Mr. Geoffrey Smith, a director of Iliffe and Sons Ltd., who has taken a keen personal interest in the preparation of the design, and in

the building of the body. The original design appeared in an article " The Benefits of Streamlining," in *The Autocar* of January 12th. It is mounted on a 3½-litre Bentley chassis.

Naturally with such a car the important feature as regards appearance is to obtain a pleasing outline which will allow adequately roomy and comfortable seating accommodation to be incorporated. This is not an easy matter when it is considered that not only is the body tapering in a vertical plane, but also in a horizontal plane; yet it will be agreed that in this instance an excellent outline and well balanced proportions have been achieved, together with comfortable accommodation for four passengers within the wheelbase, as one of the scale perspective drawings shows.

Another difficulty concerns the rear aspect, for with a body which tapers in a horizontal plane it is obviously necessary for the rear wings to merge gracefully into the

In this side view the graceful lines and good proportions are very evident.

general lines of the tail. To achieve a good result demands considerable skill in the designing of the body, and in its actual construction, particularly as regards the panels, and the coachbuilders are to be congratulated on the result.

It should also be noted that the tapering tail does not involve a greater overhang at the rear, but, at the same time, it has the advantage of making available an unusual amount of luggage space. Two panels in the tail are hinged at their upper and lower edges, respectively, and the lower panel is supported by side stays which allow it to lie so that its flat inner surface is horizontal, thus forming a luggage grid should it be desired to carry unusually bulky cases, such as a cabin trunk. Actually, five suitcases of large size can be accommodated in the rear locker with the lids closed and locked. Tools, nested in rubber, are accommodated between the inner and outer panels of the lower lid, and there is also a wide, deep well for large tools immediately behind the recessed number plate, which is illuminated from behind.

Good Visibility for all Passengers

Another feature of the design is the elimination of the upper portions of the door hinge pillars and centre standing pillars, giving the effect of a single wide window on each side, although there is, of course, a division between the door glass and the quarter glass. The quarter lights slide backwards under the control of winders. Visibility is, therefore, unusually good for all passengers, especially as the screen pillars are kept thin. In spite of the curvature of the roof, it has been possible to include a sliding panel, giving an opening over the front seats. The colour scheme is stone grey, with a darker shade for mouldings and wings, fine blue lines being used as relief, and the interior is upholstered in soft fawn Vaumol leather in a plain, stretched style, relieved by narrow blue piping.

The seats are composed of Dunlopillo with down overlays. Arm rests are provided on the doors and to the rear seat, which also has a folding centre arm rest. Behind the rear squab there is a useful shelf for parcels, maps, and so on. The instruments are specially grouped and have white dials with blue figures and needles. The steering wheel and control knobs are likewise finished in blue to match the upholstery piping, and the cabinet work is finished in "bird's eye" maple veneer to tone.

Particular attention has been paid to one or two details that do not as a rule receive much consideration. One of these items is the front dumb iron casing, which is so

This perspective drawing of the framework is to scale and shows how the four passengers sit comfortably within the wheelbase.

arranged that it conceals the tubular tie-bar common to Bentley and Rolls-Royce chassis, and is downswept to the bottom of the radiator. This casing is louvred, and its forward face, which carries the number plate, is rounded under to correspond with the general lines of the body. The front wings, too, are carried well over the wheels, which N.P.L. tests have proved to offer less wind resist-

Showing the generous luggage accommodation, nested tool locker, and rear wing treatment.

ance than the so-called "sporting" wing, and merge into the running boards with a long gentle sweep, while the rear wings, which are of streamline form, correspond with the shape of the rear panels, which it should be noted are curved under to enhance the streamline effect. The windscreen with its curved top rail is free from obstruction, the Klaxon wipers operating from the bottom of the glass and having concealed mechanism. Lucas lamps are fitted, including four of the new streamline side lamps, two of which on the rear wings serve as stop and tail lights.

One of the latest Philco Transitone car radio sets is installed, and it is interesting to note that the aerial is mounted beneath the running board, owing to the fact that the roof is fully panelled. To give adequate head room for the rear seat occupants and yet preserve a low roof height it was considered advisable to recess the roof above the rear seats, and thus there is no inner panel at this point, the head lining being applied to the underside of the outer metal panel. Accordingly, a short sunshine roof is necessitated, giving a maximum opening of 14in. It might be imagined that the body weight would be above the average, but actually this is not the case, owing to careful design.

The rear framework and luggage compartment.

The T.T. Bentley

Special Offord Coachwork for E. R. Hall's Private Entry

THE entry of a Bentley for the Tourist Trophy Race has aroused great interest. The name of Bentley conjures up visions of great British successes in the past, but at the outset it must be stated that the lone entry for the 1934 Ulster T.T. is by Mr. E. R. Hall, a private owner, not by the works. The consent to run the car and a certain amount of backing have been received from the works, but it is in no sense a works entry.

A special light body conforming to the A.I. regulations has been constructed for Mr. Hall by Offord and Sons, Ltd., the well-known coachbuilders, of 67, George Street, Portman Square, W.1. The framework is made entirely of duralumin, with panelling of aluminium, and the body is so constructed, with a five-point mounting on Silentbloc bushes, that it can be removed in half an hour.

The body is a four-seater in the A.I. sense of the term, and, whereas the rear seats are mounted on the body framework, the front seats are mounted direct on a wooden platform bolted to the chassis frame, and would thus remain in position if the body were lifted off. This wooden platform and the wooden floorboards are the only wood used.

The tubing for the seats is of elektron, giving an extremely light construction, and the hood brackets are also of elektron tubing. The hood itself is detachable, and its brackets, when in use, bolt on through a hole in the side of the body. When not in use the hood frame is clipped to a cross-stay running behind the front seats, with the hood fabric furled round it. The regulations for the race, by the way, require that a hood shall be capable of being erected and furled again by two persons in five minutes, though no actual running is done in the race with the hood up.

The front passenger's seat—no mechanic will be carried—is enclosed by

E. R. Hall's privately entered Bentley for to-morrow's T.T. race.

a half-tonneau cover, and this is secured in front not by the usual fasteners but by a beading, which prevents any air getting in and forming a pocket. A beading also secures the front edge of the rear tonneau cover.

Streamlined Lamps

A stoneguard is fitted over the Bentley radiator, and the small 6in. lamps have streamlined covers of an extremely light metal. The wings are of duralumin, mounted on spring-steel brackets, but the wings shown in the photographs, which are of the minimum A.I. dimensions, will not necessarily be those used in the race. A wire mesh screen, which will be folded flat, is also constructed to comply with the regulations; the screen framework is of elektron. Hall will actually be protected by a small aero type of screen.

The rear of the chassis, where there is a very large petrol tank, is covered by a streamlined fairing, cunningly devised so that air is thrown on to the rear brake drums for cooling purposes.

THE NEW

A Run With the Latest Barker-bodied

SOME cars are in a class apart. To own them is a sheer joy, available, alas! to only a limited few whose pockets are deep enough. The performance that they give varies according to the type of machine. It is said that money can buy anything. In the car world it can buy superlative performance, or sheer luxury, or a combination of the two. In this latter class is the new 3½-litre Bentley.

My old friend, Mr. Oliver Bertram, the well-known Brooklands driver, is in the fortunate position of being able to drive, in the course of business, many luxurious and powerful cars, but even he had been impressed by one of the new Bentleys to which had been fitted the latest thing in drop-head foursome coupé coachwork by Barker and Co. (Coachbuilders), Ltd., 66, South Audley Street, London, W.1, the whole car costing £1,680.

By a coincidence another friend of mine, Mr. W. J. Clennell, just home from Bangkok, had acquired an old 1924 3-litre Bentley for use during his stay in England, and had many times told me how well this old veteran was going. The old 3-litre was the car with which Bentleys made their name—the new Barker Bentley is one of the latest productions of the famous firm under their new management. What could be more apt than a comparison of the two?

First of all, by courtesy of Barker's, I went out with Oliver Bertram in the new car, a beautiful red coupé. It attracted from the very first by its distinctly sporting lines, allied with a sense of power and luxury. A splendid view is possible from the driving seat, so that the driver can see not only both side lamps, but both wing tips also—and that without any feeling of the seat being perched unduly high. Twin screenwipers are built into the scuttle, with a "remote" motor well out of the way under the dash.

Work of Art

The wings themselves are of particularly pleasing design. One can rarely say exactly what it is that pleases the eye in a work of art, but these wings are just right. So is the well-shaped luggage box at the rear, in the lid of which the tools are neatly laid out.

The head is so arranged that either the front seats or the whole car can be opened, the supporting arches being detachable and fitting into special clips in the floor of the luggage box. An interior light is also fitted over the rear seats, with a switch on the dash. Thus with the head erected the car gives full saloon comfort.

The engine (six cylinders, 82.5 × 114 mm., 3,669 c.c., 25.3 h.p., £26 tax) has a 1½-gallon sump, and the petrol tank holds eighteen gallons; the fuel consumption is approximately 15 m.p.g. A spare coil and contact-breaker points are provided, and the radiator shutters are thermostatically controlled. The gear lever is on the right—a point many drivers will like—and a synchromesh mechanism is used for top and third gears, with a constant-mesh second as well.

As regards the chassis, the wheelbase is 10ft. 6in. and the track 4ft. 8in., and an exceptionally good lock is available for so large a car (39ft. turning circle left hand, and 41ft. right hand). A hypoid rear axle is used, and at the front there are brake torque reaction members. The wheels are of the Rolls-Royce quickly detachable serrated-ring centre-lock pattern. The chassis weight is approximately 22 cwt.

The day was extremely cold, and I had earned much scorn from the lordly coachbuilders through arriving clad in a leather coat in an open sports car. I was so cowed that I hid my coat in the back of the Bentley, which had the head erected, and set off in an ordinary lounge suit. Now, we all know how cold it can be when, as was the case at the time, a biting east wind is blowing. But, in London at any rate, the comfort of the draughtproof body was such that neither I nor "Bertie," who was similarly clad, felt unduly cold, and it was not until, having picked up a third passenger, we got out into the open country that we donned our overcoats.

Steering Unaffected by High Wind

There was "half a gale" blowing—or it might almost have been a full gale, whatever that may be—straight sideways across the road. Most cars would, at all events, have needed some keeping straight in such a wind, but when I took the wheel I found the steering not at all affected at either high speeds or low.

A striking feature of the new Bentley is that it is almost impossible to estimate at once the speed at which the car is travelling; 70 m.p.h. literally felt like 40, and at 90 m.p.h. the car was not fussing at all, purring along smoothly and with an absolute lack of effort. On a long, straight, deserted stretch I reached 95 m.p.h. with absolute safety.

Safety introduces the braking element. The new Bentley is fitted with the mechanical servo mechanism as for the brakes used on Rolls-Royce cars. We are familiar with the giant figures, seen in some advertisements of brake linings, taking a mighty grip on a car and hauling it to a standstill. Never before have I actually received such an impression—but a little earlier in London, while Oliver Bertram had been driving, a cyclist had suddenly decided

AND THE OLD

Bentley Compared With a Ten-year-old 3-litre

By BRIAN TWIST

to turn in front of us without warning. " Bertie " put his foot gently on the brake pedal, and there was scarcely even a " phenomenal avoidance "—the car just stopped, not as though it had run into a mass of soft wool, as some have described good braking, but literally as though a giant hand had suddenly closed on the car and pulled it up, giving a sense of control which placed the car still further in a class apart.

The gear change, too, was entirely remarkable from second to third and from third to top. First to second, if necessary, could be effected quickly, but normally was just an ordinary, easy change.

Acceleration Figures

Then Bertram took over the car, and I grasped a handful of stop-watches for some unofficial acceleration figures. From 0-60 m.p.h. took $13\frac{12}{100}$ sec., 0-70 $17\frac{1}{4}$ sec., 0-80 $24\frac{46}{100}$ sec., and 0-90 $37\frac{12}{100}$ sec., these figures representing the best of a number of runs under varying conditions of wind and a slight gradient—the wind was against downhill and with on the uphill ; 10-30 m.p.h. took $3\frac{64}{100}$ sec. in first gear (11.3 to 1), $4\frac{12}{100}$ sec. in second (7 to 1), $7\frac{15}{100}$ sec. in third (5 to 1), and $9\frac{8}{100}$ sec. in top (4 to 1). Note, owing to the weather and other conditions these figures (uphill and wind with) are not entirely comparable with those set up by other cars in other circumstances.

Meanwhile, I was sitting in the back, and, having folded down the armrest in the centre, was extremely comfortable. This feeling of complete comfort and security prevailed even when I noted that the speedometer once touched the 100 mark ! On one occasion, when we were actually travelling at 90 m.p.h., I leant forward, noted the readings of the rev counter and speedometer, and, resting a pad on the armrest of the car, wrote down, perfectly steadily and legibly, " 4,200 at 90."

A greater tribute to the springing might not have been possible, but Bertram was not satisfied. We took the car to a certain little used " road " in the north of London, frequented by inventors of patent wheel suspension systems, and drove up this rutted and pot-holed surface, with great steel man-holes projecting in places, at a steady 40 to 45 m.p.h., actually touching 50 m.p.h. in one place. I was amazed. I can say no more. The Bentley's suspension is perfectly normal, but even had it had the most highly developed independent wheel springing the comfort could scarcely have been greater and I was still sitting in the back !

Next day, with the magnificent handling of the new car fresh in my mind, I met Mr. Clennell, and we set out in the ten-year-old 3-litre Bentley. I am prepared to wager that no one would take this for a ten-year-old machine either at a first or at any other glance—save, of course, those Bentley enthusiasts who know each detail that has distinguished the famous marque year by year. Neither the appearance nor the running gave any sign of senility. The smart two-seater body, fitted about 1928, was polished up to the nines, and the engine gave forth that impressive rumble which all enthusiasts love so much.

We called at the Bentley service station, however, for an adjustment to the starter motor pinion, and while the job was being done I looked at the past history of the car in the Bentley record book, where full details are kept of all the chassis that have ever left the works, as far as information is available when the car passes out of the original owner's hands. There was no question of the vintage of this particular model—there it was with all its history, dating back from 1924.

The old 3-litre has, of course, a four-cylinder engine, 80 × 149 mm., 2,996 c.c. It has two magnetos, feeding two plugs per cylinder, and two S.U. carburetters, altered on this car to the later type. The engine has a five-bearing crankshaft, four valves per cylinder, and a $2\frac{1}{2}$-gallon sump. There is an 11-gallon petrol tank, and the petrol consumption has been accurately checked by Mr. Clennell to be exactly 20.2 m.p.g. The oil consumption is negligible, in the region of a quart for 3,000 miles ! The wheelbase is 9ft. $9\frac{1}{2}$in. and the track 4ft. 8in. ; the weight of the speed model chassis is $22\frac{3}{4}$ cwt.

Tractable in Traffic

Unfortunately—or fortunately—no cyclist turned in front of us this time to test our brakes, but the car (one really hesitates to say " the old car ") ran beautifully and steadily. More pressure was needed on the pedal, but the brakes were entirely adequate, even if not comparing with the gigantic efficiency of the new car. By using the close-ratio gears, which were even higher than those of the new Bentley—first, 10 to 1 on the old, 11.3 to 1 on the new ; second, 6.18 to 1 against 7 to 1 ; third, 5.05 to 1 against 5 to 1 ; top, 3.78 to 1 against 4 to 1— one could travel nicely through the traffic, and when we got out on the open road again the high top gear and the big, slow-revving four-cylinder engine made 60 m.p.h. a pleasant cruising gait.

It is interesting also to compare the theoretical speeds at peak revs on the gears, though one must point out first that the new car would actually exceed these speeds, but the old car, after its ten years' usage, fell short. As a matter of fact, the 3-litre had a thick compression plate for ordinary touring purposes, the removal of which might have necessitated benzole in the fuel, but would probably have increased the efficiency a great deal.

First, the new Bentley, with peak revs 4,500, first 35 m.p.h., second 56, third 77, top 97 ; then the 3-litre speed model, at 3,500 r.p.m., first 34, second 54, third 67, top not stated. Actually, the old 3-litre would still do 30 on first, 45 on second, 60 on third, and we reached about 78 m.p.h. on the speedometer on top gear.

Also, naturally, the new car would reach its speeds very much more quickly, and at the lower speeds on each gear was considerably more flexible. In a series of acceleration tests with the 3-litre, 0-60 m.p.h. took $23\frac{75}{100}$ sec., with the wind behind, and 0-70 m.p.h. 38 sec. (i.e., about the same as the new Bentley's 0-90 m.p.h.). 10-30 m.p.h. took $5\frac{75}{100}$ sec. in bottom, $8\frac{1}{100}$ sec. in second, $10\frac{65}{100}$ sec. in third, and $14\frac{73}{100}$ sec. in top gear.

There was no point in trying Mr. Clennell's old veteran over our appalling " colonial " section—no extraordinary claims are made for the suspension ; it is just perfectly comfortable on ordinary roads. The old car was not outclassed. It reflected the glory of the new model, holding its own manfully. Either car is a machine anyone would be proud to possess.

TALKING OF SPORTS CARS (No. 255)

High Performance

Experiences of an Open-bodied 3½-litre Bentley Used

FOR a long while I have been wanting to include in this series an open-bodied example of the modern Bentley, as distinct from the various vintage examples of the "old" company's production which have been dealt with here from time to time. As a personal view I place such a car in a category by itself. The modern Bentley, as built by Rolls-Royce, is a sports car—sporting car might perhaps be a better term—irrespective of what style of body happens to be fitted, for it possesses all the latent performance appropriate to the term, and the suitable handling qualities as well. As a saloon or drophead coupé it is well-nigh silent. In open form, as I can say from personal experience, it approaches as near to silence in road progression as has yet been seen—or heard! Air noise is the only prominent sound accompanying its movement.

Contrasts

To my way of thinking that is a most desirable kind of sports car to have, providing performance without fuss of any sort, although I will admit against my case that there is something exhilarating, in an entirely different kind of car, in the blend of mechanical noises and self-obvious efficiency which is found, for instance, in a "two-three" Bugatti. The one, meaning the silent sports car, is restful, however, and the other can prove wearing in day in, day out use, even though it may somehow be satisfying to the enthusiast.

The modern Bentley—never, by the way, referred to officially as the "Rolls-Bentley," though most people call it that and the name is descriptive—is represented by notes on a 1934 model 3½-litre sports tourer used extensively on duty service during the war by a Naval officer. He has had plenty of opportunity of using its high performance and of making comparison with an entirely different type of car such as I have cited myself, for he also owns a

"two-three" Bugatti. His Bentley is a 1934 model of the second series. The 3½-litre was first announced in the autumn of 1933, and deliveries commenced early in 1934. In this series the 3½ has not previously had a proper show, though a Portuguese-owned sample, fitted with a Paris-built convertible body, was described in one of these articles in March, 1944.

Later, of course, the 3½-litre was superseded by the 4¼-litre, on the same general lines of design, but benefiting materially in acceleration over the smaller-engined car. There never seemed to be quite the same proportionate difference between the maximum speeds of the 3½ and the 4¼. The first 3½-litre I tested, almost exactly eleven years ago, did 94.24 m.p.h. in the favourable direction of the wind over a half-mile at Brooklands, and a mean speed over various half-miles round the track of 91.84. That was a saloon and I have never put an open version of the modern Bentley over the same test. Just two years later, by which time the 4¼ had been introduced, I timed the larger-engined model, again as a saloon, at 94.74 m.p.h., this time over a quarter-mile, the mean maximum speed by stop-watch being 90.91 m.p.h.

Thus maximum and mean timed speeds of the particular cars tested were within 0.5 m.p.h. and less than 1 m.p.h. respectively with the two sizes of engines. In making such comparisons it has to be

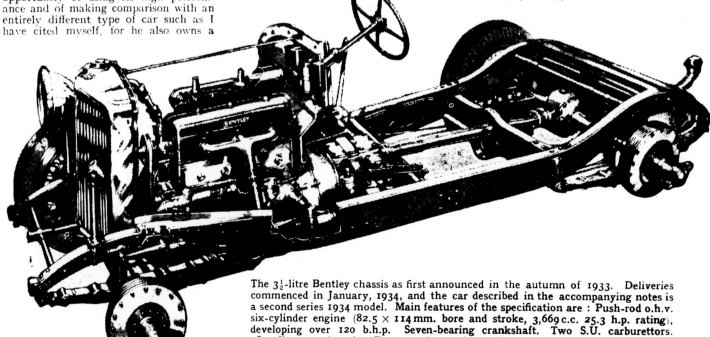

remembered that seldom are two days alike at Brooklands as regards wind and atmospheric conditions, and most improbably so at an interval of two years, though as it happened the season of year was the same in the two cases concerned.

Acceleration Comparison

Yet again considering the same two cars tested, the difference in acceleration was as great as between 13.4 sec. from rest to 50 m.p.h. for the 3½-litre and 10.3 sec. for the 4¼-litre, and 20.4 sec. from rest to 60 m.p.h. on the 3½, reduced to 15.5 sec. by the 4¼-litre.

The 3½-litre Bentley chassis as first announced in the autumn of 1933. Deliveries commenced in January, 1934, and the car described in the accompanying notes is a second series 1934 model. Main features of the specification are : Push-rod o.h.v. six-cylinder engine (82.5 × 114 mm. bore and stroke, 3,669 c.c. 25.3 h.p. rating), developing over 120 b.h.p. Seven-bearing crankshaft. Two S.U. carburettors. 18-gallon petrol tank. Four-speed gear box with synchromesh on top and third. Overall gear ratios : 4.10, 5.10, 7.09, and 11.30 to 1. Tyre size : 18 × 5.50 in. half-elliptic springs. Rod-operated brakes with Rolls-Royce disc-type mechanical servo and full compensation. Wheelbase : 10ft. 6in. Track : 4ft. 8in. Chassis price (in 1934), £1,100 ; open four-seater £1,380.

De Luxe

on Service Duty

Views from various angles of the 3½-litre Bentley **Vanden Plas**-bodied open tourer described—a car for any motoring enthusiast to covet !

Apart, however, from quoting a few figures which I think are of interest I am not seeking to show in detail that the 4¼ is a faster car in the general sense than the 3½—the real point is how speedy the smaller car was in relation to the larger.

My own memories are sufficiently vivid to make me agree very definitely when the owner of the 3½-litre speaks of the deceptiveness of the performance, a factor calling for real care until one becomes accustomed to the car. Brake fading such as he mentions I have not encountered with a modern Bentley. The 3½-litre I never drove far and hard enough to strike this point, if indeed it existed with a comparatively new car as was usually tested, but I have handled several examples of the 4¼ under conditions that would show up such a feature and have not experienced it. An outstanding instance of such fading with a fast, heavy car that I can recall was with a supercharged 5.4-litre Mercedes-Benz at night, on the Hog's Back, Surrey.

Now I will leave the Bentley owner to recount his impressions and experiences. How I would have liked to have been able, time permitting, to accept a suggestion he made that I should accompany him in his car on a duty journey some little while ago.

VIZOR.

●●●●●●●●●●●●●●●

"THE car which is the subject of these notes has for the past three and a half years been used solely on 'the King's Business.' That business has involved a very considerable amount of long-distance travel which, of necessity, has had to be undertaken at high speeds. Certain vital matters connected with the war have had to be attended to without delay and the Bentley has played a most prominent part in ensuring that as much of that undesirable element as was humanly and mechanically possible was eliminated. It is the writer's conviction that there are few cars which could give such unfailing service as has been

asked of, and given by, the car here discussed.

"My 'stable' at the time of purchasing the Bentley consisted of a much beloved Rolls 20 open tourer, and a blown 'two-three' Bugatti. Anyone who has driven a 'two-three' will appreciate that this is hardly the ideal car for sustained long-distance high-speed duty travel! At the same time it will also be appreciated that neither was the Rolls 20 designed for such work. Accordingly, one fine frosty morning the old Rolls 20 was traded-in at the wartime H.Q. of Paddon Bros., and the new love taken over.

Hall-marks

"The Bentley was of the second series of the so-called 'Rolls-Bentleys' and its speedometer showed that it had done just over 40,000 miles. The first impression, and one never since lost, was that here was a thoroughbred car: a car with that tautness and vivacity which set it in a class apart. It seemed to be made for 'having fun with,' and it gave that indefinable feeling of security which is among the hall-marks of all really good cars. Perhaps the comparison was more impressive to the writer as he was fresh from handling the Grand Prix Bug. and the Rolls 20 by turns.

"The first trip undertaken in the Bentley involved a matter of some 200 miles on ice and snow, and the way the car handled on the slippery surfaces was most encouraging; it was with something of elation that the solid roadworthiness was realised. In these conditions of ice and snow the 'loud pedal' was not used at all, so the petrol consumption was expected to be reasonable, but it was with real pleasure that it was found that the car was doing almost 24 m.p.g. This figure has been repeated so frequently since that first trip that there is no question of its being a freak, and it should be stressed that throughout this account I am speaking of wartime conditions as regards fuel, materials and road conditions.

"It was only later, when I was in a violent hurry, that the other side of the picture became apparent; when cruising between 55 and 65 the fuel consumption rises to the neighbourhood of 16 m.p.g.., but then a curious phenomenon manifests itself; if the cruising speed is raised still farther the consumption improves again to the region of 20 m.p.g. It is my opinion that this is not a purely mechanical matter, but that one's whole mode of driving changes when cruising between 70 and 80 m.p.h. and that this is the real cause of the improvement. It is as though the whole car were able then to take things in its stride.

"As to the matter of speed it may be as well to pass on to any prospective buyers of this type of car the advice given by Mr. Paddon as I took the car over: '. . . and don't for goodness' sake forget that that car has a bonnet 200 yards long!' It was not till the car was being driven as a modern Bentley *can* be driven that the real meaning of that advice became apparent; the car has such a deceptively quiet and smooth way of 'batting' that until one is well used to it there is a definite tendency to go far faster than one is aware: this applies particularly after a spell at any considerable speed. Actually the car in question has on several occasions almost reached the 100 m.p.h. figure. This needs good conditions, but it is not necessary to 'cheat' by downhill or following wind methods to achieve it; all that is needed is a good straight and a firm right foot. The makers do not claim a maximum, but if you ask nicely you will probably be told that the car should do an honest 90. It will.

Indefinable Margin

"Regarding average speeds, it is not desired to start up any argument as to what is or is not possible in these cars. It seems to me that the whole thing depends upon that indefinable margin where fast driving degenerates into dangerous driving. When necessity demanded, averages of just over 55 m.p.h. have been put up in the Bentley without (so the driver believes and hopes) crossing that margin.

"Tyre life has worked out at about 12,000 miles per cover and in this connection it may be of interest, in view of the kind of driving the car was receiving, to record experience of the Avon 'silent' type of tyre. The change in noise was most impressive and the whole car seemed to proceed in an even more effortless manner than usual. On the other hand there was in my experience on the Bentley a noticeable reduction in tyre adhesion. It is not possible to assess such a reduction as a percentage, but it was manifest that with the 'silent' type one could not take the same liberties in handling the car as with the more normal type of tread.

"The Bentley is most sensitive to wheel balance and it is well worth while spending an hour or two ensuring the correct balance after a change of tyres. I had not fully appreciated this point and spent a few anxious days in trying to discover the cause of unsatisfactory steering and uncomfortable running whereas, had it been realised sooner, less than an hour's work would have cured the trouble.

"When the car had done about 55,000 miles it became necessary to have the brakes and clutch relined, as the whole of the adjustment on these components had been used up. After about 60,000 miles a new symptom began to appear: after a few miles at 70 m.p.h. or over, that hot oily smell which to the initiated whispers . 'Rebore' began to be apparent and as oil consumption had fallen to 800 m.p.g. it became necessary to face up to the question of 'to overhaul or not to overhaul.' We overhauled.

"It was an expensive and lengthy business, costing, I suppose, double what it would have cost before the war. In the course of the overhaul the chance was taken to attend to everything that showed any sign of needing attention, and in addition certain internal modifications were made so as to bring the engine into line with the latest practice. Further in the interests of wear—or rather freedom from wear—a large-size Fram filter was fitted.

Careful Running-in

"The car was run-in largely by 'feel.' The engine was very stiff at first and this necessitated very gentle treatment during the early stages. Actually 25 m.p.h. was not exceeded for the first 200 miles; my rather acute mechanical sense objected that I was forcing things if this speed were exceeded. The engine began to free perceptibly when the first 90 miles were logged. After the 200th mile the maximum was raised to 30 m.p.h. and this was maintained till the car had done 500 miles.

"At this time a careful petrol consumption record was kept, and, with the stiff engine,

The Bentley from three-quarter rear view, a recent photograph of the car which suggests "showroom" condition in spite of the hard service it has seen on duty journeys during the war.

the first figure recorded was only 17.8 m.p.g.; as the engine freed this figure improved steadily to 21.3 m.p.g. It was noticeable, however, that when at 500 miles the speed was increased to a maximum of 35 m.p.h. the petrol consumption figure dropped to 20 m.p.g. During the next 250 miles this gradually improved to 21. At 1,000 miles the figure had increased to 22 m.p.g. at a maximum speed of 40 m.p.h. The engine was far from free, however, and it was not till more than 5,000 miles had been put in at a gradually increased speed that the engine was deemed to be free.

A Regular 20 m.p.g.

"As a check on the petrol consumption figures it was decided to do a test at the same speed as was employed at the start of the running-in period. Over ten gallons this resulted in a consumption of 25.3 m.p.g., but it was a wearisome business at 25 m.p.h. in a fully run-in car! For the last 200 gallons the car, fully run-in, has averaged 20.1 m.p.g.

"The following views may be of interest to the enthusiast:—

"Tappets: The makers' recommended clearances seem to be entirely suitable for all normal road work, and once the cylinder head has been finally tightened down and given a chance to settle the clearances require very little attention, but it should be stressed that frequent checking is advisable until the head has settled and the valves themselves have settled, too.

"Carburettors: The engine is far more sensitive to carburettor adjustment than usual. Extreme care and constant attention

in obtaining the ideal setting are amply repaid both in petrol economy and in performance. It has been my experience that the setting which gives the best running (vide the instruction book), once achieved, also gives the best economy and performance. There is no need to 'cut down' the mixture to obtain the best economy; all that is needed is to get the mixture right. As will be apparent from the foregoing notes the driver really holds the keys of good fuel consumption in his right foot!

"Tyre pressures: The makers' recommendations seem suitable for all but the fastest driving, for which I prefer to increase the pressure in the rear tyres by 5 lb.

"Brakes: Maintaining the proper adjustment is amply repaid but it should be stated that when the car is driven really fast the brakes of the 3½-litre are not immune from fading when used a lot. Once one is aware of the tendency it is easy not to be caught, but to the uninitiated it might be disconcerting. (I must admit that my Bugatti does it, too.)

"Shock absorbers: These are on the whole trouble free, but I have a criticism of the mounting of the front shock absorber links; I consider this too flimsy and I find frequent adjustment is needed to avoid an irritating rattle.

Pipe Line Failure

"The centralised chassis lubrication is a godsend and has never caused a moment's trouble, except when one of the pipes chafed through, with the result that one of the shackle bushes suffered. It is worth while operating the pump and looking underneath occasionally to make sure that there is no failure in the pipe line.

"Plugs: The maker's recommendations are all that could be desired for driving fast or slow.

"In conclusion, one more criticism: the whole car is too nice! There comes a time in the affairs of men when they have to go where Bentleys may not follow. It is going to be very hard indeed to have to part with one who has served so faithfully and well, but as we have a real mutual understanding I know my Bentley will understand that the old explanation of some merciless caning still applies.

"... There's a war on...."

The engine from the carburettor side. Maintained high finish and general cleanliness are as evident in this under-bonnet view as in the external pictures of the car.

BENTLEY
The Silent Sports Car

BENTLEY MOTORS (1931) LTD. 16 CONDUIT ST. LONDON W.1. PHONE: MAYFAIR 4412

A Thrupp and Maberly drop-head coupé on a 3½-litre Bentley. The front wings are grey to blend with the bonnet and body sides—a new note.

A DISTINCTIVE BENTLEY COUPÉ

Drop-head Coachwork Having a Number of Novel Features

THE convertible body of drop-head style becomes increasingly popular, and amongst the latest examples is the 3½-litre Bentley sedan coupé shown in accompanying illustrations. The body has been built by Thrupp and Maberly, Ltd., for Mr. G. Geoffrey Smith, Managing Editor of *The Autocar*, and one of its principal characteristics concerns the

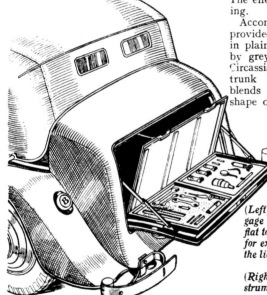

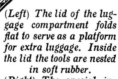

style of exterior decoration employed, which strikes a new note. The exterior panels are cellulosed in Oxford blue and grey, and all above and behind the down-swept bodyside swaging, including the rear wings, is finished in the darker colour with head material to tone, the front wings and running boards, in common with the lower bodyside and bonnet panels, being matched in grey. The effect generally is regarded as pleasing.

Accommodation for four passengers is provided, blue Vaumol leather applied in plain style being attractively relieved by grey piping. The woodwork is in Circassian walnut. A capacious luggage trunk having well-rounded contours blends harmoniously with the excellent shape of the hood, and has its rear lid

to let down horizontally, forming a platform for additional luggage. Tools are separately nested in two rubber trays in the luggage lid. To avoid damage to the paintwork by petrol pump hoses, twin petrol fillers have been mounted flush, one on each rear wing.

Let into the near-side front wing is the spare wheel, which is entirely concealed by a neat metal cover. Ace discs are employed throughout. The hood neatly falls flat into a recess formed between the rear seat and the trunk, being covered by an envelope. When the car is used fully open with only the front seats occupied, a tonneau cover protects the rear compartment. The car is equipped with a Phillips radio set, and new pattern Lucas trumpet horns are fitted.

(Left) The lid of the luggage compartment folds flat to serve as a platform for extra luggage. Inside the lid the tools are nested in soft rubber.
(Right) The special instrument panel of A.T. instruments with silver finish dials.

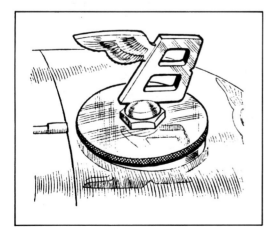

A CHANCE TO WIN £50

HERE is a chance for artistic people to design a mascot for a famous car. Bentley Motors, Ltd., are not quite satisfied with the present mascot (shown in the illustration) and are offering the very tempting prize of £50 for a design which they consider more suitable.

The design should be drawn to full size, and birds and the female form are barred. What is wanted is a mascot to convey flowing lines and speed, and it must be as low as possible so that it will not interfere with the driving vision. The last date for designs to be sent in is Saturday, March 30th, and they should be addressed to Bentley Motors, Ltd., 16, Conduit Street, London, W.1.

[Opposite] TT incidents captured by F Gordon-Crosby.

[Top] E.R. Hall in his privately-entered 3½ litre Bentley holds off the Hon. Brian Lewis (Lagonda) in 1934. They finished second and fourth.

[Lower] Von der Becke (Riley) rams the sand bank in Newtownards as Hall presses on to another second placing, in 1935.

The Autocar Road Tests

No. 1030. 4¼-LITRÉ BENTLEY SALOON

New Model with Enlarged Engine Establishes a Fresh Standard of Fine Car Merit

The new Bentley at Tyneham, in Dorset, during its test: this district, near Wareham, offers an entirely unspoilt coast line.

IT is not too much to say that, with the introduction of the 3½-litre Bentley some three years ago, a new standard of car values was set, for never previously had a car of similar size given so high a performance with such remarkable ease and quietness of running. The recent announcement that a bigger engine, of 4¼ litres, was to be made available instantly caused those who knew the 3½-litre to speculate upon the probable advantage, not so much from the point of view of sheer maximum speed, which already was satisfying enough, but from that of all-round performance, and acceleration in particular.

The 4¼-litre Bentley, rated at 30 h.p., is now being delivered, and an example has been put through the usual exhaustive tests carried out by *The Autocar*, involving timed records of the performance figures at Brooklands track and over 400 miles of road driving under owner conditions.

It is not easy to know where to start in apportioning full and proper credit to this altogether remarkable motor car. Analysed, its individual features show up exceedingly well, but it is as a whole that the car must be judged, and as one costing £1,500, backed, of course, as everyone knows, by the most famous firm of car manufacturers in the world. One cannot help feeling when handling this car that it represents the accumulated store of knowledge of that firm in high-class car production, put together to evolve a machine that shall meet every requirement of the most fastidious driver interested in performance—but refined performance.

In a way it seems almost purposeless to go point by point through this car, and to say, for instance, that the steering is very good and the springing extremely comfortable, or that the brakes give exceptional power, since, in the eyes of the makers, these are nothing more than a car to satisfy their rigid standards must necessarily possess from the commencement. It is the combination of

features, the manner in which one supports another, that gives the car an incomparable "feel."

Whilst the performance figures speak for themselves, the quality of the important top gear acceleration will be particularly observed. What is not apparent from cold figures is the fact that everything the car does is achieved with amazing ease and in a degree of quietness that approaches dead silence. Yet there is all the liveliness of a first-class sports car derivable from the engine, with hardly a hint of exhaust note, no fuss, no vibration, not even hiss from the twin carburetter intakes. An exhaust cut-out is no longer fitted, by the way.

This car can be driven almost entirely on two gears—first or second for starting, and top for most of the time in ordinary running, so flexible is the engine and so much silky power does it give even at low speeds. On the other hand, a really quick getaway can be achieved, and second and third gears provide an exhilarating performance. Second is so quiet as not to be noticed until nearing the limit on that ratio; third is literally indistinguishable from top, and at lower speeds one may go to change down from top only to find that third is already engaged. Passengers are certainly unable to detect the difference.

A right-hand lever, working in a gate and with the very best form of synchromesh on top and third, provides the most highly developed lever gear change that has yet appeared on a car. The action is beautifully balanced, and the gears go in imperceptibly. From second up to third and from third to top, also down from top to third, in all of which the synchromesh operates, changes can be made as rapidly as the lever can be moved. It is almost as though the car had two top gears. Fierce, rushing acceleration is given on third, yet the engine remains entirely soft, and the evidence of the speedometer is hard to believe. Even more remarkable is the acceleration on top gear from speeds around

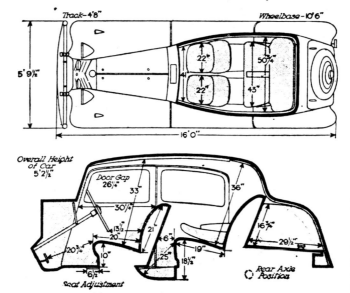

50 m.p.h., there being a great reserve from that middle range onwards which quickly sends the speedometer needle soaring towards the 80 mark.

It is a wonderful experience to handle this car over main roads which give opportunity for employing the performance. The throttle goes down, and the speedometer needle sweeps round the dial; the landscape rushes past, but nothing else emphasises the rate of travel, and conversation in a normal voice can be continued.

In favourable conditions it is only the will of the driver and the nature of the road that decide the speed, up to a figure within close reach of 100 m.p.h.

Noteworthy features of the under-bonnet compartment are, first, the beautifully finished engine, and the very big air cleaner and carburetter intake silencer, the snap-catch oil filler, and the secure yet neat mounting of the wheel tools.

The whole running is so exceptionally easy, even to a seasoned driver acquainted with the best fast cars there are, that speeds up to 70 m.p.h. are automatically used. Within this range the car almost takes itself along, the driver not having to concentrate upon his handling of it.

The speedometer proved to be 2.5 m.p.h. fast at a reading of 30, and 4 m.p.h. fast at a reading of 50, which margin was maintained approximately consistently up to the limit, the highest reading being 100-101 when the car was timed at nearly 95 m.p.h. Conditions at Brooklands for these speed tests were not actually adverse, but were not helpful to the car.

With all this performance, it is a characteristic that the car feels eminently safe. The driving position and all the controls are admirably arranged, whilst vision is all that can be desired. Also, there is a surprising feeling of compactness, so that the car is easy to handle. The steering allows the driver to put it exactly where he wishes; the springing is controllable in accordance with the speed, road surface, and load by means of a finger-operated control at the centre of the spring-spoked steering wheel. This regulates the damping provided by the special hydraulic shock absorbers. Even at the maximum position of the shock absorber control there is no actual harshness about the suspension, and the comfort afforded in the back seats as well as in the front is exceptionally good.

The braking system embodies the Rolls-Royce mechanical

POSITIONS OF THE VARIOUS CONTROLS

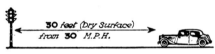

30 feet (Dry Surface) from 30 M.P.H.

servo, driven from the gear box and assisting the action, so that light pedal pressure is intensified and extremely powerful braking applied to the wheels. They are extraordinary brakes, smooth to the last degree, but relentless in their power to pull the speed of the car down, and they afford the uttermost confidence. The steering mechanism is quite high geared, 2¼ turns of the wheel giving the full lock-to-lock movement, but the balance between lightness for ease of control and accuracy for safe steering at speed has been exceptionally well struck. At no time is more than the mildest amount of road wheel movement felt through the steering, whilst the caster action to return the front wheels after a corner is just right. Unusually good steering lock is provided.

The average speed capabilities are, of course, altogether beyond the ordinary, and a long day's run leaves the driver not only fresh but willing to go on still farther. Most ordinary climbing is carried out swiftly on top, and third will deal with almost any gradient on main roads. It is interesting, too, as showing another side of the car, that a narrow hill with a maximum gradient of 1 in 4¼, and an awkward "S" turn, which until recently was an observed test in one of the classic trials, but which now has a good surface, was climbed with the greatest of ease, with a full load on board.

There is hardly a tremor from the engine, even when accelerating from crawling speeds on top gear; it can, however, be felt a little when ticking over with the car stationary unless the ignition control lever be retarded a notch or two. There is a host of interesting details that ought to receive mention, for every single item has been closely studied, and each does its appointed work in an exemplary manner. The controls on the steering wheel are an instance.

The body on the car tested is the standardised Park, Ward four-door four-light saloon, which, of course, is extremely well finished, and which has exceptionally comfortable seats.

Experience of this remarkable British car makes one realise afresh that it is not only sheer performance which counts—and the Bentley has that in full measure—but the manner of it.

DATA FOR THE DRIVER

4¼-LITRE BENTLEY SALOON.

PRICE, with standard saloon body, £1,510. Tax, £22 10s.
RATING : 29.4 h.p., six cylinders, o.h.v., 88 × 114 mm., 4,255 c.c.
WEIGHT, without passengers : 33 cwt. 1 qr. 22 lb.
LB. (WEIGHT) PER C.C. : 0.88.
TYRE SIZE : 5.50 × 18in. on knock-off wire wheels.
LIGHTING SET : 12-volt. Automatic voltage control.
TANK CAPACITY : 18 gallons ; fuel consumption, 17 m.p.g.
TURNING CIRCLE : (L.) 39ft. 7in. ; (R.) 40ft. 11in.
GROUND CLEARANCE : 6in.

ACCELERATION				SPEED	
Overall gear ratios	From steady m.p.h. of 10 to 30	20 to 40	30 to 50		m.p.h.
4.10 to 1	7.4 sec.	7.5 sec.	7.7 sec.	Mean maximum timed speed over ¼ mile	90.91
5.10 to 1	6.2 sec.	6.1 sec.	6.5 sec.	Best timed speed over ¼ mile ...	94.74
7.08 to 1	4.5 sec.	4.7 sec.	5.6 sec.	Speeds attainable on indirect gears :—	
11.30 to 1	3.4 sec.	—	—		
From rest to 50 m.p.h. through gears, 10.3 sec.				1st	33
From rest to 60 m.p.h. through gears, 15.5 sec.				2nd...	52
From rest to 70 m.p.h. through gears, 21.1 sec.				3rd	74
25 yards of 1 in 5 gradient from rest, 4.8 sec.				Speed from rest up 1 in 5 Test Hill (on 1st gear)	22.66

Performance figures for acceleration and maximum speed are the means of several runs in opposite directions.

Distinctive Bentley Saloons

Two Park Ward Bodies Making Interesting Comparison

These two 4¼-litre Bentleys with Park Ward bodies offer an interesting comparison in both colour and detail finish, for they differ considerably.

EXAMPLES of the new 4¼-litre Bentley are now steadily passing from the works of coachbuilders into the hands of private owners. Amongst the first to be delivered are two carrying special Park Ward four-door saloon bodies, one finished in battleship grey with indigo blue for the waist moulding and wheel discs, the other finished all-black, relieved by a chromium waist moulding. The grey saloon has been supplied to Mr G Geoffrey Smith, Managing Editor of *The Autocar*; the other is the property of Mr. C. E. Wallis, a Director of Iliffe and Sons Ltd.

These two cars provide a series of interesting comparisons, for while, as the illustrations show, they appear vastly different, the bodies are almost identical in design, illustrating the manner in which slight rearrangement of mouldings and fittings and different colour treatment can greatly alter appearance.

Constructionally these Park Ward bodies represent something distinctly new in specialised body production, for steel enters largely into their manufacture, and amongst other things is responsible for the narrow section of the screen pillars, which great assists visibility. Steel is also used for the panels and wings.

The main external difference to be observed between these two cars is the mounting of the spare wheel in the more usual position at the back of the trunk in one case, and sunk into the near-side front wing in the other. This affords a clean tail design with a return sweep. A continuous moulding commencing at the radiator, increasing in width at the screen pillars, and tapering off as it sweeps down to the extremity of the tail, is used on the grey saloon; the other example has a downswept splayed moulding terminating behind the rear door and surmounted by a bevel-edged chromium-plated moulding. In addition, the drip moulding on the grey saloon is continued by a swept bead following the inclined rear line of the roof.

The absence of a rear-mounted spare wheel makes possible a built-in number plate of the Ace prismatic type on one of the cars, the other having an external plate of similar pattern. Ace spare-wheel covers are used on both, and one has Ace wheel discs, finished indigo blue. Differences are to be noted in wing design, those used on the grey saloon being of a more heavily domed pattern and having swaged edges, and the wing lamps are of the built-in design. An impression of increased bonnet length is given to the grey saloon by the extension of the bonnet louvres to the scuttle.

Concerning luggage accommodation, on the black saloon the rear panel spare-wheel mounting precludes the use of the boot lid as a luggage platform, a method which is adopted in the case of the other car. On the grey car to protect luggage within the

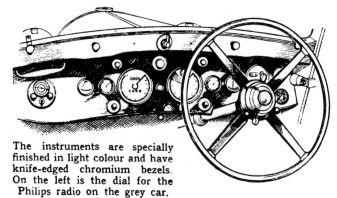

The instruments are specially finished in light colour and have knife-edged chromium bezels. On the left is the dial for the Philips radio on the grey car.

boot when the platform lid is in use there is an inside dust flap. The platform lid is rubber-covered on the inside, and has sunk into it two trays in which are small tools, nested in rubber. There is a light inside the boot, and also a first-aid outfit. The new Bentley external petrol filler cap is used on the black saloon, but the other has a filler cap in each rear wing, a point the usefulness of which Continental tourists will appreciate.

These two bodies possess a number of practical interior fitments, and both are equipped with radio, one having a Philco and the other a Philips set. On Mr. Smith's car the backs of the front seats embody folding glass-topped tables, above

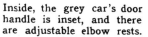

Inside, the grey car's door handle is inset, and there are adjustable elbow rests.

A central armrest for the driver is an unusual fitting on Mr. Wallis' car, and the seats have high backs.

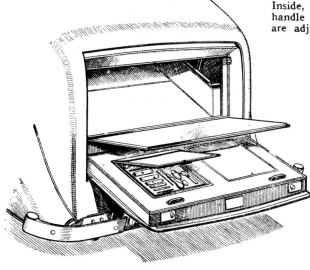

The luggage boot lid serves as a grid on Mr. Geoffrey Smith's car, the cases inside being closed in and thereby waterproof.

which are ash-trays, and over each rear door, set within easy reach of the rear-seat passengers, is a cigar lighter.

On the all-black saloon, behind the hinged rear seat

backs, special compartments have been devised for the accommodation of a Thermos flask, bottles, and so on, and beneath the rear window is a full-width recess to house a folded rug or coat. Both cars are fitted with sunshine roofs—that in the case of the grey saloon being of the Weathershields dual-opening type, giving both front and rear openings; this body also has glass ventilation eaves above the windows.

Door-handle Details

Connolly's Vaumol leather in a light blue shade is used for the sumptuous upholstery of the grey saloon, and is carried out in an attractive plain style, relieved by blue piping, interior woodwork being in burr walnut. Both interior and exterior handles are of unusual design, the former being of special sliding pattern; the exterior handles, instead of having the usual T-section, are of continuously curved design, forming a particularly convenient grip, since when opening the door the fingers do not need to be parted to accommodate the handle spindle.

The other equipment on this car includes twin Klaxon wipers, twin Lucas Mellotone horns, and a centrally mounted Notek lamp. This car has a special instrument-board layout embodying A.T. instruments with knife-edge chromium-plated bezels, and an interesting point is the manner in which the intensity of the instrument-board illumination can be varied.

Trimming used on the all-black saloon is in beige, and notable interior details are front-door armrests with hinged tops disclosing cigarette boxes, and a small folding armrest on the near side of the driver's seat. In each case the seats and upholstery are of generous and comfortable dimensions.

Showing how the location of the spare wheel influences the design as a whole.

$3\frac{1}{2}$ and $4\frac{1}{4}$ Litres Compared

Ascending Applecross, a long, rough and winding climb in the West Highlands.

Some Comparative Figures Based Upon the Two Types of Bentley Chassis
By G. GEOFFREY SMITH

FREQUENTLY on my travels I have been asked to compare the 3½-litre Bentley with the more recent 4¼-litre type. Although in general design they are the same, with a chassis of similar wheelbase and track—that is, 10ft. 6in. and 4ft. 8in. respectively—naturally the difference between the 3,669 capacity of the 3½-litre and the 4,257 c.c. of the 4¼-litre exercises a great influence upon performance. In a nutshell, the effect of the extra c.c. is to give the 4¼-litre model the same acceleration powers on top gear as the 3½-litre possesses on third gear, due, of course, to its superior power-weight ratio. And that is saying a great deal, for the nippy acceleration and general liveliness of the Bentley chassis has long been the envy of thousands of motorists.

Performance Figures

From a speed of 10 to 30 m.p.h. on top gear takes 7.4 sec. with the larger model, and from rest through the gears to 50 m.p.h., 10.3 sec. As to the ultimate speed there is little noticeable difference, which is not perhaps surprising as speed is governed entirely by gear ratio and the r.p.m. an engine will attain. Weights are approximately the same, viz., 33 cwt. for the 3½-litre and 35 cwt. for the 4¼-litre fully equipped. The gear ratios remain the same in both types, 4.1 to 1, and the speed attainable by the engine is also approximately similar, 4,500 r.p.m., so that in either case one can attain 90 to 95 m.p.h., depending upon the conditions prevailing, and this even with a saloon body.

Of course, the 4¼-litre is able to attain its maximum quicker, as it should do, and obviously, therefore, it is faster in regaining its normal cruising speed. This is indeed the most satisfying characteristic of the latest car, for, as traffic increases, constant stops and restarts are the rule, and even on the open road, when traffic is spaced out along the roads in each direction, it is the ability to overtake promptly and rapidly as opportunity offers that is so satisfying.

Silent Speed

Nor is this crescendo of acceleration attained with fuss and bother or clatter. It is a progressive surging forward accomplished with comparative silence no matter the gear ratio employed. In my experience, high-geared cars with a high maximum speed attained only by dint of noise and pother do not, on a long day's run, enable the same high average to be maintained as a silent, reasonably geared car of similar size.

Various factors contribute to this, but in any such comparison quite obviously the quieter the car and the smoother the power output the less tiring the car is to handle. In brief, a car of high stamp to-day must not be judged by sheer maximum speed, but by its general silence, lightness of handling and responsiveness following traffic checks. Such are our road conditions to-day that fast cars are only able to attain their ultimate speed perhaps once a month. Obviously, therefore, one can place far too much stress upon speed propensities in choosing a car to own. It is not without interest that the Philips wireless set on my car can be heard at 80 m.p.h., a point I tested especially on one occasion to prove the fact. Curiously, the tyre treads are the noisiest part of the car.

A far more important attribute than speed is ease of handling. Years ago, a light car which conveyed to the driver a "big-car" feeling was a type to acquire. To-day, the opposite effect is sought, but not by any means always attained ; that is, a big powerful car with a "light-car" feeling, conveyed by easy two-finger steering, servo brakes which are smooth in action, and require a minimum of effort, gears that change silently by the simple act of moving the lever from one position to another. Therein the Bentley scores, for on long day runs up to 400 miles no ordinary driver would be in any way fatigued. London to Glasgow is a comfortable day's jaunt between breakfast and dinner.

Fuel Consumption

Two S.U. carburettors are fitted, and, as to consumption, the 4¼-litre shows but 1 m.p.g. less economy than the figure given by the 3½-litre, which regularly showed 18½ m.p.g., and on long straightaway roads, such as the Great North Road, 20 m.p.g. has several times been achieved without any attempt to economise. Oil consumption with the bigger engine is about 800 m.p.g.

Here I would interpolate a plea for the fitting of a two-way petrol reserve tap on all cars. Even with dashboard gauges a two-gallon reserve is most useful, as I have often proved with the Bentley. Too many cars are not possessed of this desirable item of equipment.

The "4¼" Bentley in Bridgnorth, Shropshire

This view of the back compartment shows the double sunshine roof, window ventilators, tables behind the front seats and the plain light blue upholstery with dark blue piping.

I also find a filler-cap on each side of the tank most handy for pumps on either side of the road, and on the Continent, whilst twin fillers also give a balanced view of the rear.

Tyre wear must enter into this comparison of types. As might be expected, the extra power of the 4¼-litre wears out the covers more quickly, and I estimate 15,000 to 16,000 miles as a fair life, with an added 2,000 for the 3½-litre. Tyre wear is, of course, governed largely by one's methods of driving. Fast cars, too, should never be run with covers worn smooth, and herein the Pneugrippa process scores in restoring non-skid properties.

Double-action Roof

My present car has a Park, Ward metal-frame saloon body with a Weathershields double sunshine roof, that is, either the front or the back passengers may slide the roof away. In summer this is a great advantage and assists ventilation considerably, but the roof must be well fitted to avoid rattle at speed.

With the improved speed qualities of modern cars, a new complaint is coming to the fore, but one which big-car and specialist bodybuilders grappled with successfully years ago. I refer to wind shriek from the front portion, which may be due to bad line or excrescences around the windscreen, or to defective bonnet and louvre design or other causes. Makers of fast cars encountered these difficulties quite early, smoothed out excrescences and eliminated nooks and crannies. Only by long experiment can wind noise be practically eliminated when travelling at speed as in the case of the car to which I refer.

The AUTOCAR ROAD TESTS

No. 1,149.—30 h.p. 4¼-LITRE BENTLEY SALOON

Something More Than a Mere Car—a Patrician Machine That is a Joy to Behold and to Handle

IT is impossible to think of the Bentley as no more than a means of transport, even a highly refined and luxurious means. Rather, after renewal of acquaintance with it in a long test run, is one inclined to become rhapsodical about a machine which really is incomparable. No one free from prejudice could fail to come under its spell, given experience of the car.

An adequate impression is in no wise rendered by analytical description of the various features of behaviour, for these are so balanced that one does not necessarily stand out above another. They combine to make up a car which in each respect is as good as a very famous firm of great practical experience can make it at the present stage of development.

While perfection has never been their claim, it would be a curious-minded or biased driver who could find cause for real criticism in the car. It achieves a very great deal in sheer performance, but is what it is because of the manner of the doing. Every control, every facet of the performance, attains a lightness, a positiveness, a softness, or a quietness, as the need may be, which shows unmistakably that unusual care and thought have gone to the evolving of every single item. The smallest detail seems to have received as much attention as, for instance, the engine itself, and will bear the closest examination.

Those are some outstanding impressions of the 4¼-litre Bentley which persist. Though by no means telling the whole story, to the experienced owner they go to show what sort of car this is in return for an outlay of some £1,500. Then, again, the quality of day-in, day-out regularity, consistency, whatever it may be called, which is not quite as common as might be supposed, especially if a car is driven really hard, is certainly one of the Bentley's foremost attributes. As to general engine behaviour, there

is never any pinking, but at a tickover the engine can be felt a little unless the ignition lever is retarded. Starting from cold is sure with use of the mixture control on the steering wheel.

This car would make a new motorist feel at home, and probably quickly turn him into a good driver. It is so beautiful a piece of machinery as somehow to encourage a driver to develop a delicate touch and to behave in a more than usually reasonable manner on the road.

Perhaps some part of that comes from the knowledge of the great power in reserve. Although one may hold back behind other vehicles, or take a village unnecessarily slowly, the speed can soar again in an effortless fashion as soon as the way is clear. As illustrating this point, it is found that the Bentley will average over 40 m.p.h. in spite of other traffic and fairly frequent urban stretches, much more, if the driver so chooses, where the going is favourable. The speedometer showed a highest reading of 98 during the timed tests, and at 70 and 50 was 4.8 and 3.6 m.p.h. fast respectively.

There is no cruising speed as ordinarily understood. The road and the driver's wishes are the only limiting factors up to the maximum. No fuss or effort is apparent

---

DATA FOR THE DRIVER

30 H.P. 4¼-LITRE BENTLEY SALOON.

PRICE, with four-door all-steel saloon body, £1,510. Tax, £22 10s.
RATING: 29.4 h.p., six cylinders, o.h.v., 89×114 mm., 4,257 c.c.
WEIGHT, without passengers, 34 cwt. 1 qr. 20 lb.
LB. (WEIGHT) PER C.C.: 0.91.
TYRE SIZE: 5.50×18in. on centre-lock wire wheels.
LIGHTING SET: 12-volt. Automatic voltage control.
TANK CAPACITY: 18 gallons; approx. normal fuel consumption, 16–17.5 m.p.g.
TURNING CIRCLE: (L.) 39ft. 7in.; (R.) 40ft. 11in. **GROUND CLEARANCE**: 6in.

ACCELERATION

Overall gear ratios.	From steady m.p.h. of		
	10 to 30	20 to 40	30 to 50
4.10 to 1	7.3 sec.	7.4 sec.	8.0 sec.
5.10 to 1	5.9 sec.	6.0 sec.	6.6 sec.
7.08 to 1	4.4 sec.	4.7 sec.	5.9 sec.
11.30 to 1	3.5 sec.	—	—

From rest to 30 m.p.h. through gears ... ... 4.9 sec.
To 50 m.p.h. through gears 12.7 sec.
To 60 m.p.h. through gears 17.1 sec.
To 70 m.p.h. through gears 24.2 sec.

25 yards of 1 in 5 gradient from rest ... . 5.3 sec.

SPEED

	m.p.h.
Mean maximum timed speed over ¼ mile	88.02
Best timed speed over ¼ mile ...	91.84

Speeds attainable on indirect gears (normal and maximum):—

1st	21—32
2nd	37—51
3rd	61—71

Speed from rest up 1 in 5 Test Hill (on 1st gear) 21.44

BRAKE TEST: Mean stopping distance from 30 m.p.h. (Dry concrete). 30ft.

Performance figures for acceleration and maximum speed are the means of several runs in opposite directions.

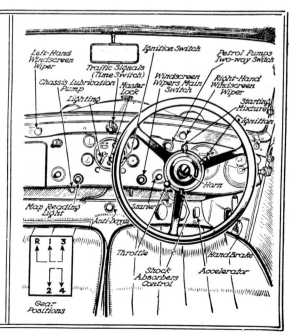

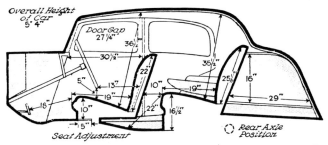

at 80 m.p.h., a figure rapidly obtainable wherever the road is clear sufficiently far, whilst about 70 m.p.h. is unnoticed. The driver is often surprised on looking at the speedometer to find how fast he has been travelling. The whole running of the car, its stability, and its feeling of solidity engender the utmost confidence in passengers as well as in the driver. On a journey at night passengers, indeed, are more than usually inclined to go to sleep at quite high speeds, which says a great deal for the mechanical side as well as for the comfort of the suspension and the seats.

It is a car that one wants to go on driving. At the end of a good day's mileage one has not had enough. It is always revealing some fresh and pleasing aspect of performance or behaviour.

Top or Third—As You Will

The car is almost a practical embodiment of top-gear ideals, gliding through a town, or taking right-angle turns without a change down, or, again, sweeping up long hills, accelerating all the way. Yet the indirect gears are of great potential value. Third is literally indistinguishable from top, either by any noise produced of itself or by engine effort, up to about 60 m.p.h. Second is almost equally silent, and only first gear can be heard at all, but is practically never used, and in any case produces no more than an expensive-sounding hum.

It would not be an exaggeration to say that this right-hand-lever gear change has no equal at the moment for lightness, smoothness, and sureness of movement, particularly where the two upper ratios are concerned. There is synchromesh on third and top only. Thus, all normal upward changes are synchromesh-assisted, since it is general practice to start the car on second gear.

As to control in general, the steering provides accurate "feel" of the front wheels at the highest speeds of which the car is capable, and at ordinary rates steering is an unconscious process. The ratio is distinctly moderate, about 2¼ turns being required from lock to lock. At times a slight road-wheel reaction is felt, but this never develops into any irritating tendency, nor is the steering heavy at low speed.

On the wheel is a finger-moved overriding control for the special hydraulic shock absorbers. As speed rises, the damping provided is in any case automatically built up by a pump driven from the gear box, but the stiffening effect upon the springs can be directly regulated according to conditions by means of this small lever, the result of moving which is very definite.

Surer and more easily secured control than is given by the brakes, with the Rolls-Royce type of mechanical servo, is hardly to be imagined. They are not in the slightest degree fierce or sudden, but speed is reduced almost uncannily by a light pressure on the pedal, from 75 m.p.h. down to 30 m.p.h., for instance, without the car's occupants being actively aware of the considerable deceleration that is taking place. The driver experiences the inestimably valuable feeling of being always able to cope with an emergency. There is a slightly delayed braking action when running backwards.

It is always interesting to observe how the driving position is arranged in the best cars. In the Bentley the spring-spoked steering wheel is at an ideal angle and height for confident handling, and to reach every control is a natural movement. All seats have high back rests extending well up to the shoulders, and they can be occupied

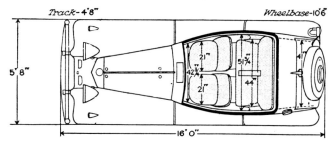

Seating dimensions are measured with cushions and squabs uncompressed.

for hours on end without causing driver or passengers to become tired. The driver is free to use the near-side door; the gear lever gets somewhat in the way of right-hand door entry, but not really seriously.

There is no opportunity to refer to all the numerous details of interest in both the mechanical side and the coach-work—the beautifully finished engine, the sensitive gauges on the instrument board, for instance, but a point to mention is the provision now of twin electric fuel pumps, with a dual switch for checking purposes on the instrument board. Another important item of the equipment is a centralised system of chassis lubrication, operated by a pedal in the driving compartment. A reserve petrol tap is no longer fitted, but a brilliant red warning lamp on the instrument board shines when the supply is at about two gallons. In the switch panel is a master lock, which secures the lighting and ignition switches against interference.

BENTLEY

A fairly long bonnet, but a wide, deep windscreen are indicated, also sufficient vision of even the near-side wing.

Someone's Ideal

Comfortable Two-seater Specially Equipped for Continental Touring

The Vanden Plas Bentley open and closed.

IT is always interesting to examine a body specially built to conform to an enthusiast's requirements. The 4¼-litre Bentley two-seater illustrated has been built by Vanden Plas (England), 1923, Ltd., and incorporates the owner's practical ideas to render the car specially suitable for long-distance Continental touring.

While the complete car was required to have a pleasing appearance, it was also necessary for it to provide an exceptional amount of luggage space, and appearance has, therefore, been placed second to practicability. Thus, the tail or luggage boot is rather on the large side in relation to the general proportions of the body. The colour scheme also is serviceable rather than ornate, for it is the authentic battleship grey of the Home Fleet, and is relieved only by chromium-plated fittings. It is a colour pleasing enough in itself, but one not often seen nowadays on fine coachwork.

For Use in Hot Climates

As regards the character of the car, it might be described as a drop-head coupé, but a more fitting description would be a convertible coupé. Not only do the door windows lower completely, but the head is concealed when folded, and also has an opening rear panel so that ample ventilation can be obtained if the head is used for shade in a hot climate. Indeed, this car should be considered as an open two-seater which can be closed in, rather than as a closed car which can be opened.

Those who drive open cars know well how draughts can whistle round the seats from the open space behind them. Even the best-fitting tonneau cover will not prevent this. Accordingly, the front seat is a single unit, but it has a broad folding central armrest, and the passenger's side of the cushion has a greater thickness of upholstery than the driver's side. In addition, the tonneau cover is continued downwards round the side edges of the seat, and there are also draught-excluding slips which come in contact with the sides of the body when the seat is in its normal position.

Behind the seat is a large space for luggage, the floor being flat. Indeed, an occasional seat is concealed in each side

panel, for use when no luggage is carried, and leg room for their occupants is provided by taking up panels in the floor

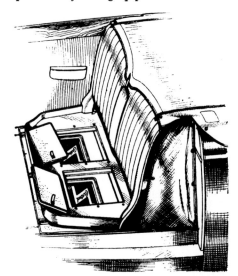

(Above) The tonneau cover fits down the side of the seat to prevent draughts. Lockers for spare oil tins are fitted beneath the seats.

(Right) The space behind the seat is for luggage, but has folding occasional seats in the side panels and covered wells in the floorboards. Over the luggage a strong net can be fitted to carry coats.

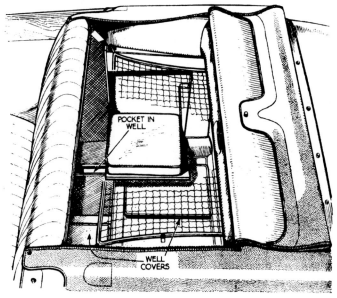

POCKET IN WELL

WELL COVERS

over two foot wells. In the sides of these wells are recesses for small spares. There are also lock-up wells in the front floorboard for carrying spare oil tins.

Normally, however, the space behind the seats is for luggage, and it may be loaded up without removing the tonneau cover, for in the cover is an opening panel with lightning fasteners. An interior light is fitted in the back rail above the luggage space. When the luggage is in position a strong parcel net can be drawn out of a recess and hooked into position above the luggage, as a receptacle for coats and small parcels.

The main luggage space is, however, in the tail. Actually this is so roomy that when the car was on test an observer rode in it to listen for body noises! The lid of the tail carries an illuminated G.B.

plate, and a light is provided in the tail for ease in unloading the luggage at night.

There are many other interesting details. For example, beneath the bonnet there are two lights, one so positioned that it illuminates the sump oil gauge, while the other throws light on to the fuse box. Then the spare wheel is secured by a padlock, the latter being held by a leather band so that it cannot rattle.

Some thought has been given to the instrument board, which has a dull ebony finish, there being a lock-up cubby hole in front of the passenger, and all gauge dials and switches being placed for easy reading and handling by the driver. The switch box is of Rolls-Royce Phantom III type. Small tools are carried in a lift-out panel in the side of the scuttle.

Naturally the single-panel screen has been made to open fully, but it can also be rigidly supported in a partly open position, an important point on a car capable of high speed. The screen pillars are of commendably thin section, giving excellent visibility.

New Cars Described —

Overdrive for the Bentley

New Gear Box Development Increases Maximum Speed for Same Engine Speed as Before : All-round Ease of Running Improved Some Road Impressions

AN extremely interesting development made in the 4¼-litre Bentley, and now announced for the first time, is the introduction of an overdrive or extra-high top gear in the gear box. The manner in which this is incorporated is interesting, for it is not an overdrive automatically engaged or disengaged according to the speed of the car, or one that steps up in ratio an existing gear, but an indirect ratio under the precise control of the driver according to his wishes.

This has been incorporated with the object of reducing engine speed for a given road speed, and it is obtained by a definite position of the gear lever in its gate. The car still has four forward speeds, not five, and third is now the direct drive, a ratio of 4.3 to 1, thus closely corresponding to the Bentley's former top gear of 4.1 to 1, with the overdrive ratio of 3.65 to 1 as the alternative according to conditions.

Without exceeding the maximum recommended engine speed, 4,500 r.p.m., road speed can be very considerably higher on the new overdrive gear. This latest system should also certainly have the effect of improving petrol consumption and of reducing general wear and tear, besides its advantages in greatly improving the general ease of running at medium and high speeds.

As a trial of one of the latest cars—a drop-head coupé—fitted with the overdrive has shown, it transforms what was already a remarkable high-speed machine from the point of view of effortless fast motoring. Approximately 26 m.p.h. per 1,000 r.p.m. is given on the new gear, so that it is easy to see what range of speed is available when it is remembered that 4,000 r.p.m. is a thoroughly comfortable engine speed for this car, and

4,500 r.p.m. within the safe limit of crankshaft speed.

A surprising feature is the flexibility of the engine even if the overdrive gear is left in engagement at comparatively low speeds. It is not the purpose of this new gear to be used at traffic speeds, but even from a crawl the pick-up on it is quite remarkable, and from around 30 m.p.h. is brisk. On the other hand, the 4.3 to 1 direct drive obtained in the third-speed

The sports four-seater tourer has similar lines to previous models and is the least expensive body type of the Bentley range.

position of the gear lever is a capital ratio for ordinary running around, and gives really rapid acceleration.

Another change is that first and second gears are now of higher ratio, first being 10.3 to 1 against 11.3 formerly, and second 6.45 to 1 against 7.1 to 1 before. Thus, within the recommended engine speed limit the maxima on first and second are appreciably higher, being approximately 38 and over 60 m.p.h. in these two cases, while third (direct drive) gives the outstanding maximum of over 90 m.p.h., and on the overdrive or new indirect top 107 m.p.h. is claimed. There was not an opportunity on this occasion to make timed tests of all-out speed, but the second and third gear figures were verified.

Ease of Control

No difference in handling is introduced by the new transmission. A driver accustomed to the Bentley finds the same type of right-hand gear lever to which he has been used, and synchromesh on third and the new top. A start from rest is made in the usual manner, second gear being engaged almost at once, and then third in a short distance, according to circumstances.

Third suffices for most town work and, in fact, can be used for " by-pass "

The Bentley two-door saloon gives excellent side vision and accommodates four.

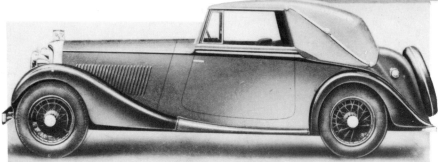

Two drop-head coupé models : (Above) The four-seater coupé at £1,820, which has particularly good lines when folded, and (below) the standard coupé at £1,535.

driving, the rapid acceleration it affords being valuable. There is no suggestion of the engine becoming fussy even if third is retained up to 70 m.p.h. and over. Nor is this surprising, for, as has already been indicated, the new direct-drive third is a close parallel in ratio to the former ordinary top gear of the Bentley.

The engine is mildly apparent at all only when allowed to come down with somewhat abrupt release of the throttle pedal from speeds around 70 m.p.h. on third, and such evidence of it as is then observed would pass unnoticed in most other cars of a less highly refined all-round standard.

Even in and around a town, and certainly out on the open road, there is a decided inclination to put the car into the highest gear available—solely because it is the natural thing to do—and seldom

even on the new high gear does it seem that acceleration is lacking.

It is a singularly easy and pleasing movement to change up and down between the two higher gears at any speed, and impossible to detect any additional transmission noise on the overdrive as compared with direct drive, which is a notable achievement on the part of the Derby engineers and craftsmen.

Clearly, one of the advantages of the new transmission, quite apart from the added sense of ease at ordinarily fast speeds, is that the car can be driven on full throttle for indefinite periods on the Continental roads in the knowledge that the engine is not being overstressed.

Additionally, there are improvements to the steering, which is appreciably lighter than before, though no less definite in " feel," whilst bigger tyres—of

6½in. section compared with 5½in. formerly—give more comfortable riding.

As to other points in the latest car, there is an alteration in the arrangement of the thermostatic water control for the engine, this now being applied to the water circulation system itself instead of to the radiator shutters, providing more rapid warming from cold and maintaining a more uniform engine temperature. The shutters are now fixed permanently open and form an embellishment only.

A new arrangement of the instrument board has been adopted, the instruments having concave dials and improved illumination for night driving, and the speedometer being placed centrally, with the rev counter still immediately in front of the driver. The switch box now contains a master switch and lock. Existing features are centralised chassis lubrication, and hand over-riding control of the hydraulic shock absorbers from the steering wheel. Two S.U. carburettors are fitted, and there is a control lever for ignition advance and retard on the steering wheel.

The wheelbase is 10ft. 6in., the track 4ft. 8in., and the six-cylinder engine has dimensions of 89 by 114 mm. bore and stroke (4,257 c.c.), the rating being 29.4 h.p. and the tax £22 10s.

Prices remain as follows: Sports four-seater tourer, £1,430 ; saloon, £1,510 ; all-weather four-seater, £1,645 ; drop-head coupé, £1,535 ; sedanca coupé, £1,780 ; two-door four-seater saloon, £1,805 ; four-seater drop-head coupé, £1,820.

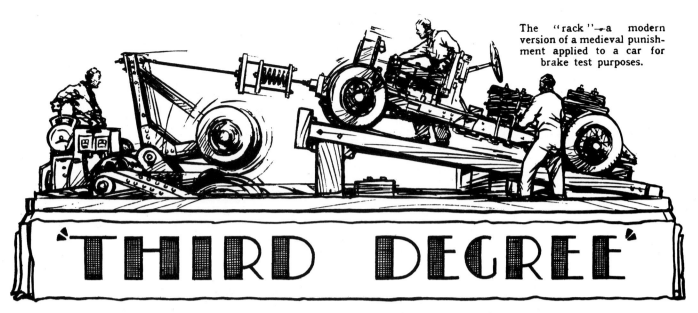

The "rack"—a modern version of a medieval punishment applied to a car for brake test purposes.

'THIRD DEGREE'

Details of the Methods Employed by the Rolls-Royce and Bentley Experimental Division to Wring the Stark Truth Out of New Designs

By
MONTAGUE TOMBS

With Illustrations by F. Gordon-Crosby

UNLESS you have witnessed it you could scarcely conceive what excruciating tests are performed upon metal in the processes of "proving" the soundness of new type cars and components by the Rolls-Royce and Bentley experimental engineers. There is a passion for the truth in that historic factory in Derby—home truths, and the truths about other people's products, too. Neither time nor expense is allowed to stand in the way of getting at the truth. Hence the pinnacle upon which that reputation without parallel so securely rests.

In America a suspected person is liable to be subjected to a painful process called the "Third Degree." In England that process has its counterpart in the treatment given by engineers to metals and metal structures. And in the Rolls-Royce factory it is raised to a fine art. New jobs are suspect until they have proved their innocence.

Imagine a chassis stripped naked, fastened down on a rack, and then subjected to relentless heavy blows, upon its rotating wheels, which cause it to writhe and twist and shudder. This heartrending torture is continued until one or other of its poor bones breaks with fatigue.

The picture is not overdrawn, it is the truth. But the process is, in fact, no more severe than conditions which are met in the daily life of a car used in rough country. The difference is that the worst that may occasionally happen on the road is made to happen continually on the rack, so that it is got over fairly quickly and the weak spots found, traced, and eliminated. That is how the perfect car is sought.

The spectacular apparatus referred to as the rack is officially described as the bump-test equipment. At one side, concealed below the surface of the floor, is a pair of 4ft. diameter drums capable of being rotated at various speeds by an electric motor. The top of each drum is level with a gap in the floor, and the front wheels of the chassis to be tested are set to rest upon the drums. The rear wheels are chocked to secure the chassis.

Bolted to each drum is a cam three inches high. When the drums are rotated, the cams strike the revolving front wheels repeated blows equivalent to running the car continuously over a series of enormous pot holes.

Some idea of the severity of this test is given by the fact that with the surface of the drums running at 18 m.p.h. each cam strikes the tyre with a force of 2,100lb., and imparts an upward acceleration to the wheel of 600ft. per sec. per sec.

One of the principal objects is to prove the strength of all parts of new suspensions or steerings, since a failure on the road might endanger the life of a tester at his work.

The test produces a great many more results than that, however. It is amazing to see how massive-looking components twist and turn, weave and vibrate, from one end of the frame to the other.

"A chassis . . . subjected to relentless heavy blows . . . which cause it to writhe and twist and shudder."

The front wheels flip violently from side to side under gyroscopic forces induced by the sudden rise and fall. The test is so severe that tyres and shock absorbers have to be cooled by water sprays.

If a part will stand up without fracture to 50 hours of this intensive maltreatment, it will run indefinitely on the road.

Another important feature of this test is that everything going on can be measured with precision as to frequency, amplitude, and so forth, so that reliable data are established.

In the same building another process is carried out which is equivalent to vivisection, for the chassis may be dismantled piecemeal whilst it is running. This is done to track down and analyse vibrations of all kinds. Drums similar to those used in the bump test are driven by an engine of 150 b.h.p. up to speeds equivalent to 80 m.p.h. or so.

By placing the rear wheels of the chassis on the drums, its whole working mechanism can be driven, and every component can be dissected.

It may happen that there is an irritating little vibration in evidence on a new design, incited by some unexpected cause. It may be in the valve gear, or the crankshaft, or some lesser component. So the engine is stripped piecemeal until the offender is traced. Actually, vibrations due to crankshaft dampers, flywheels, and clutch parts have thus been determined.

Shimmy and Tramp

Conversely the front wheels may be placed on the drums, and information with regard to "shimmy" and high-speed wheel wobble obtained. "Tramp" can be aggravated by fastening cams and irregularities to the drums. Synchronous movements of the frame, radiator, wings, road springs, or wheels can be examined with exactness by the aid of the Stroboscope, which is an optical instrument designed for producing a slow-motion picture effect.

There is something else in the daily work of a car which imposes stresses of a high order upon the suspension and frame, namely, braking. So the chassis is subjected to a brake test rig which is uncommonly like the medieval rack.

In this test the wheels are locked to the axles by plates and bolts so that they cannot revolve. Then a coupling rod is fastened to the front of the chassis, and is passed through an enormous coil-spring. The latter is suitably connected up to a heavy framework which is caused to rock back and forth over an adjustable distance.

Adjustment of the spring enables a draw-bar pull to be applied to the front of the chassis equivalent to the maximum torque of which the brakes of the car would be capable. This pull is repeated and released at intervals of a few seconds for hour after hour. The test is responsible for analysing a host of problems relating to the brakes themselves, and also to their reactions upon the chassis.

Twenty degrees below zero, "Observers, who go into the cold chamber through a 'sealing' chamber have to wear arctic clothing whilst carrying out their work."

When the lining of a stationary brake shoe is forced into contact with the rotating brake drum, friction is produced which tries to arrest the movement of the drum. Omitting for the moment such factors as loads and speeds, the degree of friction also varies with the nature of the two materials causing it, and with the changes in the temperature which result.

The degree of friction is normally known as the "co-efficient of friction," and is usually designated by the Greek letter μ. The co-efficient of friction of brake linings, and the ability of the latter to maintain their standard, is of paramount importance to the efficiency of brakes in actual use.

A falling off in μ as the effect of continuous brake use down a really long hill, such as is common in the Alps, is the cause of brake "fade out." On cars of the Bentley and the Rolls-Royce calibre such things just must not happen; hence the extremely careful watch kept on brakes and linings.

Keeping a Check on "Mu"

One piece of apparatus used for the purpose consists broadly of a single wheel, tyre, and brake mounted on a framework which can be moved into position with the tyre in contact with the jacked-up rear wheel of a car. The car engine then drives the testing apparatus, which is provided with means of adjustment of brake application and with reaction-measuring devices, and is fitted with chronograph pens which trace on a strip of paper a record of what is happening to the co-efficient of friction during the test. This is a brief description of what is actually a somewhat complicated piece of scientific apparatus.

What is brake horse power to the owner of a car? Does the ability of one cart horse to raise a weight of 33,000 lb. through a height of one foot in one minute mean much to the average lady driver? When we buy a car with an engine rated at 20 h.p. and are informed that this engine can develop 70 brake horse power, are we much wiser?

What does really matter to the owner is the amount of useful tractive effort exerted on the road by the back wheels of his car as the result of putting his hand in his pocket to buy gallons of petrol. In short, brake horse power delivered at the road wheels is the real criterion of the efficiency of a car. That is the common-sense attitude towards power, and although exhaustive bench tests of engines are carried out for comparison, when it comes to hard facts the tests are applied at the road-wheel end of the car.

Such tests are carried out once again upon a pair of sunken 4ft. diameter drums, which are coupled to a large Heenan and Froude water brake, this constituting the road-wheel dynamometer. A car of any make can be run on to this dynamometer and tested extensively on all gears, with provision made to cool those parts which normally would be cooled by moving through the air.

To run a car on a low gear under full torque conditions for an indefinite period is an extremely severe test. One of the difficulties in connection with transmission tests is to ascertain quite how much of this intensive maltreatment should be withstood, since, in the normal life of a car, full torque on first gear is seldom employed for long. This ratio can only be determined by running in conjunction innumerable endurance tests on the road.

I enquired as to the relationship disclosed between the b.h.p. of the engine and the b.h.p. delivered at the wheels. The reply was that a good car delivered rather over 80 per cent. of the engine b.h.p. to the road, counting all losses, including tyres. Further, I gathered that very wide differences are exhibited between cars of all makes.

Some years ago a case was recorded of a foreign car which delivered only a shade over 50 per cent. of its engine power to the road wheels. This was traced to the fact that its particular form of worm final drive did not lend itself happily to such extremes of testing, although it performed reasonably under less arduous road test conditions.

Despite our grumbles at the weather we do not know what it is to be really hot or really cold in this country, but Rolls-Royce cars have to perform faultlessly in any and every climate. Hence the experimental department has a large cold chamber, which can also be used as a hot spot.

This room, with its foot-thick insulated walls and doors, is big enough to take any two of the largest passenger cars produced to-day. The temperature can be reduced to rather lower than 20 degrees below zero, a process which takes the greater part of 24 hours if cars are inside, because the cars themselves have to grow cold. Observers who go

Investigating chassis vibrations and steering phenomena. "The 'joggler,' when in full frenzy, looks as if it were able to shake the teeth off the gearwheels."

into the cold chamber through a "sealing" chamber, have to wear arctic clothing whilst carrying out their work.

In addition to ensuring that cars will start under conditions of low temperature, the cold chamber is invaluable for testing piston "scuffing" and crankcase oil dilution from wet residual petrol, which are by-products of cold starts. Conversely, by circulating hot instead of cold air, conditions may be raised in the chamber suitable for the causing of vapour locks in fuel pipe lines or fuel pumps, such as may occur in hot climates. Lastly, as the chamber is so heavily insulated, it is also used for silence tests.

With the apparatus known as the "joggler" many readers will already be familiar, because many wise garage proprietors have it installed. It consists of four troughs into which the wheels of the car are placed. Each trough is carried on a battery of half-elliptic springs, between which is mounted a bob-weight driven by a jointed shaft from an electric motor.

When the motor is started the rotating bob weights causes an oscillation of the troughs. The frequency of this oscillator can be varied from 100 to 700 per minute. Primarily this rig is employed for the purpose of inciting frame and road-spring resonance, with the object of investigating chassis vibrations and steering phenomena, but it can also be used for chasing bodywork squeaks and rattles. The joggler, when in full frenzy, looks as if it were able to shake the teeth off the gear wheels!

(To be continued next week.)

BEHIND THE SCENES

Rolls-Royce and Bentley Testing Equipment

(Above) A specially made chronograph for obtaining accurate data of car acceleration and deceleration.

(Right) Brake - lining analyses, for determining the coefficient of friction.

'THIRD DEGREE'

Concluding the Article on the Methods Employed by the Rolls-Royce and Bentley Experimental Division to Wring the Stark Truth Out of New Designs

By
MONTAGUE TOMBS

With Illustrations by F. Gordon-Crosby

ONE of the largest sections of the development department of the Rolls-Royce-Bentley organisation is a form of clinic for engines. It is the engine unit test, and the test beds are equipped with every modern measuring device—indicators, exhaust-gas analysers, air-measuring apparatus, multiple thermometers, the Stroboscope, vibration analysing and recording meters, and one hundred and one truth-seeking instruments.

Endurance running of engines goes on almost continually. One of the standard intensive tests consists of 25 hours' running at full power, 15 per cent. over speed, which has been found to produce the same results as 15,000 miles on the road. Many hundreds of hours of such tests are completed in the year's work. Exactly what is accomplished by this research work is illustrated by the fact that during the past fifteen years the power output per pound of engine at Rolls-Royce, Ltd., has been increased by 200 per cent.

Every Combination Tested

In most of the progressive car factories the engineers have "something on the shelf" in the way of new engines, but I was considerably surprised at the extensiveness of the Rolls-Royce "shelves." There is hardly a known and promising combination of valves, valve gear, combustion chamber, and so forth, that has not been made and subjected to exhaustive tests. I saw one such combination which, when applied to the 4¼-litre Bentley engine, would raise the maximum b.h.p. at any given compression ratio by as much as 20 per cent. It has never been put into production because it produces minor effects at the other end of the power range which would not preserve the silkiness associated with that famous car. Supercharging

---

The illustration in the heading is the "skid pan" on which cars are tested for steering accuracy.

has been thoroughly investigated up to the final point of comparative tests on the road.

Another particularly interesting feature of the "clinic" is a section devoted to research on single cylinders, consisting of a crankshaft and crankcase upon which different types of single cylinders may be dropped. This unit is also equipped with variable valve lift and timing. Single-cylinder running is confined mainly to the investigation of combustion chamber design, but reliance cannot be placed upon the results until they have been confirmed on a complete multi-cylinder engine.

If the weighbridge is not exactly a spectacular method for extracting the truth out of road springs and frames, it is not the less effective. It consists of a rectangular platform with a weighbridge at each corner to accommodate each wheel, or a support in lieu thereof, with large screw-down jacks at the ends. Chiefly it is used for determining the rate of the frequencies of road springs, and their working deflections. The chassis is pulled downwards by means of the jacks, and the increase of load for any increase in spring deflection may be accurately measured. Frame deflections for different loads variously applied may be measured in the same way, a process extremely useful in developing frame designs.

"Water Clock" Braking

Quite another phase of brake testing is employed for research into brake mechanism as a whole. When it is desired to duplicate constantly the effect of a driver using his brakes for medium-length hills, the whole car is mounted on drums which it drives under its own power, as during the testing of b.h.p. at road wheels. Then a contrivance is brought alongside which takes the place of a driver's foot and which applies the neat little servo-motor characteristic of Rolls-Royce brakes.

This device is a form of water clock. A stream of water is directed into a small tank, balanced on trunnions, and having on one side at the top a shallow annexe. The weight of this tank and its water content is arranged to provide

Research by means of single cylinders—the "clinic" where various cylinder designs are tried.

the equivalent of pedal pressure. As the tank fills, the water flows into the annexe, puts the tank out of balance, and causes it to tip over and empty itself. Thus a pedal pressure is obtained which gently rises to a maximum, is then released, and then gradually builds up again, repeating the process without cessation if necessary.

"Physical Endurance"

Then there is the large R.-R. physical laboratory where luckless components are taken for test to destruction. Imagine the whitewashed interior of a large building, rows of queer machines along the sides, brilliant lights down the centre and the ceaseless movement of gleaming crank and rods and wheels all around you. Here you see a shock absorber, absorbing what must seem to it to be all the shocks in the world, there an axle shaft receiving shrewd and irresistible twists from end to end, or perhaps a steering wheel having its rim persuaded to part from its spokes. Close to the floor over in that direction is a large connecting-rod securely held at some points, and enduring intolerable squeezes on its big-end. Behind is a great metal box with windows, vapour issuing from a funnel in the top. Inside you can see a water pump apparently trying to pump the ocean dry. On your left is a steel cage covered with torpedo netting, which is placed over components such as flywheels or clutches when they are run up to speeds at which they may perhaps burst. One hundred and one tests are going on all the time, to ascertain the working life of this and that, to determine its factor of safety by pushing and pulling and prodding and twisting and rotating relentlessly until the truth is dragged forth. Every single new component has to go through it.

To exact the truth, in its unity, about certain aspects of road performance, a most intriguing instrument has been devised and is in regular use. It consists of a chronograph with a choice of some four recording pens which apply their marks upon a moving strip of paper. Suppose an accurate brake test is required. The instrument is placed in the back of the car, and electrical contacts are provided on the brake pedal and on cams attached to the road wheels. The clockwork of the chronograph moves the strip of paper. One pen makes a mark for every second. The car is

driven at the desired speed, and the second pen marks each revolution of the road wheel, or a part thereof, on the paper. The brake pedal is applied, and the third pen records the fact. Then as the brakes pull the car up the exact happenings of a complete stop are marked down.

When the strip record is examined it shows all details of time and distance, and thus provides unassailable testimony of the whole of that test deceleration. Acceleration can be accurately measured by the same instrument, and it eliminates speedometers and human error. It was made to R.-R. specifications by the Cambridge Scientific Instrument Co., and adapted by the test section to their needs.

Besides this extensive physical laboratory, there is also an electrical laboratory, wherein research into present and future equipment is carried out. It is not generally known that Rolls-Royce and Bentley make their own dynamos, starting motors, distributors and coils, and do it with that care for details so typical of their search for durability.

If you make a car with no real springing and fit the wheels with extra hard tyres, it may perhaps go round corners at high speeds exactly in accordance with the movement of the steering wheel. But if you desire a car which has pre-eminently comfortable springing and soft tyres, and safe into the bargain, and you expect to be able to drive equally fast and steadily round curves and corners, the proposition is much more difficult to tackle. As an example of extremes imagine a car on full lock being driven round at a speed of 2 m.p.h. The car will follow its steering fairly accurately, but if the speed were increased to 20 m.p.h. it would begin to roll and the tyre treads to creep, so that the turning circle became much greater and the vehicle would be to a considerable extent out of control. In order to study this waywardness, and thereafter exorcise the evil influences which cause it, Rolls-Royce and Bentley have constructed a large concrete arena about 80 yds. in diameter at a cost bordering on £4,000, which is called the "skid pan." On this flat surface the problems of under-steering and over-steering are examined. "Under-steering" means that when rounding a fast curve the front of the car has the greater tendency to swing outwards, and hence the driver has to increase the helm he is applying. "Over-steering" is brought about when

Testing frame torsion—"thumbscrews" are being applied to a competitor's frame.

the tail of the car tends to swing first, and therefore the helm has to be relieved. The ideal condition lies midway.

It would be of little use to extract with great pains the truth out of every part and component unless records were kept for ready reference. Rolls-Royce and Bentley maintain a remarkably efficient records section. Just to give one small instance of its thoroughness, suppose that you wished to know the weight of the rear axle of a certain model. Records will produce for you the total weight, the detail weight, comparisons with weights of similar parts on other cars, accompanied by photographs showing the actual parts which were weighed, laid out so that you could see every detail and obtain a shrewd idea of the construction and proportions.

Forty Years' Experience

Although these notes have, in fact, only covered the broadest outlines of this immensely impressive organisation for discovering the truth about cars and every single part of them, I hope that I have succeeded in conveying a clear picture of the intensive research which is continually in progress. It is the collation of first-hand evidence and reliable data which places the engineering department in a position to form sound judgments. In every one of these many departments there are literally hundreds of precision instruments in constant use. It must be remembered that the existing equipment has been built up and regularly modernised over a period of 40 years.

All this experimental equipment is largely engaged in ensuring that before a Bentley or a Rolls-Royce car is subjected to road test—which must be successfully completed before any part is standardised—every reasonable effort is made to ensure that the test will be entirely successful.

Road tests have never been subordinated to laboratory or rig tests, and, in fact to-day more mileage is being run than ever before. The present requirement is that any alteration to chassis, no matter how minor, shall have successfully completed 15,000 miles before it can be put on to production, the 15,000 miles to have been run on the same parts.

Where the alteration is of a major nature, such as a new gear box, steering or axle the distance which has to be run is increased to 50,000 miles, all of which is carried out under road, and not track, conditions. Continental roads are used almost exclusively for these endurance tests owing to the fact that they have, generally speaking, worse surfaces than English roads and permit of far higher average speeds. Every standardisation run, however, includes one or two thousand miles under London traffic conditions, which throws exceptional loads on the clutch and transmission.

Competitors' products are always being subjected to tests in parallel with the products of the R.-R. factory, and occasionally one is selected to undergo a full road endurance run. This is the only way to determine the relative durability of other makes.

In view of the fact that Rolls-Royce have such an extensive research division, one may naturally be tempted to ask what they do with their facilities, seeing they seldom introduce any new model to the public. The answer is that for every new unit of the chassis which is put into production, half a dozen others are likely to be made, tested and rejected as being deficient in one or other of the qualities considered to be desirable.

As an example, I saw complete engines built with overhead camshaft and other varieties of valve arrangement which have actually been put in cars and run on the road, quite apart from a multiplicity of valve arrangements which have been tried on single-cylinder units.

The Best Compromise

The fact that the existing type of engine has remained in production almost unchanged during the past 15 years merely indicates that Rolls-Royce consider it to be the best type of unit they have tried for giving reliable service combined with maximum output in the hands of the customer.

The test equipment could not be used to the utmost advantage unless it were backed by extensive facilities for producing experimental parts accurately in the minimum time. One of the "articles" of the experimental department is that part of its efficiency lies in its capacity for meeting emergencies in the minimum time. As an example, during the Schneider Trophy Test it was decided that the diameter of the crankshaft would have to be increased in the interests of reliability. The time was short before the race, but drawings were completed, crankshaft forgings obtained, the shafts machined, fitted and tested in the engines all within the space of six weeks. When it is remembered that the dimension of the crank was unlike anything manufactured in the country at the time, the magnitude of the achievement will be appreciated.

Another example of the speed with which the work can be carried out was given when a new model set out for a Continental test, and some 50 miles from the works ran a bearing. Some 48 hours after this event the car, insured against further trouble of the same kind, was in the South of France being tried by Sir Henry Royce.

Testing the rating of front shock absorbers.

EVERY COMPONENT WELL TESTED

Even oil filters are put to exhaustive tests in the search for efficiency.

After a high-speed run on the autobahn : beside the car are John Dugdale, of "The Autocar," V. E. Morgan and A. W. Sleator, manager of Bentleys in Paris.

'Ware ice at 80 m.p.h.!

What Car is This?

Cruising at 100 m.p.h. : Fuel Consumption of Over 20 m.p.g. at 80 m.p.h.

FEW readers will guess the identity of this modernistic streamlined saloon at first glance. A careful examination, however, reveals the familiar winged emblem on the radiator cowling denoting that it is a 4¼-litre Bentley from the Derby works.

This car, the prototype of an additional model, has been undergoing long-distance and high-speed tests on the Continent at which *The Autocar* was represented. The results obtained from the car illustrated here, which was actually built to private order, have been so successful that the Bentley company are preparing to supply replicas.

The specification of the new car includes a more powerful version of the 4¼-litre engine and higher gear ratios. A carefully streamlined body has been developed by means of models and with the co-operation of Rolls-Royce aircraft experts. Details of the outstanding performance of this Continental Bentley will be given in a forthcoming and exclusive article.

TOURING
at
100 M.P.H.!

(Above) The two Bentleys at Metz, France. (Left) In Ulm S. Germany.

LAST week *The Autocar* gave readers something in the nature of a strong *apéritif* by publishing in the Photogravure section some preliminary pictures of an outstanding car, tests of which I have been observing on the Continent. The car in question is the prototype of an additional model to the $4\frac{1}{4}$-litre Bentley range.

In brief, its performance includes cruising speeds up to 110 m.p.h., a maximum speed approaching 120 m.p.h., a most economical petrol consumption (I need only mention now the figure of over 20 m.p.g. at 80 m.p.h.), and Bentley standards of silence and road-holding. With these appetising reminders I will describe our run across France and Germany from its starting point in Paris.

It was a spring-like, sunny day as we assembled outside the Rolls-Royce showrooms in the Avenue George Cinq. Not unnaturally, with the prospect of a Continental tour in such weather, the party was in good spirits, and after a cheerful send-off from a gathering of French Press men, including the great Faroux, of *L'Auto*, we left about midday.

As usual, the fast "fly-under" tunnel crossings which now ring Paris were a source of wonder to those in the party who had not seen them before, and we halted not far beyond the gate of Paris to fill up with standard Azur (which has about the highest octane value of French fuels) in preparation for the long drive ahead.

Two Cars Taken

Two $4\frac{1}{4}$-litre Bentleys were taken, a standard chassis fitted with a four-door pillarless saloon and the special streamlined car which we were going to test not only for its general practicability for Continental touring, but for its performance capabilities on the German *autobahnen*, which lie only just across the French border. These roads have received much publicity, but deservedly so, for they form one of the few places where such a car as this streamlined Bentley can be tried at its maximum speed in safety. Both cars have French-built bodies, the four-door saloon being by Vanvooren and the two-door by Paulin.

Although we did not really leave Paris until 12.29 p.m., the streamlined car was in La Ferté, thirty-eight miles away, by 1.10 p.m. This represents an average speed of 55 m.p.h., maintained, as I will vouch for, as an ordinary matter of course with every consideration for the various small towns along the straight, flat roads leading eastwards across the French plain from Paris.

Tucked away down a side road to the left of the main road through La Ferté-sous-Jouarre is the Hôtel de l'Épée, where we paused for lunch.

Snow in the mountains near Wiezenstein. The "autobahn" becomes a single track here.

High - Speed Continental Test with the Prototype of an Additional 4¼-litre Bentley : Remarkable Performance Revealed : Important Effects of Streamlining

 by

JOHN DUGDALE

(Above) 110 m.p.h. on the speedometer on a French highway. The equivalent engine speed is 3,500 r.p.m.

(Centre) By the Danube. (Above) The streamlined and standard Bentley radiators, in Homburg.

always something of a ceremony in France. The ordinary motorist would scarcely have noticed the inconspicuous hotel, but those who know their France or who are armed with one of those little booklets for gourmets would not have passed it by. The proprietor, M. Truchet. was *chef de cuisine* to Marechal Joffre during the war, and his hand has by no means lost its cunning, while his cellar will long be remembered for its *champagne natur*, the still champagne so popular in France.

After such an excellent luncheon we felt quite up to some fast motoring, and proceeded to cover the next sixty-four miles in fifty minutes, which represents an average of 76 m.p.h. and is the highest average speed I have ever maintained for such a distance on the road. Once more I would reiterate that this speed was achieved with every consideration for road conditions, and the driver knew the road intimately.

We paused to allow the four-door saloon to catch up, and continued the remaining 106 miles to Metz for the night. The average speed, not including stops or the time taken for the first eight miles before filling up in Paris, worked out at precisely 60 m.p.h.

I covered the whole of that distance in the streamlined car and well remember my first impressions. This, I thought, is a new aspect of motoring; it is the nearest thing to flying. Indeed, in many ways I was reminded by the sleek lines of the car of the Lockheed Electra with which British Airways had carried me so rapidly to Le Bourget the previous day. The parallel may also be carried beyond appearance to the smooth, rapid 100 m.p.h. progress of the car on the road.

Engine and Chassis Modifications

Now, how has this high performance been obtained? The chassis used, I am assured, is a standard one fitted with an engine modified to give more power, with higher gear ratios, and with shock absorbers set somewhat harder for high-speed work. Alterations to the engine consist of raising the compression to 8 to 1 by means of raised-crown pistons of a new Bentley design, although the cylinder head is standard. Larger-type S.U. carburettors are another important fitting, and these have oil dashpots on the pistons to minimise the likelihood of flat spots. In this condition the 4.257 c.c. six-cylinder o.h.v. engine gives over 140 b.h.p. on the bench, compared with the 125 b.h.p. usually given by the standard Bentley engine of 6.5 to 1 compression.

As to the gear ratios of the streamlined saloon, these

Details : (1) How the spare wheel is carried. (2) A side view showing the flowing lines. (3) The streamlined tail. (4) The spare wheel pivots forward for removal of luggage. (5) Flush-fitting door handle. (6) Operating the handle.

are high, being 8 to 1 in first gear, 5 to 1 in second gear, 3.41 to 1 in third or top gear, and 2.87 to 1 in overdrive. All Bentley cars have been fitted with a similar type of overdrive gear box since October, 1938, but use lower ratios. The speeds given on the various gears are approximately 50 m.p.h. in first, 80 m.p.h. in second, 115 m.p.h. in third, and 118 to 120 m.p.h. in overdrive.

The engine performance figure with which the Bentley engineers are justifiably most pleased is the m.e.p. of 130 lb. per sq. in. at 2,000 to 2,500 r.p.m.

Tunnel-tested Bodywork

As to the body, this in itself is a most interesting production and was developed in France by Monsieur Paulin with the full co-operation of Rolls-Royce. A model was submitted to wind tunnel tests, and the result is a particularly good body from the point of view of wind resistance. The familiar Bentley radiator is now cowled in the most modern style, the head lamps are flush-fitting, the mudguards are tapered, the rear wheels are enclosed and the two-door body slopes gracefully back to a point, as can be seen in the illustrations. The undersides are also rounded with a more extensive undertray than usual. Finally, eddy-making excrescences such as hinges, door handles, window frames and number plates have been made flush-fitting.

An important effect of such efficient steamlining is that the help of wind resistance while decelerating is much reduced. This fact, combined with the screening of the brakes by the streamlined body, has made the fitting of light alloy brakes advisable for greater cooling. The alloy drums have steel liners. The difficulty is not so much to find a heat-resisting lining as to find a lining which combines good non-squeak properties with ample heat resistance. An air intake, deflecting a draught on to the sump, is another point designed for extra cooling.

The body is well equipped with four comfortable tubular-framed seats, though head room in the rear seats is some-

what restricted. This particular design is only intended as an occasional four-seater. The construction is extremely light, Duralumin being extensively used. The overall weight of the car is just over 31 cwt., which represents a saving of some 3 cwt. on a standard Bentley. A wireless set is carried with outside telescopic aerial, and there is room for suit cases in the rear in front of the spare wheel, which is supported on a hinged bracket in the tail.

In spite of the cold weather the car remained comfortably warm within, an effect no doubt helped by the undertray. Yet it is possible adequately to cool the interior by means of the two very small rear-quarter panels only. The extractor effect of these is powerful. With such a speedy machine more than usual care must be taken with the window openings or draughts might result, and streamlined cars are, in fact, revealing the need for a scientific investigation into car interior air conditioning. Experiments have already been made on the lines of a sealed interior with air supplied by a fan.

From France to Germany

Having learnt these instructive details of the car and having gained a striking insight into its capabilities on that first day, I looked forward to our runs on the *autobahnen* next day with keen anticipation.

We reached the frontier in the Saar district, where the Nazis made one of their famous occupations in 1935. The Franco-German feeling could not have been more graphically illustrated than by the horrible first and only sign of the subterranean Maginot line, where a 20ft. wide wall of steel anti-tank posts stretches across the fields like the Great Wall of China. The Frenchman has indeed sown dragon's teeth.

The German Customs house is a palatial affair, comparing well with the French, but I should hate to see the bill incurred for public works in Germany over the last four years.

Most striking of all the extensive building in Germany—

more striking than the lavish new sports arenas in every town, more striking even than the monumental party centres at Nuremburg or the vast palace of a Chancellery in Berlin—are the new motor roads or *autobahnen*. One of us described them as "a wonder of the world," and, indeed, he is not far wrong.

We joined the *autobahn* at Mannheim, and here the tank was emptied for a rough consumption test, to repeat figures obtained on an earlier occasion. On four and a half litres (4.543 litres = 1 gallon) we covered 23.7 miles. I timed 21.8 miles of these to be covered at an average of 76.4 m.p.h.; also over 13.5 miles of the total were covered at 81 m.p.h. A certain distance had to be driven at lower speeds in order to get from the filling station on to the *autobahn* by means of the clover-leaf crossing, and, unfortunately, after about fourteen miles the *autobahn* suddenly came to a dead end and we had to reverse and return down the parallel track. Still, 20 m.p.g. at 80 m.p.h. is within the capabilities of the car, and Bentleys in their previous tests have obtained 32 m.p.g. at 40 m.p.h.; 26 m.p.g. at 60 m.p.h; 21 m.p.g. at 80 m.p.h.; and 17 m.p.g. at 90 m.p.h.

After refuelling we ran down the *autobahn* that evening to Ulm, the roads farther south being covered with ice and snow on the last section over the foothills of the Bavarian Alps. In Ulm, I am glad to say, the sarcastic remarks of the pro-French wing of our party, which had been greatly encouraged by a very plain *wiener schnitzel* at Mannheim, were much reduced by a miraculous blue trout (about the only blue thing ever to come from the near-by Danube) and by peach cup as the Germans really can make it.

We had a rapid glance at the Danube, which at Ulm has scarcely begun its 1,000-mile course towards the Black Sea, before rejoining the *autobahn* next morning. Then, with the fine single spire—said to be the tallest in the world—of Ulm behind us, we proceeded to put in some more intensive speed work.

First we stopped at an official fuel depot called a *tank*, pumped the tyres up to 45 lb. all round and then soon warmed "La Streamline" up to an average of 89 m.p.h. for ten minutes. She could do better than that, however, for the next five miles were covered at 110 m.p.h. and a further 4.2 miles at 112 m.p.h. This made an overall average of 96 m.p.h. for a total of 24 miles covered in a quarter of an hour. During this time the fastest speed recorded was 118 m.p.h.

Wonderful as are the *autobahnen*, such high speeds are a strain to maintain. Inevitably one must come up with slower-moving traffic, and in the unlikely event of motorways being built in this country they will have to be much wider than the German examples to carry our volume of traffic. Again, it is a fallacy to say that the 'bahn is designed for 120 m.p.h. One curve we found could not have been taken at more than 90 m.p.h. I remember another fast, slightly banked curve, however, which we actually took at over 110 m.p.h., a speed which amply demonstrated the road-holding abilities of the car.

On driving one notices the lack of deceleration due to the streamlining. Carried to its extreme, this effect can be disconcerting, and, for instance, Major Gardner on switching off the engine of his streamlined, record-breaking M.G. at over 150 m.p.h. coasted for over two miles. The 357 m.p.h. Thunderbolt has, therefore, additional air brakes, and for the streamlined high-speed tourer of the future I predict air brakes as a standard fitting.

In the afternoon we left the *autobahn* at Karlsruhe and crossed the frontier at Strasbourg, where the company once more delighted in French cooking at the Maison Rouge.

For a short stretch on the final day we met fog, though the weather as a whole for early February had been beautifully sunny, but cold. We covered 210 miles before stopping for lunch at the Hôtel de France, in Sezanne, another inn well known to the discerning traveller.

In over a thousand miles under hard touring conditions the car had proved itself as a practical and remarkably fast machine

(Right) Through the narrow streets of Ulm, on the Danube.

The Original Bentley Corniche

Over a number of years there has been confusion about the identity of the car known as the Bentley Corniche; many people have confused it with the special car built for N. S. Embiricos. Recently there has been a resurgence of interest in the car and we have published several letters from readers (see *Autocar* 21 June and 19 July). We are, therefore, greatly indebted to Rolls-Royce Motors Ltd. for supplying a photograph of the Corniche and thus enabling us to show it and the Embiricos car together. We hope this and the following will put the record straight.

IN 1938 a special Bentley 4¼-litre car with streamlined body designed by M. Paulin and executed by Van Vooren was evolved by Walter Sleator, manager of the Rolls-Royce Paris branch, for the Greek racing driver N. S. Embiricos for high speed touring and *autobahn* use. At 31cwt it was about 3cwt lighter than the standard Bentley saloon and was quite a departure from the orthodox Bentley of the day in that it had a streamlined radiator shape. It also had a very low wind resistance and when fitted with an overdrive gearbox was very fast for the time — as demonstrated to John Dugdale of *The Autocar* on a Continental trip in February 1939 when, with Walter Sleator at the wheel, 112 mph was averaged for five minutes and a maximum of 118 mph was seen. Fuel consumption was not bad either, with 26 mpg obtained at a constant

Above: The four-door Bentley Corniche
Right: The Embiricos Bentley at Brooklands in 1939 on the occasion of Captain G. E. T. Eyston's record run. Left to right are: Rolls-Royce mechanic George Ratcliffe, Captain G. E. T. Eyston (in car), Rolls-Royce chauffeur Wally Garner, Rolls-Royce publicity manager Millard Buckley, J. A. V. Watson of Wakefield (Castrol), unidentified gentleman, John Dugdale of The Autocar, *and W. A. Rowbotham.*
Below: Captain G. E. T. Eyston driving the Embiricos Bentley in 1939

60 mph and 21 mpg at 80 mph. Later the same year Captain G. E. T. Eyston, drove the car at Brooklands and covered a very creditable 114.63 miles in an hour with a fastest lap of 115.02 mph and an average of 115.05 mph for 10 miles. These tests with the car proved so successful that Rolls-Royce decided to produce a modified version of it as a production model with a four-seater body.

This resulted in the prototype Bentley Corniche which was evolved by H. I. F. Evernden of Rolls-Royce in conjunction with M. Paulin and bodied by Van Vooren of Paris. The intention was that Park Ward, Rolls-Royce's coachbuilding subsidiary, would build the bodies for the production versions of the Corniche. There were quite a number of mechanical differences between the 1938 Embiricos Bentley and the 1939 Corniche, not least of which was the fact that the Corniche was based on the later 4¼-litre Mark V Bentley chassis and had independent front suspension and a semi-floating rear axle and was fitted with an experimental 4,257c.c. engine with overhead inlet and side exhaust valves. Also

the Corniche had steel disc wheels as opposed to the wire wheels of the "Embiricos", standard 4¼-litre and Mark V. High speed testing of the Corniche was carried out on the Continent successfully and then according to Ivan Waller, who was one of the Rolls-Royce engineers involved in testing the Corniche (see *Reader's Letters, Autocar* 19 July page 51), the car was seriously damaged while on endurance testing. Consequently it had to be transported to Dieppe and it was then that the outbreak of World War II intervened and prevented it being shipped back to England. During the War the Corniche, chassis number 14BV, sustained a direct hit from a bomb and was completely destroyed.

The Embiricos car on the other hand passed into the private ownership of H. S. F. Hay in July 1939 and was raced by him at Le Mans in 1949 and finished sixth averaging 73.56 mph. Soltan Hay entered again in 1950 finishing 14th, and was 23rd in 1951. The car appeared at a Sotheby Auction in London in October 1968 and so far as is known is still in existence.

Warren Allport

Bentley Mark V 4¼-litre, of which less than 20 were produced between 1939 and 1940.

The AUTOCAR ROAD TESTS

No. 1,269.—30 h.p. 4¼-LITRE BENTLEY SALOON

IT is easy to shower superlatives upon the 4¼-litre Bentley, but difficult to render a true word picture of its exceptional blend of qualities. To appraise it a critic needs to have a faculty of comparison built up by trial of all the outstanding cars produced in recent years. Then proper valuation can be made of the presentation in one machine of the principal car virtues.

Speed is only one feature, deriving naturally from the high engine power developed. It is as near silent mechanically and as smooth running as a motor car is likely to be on the present-day universal lines of design. From the passenger point of view it ranks with the most comfortable cars that have been tried, yet is stable to exactly the degree required of a machine to which maintained speeds between 70 and 90 m.p.h. are natural on suitable roads. Not least, it is of compact overall size, and does not feel unduly large or unwieldy. The type of body fitted is, of course, a matter of choice, the lowest priced saloon costing £1,510.

One of the most impressive points is the controls. Their light and silky action makes the Bentley more easily driven than the majority of machines, and also contributes immeasurably to its charm. Not just because it gives swift acceleration and can travel from one place to another more rapidly than most cars, but because of the way in which each part of it works; every minute spent in driving it is a pleasure.

These are things that make it worth while in the eyes of those who can buy the ultimate in car behaviour.

A long journey brings out its advantages to the utmost. To-day a 1,000-mile run in comparatively short time is not a destructive test of any modern car, but the experiences of almost this distance covered within two days during the present test show the calibre of the Bentley convincingly.

For such a distance to be possible within the time, a car must make high averages for this country, 50 miles in the hour being achieved, but, still more important, a 45 m.p.h. running time average over a distance exceeding 300 miles, largely after dark. Although for some considerable distance weather conditions were not of the best, the driver was appreciably less tired afterwards than following some other runs shorter by 200 and 300 miles made in the same time, whilst the two passengers were fresh, too.

In motoring such as this a car must answer exactly, swoop up to high speeds, and be under precise steering control and instant regulation by the brakes, and maintain speed practically regardless of road surface.

No practical illustration of true innate quality would be afforded by a forced journey which left a car in some way "below par." Here the Bentley proved its worth in perhaps the most impressive manner possible by consuming barely any oil, starting up at once on the following morning and ticking over in its subdued manner, and also by still possessing the full power of its brakes.

DATA FOR THE DRIVER
7-4-39

30 H.P. 4¼-LITRE BENTLEY SALOON.

PRICE : Chassis, £1,150 ; saloon from £1,510. Tax, £22 10s.

RATING : 29.4 h.p., six cylinders, o.h.v., 89 × 114 mm., 4,257 c.c.

WEIGHT, without passengers, 35 cwt. 0 qr. 23 lb. LB. PER C.C. : 0.93.

TYRE SIZE : 6.50 × 17in. on knock-off wire wheels.

LIGHTING SET : 12-volt. Automatic voltage control.

TANK CAPACITY : 18 gallons ; approx. normal fuel consumption, 16–18 m.p.g.

TURNING CIRCLE : (L.) 39ft. 7in. ; (R.) 40ft. 11in. GROUND CLEARANCE : 6in.

ACCELERATION

Overall gear ratios.	From steady m.p.h. of		
	10 to 30	20 to 40	30 to 50
3.64 to 1	9.7 sec.	9.8 sec.	10.6 sec.
4.30 to 1	7.8 sec.	7.7 sec.	8.2 sec.
6.43 to 1	5.2 sec.	5.3 sec.	6.1 sec.
10.25 to 1	3.8 sec.	—	—

From rest to 30 m.p.h. through gears ... ... 5.2 sec.
To 50 m.p.h. through gears 11.5 sec.
To 60 m.p.h. through gears 16.1 sec.
To 70 m.p.h. through gears 23.5 sec.
25 yards of 1 in 5 gradient from rest ... ... 6.2 sec.

SPEED

	m.p.h.
Mean maximum timed speed over ¼ mile	90.68
Best timed speed over ¼ mile ...	92.78

Speeds attainable on indirect gears (normal and maximum) :—

	normal—maximum
1st	32—38
2nd	51—60
3rd (direct drive)	77—89

Speed from rest up 1 in 5 Test Hill (on 1st gear) 21.07

BRAKE TEST : Mean stopping distance from 30 m.p.h. (dry concrete), 32ft.

WEATHER : Dry, mild, bright ; wind fresh, W. Barometer : 29.80in.

Performance figures for acceleration and maximum speed are the means of several runs in opposite directions, with two up.

(Latest model described in " The Autocar " of October 7th, 1938.)

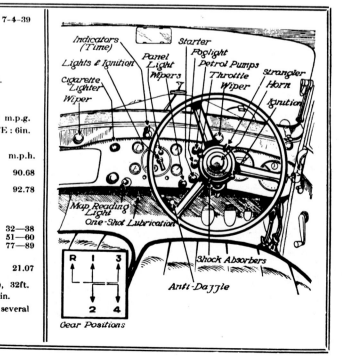

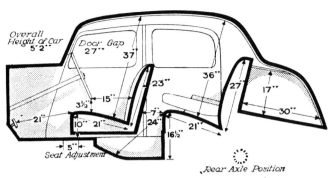

Overall Height of Car 5′2″ *Door Gap 27″* 37″ 36″ 27″ 17″ 23″ 15″ 3½″ 30″ 7″ 21″ 10″ 21″ 24″ 21″ 16½″ 5″ Seat Adjustment

Rear Axle Position

Seating dimensions are measured with cushions and squabs uncompressed.

In other words, it was fit for a similar journey straight away. Bare figures of performance, however good they may be, cannot convey such qualities as these.

As to mechanical features which make up this remarkable machine, one of the most interesting is the new gear box with a high-ratio indirect top gear, termed the overdrive. This is not an overdrive in the sense in which the description has now become recognised, though productive of the same important result of reduced engine speed for a given road speed.

First and second gears are slightly higher in ratio than formerly, affording appreciably increased maxima ; third-speed position of the lever now gives direct drive on a ratio only slightly lower than the previous ordinary top gear. Nearly 90 m.p.h. is available on this gear. Fourth-speed position engages the new overdrive top of 3.64 to 1, compared with the 4.1 top of the earlier model.

The gear change handles exactly as before, there being synchromesh on the third and fourth speeds. Only finger pressure on the lever is necessary. The upward change from first to second, and downward from third (or direct drive) to second, and from second to first, require double-declutching treatment. The synchromesh changes can be made perfectly quietly as quickly as the lever can be moved, and the car has three silent ratios.

At the moderate engine speed of 3,500 r.p.m. on the new overdrive top gear the Bentley is travelling about as fast as British roads commonly permit—above 85 m.p.h. The entire absence of effort and noise makes the higher speeds seem hardly credible, whilst the low engine revs lead to materially reduced wear and tear.

There is no question of a free wheel being used in conjunction with this transmission. A natural tendency is to run through the changes upon moving away and thus bring the lever back into high top or overdrive. If this is done flexibility does not suffer noticeably until the speed

is brought down to a crawl, and it is an easy change to third or second for an accelerating spurt or rapid hill-climbing. Actually, the car will pull smoothly from under 10 m.p.h. on the high-ratio fourth.

The steering is strikingly free from heaviness at any time, especially considering its complete accuracy and freedom from kick-back up to the highest speeds. Three turns of the wheel are required from lock to lock. The mechanical servo-operated brakes check the car or stop it suddenly if necessary with astonishing smoothness in relation to the retarding power exerted, and are a potent factor in confident use of the high performance.

Considerable range of adjustment of the suspension is afforded by means of a steering wheel control for the shock

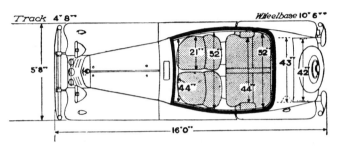

Track 4′8″ *Wheelbase 10′6″* 5′8″ 21″ 52″ 52″ 43″ 42″ 44″ 44″ 16′0″

absorbers, overriding a pump driven from the gear box that increases the shock absorber pressure hydraulically as the speed rises. With the control towards "hard" a capital firm effect is obtained, the car feeling taut and solid.

A first-rate position is obtained behind the spring-spoked steering wheel. The right-hand brake and gear levers are extremely satisfactory controls, though the gear lever does interfere to some extent with use of the driver's door.

Both speedometer and rev counter are of large diameter. The speedometer showed a highest reading of between 97 and 99—approximately 3,800 r.p.m. on the overdrive—during maximum speed timing, ranging from 4.3 m.p.h. fast at 70, and 3.4 at 50, to 2.5 m.p.h. at 30.

Not one of the least delightful things about the car is its manner of starting. The engine fires instantly from cold, and soon accepts closing of the mixture control on the steering wheel for the two carburettors, gaining water temperature quickly. The engine and its auxiliaries have that clean finish and air of planned arrangement that round off the other and more obvious qualities of the machine.

One-shot lubrication of a large number of points on the chassis is operated by a plunger in the driving compartment. A reserve petrol tap is not now fitted, but a green warning signal flashes when only about two gallons remain.

Apart from the sensible width and depth of the windscreen, a notable feature shown by the Visibility chart is that vision over the front and sides of the bonnet is good. Also, enough of the near-side wing is seen to be useful.

Bentley's 114 Miles in the Hour

Impressive Performance of Streamline Saloon Tested Early This Year

The streamlined Bentley shows to advantage at speed on the banking.

DRIVING the 4¼-litre Bentley which early this year put up an outstanding performance on the German *autobahn*, Capt. George Eyston, on Tuesday morning last, averaged 114.63 m.p.h. for an hour on Brooklands track. His fastest lap was at 115.02 m.p.h.

This is a very fine performance, since such an average at Brooklands means that the maximum of the Bentley must be about two miles a minute. The car was a four-seater streamlined saloon, and ran on standard B.P. ethyl fuel and Castrol oil. Modifications from the standard Bentley chassis include a higher back axle ratio, track racing Dunlop tyres, and an engine of increased power having a special air intake to counteract increasing under-bonnet temperatures at high speeds.

When the car proved its speed and especially its economical performance in Germany it was observed for *The Autocar* by John Dugdale, of the editorial staff. On Tuesday morning during the warming-up lap he also lapped Brooklands with Capt. Eyston at over 110 m.p.h., again reporting favourably on the track-holding considering there was some rain and wind at the time. The petrol consumption of about 11 m.p.g. at 115 m.p.h. must also be considered exceptional.

Finally, Capt. Eyston covered 10 miles at an average speed of 115.05 m.p.h. It is understood that this 4¼-litre Bentley is the prototype of a new model to be announced later this year.

Discussing the 114 miles in the hour. (From left to right), W. A. Robotham, in charge of the technical side for Bentleys ; Captain Eyston, the driver ; J. A. V. Watson, of Wakefields' ; and Millard Buckley, Rolls-Royce publicity manager.

"HI"

A 4¼-Litre Bentley with Saloon Body Designed to Give as Nearly as Possible the Effect of an Open Car

November 8th, 1940.

Clean-cut and business-like from the rear view is the special 4¼-litre Bentley. The tank holds thirty-two gallons.

A CORRESPONDENT of *The Autocar*, Mr. H. de Yarburgh Bateson, wrote recently mentioning a special modern Bentley he had seen in London, carrying the distinctive registration number H1. His letter was published in the Correspondence columns, and he hoped, as I did, that it would catch the owner's eye and produce some details of an interesting-looking car. As in a rather similar instance not long ago, this had the desired effect, showing again that *The Autocar* penetrates to all motoring circles.

As a matter of fact, the Bentley's owner, Mr. R. G. McLeod, had missed his usual reading for a week or two owing to a little difficulty in connection with bombs on and near certain of his interests, and had not seen this letter in the issue of September 27th. Twice on the road he was addressed by other drivers who had recognised the Bentley from the description given, and who asked him if he knew that he was "wanted" by *The Autocar*. One of them was driving an elderly Lea-Francis. Thus the registration number of the Bentley, an exclamatory "Hi!" at a quick glance, proved rather appropriate.

Its owner, a busy man, was kind enough to bring it along for me to see last week. Even if anyone should consider that a 4¼-litre Bentley saloon is not a sports car in the sense that is usually meant, this one qualifies, I think, if only for the reason that it is entirely free from trimmings. Stark is the word, and there is something particularly attractive about its severity.

Mr. McLeod is by natural preference an open car man, but for everyday motoring, long journeys being frequently necessary, he has found that the inevitable exposure and draughts do him no good as regards an occasional touch of rheumatism. He therefore decided to have a saloon body built to his own design that would give as nearly as possible the feeling of light and freedom of an open car. Also, he does not like a car to be decked out in the manner of a Christmas tree.

The full-width rear window is seen, and an impression obtained of the exceptionally thin windscreen pillars.

The result of his ideas, carried out by the coachbuilders, H. J. Mulliner, is a modern Bentley that would always attract notice, yet one that could never be criticised as being sensational, for it is essentially practical. It reminded me of the rather bare but decidedly "right"-looking sports cars of ten years or so ago, plus all the refinement and comfort and high performance of the "4¼." The business-like appearance was added to by the present finish—camouflage colouring devised by Mulliner's, a scheme that is more pleasing to the eye than any I have seen on a car, yet also effective, I should say. It includes the plating, of course, and the whole appearance is altered by it, helping to impart a "ready for action" atmosphere which the "cleanness" of the car in itself suggests.

Unusual Lamps

The thing that first strikes you after the camouflage is the absence of ordinary head lamps. Mounted low down are a Marchal hooded type of lamp and a lamp of fog-light size, fitted with the present A.R.P. mask. Also, the side lamps are an unusual pattern. They consist of small-diameter pillars in which

a festoon bulb is hung vertically. Mr. McLeod, who has specialised knowledge of the subject, finds that the life of such bulbs, suspended thus instead of being carried horizontally in the ordinary manner, is greatly lengthened.

The two-door body is plain in lines, and the rear shape is somewhat reminiscent of the Voisin and Ballot of other days. The tank, which is separate from the body, holds thirty-two gallons, and has two snap fillers. The wings have a good deal to do with this car reminding one of sports models of several years ago. They are of the comparatively narrow semi-flared pattern that allow the underwork of the chassis to be seen, and the tyre treads to be inspected, rather like the 2-litre Lagonda's wings, you remember.

Then there are other interesting points about the body. To obtain all possible light inside, a panel of safety glass, similar to the windscreen, has been inserted in the roof. The effect is remarkable; there is no "shut-down" suggestion, and on a dull day it was an exceptionally light interior. This result is helped by the thinnest screen pillars I ever remember seeing, as well as by a rear window of maximum width.

Showing the glass panel in the roof, which is one of the Bentley's special features.

It might be supposed that there would be a somewhat overpowering light in bright weather. Mr. McLeod has his own system of anti-dazzle screens. He regards the usual pattern as unduly limited in range and a nuisance when not actually needed. His own arrangement is simple but provides all the latitude of adjustment that is required. It consists of two pieces of thin opaque card, which are slipped through a space formed by a light wooden slat extending across the top of the windscreen.

Primarily a Two-seater

The body was designed as a two-seater primarily, with occasional but none the less comfortable back seats, the cushions and squabs of which are made easily removable to give a very large luggage space. Either one half or both sides can be taken out. This body was previously fitted on a 1938 Bentley chassis Mr. McLeod owned, it being transferred to his present 1939 overdrive chassis. The car weighs 31 cwt.

Mechanically, the car is to standard specification; the instruments are normal, too. The owner is yet another who has found the overdrive gear box an improvement over the previous ordinary

The absence of ordinary head lamps gives the front of the car an unfamiliar touch.

box. He treats it entirely as a "one, two, three, four" gear change: that is, he goes straight through in sequence into the indirect top, and uses this ratio down to quite low speeds. He can regularly obtain a 97 m.p.h. speedometer reading ; the absence of big head lamps in a position where they cause wind resistance should give this particular saloon some advantage over more normal types, though there has been no attempt at streamlining, as the tail photograph shows. This Bentley, consistent in petrol consumption as in other things, does its 18 m.p.g. regardless of conditions, in town driving and on fast main road journeys equally.

It was a pleasure to meet one who has been a reader of The Autocar for many years, and who finds that the subjects it can still keep in front of motorists provide relaxation from the peculiar worries of the present time.   V.

Rolls-Royce and Bentley Plans

AN announcement has been made this week by Sir Arthur Sidgreaves, managing director of Rolls-Royce, Ltd., regarding the post-war manufacturing plans of the company.

It is their intention to resume the manufacture of Rolls-Royce and Bentley cars immediately conditions make it possible to do so. Development work to this end is already being undertaken, although this must remain limited in scope until more progress has been made with the liquidation of wartime commit-

ments. It has been decided, however, that the cars to be produced in the immediate post-war period will be basically similar to those which were current at the outbreak of war, except that full advantage will be taken of the improved means of production and further engineering experience resulting from the company's intensive wartime effort.

No Smaller Car

The post-war cars will be available either with standardised coachwork, approved by Rolls-Royce, and of a more modern design, or as chassis only for which the purchaser can specify any

individual form of coachwork. At this stage Rolls-Royce, Ltd. have decided not to enter the market in the lower horse-power range. They believe that they must continue to offer cars which remain exclusive in type, and for which there exists a demand amongst those who value refinement and a highly developed engineering product resulting from many years devoted to the manufacture of cars of superlative quality.

It is not yet possible to quote prices, nor to give any information as to when deliveries of post-war cars will commence. A further announcement will be made whenever this information can be made public.

A motoring idyll, such as might have been
evoked in the daydreams of deprived
motorists during the long years of World War II.
The car is Barnato's 8-litre, photographed in
the summer of 1931.

NEW CARS DESCRIBED

Post-War
4¼-litre Bentley

*Features of the Latest Design Include
Overhead Inlet Valve Engine.
Bentley-built Bodywork now Offered*

Inlet side of a superb 4¼-litre engine, that of the new Bentley. A massive air cleaner and silencer is mounted above the twin S.U. carburettors and the inlet manifold is water-jacketed.

HOWEVER carefully the designer may seek perfection, the ultimate test which his result must pass is the approval of those who have ownership under consideration. That being so, personal impressions of the characteristics of the car on the road take precedence over description of the engineering means by which refinement of behaviour has been won.

Here, then, are the first impressions of the new Bentley, recorded by a member of the technical staff as the outcome of driving it over a distance far too short, but curtailed only by reasons of present circumstances and time. Even so, a short run is enough to be most impressive. There is a fascination about the car.

Refinement in a car is the subtle combination of many qualities, and is something which cannot well be measured. The refinement of the Bentley lies in the consummate ease and the perfect certainty with which it obeys the driver's wishes. He knows beforehand that this is a powerful and very fast car, representing a considerable sum of money. Hence his approach to handling it for the first time will very likely be tinged with considerable respect. Yet, in the first two hundred yards or so he realizes that he has found a friend. The respect is deepened because it has become informal. As acquaintanceship ripens one finds that this car always does exactly what is asked of it, but at the same time conveys the idea that it has the capacity to do considerably more.

Silent Power

In an attempt to particularize impressions the following comments are offered. The Bentley is so quiet that wind noise is chiefly noticeable, and that only to a small degree. The engine is completely unobtrusive, as regards either vibration or noise, and yet there is a reserve of power under the bonnet which seems inexhaustible. When there is opportunity to keep the throttle pedal right down the car continues to accelerate strongly, right up the scale, in a most impressive way. The suspension is superb, because not only is the riding exceedingly comfortable, but also the car feels completely stable. One hardly notices whether road surfaces are good or indifferent. Curves can be taken fast and with perfect confidence, and very fast indeed by a driver accustomed to the capabilities of the car.

The steering is admirable. Although the car is large and powerful, it is quite light, even for manoeuvring,

and is accurate and definite under all conditions.

The brakes, too, are superb. They go on smoothly, and need little pressure on the pedal, but they take hold of the car in a giant's grip, and can be used at high speed with confidence. Indeed, that word confidence typifies the major characteristics of the car. It feels supremely safe.

The gear change, with an unobtrusive and rather short lever tucked away on the right-hand side, is so very convenient and easy to handle that one quickly aspires to the art of the confirmed Bentley fan, which is to change gear without anyone in the car knowing that one has made the movement. The indirect gears are naturally very quiet running, and the synchromesh cannot be caught out by careless handling. The clutch pedal is

SPECIFICATION

Engine.—Rating 29.4 h.p., 6 cylinders, 89 x 114 mm (4,257 c.c.). Overhead inlet and side exhaust valves. Detachable aluminium cylinder head. Seven-bearing counterbalanced crankshaft with spring centre flywheel and torsional vibration damper. Steel connecting rods.

Twin horizontal S.U. carburettors with hand mixture control. Pump water cooling with thermostat and by-pass temperature control. Flexible power unit mounting.

Transmission.—Single-plate dry clutch, centrifugally assisted. Four-speed gear box with synchromesh. Overall ratios: Top 3.727, third 5.002, second 7.514, first 11.125 to 1. Divided propeller-shaft to hypoid bevel in rear axle with semi-floating shafts.

Steering.—Cam and roller follower.

Suspension.—Independent front suspension with cross-coupled hydraulic dampers. Half-elliptic rear springs. Rear hydraulic dampers controlled from the steering wheel.

Brakes.—Mechanical servo. Special form of hydraulic front and mechanical rear operation of Girling expander shoes.

Tyres.—6.50 x 16 in tyres on 5 in wide-base rims. Disc wheels.

Main Dimensions.—Wheelbase 10 ft. Track (front), 4 ft 8 in; (rear), 4 ft 10 in. Turning circle, 45 ft (over wings). Overall length, 15 ft 11¼ in. Height, 5 ft 4 in. Width, 5 ft 9 in.

When the doors of the Bentley body are closed the hinges are invisible. They automatically operate on controlled slides and disappear into the door pillar.

light and the take-up very smooth. Mention of the gear change has to be made, but in point of fact a minimum of gear changing is necessary, for the engine is extremely flexible on top gear.

• • •

Measured facts of the road performance cannot yet be given, but *The Autocar* understands that the chosen limits of performance are slightly higher than those of the previous 4¼-litre Bentley and that the acceleration is more rapid, but that the rise in the power curve obtained from the new engine has been devoted to the use of a higher gear ratio, which ensures more pleasant motoring. With such a car the stability, steering, brakes, acceleration, and quietness of running combine to produce high averages without apparent fast driving or inconsiderate behaviour.

Before turning to the mechanical description there is an interesting departure to note. The new Bentley will be available in chassis form for specialist coachwork, but also a Bentley-built all-steel four-light saloon body is being put into standardized production. This is the coachwork shown in the accompanying illustrations.

The Bentley chassis is an entirely new design, in which, however, the features of previous developments are either retained or improved upon. The same general principles inherent in the new Rolls-Royce Silver Wraith (described in *The Autocar* of April 5) have been applied to the Bentley chassis, but the main differences are a shorter wheelbase, a special camshaft which increases the power output at the top end of the speed range, twin S.U. carburettors, and thermostat and by-pass water temperature control instead of thermostatically controlled radiator shutters.

Monobloc in construction—that is

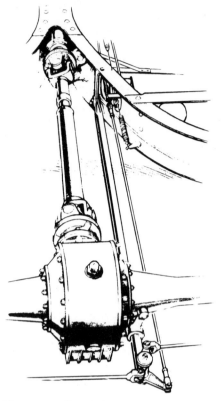

To ensure undisturbed compensation, the rear brake linkage is carried on a tube pivoted on the frame at its front end and suspended on a flexible link from the rear axle.

to say, the six cylinders and the crank chamber are formed in a single stiff casting—with a light alloy oil sump and a special light alloy detachable cylinder head, the engine presents a distinct departure from the previous design in that it has large overhead inlet valves and side exhaust valves. There are many technical reasons for this valve arrangement. Primarily it allows larger valves than could be used in the overhead valve in-line type, without making a wastefully long engine. Additionally it becomes pos-

sible to employ large clean-running inlet ports and to obtain free breathing with a more complete filling of the cylinders. Moreover the valve seats can have more even thickness of metal and a free space for water cooling.

Those, however, are not all the factors involved ; a combustion chamber shape with its greater volume above the exhaust valve and its lesser between the inlet valve and the piston crown gives high efficiency with minimum tendency towards detonation. The easy breathing and good cylinder filling permit a high torque to be obtained at lower as well as higher revolutions, and a relatively moderate compression ratio can be used.

To return to the valve arrangement : the overhead inlet valves, which are of considerably larger diameter than the exhausts, have nickel chrome molybdenum seats inserted into the light alloy head. They are returned by volute compound coil springs, the inner one of which controls a sealing device to govern the amount of oil entering the guide. Operation from the camshaft at the side of the cylinder block is through barrel-shaped tappets, hollow push rods and adjustable ball-ended rockers.

The exhaust valves, which seat in the cylinder block, are operated direct from the tappets. The overhead inlets are arranged in line and the gear is enclosed in a neat detachable cover, with the sump oil filler accessibly situated towards the front.

Inlet Manifolding

It is interesting to observe that the carburation treats the engine as two sets of three cylinders. The end cylinders have single ports and the inner pairs siamesed ports, an arrangement which equalizes the lengths of the manifold passages.

This engine has been designed not only to produce good power from a light weight, and to be smooth running—it might be said supernaturally smooth running—but also to be capable of running at least 100,000 miles without need of a rebore or major overhaul. This aim is achieved in many ways, the latest of which is the adoption of a process used in aircraft engines. The cylinder bores have their

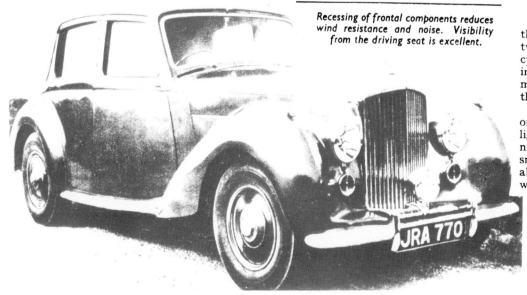

Recessing of frontal components reduces wind resistance and noise. Visibility from the driving seat is excellent.

JRA 770

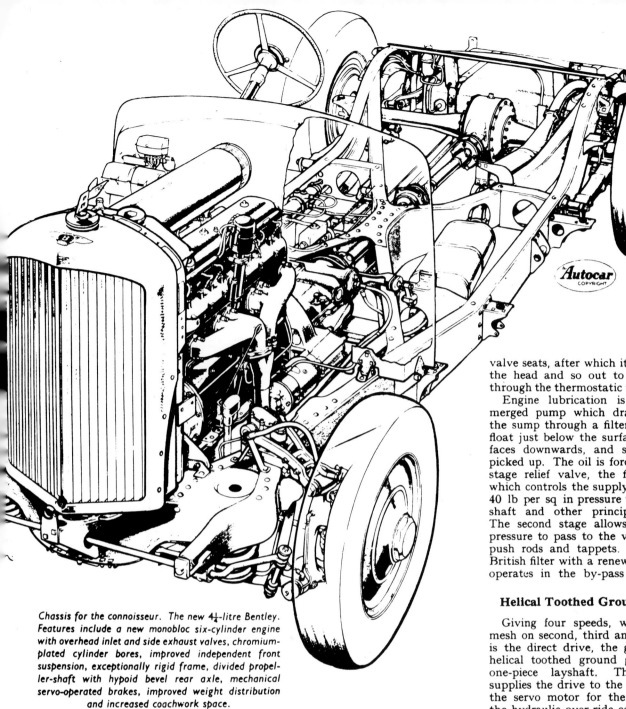

Chassis for the connoisseur. The new 4¼-litre Bentley. Features include a new monobloc six-cylinder engine with overhead inlet and side exhaust valves, chromium-plated cylinder bores, improved independent front suspension, exceptionally rigid frame, divided propeller-shaft with hypoid bevel rear axle, mechanical servo-operated brakes, improved weight distribution and increased coachwork space.

upper ends protected against corrosion and wear by a lining of chromium plating, about 0.00075 in thick—or perhaps thin! Another matter is that an engine cannot stand up against uneven wearing unless it is rigidly designed to avoid distortion from either work or heat. To guard against distortion the cylinder barrels of the Bentley are entirely separated, with water spacing between adjacent cylinders.

The crankshaft and connecting rods are a study in design and workmanship. They are machined all over, and the crankshaft is counterweighted and balanced, and has hollow crank pins closed in by end plugs to form oil ways. Down the centre of the rod is a web through which an oil way is drilled, as the forced feed from the crank journals and the crankpins is carried right up to the floating type gudgeon pins. The crankshaft and big-end bearings are of the steel backed Vandervell type, with

lead-bronze indium-faced linings. The aluminium alloy pistons are the Aerolite type, with fluted skirts.

In addition to the torsional vibration damper at the front of the crankshaft, at the rear end the flywheel has a spring centre which is specifically designed to damp out oscillation caused by the rocking couples of the throws near that end of the shaft. There is a separate face plate for the 10-inch dry single-plate clutch, which has bob weights on the extension of the operating fingers in order to give centrifugal assistance to the springs as the engine speed rises. The pedal is insulated from movements of the engine by balance beam linkage.

In the cooling system water is circulated by a leak-proof centrifugal pump, which feeds into a flat tube passing from end to end through the cylinder block and which directs the water straight around the exhaust

valve seats, after which it passes up to the head and so out to the radiator through the thermostatic valve.

Engine lubrication is by a submerged pump which draws oil from the sump through a filter arranged to float just below the surface; the filter faces downwards, and sludge is not picked up. The oil is forced to a two-stage relief valve, the first stage of which controls the supply under 35 to 40 lb per sq in pressure to the crankshaft and other principal bearings. The second stage allows oil at 5 lb pressure to pass to the valve rockers, push rods and tappets. An external British filter with a renewable element operates in the by-pass circuit.

Helical Toothed Ground Gears

Giving four speeds, with synchromesh on second, third and top, which is the direct drive, the gear box has helical toothed ground gears, and a one-piece layshaft. The box also supplies the drive to the speedometer, the servo motor for the brakes, and the hydraulic over-ride control for the spring dampers.

Engine and gear box form a unit carried on torsionally flexible rubber mountings at two points, the front fairly high, and the rear below the tail of the gear box. A tie is fitted to prevent fore and aft movement of the mounting. The unit is mounted rather farther forward than earlier designs in order to increase coachwork space, and obtain a good distribution of weight.

To obtain a low floor level the open propeller-shaft is divided into two parts. As the final drive is by hypoid bevel gear, the propeller-shaft is low. One of the most interesting matters from a mechanical point of view is found in this shaft arrangement. At the point where the division is made there is a central locating bearing, but this is given considerable freedom to float in order to eliminate vibration.

The frame side members are of deep section and braced together by a long and short cruciform central member, the extremities of which are riveted and welded into the side members to form box sections. Across the extreme front of the frame is a curved cross-member, and this provides the necessary stiff mounting for the components of the independent front suspension.

Improved Front Suspension

In this suspension a long link from the stub axle yoke runs almost to the centre of the front cross-member, and is inclined diagonally rearwards. A second short link at the head of the yoke has its fulcrum in an hydraulic damper on the top of the frame. Then from the foot of the yoke a long arm runs backwards and inwards to meet the side member at a point close to the dash, where its ball end is carried in a rubber-lined housing. Between the lower link and the cross-member a stout coil spring is mounted. The development of this suspension has been to extend the length of the links and arm so as to enlarge the base of the triangulation. This renders it possible to make a more free use of rubber bushings and so to obtain insulation from road noise and shocks without introducing too much flexibility in the system.

The rear springs are long underslung half-elliptics with rolled section leaves which are shot blasted to increase the resistance to fatigue. The leaves are indented

When not in use the sun vizors are out of sight. They consist of blinds operated on lazy-tongs, and pull out of recesses in the roof.

and are lubricated from the central chassis lubrication system; they are also enclosed in gaiters. The hydraulic dampers are of the vertical piston type and the front pair are cross coupled by a torsion bar to prevent roll. The rear pair have an hydraulically operated over-riding control, set by a small lever at the steering wheel centre.

For the steering a cam and roller follower of the Marles type is used. The track rods to the swivels are divided and jointed to a central lever, which is linked back to the steering gear drop arm.

The front brakes are hydraulic and the rear are mechanically operated. Both sets are applied through a mechanical servo drive from the gear box, which adds to the light pressure put by the driver upon the brake pedal. Girling type transversely expanding wedges, adjusters and shoes are used at back and front, but the front brakes are operated through Lockheed hydraulic equipment in order to avoid what might otherwise be a complicated system of linkage. To equalize wear between the two shoes of each brake a mechanical balance linkage is added at a point close to the expanders, each shoe thus being equally applied.

An 18-gallon tank is mounted at the rear of the chassis, and twin electric

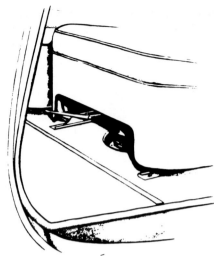

Besides entirely separate de-misting and de-frosting equipment below the windscreen, there is a separate electrically controlled heater, beneath the front seat.

pumps carry the supply to the carburettors, which are fitted with a very large size of air intake silencer and cleaner. Distinctly an important feature of the car is the provision of a centralized system of lubrication, which attends to all the important parts of the chassis, and which is operated by a pedal. The electrical equipment is a 12-volt special Lucas system, with automatic regulation of the dynamo output by vibrator control.

The Standardized Body

Next to describe the standardized Bentley four-door four-light saloon. In the first place this new coachwork has a clean-cut style of its own, graceful and characteristic, as might be expected. Secondly, it is fabricated out of steel, so as to combine strength with minimum weight. The complete 4¼-litre saloon weighs 35 cwt. The interior is larger than a first glance suggests, because the seats are generous in size and the upholstery is deep. There is about the interior trim that atmosphere of good taste and luxury which is not easy to produce, and which relies largely upon simplicity, the use of straight lines, and attention to small details. For instance, there is scarcely a screw head to be seen.

A point at once noticeable when driving the car is the clear forward visibility, which is enhanced by the slenderness of the screen pillars made possible by the fact that the windscreen is fixed. Twin Berkshire screen-wipers, with a remote motor and independent drives, are fitted. In addition there is a defrosting and de-misting unit in the scuttle. An electrically operated heater is concealed below the near-side front seat. Provision is made for the fitting of a radio set, and a small lever above the centre of the screen swings up into a vertical position a short and slender flexibly mounted aerial.

Prices of the new model are given on another page.

Typically Bentley lines are formed by the all-steel body. Locking handles for the bonnet are placed centrally on either side.

Foursome Coupé Bentley

Different again is the James Young body produced for the Mark VI Bentley chassis, this being a two-door foursome coupé of which a notable feature is the manner in which the front wings are merged into the wide doors, there being no running boards. The wings also merge into the fixed bonnet sides and in so doing form fairings for the head lamps and the twin horns, then sweep forward to form an apron in front of the radiator.

In this design also the panelling presents sharp edges, and it should be noted that the screen pillars are swept inwards slightly and that the side windows have a slight curvature, as has the rear light. The screen pillars and the upper half of the door hinge pillars are of the minimum section so that there is as little obstruction to vision as possible for both the driver and the passengers.

The wide doors give easy access to all seats and have a special hinge which results in the door remaining stationary without any tendency to swing open or closed. The windows are operated electrically and the front ventilating windows and sliding quarter-lights by hand. There are also purdah glasses for the rear quarter-lights which slide back into the quarters when not required. The front adjustable bucket seats have the squabs adjustable also, and in the back of them are folding tables. The rear seat has a wide centre folding armrest. The flat floor of the rear compartment is a good feature. In the graceful tail there is ample luggage accommodation, with beneath it a special compartment for the spare wheel.

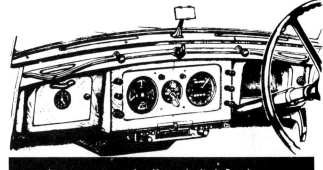

Instruments on the Young-bodied Bentley are very neatly arranged so as to be readily seen by the driver.

(Right) Razor edge panels accentuate the sleek lines of the foursome coupé. Detachable panels to the wings enclose the rear wheels.

No. 1340
4¼-LITRE
BENTLEY
MARK VI
SALOON

The *Autocar* ROAD TESTS

DATA FOR THE DRIVER

4¼-LITRE BENTLEY MARK VI.

PRICE, with four-door sliding-head saloon body, £2,595, plus £1,443 3s 4d purchase tax. Total £4,038 3s 4d.

RATING : 29.4 h.p., 6 cylinders, overhead inlet, side exhaust valves, 89 × 114 mm, 4,257 c.c. Tax (1947) £43. **COMPRESSION RATIO** : 6.4 to 1.

WEIGHT, without passengers, 35 cwt 3 qr. **LB PER C.C.** : 0.94.

TYRE SIZE : 6.50 × 16in on bolt-on steel disc wheels.

LIGHTING SET : 12-volt. Automatic voltage control.

TANK CAPACITY : 18 gallons : approx. fuel consumption range, 16–18 m.p.g.

TURNING CIRCLE : (L) 44ft 11in ; (R) 46ft 5in. **MINIMUM GROUND CLEARANCE** : 7½in.

MAIN DIMENSIONS : Wheelbase, 10ft. Track, 4ft 8½in (front) ; 4ft 10in (rear). Overall length, 15ft 11½in ; width, 5ft 9in ; height, 5ft 4½in.

ACCELERATION

Overall gear ratios	From steady m.p.h. of		
	10 to 30	20 to 40	30 to 50
3.727 to 1	8.5 sec.	8.6 sec.	9.4 sec.
5.001 to 1	6.5 sec.	6.6 sec.	7.4 sec.
7.520 to 1	4.5 sec.	5.1 sec.	6.6 sec.
11.113 to 1	3.9 sec.		

From rest through gears to :—

to 50 m.p.h.	..	..	12.5 sec.
to 60 m.p.h.	..	..	17.5 sec.
to 70 m.p.h.	..	..	25.8 sec.

Steering wheel movement from lock to lock : 3½ turns.

Speedometer correction by Electrical Speedometer : 10 (car speedometer) = 9 ; 20 = 18.5 ; 30 = 27.5 ; 40 = 37 ; 50 = 47 ; 60 = 56 ; 70 = 65 ; 80 = 74.

Speeds attainable on indirect gears (by Electrical Speedometer)

			M.p.h. (normal and max.)
1st	..	..	21–32
2nd	..	..	37–50
3rd	..	..	62–73

WEATHER : Dry, mild ; wind negligible.

Acceleration figures are the means of several runs in opposite directions.

Current model described in " The Autocar " of May 24, 1946.

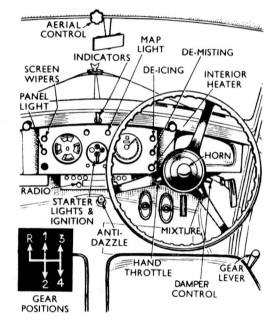

THE current 4¼-litre Bentley is approached as regards trial on the road with very special interest, in the first place on account of the calibre of the car and its reputation, and in the second because the character of the post-war model has been deliberately modified to a certain extent by comparison with the pre-war edition. It is still the Bentley that one knew formerly in the superb quality of construction and engineering qualities to R.-R. standards. It is still a car with a very high performance indeed, in fact, showing advance in this direction with the new overhead inlet valve engine ; but it has been given an additional appeal to those who appreciate an enlarged body and supreme comfort of riding. In some eyes the resultant car is very much an improvement ; in others, those who want to look upon it as a sports car with a roof, it has probably lost something by becoming bulkier and having a suspension of softer characteristics. But no one can deny its magnificent qualities on the road, representing a pinnacle of motoring experience.

The behaviour of the car as a whole can be dismissed in two sentences, or, alternatively, a small book could be devoted to it. In brief, a superlative form of road travel is provided from very little above walking pace on top gear without snatch to a genuine speed well exceeding 90 m.p.h. The manner of the achieving of each aspect of its performance, the responsiveness and delicacy of the controls, and the beautiful way in which they move, make everything the car does different from the behaviour of the ordinary good car.

In town it can be handled with the greatest of ease in spite of its size, for it is not unwieldy. The driver can see the wings and, because of the precision of control afforded and the fact that third and top gears suffice unless the car is actually brought to rest, it is easier to handle in traffic than some other cars. The present Bentley is indeed a wonderful combination of town carriage and mile-eater on the open road. It is a satisfying experience to set out on a long journey in this car, for one knows that distance will be covered in the easiest possible fashion and with about the highest possible degree of comfort for the driver and passengers, including those in the back seat. Every mile, fast or slow, will be pleasure owing to the silkiness and quietness of the car and the minimum of effort called for in controlling it. Motoring in the Bentley is on a plane altogether different from that of the general run of cars to a degree that cannot be properly credited until one has had this experience.

Then, too, of course, there is the appeal of the actual performance, which is as high as British roads, at all events, permit. One soon comes to realize just how sinuous our roads really are, for even on a known fast route the Bentley brings the bends closer together, as it were, owing

The provision of an entirely flat floor to the spacious rear compartment is aided by the use of a divided propeller-shaft and a hypoid bevel low-level final drive. The un-pleated leather up-holstery gives a well-groomed effect.

----

to its deceptive manner of travelling at high speeds. Average speeds are very much a matter of personal needs, traffic, and weather, besides route. What one finds in this direction with the Bentley is that one can be held up by other traffic, make a stop for petrol, and still put over 40 miles into the hour concerned, whilst, given a clear route, 50 miles in the hour is its natural gait. At night, over a comparatively traffic-free road, 80 miles were covered in 1½ hours, equivalent to an average speed better than 53 m.p.h., and this was achieved without putting the speedometer past the 80 reading more than twice.

Opportunity really, to let this performance loose is obviously restricted in this country, but its practical value lies in the fact that the car travels at ordinary speeds such as 60 to 70 m.p.h. without a trace of effort. One opportunity was taken of putting the speedometer needle on to the 100 reading, when heavy braking had to be applied for a bend in the road. There was the strong impression that this reading could have been increased, had there been room, by at least 5 or 6 m.p.h. Power on gradients is tremendous, and the car will accelerate to 70-80 m.p.h. rates, in a swift sweep, over slopes that would bring other quite efficient cars below 50. A 1 in 6½ gradient was climbed on third gear at a minimum of almost 40 m.p.h.

Third Gear Almost Indistinguishable

Almost dead silence of the indirect gears is a remembered feature maintained in the latest car. Even the driver is occasionally in doubt whether he has changed up from third, so quietly does the gear run and so effortless is the engine, whilst a passenger can well be unaware that a gear change has been made, the right-hand gear lever being out of his sight.

The keynote of interest in the latest car is the suspension, independent in front by means of coil springs and therein departing from the pre-war model except for the Mark V, of which very few examples were built just as the war broke out. This suspension gives the car a very different "feel" from that which one recalls with the half-elliptics formerly. The back seat riding has been made virtually as comfortable as for the front passengers, and that in itself is a big achievement.

Some movement of the car as a whole on its springs is experienced, even with the over-riding damper control on the steering wheel moved to the "hard" position, and there are times when one considers that the ordinary suspension used before the war gave a feeling of greater stability. It should be noted that one does not say "greater stability" but "a feeling of greater stability." In point of fact, extraordinary things can be done with the current car at high speed on corners, and it sits down rock-steady at speed on the straights, feeling utterly safe, but it takes time for a driver to gain complete confidence as regards cornering at the highest speeds which are here

being considered. At the more normal rates of travel no special cause for comment arises except that even at lower speeds there is sometimes, depending a good deal on the type of road surface, protest from the tyres, the treads of which have been specially designed to give silent running on the straight and which therefore have different characteristics from the normal.

Tied up with the exceptional averaging capabilities of the car and its supreme safety factor is the wonderful R.-R. servo-assisted braking system. With this car the time-honoured phrase of a giant hand clutching the car and bringing it irresistibly down from speed, yet with a silken grasp, indeed has point. They are brakes beyond comparison and vital, in their outstanding efficiency and light application, to the performance characteristics. The operation is Lockheed hydraulic in front and mechanical at the rear, acting on Girling type shoe-expanding wedges.

In such a car points which call for particular comments on other occasions can be left almost unnoticed, such as the arrangement of the seating and the range of detail equipment, though to be noted are the standard provision of radio and similarly of a most efficient heating installation which directs warmed air from beneath the front passenger seat into the interior; also screen de-misting and de-icing are effected by a separate unit.

Specially to be noted as a feature of the present car is the entirely flat floor of the rear compartment. The body on the car tested is the standard Bentley-built steel-panelled saloon, the lowest-priced version. From the driving angle, the former spring-spoked wheel was preferred and, it is understood, can be obtained as an extra if required. The standard present wheel is, as a personal opinion, a shade too large in diameter. The hand brake is of pull-out type, in a convenient and unobstructive position, and, in Bentley fashion, superior to the general run of this modern form of "hand-brake lever."

There is æsthetic as well as practical appeal in the way in which the car starts from cold. One silently moves the control on the steering wheel to the rich mixture position, opens the hand throttle slightly, presses the starter switch, and the engine springs to life without a splutter, continues regularly, and will pull straight away.

A really large luggage compartment is provided. Rearrangement of the instruments away from the former plan of separate circular dials has resulted in cubby hole space on one side and a locker with a Yale key to its lid on the other. A sliding roof of very large area is provided.

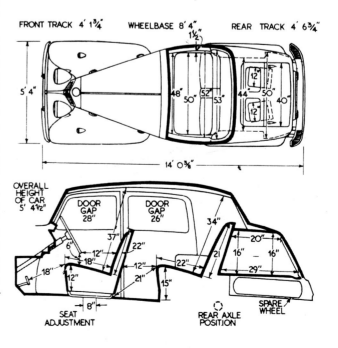

Measurements are taken with the driving seat at the central position of fore and aft adjustment. These body diagrams are to scale.

A Bentley Adaptation

Wood-panelled "Town and Country" Saloon on Mark VI Chassis

THE Kensington firm of Harold Radford and Co., Ltd., Melton Court, South Kensington, London, S.W.7, are introducing a new style of body on the Bentley chassis—the Countryman. described as a town and country saloon on the Mark VI chassis. The body is a three-seater, with a raised platform at the rear for luggage. The front seat is of the divided bench type with two arm rests to each seat; with the rests folded up, it is designed to accommodate two besides the driver. The seats, which are upholstered in leather and which can be slid back and adjusted for rake, tilt to give access to the rear of the body.

The scuttle has been modified as well as the instrument panel layout; heating and de-misting ducts are provided. The screen is fixed, and there is an electrically operated rear blind. The front windows are electrically controlled by buttons, while those at the rear are wound by hand. Rubberized felt excludes fumes from the body.

At the rear the raised platform gives luggage space capacious enough for the most exacting motorist; the space is 5ft long by 4ft 4in wide.

The body itself is of two-door con-

struction, metal panelled above the waistline and with wood framing and panelling below. The rear wings are aluminium equipped with steel stone guards. Beneath a locked panel is the filler cap.

At the rear of the body are two hinged flaps; the top one folds down to give clear access to the luggage space inside the body; chromium handles are fitted to

the flap and there is also a lock. The bottom flap lowers to allow the spare wheel to be extracted. This is housed in the normal manner.

The Countryman gives a would-be owner a comfortable three-seater car with the performance and speed of the Bentley and at the same time provides something very handsome in luggage capacity. The price is not available.

LIMOUSINE DIVISION FOR BENTLEYS

MOST of the Bentleys sold today are used for business, which frequently means that the car is driven by a chauffeur during the week and by the owner at the weekend. There is thus a good case for a winding division which can be

erected when the car is chauffeur-driven and wound away out of sight when the car is in use as a sports saloon. This requirement has been neatly met by a modification to the standard sports saloon sponsored by the firm of Charles Follett,

Ltd., 18, Berkeley Street, London, W.1.

The two bucket seats are removed and a single bench-type seat is substituted. When the seat is in the most forward position the division glass is wound up and its top edge, which is specially shaped, seats on slim sponge rubber pads inserted under the trim in the sliding panel of the roof and on the cant rail. There is a range of four inches sliding adjustment and the seat is controlled by a normal Leveroll winder. To eliminate the possibility of breaking the division glass through trying to adjust the seat while the division is erected, two locks are provided at the sides and are worked only from the rear compartment.

When the division is wound down the sliding roof can be used in the normal way, and the front seat can be slid back through an adjustment range of four inches. The division glass rises on runners attached to inconspicuous fairings mounted on the centre pillars and externally there is nothing to distinguish the car from the standard sports saloon.

The division can be specified for incorporation on new Bentleys for future delivery and can also be fitted in existing cars. In the latter case some of the existing trim material can be used, but in any case the final finish is in top quality hide and veneered woodwork to match the rest of the interior. The back rest of the bench front seat is being kept as slim as possible consistent with comfort and despite the space taken by the division glass and winding mechanism the leg room in the rear seat remains adequate. Additional toe room for rear passengers is provided by a cutaway under the front seat.

Prices are not finally fixed and will depend to some extent on whether the car concerned is new or used and hence on the state of the existing interior trim. A separate lock has to be fitted on one of the rear doors; otherwise a crisis would arise if the doors were slam-locked with the division erected.

The division installed in a Bentley saloon. Leg room is still ample.

As exhibited, the exterior of this ideal country car is in grey, with the unusual flash in maroon. A luxurious exterior impression gives little clue to the considerable luggage carrying potentialities of the Countryman, as, apart from the unobtrusive upper flap at the rear (inset) the car appears as a normal saloon.

Luxurious Countryman

SPECIAL BODYWORK PROVIDES ESTATE CAR CAPACITY WITH SALOON COMFORT

ONE of the most distinctive special coachwork designs appearing at Earls Court this year will be the Radford Countryman. With bodywork by Harold Radford and Co., Ltd., of Melton Court, South Kensington, London, S.W.7, this is a very satisfactory realization of the country-car idea. On a Bentley Mark VI chassis, the car is of composite construction in steel and aluminium, and hinged flaps at the rear give access to extra-large luggage space achieved by automatically folding rear seats. Full four-five-seater saloon layout is available if required. All the expected Bentley comfort is there, such as occasional tables for the rear passengers and a sunshine roof, and the front windows are electrically operated. Should the early morning shoot follow the all-night party there is even an "optional" electric razor!

For conversion to the layout for extra luggage, the cushions of the rear seats fold forward and the squabs fold into the floor, with electric operation if desired, and the space thus obtained is lined with polished panels and protected by rubber treads. The Countryman costs £4,245, plus £2,359 16s 8d purchase tax.

Electric operation for the rear seats and the electric razor are fitted as extras.

For normal saloon use, the rear compartment has occasional tables, with mirrors, and the side arm-rests form small cabinets of which the tops provide extra table space. As shown at the London Show this year, the upholstery is in black, with maroon piping.

Seating arrangements are flexible, and it is possible to obtain extra space at the rear and still retain a rear seat. The luggage space is well protected by treading. The upper flap is spring-loaded. Sports gear, and a prodigious array of suitcases, all go easily into the converted rear compartment.

The long wing line and slightly sloped radiator of the James Young Bentley blend sleekness into the classic styling of the car. The grilles below the head lamps conceal horns and interior heater intakes.

BY SPECIAL REQUEST: CARE FOR DETAIL WHICH

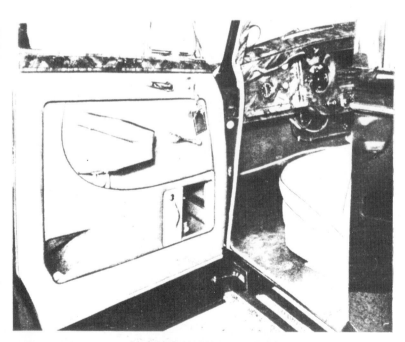

THE work of skilled craftsmen is more than ever satisfying to behold when everyday life presents so many shortcomings arising from lack of materials and labour, and often lack of care. The work of Britain's custom coachbuilders maintains its high standard, despite the millstone of double purchase tax, a measure which the Socialist Chancellor has reintroduced without any regard for the damage it may do to the builders of the best cars.

Photographs on these pages show details of a four-door six-light Bentley saloon with coachwork by James Young, Ltd., of Bromley, Kent which embodies several refinements suggested by its owner, Mr. Claude Wallis, chairman of Iliffe and Sons Ltd. The car is finished externally in dark bottle green, with hide upholstery of a paler shade, and the interior cabinet work, some of which was illustrated in *The Autocar* of April 27, is in plain and figured walnut.

Installation of detail fittings and accessories shows that meticulous attention to detail which distinguishes the work of the specialist. The door handles are blended smoothly into the slim plated moulding on the waist-line, and press buttons control the locks, which are of a new design specially produced by the coachbuilder. The tongue of the lock slides vertically and moves over two ramps mounted on the door pillar in a way which combines finger-light action with the reassuring snap of a well-made safe.

Continuous Action Winders

The window winders present another interesting point. If one continues to turn the handle after the glass has reached the top or bottom of its travel, the window smoothly reverses its action and starts on the return journey. There is thus no fear of over-straining the mechanism, however vigorously the handle may be used. Another feature worthy of note is the ingenious counter-balance for the lid of the luggage locker, by which this automatically holds itself in any position from fully closed to fully open. The

Left: There are cigarette boxes in the arm rests of the front doors and compartments are enclosed by sliding panels. A tool locker is in the floor of the luggage compartment, with small tools clipped inside. The spare wheel has a cover which prevents its soiling suitcases.

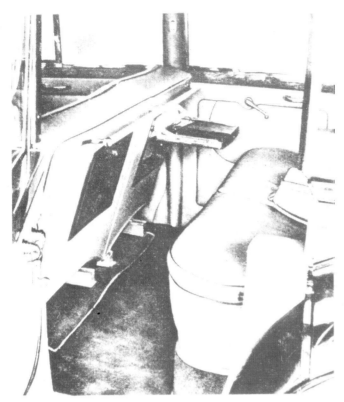

Rear passengers' tables and mirrors of the James Young body. The upholstery, in a lighter shade of green than the panels, blends well with the walnut woodwork.

DISTINGUISHES FINE COACHWORK

mechanism is completely enclosed and cannot chafe the luggage.

The ventilation system shows the results of careful study and incorporates two separate heat sources. A duct under the bonnet collects warm air emerging from the top of the radiator matrix and this is forced by an electrically driven fan through the usual demisting slots at the base of the windscreen. Separate ducts lead cold air from two grilles below the head lamps to controllable intakes in the scuttle, while the air inside the car can be heated by a large recirculating heater unit which is carried under one of the front seats and fed with hot water from the engine cooling system.

In the front doors are two roomy compartments hidden by sliding panels which can be locked. One houses a cock-tail cabinet and the other is used to carry cameras, maps and road books. These compartments are accessible from outside the car when the doors are open. Passengers at the rear have the use of occasional tables, backed with mirrors, which fold into the back rests of the front seats.

The ashtray is a simple detail which is often badly carried out. All too often it has to be withdrawn creaking from

its housing and, when open, allows the ash to blow about the inside of the car. Those on the Bentley are spring loaded, so that they fly open at a touch on a button and snap firmly back into place when not required.

The separate front seats each have folding arm rests at their inner edges and these are matched by arm rests on the front doors, which open to reveal cigarette boxes. The large folding arm rest at the centre of the rear seat has a cigar box inside it.

Another recent model illustrated on these pages is a two-door, two-three-seater, lightweight Bentley saloon with coachwork by H. J. Mulliner, which has recently been delivered by air to a customer in Switzerland. By using light alloy for the panels and for all the body frame with the exception of the main door pillars, a weight saving of about 300 lb has been achieved as compared with the standard Mark VI Bentley saloon. The front seat provides space for two or three people. The back rest is split and the two halves can be tilted forward to allow access to tip-up occasional seats in the rear.

In the ventilation system on this car, fresh air is led from two intakes beneath the head lamps direct to a pair of Smith's 3-kilowatt heater units. The control boxes allow air to be supplied to the interior at all temperatures from full heat down to outside air temperature, and there is additional provision for demisting and defrosting the windscreen.

The doors are large, but the special construction used makes them comparatively light. Wood used in the interior is plain and figured walnut, and the upholstery is in pale blue throughout with slightly darker floor coverings. A Radiomobile Model 4200 set is installed.

It will be noticed that on both these cars the Bentley radiator shell is set at a slight angle, and they both employ the long sweeping wing treatment which is the most popular style with British custom coachbuilders at the present time.

An H. J. Mulliner Bentley for Switzerland has very wide doors, lightened by the use of alloy panels. Above: Plain, readable instruments with white figures and needles in a facia of beautifully grained wood.

ELEGANCE WITH LIGHT WEIGHT

Unlike many cars of this class, the Bentley has a V-windscreen. Ducts for the interior-heating and fresh-air system can be seen under the head lamps.

The badge bar is hinged, to give access to the starting handle aperture.

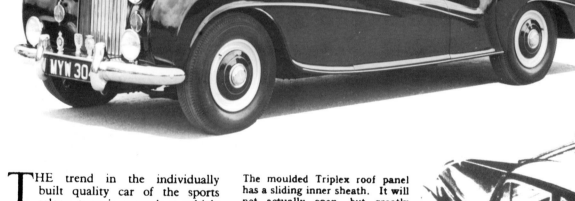

THE trend in the individually built quality car of the sports saloon type is towards a vehicle that is luxurious but also capable of high performance. This 4½-litre Bentley sports saloon by H. J. Mulliner is typical in that it achieves a high degree of luxury in appointments combined with good acceleration and maximum speed. Light alloy used for body frame and skin has reduced weight compared with previous corresponding Mulliner designs. Respectability is no longer a sufficient criterion in this kind of car; the elegance must be matched by practical qualities.

This car has a safety glass panel in the roof, which provides extra light, and there is a sliding inner sheath to blank it off when necessary. This gives an interesting sun lounge effect to the interior, especially as seen from the rear seat. Screen pillars are of what the makers call the "special light" pattern, which gives some lateral benefit and a few more degrees of visibility for the driver. Woodwork is of burr walnut veneer, and this is so worked to suggest that the minimum amount of actual wood has been used compatible with a luxurious interior. The upholstery is particularly fine. Unusual compartments are fitted in the rear doors for housing cocktail and other equipment. The car is finished in dark green, with light green upholstery.

The moulded Triplex roof panel has a sliding inner sheath. It will not actually open, but greatly adds to the lightness of the interior and to upward visibility for passengers. →

A useful cabinet, with spring-to lid, is built into each rear door. Ice for cocktails can be stowed in a vacuum flask in one of the front door compartments. The upholstered armrest conceals a cigarette box. Camera equipment is carried on the other side.

Autocar ROAD TESTS

DATA FOR THE DRIVER

BENTLEY MARK VI

PRICE, with four-door saloon body, £2,875, plus £1,598 14s 5d British purchase tax. Total (in Great Britain), £4,473 14s 5d.

ENGINE : 31.5 h.p. (R.A.C. rating), 6 cylinders, overhead inlet, side exhaust valves, 92 × 114 mm, 4,566 c.c. Compression Ratio : 6.4 to 1. 22.1 m.p.h. per 1,000 r.p.m. on top gear.

WEIGHT (in running trim with 5 gals fuel) : 36 cwt 1 qr 18 lb (4,078 lb). Front wheels 48.6 per cent ; rear wheels 51.4 per cent. LB per C.C. : 0.89.

TYRE SIZE : 6.50 × 16in on bolt-on steel disc wheels.

TANK CAPACITY : 18 English gallons. Approximate fuel consumption range, 15-17 m.p.g. (18.8-16.6 litres per 100 km).

TURNING CIRCLE : 41ft 2in (L and R). Steering wheel movement from lock to lock : 3½ turns. **LIGHTING SET** : 12 volt.

MAIN DIMENSIONS : Wheelbase, 10ft 0in. Track, 4ft 8½in (front) ; 4ft 10½in (rear). Overall length, 16ft 0in ; width, 5ft 10in ; height, 5ft 6in. Ground Clearance : 7.2in.

ACCELERATION

Overall gear ratios	From steady m.p.h. of			
	10-30 sec	20-40 sec	30-50 sec	40-60 sec
3.727 to 1	8.2	7.5	8.0	8.2
5.001 to 1	6.0	5.8	6.3	7.1
7.520 to 1	4.2	4.4	5.5	—
11.113 to 1	3.6	—	—	—

From rest through gears to :—

m.p.h.	sec	m.p.h.	sec	m.p.h.	sec
30	4.5	60	15.2	80	28.4
50	10.2	70	20.1	90	39.0

SPEEDS ON GEARS

(by Electric Speedometer)	M.p.h. (normal and max)	K.p.h. (normal and max)
1st	20-36	32-58
2nd	40-54	64-87
3rd	70-85	113-137
Top	100	161

Speedometer correction by Electric Speedometer ;—

Car Speedometer		Electric Speedometer m.p.h.
10	=	10.0
20	=	20.0
30	=	30.0
40	=	40.0
50	=	51.0
60	=	62.0
70	=	72.0
80	=	82.0
90	=	92.0
98	=	100.0

WEATHER : Dry ; negligible wind. Air temperature 36 deg F.

Acceleration figures are the means of several runs in opposite directions.

Described in " The Autocar " of April 21, 1950.

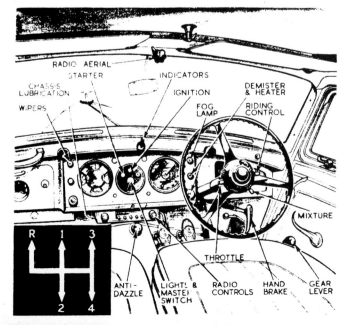

RADIO AERIAL · STARTER · INDICATORS · CHASSIS LUBRICATION · IGNITION · DEMISTER & HEATER · WIPERS · FOG LAMP · RIDING CONTROL · MIXTURE · ANTI-DAZZLE · LIGHTS & MASTER SWITCH · RADIO CONTROLS · HAND BRAKE · GEAR LEVER · THROTTLE

R 1 3 / 2 4

Outstanding is the air of quality and refinement, coupled with clean functional lines, at once suggested by the Bentley with its standard steel saloon body.

No. 1449 : BENTLEY Mark VI SALOON

THE Bentley is by no means a cheap car ; in fact, it is one of the most expensive vehicles produced in any country. Although it has often been argued that it is much more difficult to produce a cheap car of relatively good quality, the very fact that this has been done must influence the design and manufacture of the expensive product. To justify itself it must be superior in every way to a less expensive car ; there is little doubt that the Mark VI makes a good job of living up to the extremely high standards aimed at by the manufacturers and demanded by the purchasers. There is no room or excuse for defects of even a minor nature that would be perhaps overlooked in a car costing half the price. Briefly, it is a car for the connoisseur who can afford to pay the price.

As with the previous model tested by *The Autocar*, the present car was fitted with a standard steel saloon body, but with the new 4½-litre engine, which is basically similar to its predecessor, the 4¼-litre, except that the cylinder bore has been increased from 89 to 92 mm. This relatively small increase in engine capacity has resulted in a worth-while gain in performance as compared with the previous engine and without any apparent increase in total weight.

When judged from outward appearances only, the Bentley has the air of a thoroughbred, and on first acquaintance with this model, even before one has actually entered the car, it creates the impression that it must go well and possess that extra something that the others lack. Once inside, the impression produced by its external appearance is substantiated by the quiet, tasteful interior which, in spite of being functional in every way, possesses a quality obtained only by craftsmanship.

There are some cars which must be driven for a considerable mileage before the driver feels at home, while in others this process takes place in a very short space of time ; it is in the latter category that the Bentley is placed. Because of the general silence and smoothness there is often a sensation of gliding in, rather than driving, this car, and this attribute, in conjunction with the positive yet light operation of all the controls, reduces driving fatigue to a minimum. Even after frequent use of the clutch, as when journeying through city traffic in a rush hour, there is no noticeable fatigue or left-foot weariness. Also, incidentally, there is ample foot room at the side of the pedals, a point that is particularly appreciated by a tall driver.

These items combine to give the car an ability to cover long distances at high average speeds without much effort. For example, in the hands of *The Autocar* staff the car covered a distance of over 1,200 miles in just over a week,

The traditional Bentley radiator is of course retained on this latest model. Both front wings are deeply arched and, both being easily visible, provide useful sighting points from inside the car.

The semi-razor edge rear-end treatment is balanced by the rear wing line. The rear doors are provided with a generous wrap-over to prevent the rear passengers' clothes becoming soiled by contact with the rear wing. There is no interference by wheel spats with checking rear tyre pressures. The fuel tank filler is concealed by the flap in the left rear wing, which can be locked. One Yale key serves the whole car

most of this being done outside normal working hours. One trip of nearly 100 miles was covered in just over two hours, including the time taken driving through the built-up areas of two cities—an average approaching 50 miles an hour. On longer journeys it was possible to average 40 miles an hour including stops, as on a 250-mile journey from Cornwall to the outskirts of London.

On English roads it is not possible to obtain figures such as these unless a car has very good acceleration throughout the entire speed range. The ultimate maximum speed is not so important a factor as how quickly the intermediate speeds can be obtained, and here the Bentley records remarkably good figures; for example, 10 to 30 m.p.h. on second gear in just over 4 seconds, and 40 to 60 on top in a little over 8 seconds, and 0 to 80 m.p.h. in less than half a minute. Additional acceleration figures, not normally recorded—or even recordable on the average car—are:

	From steady m.p.h. of	
	50-70	60-80
	sec	sec
Top	9.9	12.1
Third	8.8	—

The excess power available for acceleration also gives the car extremely good hill-climbing ability. All normal main-

road hills can be swiftly climbed on top gear; or, if extra urge is required, the high maximum speed on third gear permits an early change down without risk of over-revving the engine. All the acceleration data were recorded on Pool petrol of approximately 72 octane; the maximum speed shown in the table was obtained in Belgium on fuel of slightly better quality. On English roads it proved possible to see speeds of the order of 91-93 m.p.h. with comparative ease; the more traffic-free straights of Continental roads enabled the genuine 100 m.p.h. mark to be exceeded. The exceptional fact of the speedometer fitted to the car tested reading *slow* from 50 m.p.h. onwards is noteworthy.

The familiar Bentley right-hand gear change is, of course, used on this model. It is very well placed and beautifully smooth and positive in operation, although perhaps a little more room between the lever and the door trim would be advantageous. Reverse gear is obtained by depressing the knob, which permits the lever to pass into the reverse position in the gate and prevents that gear being engaged inadvertently. On the car tested a slight difficulty in engaging reverse instantly was occasionally experienced.

Partly, perhaps, because of the driving position, combined with a good view of the front of the car, the Bentley very quickly creates the impression that it will handle well and

The separate front seats are well upholstered and extremely comfortable. Readily detachable arm rests are fitted inside both front doors. Movable toe boards and folding picnic tables all help to increase the rear seat luxury. There is a

pull down central arm rest in the rear seat. The fine woodwork and leather of obvious quality, but completely without ostentation, do much towards producing an atmosphere of well-being.

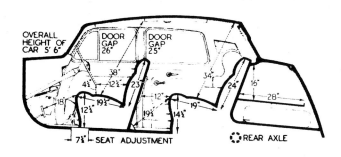

OVERALL HEIGHT OF CAR 5' 6"

DOOR GAP 26" DOOR GAP 25"

— 7⅞"— SEAT ADJUSTMENT ✛ REAR AXLE

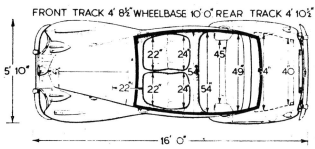

FRONT TRACK 4' 8½" WHEELBASE 10' 0" REAR TRACK 4' 10½"

5' 10"

← 16' 0" →

Measurements in these scale body diagrams are taken with the driving seat in the central position of fore and aft adjustment and with the seat cushions uncompressed.

Small tools of high quality and spare bulbs are neatly housed in a small lockable drawer below the facia cupboard, which also can be locked. A passenger's grab handle is conveniently placed alongside the left-hand windscreen wiper knob. Radio is a standard fitment.

obey the wishes of the driver. Both front and rear seat riding is good. Although the ride control lever at the centre of the steering wheel enables the suspension to be stiffened if necessary, on the car tested it was considered by one experienced driver that this gave most satisfactory results in the " normal " position for both normal and high-speed driving.

The steering is light, it has a good self-centring action, and with three and a half turns from lock to lock manoeuvrability in confined spaces is extremely good. In fact, it is possible to manoeuvre and control this car with greater ease than applies to some considerably smaller cars. When first considering the cornering qualities a driver may be a little disappointed, but this is because of the extreme silence of the vehicle as a whole, for unless frequent reference is made to the speedometer it can easily be travelling at least ten miles an hour faster than is apparent.

The mechanical servo brakes provide remarkable retarding power and can achieve, when necessary, what appears to be almost the impossible in safe stopping; also, compared with most other braking systems, the pedal pressures required are extremely low. In fact, as one member of *The Autocar* staff put it, " You have just to breathe on the Bentley brake pedal." On the test car a certain amount of initial fierceness of braking was noticed, but this disappeared by the time the performance figures had been taken, and here it should be stated that in spite of the increased number of high-speed recordings taken during this test no brake fading was experienced. At one stage there seemed to be a certain

degree of unbalance between the two front wheels, but this also appeared to right itself after a few miles.

As mentioned previously, the driving position is extremely comfortable and the well-sprung cushions provide ample support where it is most needed. All minor controls are well placed, the hub of the steering wheel containing the ride control, starting mixture control and hand throttle in a neat grouping, while the others are arranged round the speedometer and the combined unit containing the fuel, oil and water temperature gauges and ammeter. A small push button on the facia panel enables the engine's oil level to be measured on the fuel gauge, while a green light warns the driver when the fuel level is getting low. This light is rather disturbingly bright at night, if one is deliberately running with a low fuel level, and certainly it attracts the attention its function demands. A rheostat control to enable the instrument illumination to be graduated would be appreciated. There is a useful map reading lamp located under the passenger's grab handle. Although the driving mirror is rather small, the rear view is satisfactory.

The detail fittings are carefully chosen to blend with the general quality of the car. For example, in the space normally occupied by the rear quarter light in a six-light saloon, interior mirrors are fitted, each of which has concealed lighting, while on the right-hand side is also fitted a cigarette lighter. All the seats are trimmed with fine leather and there is a fold-down armrest at the centre of the rear seat. The heating unit is very efficient for both front and rear seat occupants, and ensures an ample supply of warm air for passenger comfort and demisting.

For a car of this size the enclosed luggage space is limited, but the locker lid can be secured in the open position to form a platform to which extra luggage can be strapped. In spite of their relatively small diameter, the head lamps are extremely powerful and have a very good range. The single dipped lamp system for anti-dazzle purposes was fitted, yet in the dipped position it gave ample light. Starting is at all times instantaneous. The car can be driven away from cold with the minimum of fuss and the mixture control be returned to the normal position in a surprisingly short space of time; the hand throttle is a useful and now rare fitting.

Although the luggage locker has only a moderate capacity, the lid can be secured in the open position to form a platform. A separate lower compartment houses the spare wheel and tools. The current larger engined model is distinguished by the twin exhaust tail pipes.

A large intake air cleaner supplies the twin S.U. carburettors. The tube running above the air cleaner is the demister intake. A neat inspection lamp is clipped to the bulkhead above the regulator unit and can be plugged into a socket on the facia. As always, the engine is a model of good finish.

A New High Speed Bentley

CONTINENTAL SPORTS SALOON HAS A MAXIMUM OF OVER 120 M.P.H.

AN announcement has just been made in America regarding the special high-speed version of the Mark VI Bentley which has been under development for some time. This car, to be known as the Bentley Continental sports saloon, is now going into production in very limited numbers and will be reserved exclusively for export.

The chassis is the normal Bentley Mark VI with the larger engine of 4,566 c.c. introduced last year, but various modifications, including changes in carburettors, induction and exhaust manifolds, compression ratio and gear ratios, have considerably improved both power output and performance.

The coachwork is a close-coupled two-door four-seater saloon built by H. J. Mulliner and Co., Ltd. It is panelled in aluminium, and a considerable amount of light alloy is used in the construction, profiting from the experience gained on the lightweight Bentley coupé shown by Mulliner at Earls Court two years ago. A considerable amount of weight is saved

and the Continental saloon weighs approximately 3,700lb compared with 4,070lb, which is the figure for the standard four-door saloon in running trim.

Considerable attention has been given to drag reduction both in the general form of the vehicle and in detail equipment. It will be noticed, for example, that the dummy filler cap and winged B mascot have been eliminated from the

radiator shell. In the course of development work last year the car did an officially certified lap at Montlhéry at an average speed of 118.3 m.p.h., indicating an absolute maximum speed of over 120 m.p.h.

It is expected that owners of the new model will be asked to give an undertaking that they will not use the car in competitions.

Low build and smooth lines contribute to the high performance expected of the new Bentley Continental sports saloon. The four-seater coachwork is by H. J. Mulliner.

A slim radiator shell without the usual filler cap and mascot distinguishes the Continental sports saloon from the normal model. A curved windscreen and slim pillars contribute to driving vision.

The first Continental

H. I. F. Evernden, MBE, BSc (Lond), formerly Chief Project Engineer of the Motor Car Division of Rolls-Royce, stands proudly by the car for whose design he was largely responsible.

B ENTLEY MOTORS (1931) LTD. dispose of historic prototype Bentleys about once in a month of epiphanies, so a prospective buyer, even if his credentials stand up, must be prepared to bide his time. Stanley Sedgwick's credentials were unexceptionable — he's president of the Bentley Drivers' Club — and he uncomplainingly bided more than nine years before finally making Olga his own.

OLG 490, Olga to Bentley buffs the world over, founded the Continental line and was road-test reported by The Autocar on 12 September 1952. Sedgwick coveted the car from that Friday and, in the winter of 1960, popped the question. His suitorship accepted and a price agreed, a further seven months elapsed while Olga underwent a

Olga's welcoming interior, as renovated regardless of expense by Mulliner.
Our Road Test report of this same car in 1952 described rear-seat legroom as
"ample", and headroom as "not unduly restricted". In the light of 16 years'
development, we seem to have raised our sights slightly!

With fastback bodies currently in fashion, there is little to betray Olga's 18
summers—apart from her small rear window, divided windscreen and rather
lofty skyline. This graceful tail was once in a minor shunt with a London bus,
but not the slightest trace of the damage remains

complete and exhaustive rebuild: or more exactly two rebuilds, the
makers addressing the chassis and H. J. Mulliner the body. Bentley
Motors, who don't exactly play with words, described the car as "brand
new" when it eventually darkened Sedgwick's garage door in June of
1961. Its mileage then was 200,000 and is now over 270,000.
Cherished as you'd expect it to be, it carries its 18 years jauntily
and is still sometimes taken for a youthful current model by the
unknowledgeable. Bentleys' sales manager had been right when he
predicted, eight years ago, that the car would give Stanley "a tremendous amount of pleasure, not only from its performance but also from
your knowledge of its history".

Early GT ideals

For the start of a long story we must backtrack briefly to the '30s,
when at irregular intervals Bentleys' fancy had lightly turned to go-faster
thoughts. The cars visualized would epitomize the GT genre in its true
and original sense, albeit "sports saloon" was the currently accepted
term. These pre-war exercises yielded at least four separate and distinct
prototypes, two of which are notable in our context, viz.:—

1. A one-off 4¼-litre built to the order of N. M. Embiricos, the Greek
racing driver. Developed in the wind tunnel and combining reasonable
habitability with good aerodynamic form by Georgian standards, this one
averaged over 114 mph for one hour at Brooklands in 1939.

2. The four-door Corniche of 1938/9, largely based on the Embiricos
mechanicals but roomier and more drag-making. The Corniche, fitted
with the 4¼-litre o.h.i.v. engine which the post-war Bentleys and Royces
were to share, was scheduled for limited production in 1940; but the
sole prototype, which had been on test in France when war broke
out, was smithereened by a Luftwaffe bomb, only its ignition key
surviving.

Well, a world war was won and lost, or anyway lost, and in 1950 two
leading R-R/Bentley savants, H. I. F. Evernden, chief project
engineer, and J. P. Blatchley, chief stylist, were put to work on a
second-generation Corniche job. Although the result of their labours
became publicly known as the Continental, its factory appellation was
Corniche II. This fact obliquely recognizes the fact that experience
gained from the pre-war quickie was fruitfully exploited 12 years later.

In the period separating Corniche I and Corniche II, of course, the
4,566 c.c. Mk. VI with its o.h.i.v. engine and modern running gear,
including wishbone and coil-spring i.f.s., had become established as the
bread-and-caviare norm at Crewe. Evernden and Blatchley, then, were to
take it from there, with no latitude for varying such fundamentals as the
wheelbase (10ft) or tracks (56½in. front, 58½in. rear). As conceptions, but
only that far, the objectives were simple: "a car", in Mr. Evernden's own
words, "that would not only look beautiful but possess a high maximum
speed coupled with a correspondingly high rate of acceleration, together
with excellent handling qualities and roadability".

On completion of the initial design for Olga's two-door fastback body,
a quarter scale model was made and tested in the Flight Test Establish-

ment's tunnel at Hucknall. The purpose of these experiments was not
only to determine the air drag factor in forward motion but also to study
yawing phenomena and the effect of sidewinds. (Pre-war, it had
interested Mr. Evernden and associates to discover that one of their
prototypes would be faster travelling backwards than forwards, gearing
permitting.)

If they were tempted to improve air penetration by giving the
Continental a droop-snoot prow like a Volkswagen's, this was kiboshed
in advance by a directive from on high that "the car had to be
recognizable as a Bentley". Also by order, radiator height wasn't to
undercut the Mk. VI's by more than 1½ inches. "Aerodynamically",
soliloquized H. I. F. Evernden in a Bentley Drivers' Club *Review* article,
"a front-end shape like that of the Bentley is bad, as it acts as a bluff
ploughing into the air."

Bluff or no bluff, tests at Montlhéry in 1951, timed by A. C. de
France officials, demonstrated Olga's ability to reel off five consecutive
laps at an overall average of 118.75 mph, with a best single lap at
fractionally under 120. These, in their day, were warm performances for
a full four-seater with, to quote from *The Autocar's* subsequent test
report, "generous" back seats, "ample" legroom and "not unduly
restricted" headroom for rear passengers.

Tyre pressures of 50 psi all round, compared with the 35/40 psi
normally recommended for fast driving, were run at Montlhéry, which
must have been worth a knot or two. The MDT (Medium Distance
Track) Dunlops used on the track gave "very little trouble", whereas
ordinary road tyres had been lasting as little as 20 miles at comparable
speeds. Olga's chief chaperon at Montlhéry, incidentally, was the late
Walter Sleator, head of Franco-Brittanic Autos in Paris, Bentley's leading
continental agency.   Continental Bentley owners owe Mr. Sleator a
debt that they'd never know of if we didn't tell them: it was he who, when
the R-R/Bentley directorate gave the whole project an agonizing rethink
early in 1951, and were seriously considering throwing it out of the
window, talked them into persevering.

Search for more power

In his search for an extra 20 mph and a commensurate gain in
acceleration, as compared with the standard Mk. VI Bentley, H. I. F.
Evernden put little store by boosting engine performance. There were
two unanswerable reasons for this: (a) His brief forbade souping
processes that would sacrifice refinement; (b) Calculation showed that,
to take the more or less relevant example that he himself has quoted,
raising the maximum speed of an 85 mph car to 100 mph calls for a
whacking 40 per cent increase in bhp. Prohibitive, obviously. What in
fact he did was to raise the compression ratio from 6.25 to 7 to 1 and
do a tonsillectomy job on the exhaust system, resulting in the
euphonious hubble-bubble note for which the R-Type Continentals
became famous. Thus modestly tweaked, Olga's engine, running on the
inferior fuel of 17 years ago, developed 137 bhp at 4,250 rpm. These
however were actual take-home horses, with gearbox and even final
drive losses prededucted.

Initially, prior to the Montlhéry tests, an overdrive gearbox pulling
1.226 to 1 in top (fourth) had been tried; but this, in conjunction with
an axle ratio that restricted maximum speed to 114 mph, evidently
flattered the car's overall drag, moderate as it was, relatively speaking.
While on location in France a normal gearbox with direct drive in top
was fitted and the axle ratio lowered. These changes, giving 27 mph per
1,000 rpm in top, resulted in the track speeds quoted earlier, and also of
course benefited acceleration correspondingly. The Autocar's testers,

Olga's forerunner, the pre-war Embiricos "streamliner" with o.h.i.v. 4¼-litre engine, seen at a Bugatti O.C. Prescott meeting in the 1950s. The Corniche 4¼ car was a modified inlet-over-exhaust Mark V with cross-braced chassis and i.f.s.

to take some random examples, did 0-60 mph in 13.5 secs, 0-100 in 36.0, 80-100 in top in 14.6. For the first time in their lives they were able to extend the third-gear tabulations up into three figures. Incidentally there was only a fraction of a second's difference between the top and third gear times from eighty to a hundred—14.6 and 14.4 respectively.

Indirectly, the R-Type Continental owes its good acceleration to the fact that tyre design had a long way to go in the early 'fifties. If Olga had weighed more than about 34cwt at the kerb, her tyres wouldn't have been safe at sustained speeds around 115 mph. In fact, thanks to the combined efforts of Messrs Evernden, Blatchley and H. J. Mulliner and Co. Ltd., she weighed 33½cwt (3,739lb) with five gallons on board when tested by the AUTOCAR.

Saving weight

To achieve this figure, fairly extreme measures had been taken. Not only the entire body panelling but also the window frames, bumpers and many other parts were formed in light alloy. As a tacit discouragement to buyers to add the sort of mickles that tot up to muckles, a radio was charged for but not installed unless actually bespoken. H. J. Mulliner, by dint of Wizard of Oz technique in detail design, made fractional weight economies in places where a laymen wouldn't even think of looking for them.

Appropriately, considering the services rendered by this firm at the prototype stage, Mulliner won the lion's share of R-Type Continental trade, supplying bodies for 193 out of the 208 cars built during the series' life, 1952/55 inclusive. These H. J. M. jobs were all two-door sports saloons, identical with Olga apart from their roofline (which was one inch lower) and the fact that production windscreens were undivided (Olga's, as can be seen from a photograph, has a centre parting). Also, although Mulliners themselves abhorred avoidable avoirdupois, their less spartan customers sometimes prevailed on them to make weight-upping deviations from the Olga formula.

The "R" symbol, it should perhaps be explained here, denotes the *pur sang* breed of Continentals that originated the line. All R-Types were sixes, whereas the plushier "S" models that followed on in April of 1955 *et seq* were sixes to start with, vee-8s for the remaining 11 years of Continental history. Between them, Park Ward, Graber, Franay and Farina bodied the 15 R-Types that eluded H. J. Mulliner.

Without going into sordid detail it can be said that the price Stanley Sedgwick paid for Olga was considerably less than a third of his total liability: bills for the two complementary rebuilds, that is to say, accounted for two-thirds-plus of the whole outlay. I mention this only to illustrate the point that Bentley Motors (1931) Ltd. don't describe a 10-year-old car with 200,000 miles under its belt as "brand new" on the strength of a quick decoke and a local body blow-in. On the mechanical side, mostly by a process of wholesale and ruthless replacement, everything—but everything—was restored to original condition. A new engine, of the latest 3¾in. bore size (4,887 c.c.) was fitted, also a new gearbox and back axle. And that was just a start. Spelt out in single-spaced typing, without a redundant word, the Mulliner operations filled almost a whole foolscap sheet. These included meticulous recellulosing in Olga's original gunmetal colour ("including the door shuts and bottoms inside") and ranged the entire gamut of coach builders' verbs: like retrim, reglaze, resurface, repolish, repair, replace, overhaul, band, etc., etc. Not even the "heel board" carpeting escaped attention. Trifles make perfection but perfection is no trifle, as H. J. Mulliner might have said if Michelangelo hadn't thought of it first.

Chez Sedgwick, cars come and cars go—the Bentley's running mates are currently a Ferrari 250GT, an Alfa Romeo Giulia Sprint, a Morris 1100 and a 1910 Mercedes limousine—but Olga seems set to go on forever, or anyway a long time yet. Apart from the emotional bond based on Stanley's "knowledge of her history", why should anyone contemplate parting with a car which even now, in its 19th year, is a source of constant pride and a match in most aspects of performance for about 98 per cent of the Old World's automobiles?

It isn't so much a flashy maximum as her ability and avid willingness to reach 100 mph quickly and effortlessly, and thereafter to cruise in almost stratospheric silence at three-figure speeds, that gives Olga her charm. Oddly, in spite of the 1962 engine switch and resulting gain in cubic centimetres, and also the superiority of modern petrols compared with the Pool swill of the small '50s, Olga appears to be about seven or eight miles less fast today than yesteryear. Timed over flying kilometres in speed trials at home and on the Continent, Stanley has whipped 109 mph out of her and that's about where she sticks.

This loss is not accompanied by debilitation in any general sense; the engine still idles as quietly and measuredly as ever, hasn't grown greedy for fuel and oil, still gives the old exuberant w-o-o-s-h to an indicated 100 mph in third (the speedometer, by the AUTOCAR'S test report, read 1½ mph slow at the ton, which was fairly typical of R-R/Bentley products). Although the R-Type is quintessentially a piece of machinery, with nothing of the perambulating-boudoir character of its descendants, it makes haste so unobtrusively that accurate judgement of speed is difficult. At 90 there is absolutely nothing to tell you, unless you read your instruments or check the position of the gear lever, whether you're in third or top. The Sedgwicks live at Cobham, in Surrey, about 18 miles from Hyde Park Corner, and in pre-70 days Stanley used to make an almost unconcious habit of hitting the century at least once during his daily journeys to and from town.

Perpetual youth

Money answereth all things, as Solomon sang in his Song, and it's hardly to be expected that the owner of a five-car stable that includes a Bentley and a Ferrari would keep nit-picking records of running costs. Obviously the secret of perpetual youth for a car like Olga is to entrust all significant servicing and repair operations to those best qualified to handle them, viz., the makers. In the long run, moreover, like for instance 70,000 miles since "brand new" this is also undoubtedly the most economical course, and it's the one that Sedgwick follows.

Troubles, *per se*, and displays of unladylike behaviour, have been few. The brakes, although superlatively good even by present day standards at their staple job of checking and stopping the car smoothly, powerfully, fadelessly and in a straight line from any attainable speed, emit hot smells after multiple, grilling applications. The exhaust system is prone to vibrations that transmit themselves indoors. The lack of synchromesh on first is an unendearing feature and once led to damage calling for a complete gearbox tear-down and rebuild. Apart from these griefs, not much.

Twice recently I had the privilege of borrowing Olga for a day. The object of my second trip was a visit by appointment to H. I. F. Evernden, MBE, BSc (Lond), who now lives in semi-retirement at West Wittering, the Sussex village where Royce did his last work. I hadn't said I'd be bringing Olga and the surprise and delight on the faces of Ev and his hospitable wife as the old lady darkened their hardstanding was a secondhand pleasure that I treasure. It isn't often you spend an afternoon in the company of a great car *and* the great man who designed it.

The **Autocar**
ROAD
TESTS

Long graceful lines and a special low radiator shell, without the traditional filler cap and emblem, identify the Continental Bentley saloon. There are twin Marchal head lamps with amber bulbs, and auxiliary lamps, while the side lamps in the wings act also as direction indicators.

No. 1475: BENTLEY CONTINENTAL SPORTS SALOON

THE Continental sports saloon is a new stage in the evolution of the post-war Bentley. The first major change since the introduction of the post-war chassis was made last year, when an increase in the bore brought the engine swept volume up to 4½ litres. *The Autocar* Road Test of December 7, 1951, recorded that it enabled the standard four-door steel panelled saloon to reach a maximum speed of 100 m.p.h., accompanied by impressive acceleration, without the slightest sacrifice of the smoothness or silence for which the *marque* is renowned. The next step was to raise the compression to profit by the better fuel now available in overseas markets, and to fit lighter bodywork with lower drag characteristics, which would allow the great potentialities of this chassis to be more fully exploited. The reduction in drag permitted a higher axle ratio to be employed, and a close ratio gear box was installed to give the best acceleration. The resulting car, known as the Bentley Continental sports saloon, has been subjected to rigorous testing on the Continent for about a year, and *The Autocar* has recently been able to give it an extensive trial in Britain and on the Continent. It brings Bentley back to the forefront of the world's fastest cars, and its tremendous performance makes this one of the outstanding in the long series of Road Tests.

The car is being produced in limited numbers and is reserved for export only. Its price is high, the sterling figure being £4,890 without purchase tax, which means that by the time the foreign buyer has paid delivery charges and local taxes it will probably cost him between six and seven thousand pounds. The Continental Bentley may, therefore, be the most expensive production car in the world, but it also makes a strong claim to be the fastest four-five-seater

DATA

PRICE (basic), with two-door saloon body, £4,890. Not available in Great Britain.
Extras: Radio standard if requested. Heater standard.
ENGINE: Capacity: 4,566 c.c. (278.633 cu in).
Number of cylinders: 6.
Bore and stroke: 92 × 114.3 mm (3.625 × 4.5 in).
Valve gear: Overhead inlet with push rods, side exhaust.
Compression ratio: 7 to 1.
B.H.P.: Not quoted.
Torque: Not quoted.
M.P.H. per 1,000 r.p.m. on top gear, 27.
WEIGHT (with 5 gals fuel), 33⅓ cwt (3,739 lb).
Weight distribution (per cent) 50.1 F; 49.9 R.
Laden as tested: 36.8 cwt (4,120 lb).
Lb per c.c. (laden): 0.9
BRAKES: Type: F, leading and trailing shoe; R, leading and trailing shoe.
Method of operation: F Hydraulic. R Mechanical. Mechanical servo.
Drum dimensions: F, 12½in diameter, 2⅜in wide. R, 12½in diameter, 2⅜in wide.
Lining area: F, 186 sq in. R, 186 sq in (202 sq in per ton laden).
TYRES: 6.50—16in.
Pressures (lb per sq in): 30 F; 35 R (normal). 35 F; 40 R (for fast driving).
TANK CAPACITY: 18 Imperial gallons.
Oil sump, 16 pints.
Cooling system, 32 pints.
TURNING CIRCLE: 43ft 0in (L and R).
Steering wheel turns (lock to lock): 3⅓.
DIMENSIONS: Wheelbase 10ft 0in.
Track: 4ft 8½in (F); 4ft 10½in (R).
Length (overall): 17ft 2½in.
Height: 5ft 3in.
Width: 5ft 11½in.
Ground clearance: 7in.
Frontal area: 23.5 sq ft (approx).
ELECTRICAL SYSTEM: 12-volt. 54 ampère-hour battery.
Head lights: Single or double dip, as required; wattage as required.
SUSPENSION: Front, Coil springs and wishbones with anti-roll bar.
Rear, Half-elliptics.

PERFORMANCE

BENTLEY CONTINENTAL SPORTS SALOON

ACCELERATION: from constant speeds.
Speed, gear ratios and time in sec.

M.P.H.	3.077 to 1	3.740 to 1	4.750 to 1	8.230 to 1
10—30	8.2	6.9	5.3	3.4
20—40	7.4	6.0	4.8	3.5
30—50	7.4	6.1	5.1	—
40—60	7.4	6.8	5.7	—
50—70	8.4	7.1	6.1	—
60—80	9.6	8.4	—	—
70—90	12.1	10.8	—	—
80—100	14.6	14.4	—	—

From rest through gears to:

M.P.H.	sec
30	4.4
50	10.5
60	13.5
70	16.3
80	22.2
90	28.1
100	36.0

Standing quarter mile, 19.5 sec.

SPEED ON GEARS:

		M.P.H. (normal and max.)*	K.P.H. (normal and max.)
Top	(mean)	115.4	185.7
	(best)	116.9	188.1
3rd		80—100	129—161
2nd		60—77	97—124
1st		30—44	48—71

* At 4,300 r.p.m. limit on intermediate gears.

SPEEDOMETER CORRECTION: M.P.H.

Car speedometer	10	20	30	40	50	60	70	80	90	100
True speed	11.6	21.2	30.6	40.7	51.3	61.5	71.3	81.5	92.0	101.5

TRACTIVE RESISTANCE: 34 lb per ton at 10 M.P.H.

TRACTIVE EFFORT:

	Pull (lb per ton)	Equivalent Gradient
Top	287	1 in 7.8
Third	352	1 in 6.2
Second	442	1 in 5.0

BRAKES:

Efficiency	Pedal Pressure (lb)
97.0 per cent	116
91.5 per cent	100
58.7 per cent	50

FUEL CONSUMPTION:
19.4 m.p.g. overall for 438 miles. (14.6 litres per 100 km).
Approximate normal range 16-21 m.p.g. (17.7-13.5 litres per 100 km).
Fuel: Belgian Super for performance tests; 50-50 Pool and 80 octane for road running.

WEATHER: Dry, warm, sunny.
Air temperature 95-85 degrees F.
Acceleration figures are the means of several runs in opposite directions.
Tractive effort and resistance obtained by Tapley meter.
Model described in *The Autocar* of February 29, 1952.

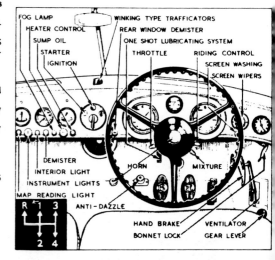

FOG LAMP
HEATER CONTROL
SUMP OIL
STARTER
IGNITION
WINKING TYPE TRAFFICATORS
REAR WINDOW DEMISTER
ONE SHOT LUBRICATING SYSTEM
THROTTLE
RIDING CONTROL
SCREEN WASHING
SCREEN WIPERS
DEMISTER
INTERIOR LIGHT
INSTRUMENT LIGHTS
MAP READING LIGHT
ANTI-DAZZLE
HORN
MIXTURE
HAND BRAKE
BONNET LOCK
VENTILATOR
GEAR LEVER
R 1 3
2 4

The special radiator shell is smoothly faired into the bonnet and the concave curves of the wings, to give a new and modern appearance to the Continental Bentley. There is a curved windscreen supported in very slim pillars.

The graceful tail sweeps down between rear wings which terminate in twin stop and tail lamps, the stop lamps being also used as flashing direction indicators. The bumpers are in heavy-gauge light alloy and the exhaust pipe is chromium plated. Twin reversing lamps are grouped alongside the central number plate.

saloon in the world. Circumstances made it necessary to carry out the maximum speed tests on brand new tyres, which increase rolling resistance, and in the middle of a hot day, with an air temperature of 95 deg F, which reduces volumetric efficiency. Even so, a mean maximum speed of over 115 m.p.h. was recorded. One run, with driver only, was timed at 120 m.p.h., and it seems probable that in more favourable circumstances this speed might be more regularly reached. The acceleration from rest to 100 m.p.h. (36.0 sec) has not been approached by any other saloon car in *The Autocar's* experience and has been equalled by very few open sports cars. Acceleration in the gears is so well maintained that the usual tabulations have had to be extended to 100 m.p.h. for both top and third gears.

However, the figures, impressive though they are, do not tell the whole story. Whatever memorable motoring experiences one may have had, this was something different. It showed what can be achieved by the single-minded pursuit of perfection, not in seeking always to incorporate the latest technical innovation, but by ceaseless, resourceful and painstaking improvement of every minute detail on well-tried basic principles. Such a car is bound to be costly, and the British, who make it, cannot own it; but it goes abroad as proof that a nation where the creators are constantly subjected to the debasement of their own living standards can still keep alive the ideal of perfection for others to enjoy.

One might think that such tremendous performance could be used only on rare occasions, but the controls are so superbly responsive that the experienced driver quickly finds himself making full use of its potentialities, to over 100 m.p.h., then effacing the speed smoothly and quickly with

a touch on the mechanical servo brakes. It is an experience that lulls the critical faculty and defies one to analyse the car step by step, but the effort must be made.

For the driver, the forward view through the wide, curved windscreen, with its very slim pillars, is excellent, the seating position is good for high-speed driving and the controls are well arranged. When the engine starts, there is a rasping noise, discreet and distant, but sufficient to indicate that this is something new in Bentleys, and there is a momentary snarl from the exhaust at the beginning of acceleration in each gear. These are absolutely the only aural concessions to high performance. Engine and gear box are slightly audible in first gear, but otherwise, throughout the performance range, there is only that uncanny silence which indicates long and careful attention to every detail of design and construction.

With the high gearing employed, third is the natural ratio to employ for mountainous country or winding roads. It can be kept in use for miles on end, and for smoothness or silence is quite indistinguishable from top. The maximum available on this gear is 100 m.p.h. without trespassing by more than the thickness of the needle into the red zone on the rev counter, so that it caters for all normal needs. Anyone not familiar with the car has to feel the gear lever occasionally to remind himself which gear he is using. If there is any mechanical noise at speeds near the maximum, it is completely lost in the rush of the wind.

There is no need to specify a cruising speed; progress seems as smooth, easy and effortless at 100 m.p.h. as at 50. Nor is there any imperative need for frequent gear changing. It is possible to make a smooth, easy start on top gear and to accelerate relentlessly away to maximum speed without using the gear box at all. This is hardly to be recommended as normal practice, however, especially as gear changing is such

The massive facia in polished walnut is almost entirely occupied by instrument dials and switches. Below are seen one of the heater elements, the pendant pedal for the one-shot lubrication and a fresh-air duct by the throttle.

There is a folding central arm rest at the rear, and below the seat is a grille supplying fresh air from the ventilation system. The generous-sized rear quarter lights can be hinged outwards to act as air extractors.

WHEELBASE 10' 0"
FRONT TRACK 4' 8⅞"
REAR TRACK 4' 10¼"
OVERALL LENGTH 17' 2½"
OVERALL WIDTH 5' 11½"
OVERALL HEIGHT 5' 3"

The spare wheel, which is carried on the floor of the luggage locker, has a special cover to prevent damage to the luggage. Jack and tools are carried in a special compartment below the floor of the locker.

Measurements in these ¼ in to 1 ft scale body diagrams are taken with the driving seat in the central position of fore and aft adjustment and with the seat cushions uncompressed.

a pleasure for the Bentley owner with any appreciation of mechanical perfection.

Hill-climbing is quite extraordinary, and main road hills can be climbed on top gear at speeds limited only by visibility and traffic conditions. The test figures were taken on Belgian " super " fuel of approximately 80 octane. On British Pool some pinking was evident, but the car is not intended for such a dreary diet.

The brakes, aided by the special Bentley servo motor which is driven from the gear box, require little comment. There are no better brakes on any car sold today, and they allow the Bentley's great performance to be enjoyed with complete confidence. A light pressure reduces speed smoothly and swiftly, and a heavier pressure produces tremendous power for safe emergency stopping; 100 per cent efficiency was several times recorded on the meter during the tests.

Variable Ride

The ride control on the steering column, which adjusts the setting of the rear hydraulic dampers, gives all the softness required for city driving and a sensation of floating gently over the worst bumps, and the harder setting gives adequate damping for fast travel without sacrificing comfort. The steering has adequate self-centring action, and there is fairly pronounced understeer, which is reflected in excellent directional stability. Rather a strong effort is required on the wheel to hold the car into sharp bends, but control is light on ordinary roads and no undue effort is required when parking. On rough roads the more severe bumps do transmit some reaction to the steering wheel, and a firm hand on the wheel is desirable when driving fast on really rough surfaces. It should not be inferred, however, that the car is tiring to drive.

To drive this car is a wonderful motoring experience, but certain questions inevitably come to mind regarding its uses. It is described by its manufacturers as a sports saloon, but the purchaser is required to give an undertaking that he will not enter it in competitive events, so the sports title goes by default. One turns next to the adjective " Continental," which conjures up visions of long, fast runs to the Riviera. But travel implies luggage, and the locker on this model, while perhaps adequate for a weekend, could not carry the luggage of four persons for any considerable period.

A few chassis only will be delivered to foreign coach-builders, and buyers who want more luggage space, and are perhaps willing to sacrifice some of the present very ample passenger space, should therefore be able to obtain what they need. The weight of the coachwork must, however, be limited to 750 lb. This is the weight of the present H. J. Mulliner saloon, and it brings the weight of the complete car to 240 lb below that of the present Mark VI standard saloon.

For the Mulliner body it must be said that it is elegant, modern, and comfortable; moreover, it represents a com-bination of lightness and rigidity which may not be easy to emulate. All panelling is in light alloy; the seats have tubular frames; there are aluminium frames for the windows; and even the bumpers are made of light alloy. Overall height has been reduced by one inch, it is under-stood, as compared with this prototype. Radio is available without extra cost, for those who require it, and right- or left-hand steering.

The front seat back rests are adjustable for angle, and both front wings are easily seen from the driving seat. The big steering wheel is admirably placed and has a horn button at the centre, but it is not necessary to remove a hand from the wheel, as there is another button on the floor which can be operated by the left foot. Facia equipment includes speedometer, rev counter, switch unit with master key, fuel and engine oil level gauge, oil and water thermometers, oil pressure gauge, ammeter and electric clock. The instrument lighting is rheostat controlled. There are an interior light and map light. The twin electric screen wipers have a two-speed control, and a windscreen spray is standard. At the centre of the steering wheel are the hand throttle, starting mixture control and ride control. There is a good rearward view in spite of the pronounced slope of the rear window.

The rear seats are of generous size, with a folding central arm rest and large fixed arm rests at the sides. Leg room is ample, and head room is not unduly restricted by the streamlined curve of the roof, as the head lining is recessed locally above the rear seat. Among the standard equipment is an elaborate heating and ventilating system which makes provision for demisting both the windscreen and the rear window.

This Bentley is a modern magic carpet which annihilates great distances and delivers the occupants well-nigh as fresh as when they started. It is a car Britain may well be proud of, and it is sure to add new lustre to the name it bears.

One side of the centrally hinged bonnet is lifted to reveal the distributor with rev counter drive, the accessible plugs and oil filler, twin ignition coils, and the fan supplying the wind-screen demister. The big air cleaner and silencer feeds two horizontal S.U. carburettors on a water-jacketed manifold.

Mark VI Standard Steel Saloon contrasted
with a rather more svelte Park Ward coupé.

MAKING IT LAST

14 Years and 180,000 Miles

By MICHAEL COLLIER

Extensive Continental touring has been enjoyed with the Bentley Continental, seen here at the gates of the walled city of Dubrovnik, Yugoslavia

THE small urchin pushed his grubby nose against the driver's window.

"This the new Series T, mister?" he inquired, eyeing the sloping tail (or fastback) with interest.

"Not really," I said, "though thank you for the compliment. In actual fact this is an R-Type Continental and is 14 years old."

"Cor," he replied, "however do yer git it to last that way that long!"

Really it's not so very difficult. The first cost is, of course, frightening when one actually comes to write the cheque, but as Sir Henry Royce so aptly put it, "The quality remains, long after the price is forgotten."

I ordered this car the moment it was announced—as an export-only model. It struck me from the first as one of those great cars which get designed and built but rarely, and I was fortunate in being allocated the second car for the home market. I do not know who had the first one—probably Jack Barclay, I should imagine—but at any rate I was ahead of all those who ordered them at the Earl's Court Show of 1952. The chassis was constructed quite rapidly and arrived at Mulliners by train at the very end of the year, but the body took another 6 months to build in those days.

As soon as I heard that things were under way, I went along to Mulliners' works near Putney Bridge to have a look, and I shall never forget the first sight I had of the chassis. I arrived in a tea break and three stalwart craftsmen, complete with traditional aprons and waistcoats, were seated along the frame, consuming the all-important British beverage and the gearbox was adorned with four empty milk bottles! I said nothing, but thought a lot and I would not advise any prospective owner to go along to see his car before it is complete. I went again on another occasion and on opening the driver's door water poured out of the drain holes along the lower edge. Probably things are more organized now that Mulliners are part of Rolls-Royce and there is no doubt that despite the excellence of their finished products they did suffer from lack of capital and premises in those days. I remember seeing even the Queen's car being worked on out in the road before the take-over.

However, my car did get completed in the long run and I duly collected her from Lillie Hall. Back in 1953, 100 m.p.h. on the road was considered quite fast and I was extremely thrilled to be the owner of a quiet, comfortable saloon which would achieve this in 3rd and quite a lot more in top.

I had owned my previous

Bentley, an early Mark VI, for a matter of six years and when the Continental was new I had no thoughts of keeping it for any exceptionally long period. However, the sad demise of the manual gearbox within a year or so made me realize that if I was to continue with my kind of motoring I had to make the car last for the rest of my life and I am still doing just this.

The prospect does not daunt me and it has the added merit of being economical once one has escaped from the bogey of depreciation that erodes capital in such a ghastly way. Spare parts, too, are reasonable, some of the smaller joints costing as little as 1d in 1953 and not much more now. Moreover, they are readily available, in contrast to those of some other makes. Actual running costs are reasonable, as the engine operates perfectly well on standard fuel, the compression ratio being only 7·2 to 1, and it is pleasant not to have to buy super 5-star or even 4-star premium. It is possible to exceed 20 m.p.g. on long runs as the high top gear of 3·07 to 1 and the near perfect streamline shape enable a 70 m.p.h. cruising speed to be maintained on a mere whiff of throttle. My car has only the 4,566 c.c. engine and for reasons of economy and a desire to keep the car in authentic original condition I have resisted all temptation to install the large engine, raise the compression ratio, fit an S.1 head or any other aids to an even better performance.

Tyres have been something of a problem and originally were easily the most expensive item to be faced. In fact the whole question of high speed tyres for road work was quite dire in 1953 and the only 16in. cover available for cars of this potential was the India Speed Special, with which it was equipped. This appeared to be a more or less ordinary cross-ply cover with only half the normal depth of tread to ensure that it did not

part company with the carcase at over 105 m.p.h. So the life of a set of tyres was hardly more than 5,000 miles and after 3,000 there was precious little tread left.

After several sets of these at some £50 a time I felt that I might forfeit the esteem of my Bank Manager if I did not find some other tyre which would be safe and have a life of about 10,000 miles. I tried the inevitable steel braced tread and found that the safety was adequate, though there was a peculiar "floating" period around 70-80 m.p.h., and that the maker's mileage claim was indeed justified. In fact I threw the covers away after 12,000 miles, long before they were worn out, as I just could not get on with the loss of the beautiful smooth silky ride at low speeds. In these days we seem to spend more and more time in faster and faster cars at slower and slower speeds, so the bottom end of handling really has to be considered.

I then turned to Pirelli: I have nothing but praise for their Speed Special cover and much lament its untimely departure from production. It was based on the racing tyre developed for the all conquering 158 Alfa which dominated the Formula 1 racing of the period. The character of the car was transformed by fitting these tyres, specially in the wet; under these conditions the Pirelli Speed cover was particularly effective and the fact that it produced a high-pitched scream on smooth wet surfaces proved to the ear as well as to the hands of the driver that the road beneath the wheels really was being swept of water. Aquaplaning was a sensation quite unknown and good as I find the grip of the RS5 which I now use, I cannot treat wet slippery surfaces with quite the lofty disdain that Pirelli could accord to them. Mileage began by being about 9,000 per set of four tyres which as I grew older and drove slower increased to 12,000 on the rear wheels and 17,000 on the front.

I have been fortunate in being able to do all work on the car, apart from really major overhauls, either entirely myself or sometimes with the weekend aid of my old racing mechanic, Ray Balcombe. I hold the only Certificate of Merit for efficient maintenance ever awarded by Bentley Motors (1931) Ltd. to an actual owner. This was presented to me by the late Roney Messervy at a lunch at the R-R works in Hythe Road.

I have therefore always done jobs like relining the brakes myself and on this basis it can be done for £3 13s 6d per drum, using Mintex M.22; the front linings last about 15,000 miles

and the rears 35,000, though this ratio of life depends to some extent on the type of lining used in the servo motor and the length of the balance lever. There are three alternative lengths and the one giving the best braking on a dry road will lock the front wheels easily on a wet surface, so it is largely a matter of personal choice to suit the owner's style of driving. While I find that cadence or stab braking is great fun and effective when there is no real crisis, it can be difficult if faced with almost certain disaster. Hence I now use the setting which does not lock the wheels in the wet.

Similarly I have always changed all oils myself, doing the sump every 2,000 miles, as it holds 2 gallons, and the filter element every 6,000 miles. This ensures what I thought was absolute cleanliness until I met another owner at the R-R Service station. When I told him I only used sealed containers of new oil, he said, "Good Heavens, you don't mean to say you put that stuff straight into your engine. I always strain it through a muslin filter before putting it in mine." Not to be outdone, I tried this myself for some months afterwards, but never managed to extract any visible impurities from Castrol.

Oil consumption has varied and when the engine first settled down worked out at 1,250 m.p.g. This steadily increased until at 75,000 miles I decided the time had come to do something about it. Attitudes to oil consumption vary and I have never ceased to be amazed by the tremendous store most people set on a microscopic consumption of this still reasonably priced fluid. Many expect cheap, mass-produced engines to cover 5,000 miles and more on a pint and are blissfully ignorant about what is happening inside them under such circumstances. Personally I never worry about oil consumption until it falls below 500 miles per gallon. A loose engine gives a better performance, but at this point it must suffer from lack of compression.

So it was at this stage that I asked Ray to come over and help me to restore the *status quo*. In approximately three days, admittedly starting at 5 a.m. on two of them, we decoked the engine, fitted new pistons and rings (in the same untouched bores) with new bigend shells. We left the main bearings alone and also the little ends, though we should have renewed the latter as they became noisy after a while. We hand-fitted each ring to its bore and I ran the engine in for 1,000 miles. The official Service Manual suggests a ring gap of ·014in., presumably to eliminate running-in, but I was brought

up to believe that ·001in. gap per 1in. of piston diameter is correct. Actually we compromised and gave them a gap of ·007in. and the oil consumption became 1,850 m.p.g., i.e. better than new. The cost of the parts was around £25 and I gave Ray a similar sum for his efforts, so we did the lot for £50.

The engine then ran for another 88,000 miles without any attention beyond routine adjustment of tappets, new plugs every 10,000 miles and new distributor points every 20,000.

As the mileage increased so did the oil pressure! A most desirable phenomenon, but puzzling, and this, together with oil consumption again around 500 m.p.g. I decided that the engine must be stripped right down, the total mileage from new then being 162,500. I felt that this was rather beyond my own workshop facilities as a rebore was quite a possibility, so I entrusted the job to Phantom Motors of Crondall. There was only ·004in. wear on the bores and no measurable wear on the crankshaft, so again for the second time new pistons were fitted to the same bores, new bearing shells, valve guides and so on. The same gap of ·007in. was used on the rings and the oil consumption is 1,700 m.p.g. The ever-increasing oil pressure was traced to blocked oilways at the front of the crankshaft for the feed to the damper which had broken up. The total cost this time was £282 10s 0d, which included a new clutch and, of course, a labour charge of 22s 6d per hour, which I normally escape.

Other expenditure has been £100 for new bearings in the rear axle, which was done by R-R at 146,700 miles to cure slight play when going from drive to overrun.

The clutch requires a new centre plate about every 50/60,000 miles according to the amount of traffic driving, and I find that the new section of M4 into London is a great saving both on the clutch and brakes as against the conditions which I used to suffer on the Great West Road. The very high bottom gear of 8·22 to 1 is another factor which demands a good clutch, but the reline is not a difficult job and I have done it with Ray in two days. The centre plate and pressure plate assembly cost £22 13s 9d and I still have the original thrust race and spigot in use.

The gearbox has given trouble twice, once after only 12,000 miles when a ball race went while I was in Wales. At the time, the car was well within its 3-year guarantee and the full might of R-R service was turned on to cope with this unfortunate

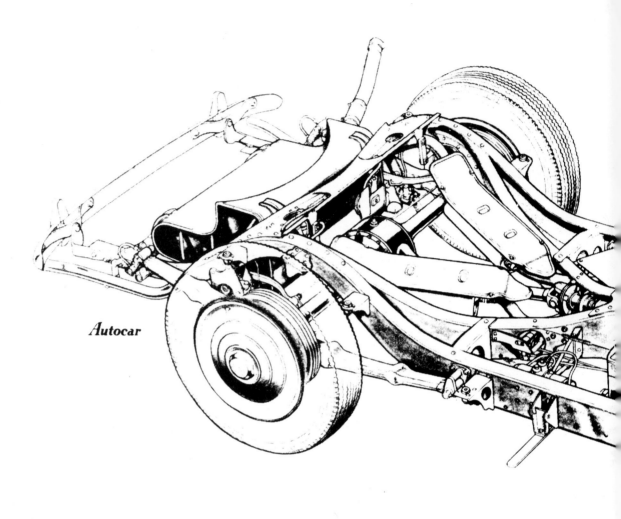

Autocar

breakdown. Fitters arrived from Crewe in the middle of the night, by which time I had been towed in to a Ford Main Dealer. What had actually happened was that part of the broken up race had become wedged in the teeth of bottom gear bringing me to an abrupt standstill in a traffic block. During the tow-in this fragment had fallen out, but naturally this was not apparent at the time and the atmosphere became positively glacial when it appeared that there was nothing wrong with the car. However, the usual perfect manners of R-R prevailed and we went out for a test run. Fortunately the trouble recurred after a time and they removed the gearbox during what was left of the night and fitted another one the following night. R-R know what a guarantee means and there was no charge of any kind for this midnight oil job or indeed for any other minor jobs during its validity.

The car has lived up to its name and I have taken her on many trips to the Continent. In early June last year before the

Alpine Passes were officially declared open, I wished to make a quick trip across France to Milan. On the somewhat indiscreet recommendation of two not very well-informed French speed cops we decided to go up the Little St. Bernard which they assured us was open. The board at the foot of the pass firmly stated *Fermé,* but nothing daunted I pressed on thinking that perhaps the road was being finally tidied up and would be passable.

On and on we went right up past the last signs of life into the snow until rounding the last bend but one we found the snow plough, complete with stainless steel chains, blocking all further progress just as we looked like getting over and down the other side into Aosta. Any idea of turning the car round was quite out of the question as the banked snow was almost touching both sides, so

there was nothing for it but to reverse a very long way to below the snow line. Later we were rewarded by an exceptionally good dinner at the Hotel Million in Albertville and the next day we spent £3 going through the Mont Blanc railway tunnel.

I made another trip later in the year and when on the way home crossing France the gear lever became stuck in bottom. I removed the floorboards and took the plates off the top and side of the gearbox, but the trouble was obscure as there were no broken or chewed up bits in the bottom of the box and even with a powerful torch it was impossible to see anything amiss. So I put it all together again and drove back across France at 22 m.p.h. in bottom gear much to the puzzlement of other road users. R-R said at first that delivery of new Continental gears would be 4 months. Would I like standard gears? I

said that most certainly I should not, as the very high 80 m.p.h. second gear gives the car so much of its charm. So they looked around again and found a reconditioned Continental box. This was £90 on an exchange basis, but I was only off the road four days which was far less than my wildest hopes as we crawled up to Calais.

An account such as this of the life of a car inevitably centres round the troubles experienced and how they were overcome, but I would not have you think that I am anything but an extremely enthusiastic owner. Perhaps the highest tribute I can pay the car is to emphasize that if she were stolen or became a total loss tomorrow I should go out and endeavour to obtain another similar model and restore it as necessary. For me, and I think others, " Age cannot wither, nor custom stale, her infinite variety."

152

Bentley Sports Saloon

Semi Razor Edge Styling for a Modified Body on the

4½-litre Chassis: New Cold Starting Device

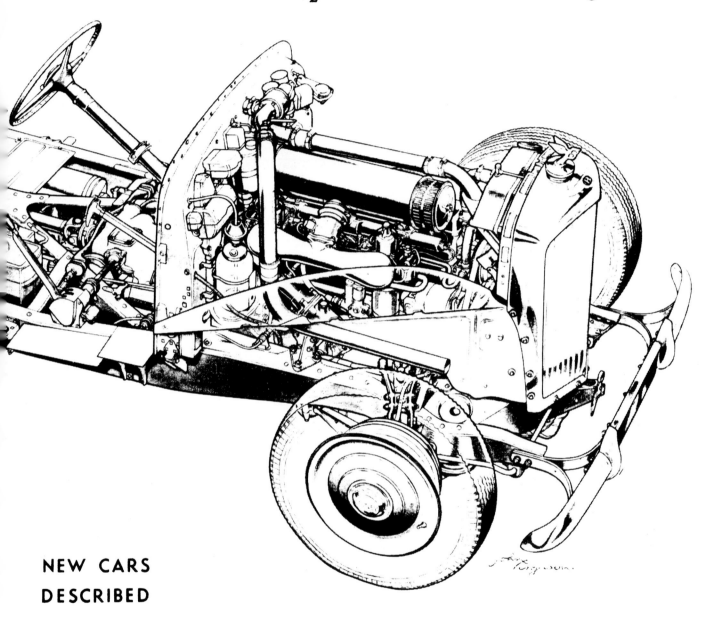

This drawing by John Ferguson of *The Autocar* shows the Bentley sports saloon chassis in an almost complete form. It will be appreciated that present-day construction methods usually result in a number of small chassis components being carried in the body structure. Above right: this view of the Bentley shows the balance of line that is obtained by the addition of a large luggage locker and a slight increase in the overall length.

THE connoisseur of cars who appreciates the best that money can buy realizes that to increase the standard of refinement by only a small amount above what may be considered as average results in a considerable increase in cost. He also realizes that the standard of workmanship, coupled with the cost of necessary development work, must result in a high price for the finished product. Consequently he accepts the fact that the Bentley is an expensive car. Analysed in detail, the tremendous amount of work involved in its manufacture will be realized.

With the introduction of a new body the model has shed its mark number and is now known as the Bentley sports saloon. Since the Mark VI Bentley with special

saloon body was last described in *The Autocar* a number of detail changes to the chassis have been made from time to time.

The Mark VI Bentley was originally supplied with the standard steel saloon body and a 4,257 c.c. engine having six cylinders and a somewhat unusual system of valve gear with overhead inlet and side exhaust valves. Later, the cylinder bore diameter was increased by 3 mm (from 89 to 92 mm); this resulted in a capacity of 4,566 c.c., or, in general terms, 4½ litres. At the same time modifications were made to the exhaust system. On the 4½-litre engine two manifold castings were attached to a Y-branch fitted to the top of the exhaust pipe. This conveyed the gas to the silencer and so to the tail pipe.

Twin Exhausts

However, for the larger engine two complete exhaust systems are used, one for each group of three cylinders. Twin pipes run to the first stage of the silencing system, which consists of two silencers mounted side by side and situated between the left side member and the cruciform section of the frame. From the outlets of the first-stage silencers two pipes feed the second-stage silencers, which are placed between, and in line with, the rear cruciform members. Finally, two tail pipes run over the top of the rear axle, under the rear of the frame, and emerge polished at the rear of the car. The twin pipes determine, in fact, the engine size of the Bentley that has just passed!

To prevent heat from the silencers reaching the occupants of the car, shields are fitted between the silencers and the floor of the body. These are formed in light alloy and consist of shallow pressings mounted back to back to form a box, with an air space inside to improve the insulation qualities. This space was originally filled with insulating material, but it was found that air was cheaper!

Perhaps the most important new feature on the engine is the arrangement of the cold starting device for use in conjunction with the twin S.U. carburettors. This device has been designed and developed by Rolls-Royce, and overcomes disadvantages found in some cold starting systems used with this type of carburettor. The operating principle is not in any way new; it consists of a strangler on the atmospheric side of the carburettors between the air silencer and the air intake T-junction. Consequently it is not necessary to alter the carburettor jet block position in order to provide the necessary rich mixture for cold starting purposes. The device is automatic and this has enabled both the choke control and the hand throttle to be eliminated, a measure that simplifies driving and provides an interesting example of control mechanism.

The operating mechanism consists of a pair of bi-metal springs mounted in a pocket in the water-heated induction manifold. Now this is interesting, as it is usual to operate bi-metal springs by means of exhaust heat. However, the exhaust heat actuation method is not ideal because the temperature of the exhaust manifold may fall quite considerably if the engine is stationary for a short period. Consequently on some exhaust-operated mechanisms there is a tendency for the fuel consumption to be unnecessarily heavy because the exhaust manifold be-

comes cool, thereby enriching the mixture while the engine itself is still warm and does not require the rich mixture.

The very much reduced temperature range necessitates the use of two springs on the Bentley. A rod connects the lever on the bi-metal spring assembly to a small lever on the cold starting butterfly valve (or strangler) spindle. A second rod, coupled to the cold starting butterfly lever, operates a cam that controls the throttle position. Mounted on the left side of the cold starting assembly housing are a solenoid and a vacuum-operated diaphragm controlling strangler and throttle stop. (Diagram on page 1161.)

Now, assuming that the car has been running and is left to become completely cold, it is first necessary to depress the throttle and release it again in order to allow the bi-metal spring to close the cold starting butterfly valve, and the rod (c) to operate the cam to adjust the idling speed. When the starter button is pressed the solenoid circuit is also energized, and this holds the strangler butterfly valve in the completely closed position, but when the starter button is released the solenoid

is no longer energized because when the engine fires it will, of course, require more air than would be obtained if the strangler remained completely closed. The vacuum-operated device coupled to the induction manifold opens the strangler butterfly to a predetermined amount and holds it there until the engine water jacket temperature has risen sufficiently to enable the bi-metal spring further to open the strangler.

It is, as previously mentioned, necessary to open the throttle and close it again in order to allow the bi-metal spring to close the strangler and permit the progressive cam to modify the throttle stop position. This cam is formed in three sections and, if the throttle is almost fully opened and released, the carburettor throttles will be set to a very fast idling position. On the other hand, if a lower initial idling speed is required, this can be obtained by depressing the throttle only as far as the quarter-open position, and then releasing it. In a similar way, if the engine is started on the very fast idling position, the induction manifold operated diaphragm, which opens the

strangler valve as soon as the engine has started to run, will also allow the progressive cam to reduce the idling speed slightly, if the throttle is quarter-opened and released again. The car can thus be started initially on a high idling speed and then warmed up on an intermediate speed; alternatively, it can be started on this intermediate idling speed.

In the event of the engine failing to start, the large jet depression caused by the closed strangler valve might cause an over-enriching of the mixture, or if flooding takes place (if a carburettor float stuck, for example) it would be necessary to open the strangler. Consequently an over-riding lever is fitted to the throttle spindle shaft so that, if the throttle pedal is fully depressed, both the carburettor throttle spindles and the strangler will be placed in the full open position. This will, of course, enable the engine to be turned over and the excess fuel cleared from the manifold.

All the control links from the bi-metal springs are of light alloy to reduce weight and improve sensitivity.

The strangler butterfly valve is offset so

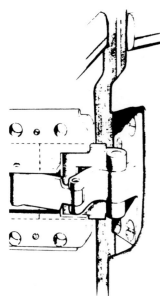

A combined sliding and pivoting motion is arranged for the door hinge to assist sealing and to enable the pivot point of the door to move farther away from the body during the initial opening period.

the limits to which the designers of this outstanding car will go in order to obtain perfection. Unlike a normal unit, the dynamo is insulated and earthed through a cable direct to the battery, while the radiator is provided with an external earth strip. This arrangement, believe it or not, has been found to reduce the silting up of the radiator tubes.

Anyone who has driven one of these cars is immediately impressed by the silky feel of the right-hand gear change, especially when it is realized that the lever is attached to a cross-shaft which must be slid in a transverse direction to the chassis centre line when the lever is moved across the gate. Now, pressure on the knob end of the gear lever would normally produce a considerable amount of friction in the sliding mechanism if a normal type of bearing were used. However, in the Bentley the smooth feel and the impos-

Rear spring shackle lubrication pipes.

Bentley Sports Saloon . . . continued

This view shows the large amount of luggage space, achieved partly by incorporating the capacity on each side of the spare wheel in the main compartment.

that the valve tends to fall open as the torque on the bi-metal spring closing it is reduced. The spring tends to keep the butterfly valve closed when the engine is cold, but open when the engine is hot. During the changeover at a certain critical temperature, therefore, there will be no load on the valve, and during this period the out-of-balance of the valve spindle and mechanism prevents the strangler valve from flapping.

Another most interesting detail shows

The semi razor edge coachwork used for the rear panels and the luggage locker is well balanced by the flowing lines of the rear wings. The adjustable number plate fixing is provided so that the locker can be used in the slightly open position.

sibility of binding are ensured by supporting the cross shaft in a number of rings of ball bearings. The balls are prevented from moving sideways by means of a retaining spring at each end. From the gear box the drive is transmitted to the rear axle by means of a two-piece propeller-shaft, supported at the centre by a flexibly mounted bearing. Although this is not a new feature, it is interesting in that it provides flexibility in two directions.

To accommodate the new body a number of chassis modifications have been carried out. The frame has been lengthened to accommodate the greatly increased capacity of the new luggage locker and the rear suspension has been modified to improve handling qualities. The rear leaf springs have been inclined so that the rear anchorage point is higher than that at the front. When the body attempts to roll on corners, the rear axle movement permitted will produce a certain amount of what is termed " roll understeer." This resists any oversteer characteristics brought about by variations in weight distribution.

The Bentley system of variable ride control is retained; it consists of a small oil pump situated in, and driven by, the gear box. A hand control on the steering column regulates the oil pump release valve blow-off pressure and a variable-pressure oil supply is therefore available. This is piped to the rear spring dampers and is arranged to vary the damper valve position. The dampers themselves use normal fluid and the pump oil pressure is utilized only to adjust the settings.

In the coachwork the most noticeable alteration compared with the previous model is the modification at the rear. In order to provide the greatly increased luggage space the fuel tank has been redesigned to enable the spare wheel to be placed as low down as possible without reducing the tank capacity—a very definite improvement on a car that may be required to transport a large amount of luggage on long-distance touring. Further, the revised body lines considerably improve appearance; in fact, the balance obtained by what is sometimes termed a " notch back " results in a car of considerably increased utility, yet one that retains the air of a thoroughbred and carries on the famous Bentley tradition.

The luggage locker lid encloses the spare wheel and tools but in a separate lower compartment so that the luggage will not be contaminated. To prevent damage to paintwork when the spare wheel is removed a small stainless steel rubbing strip is fitted to the vulnerable part of the body. The locker has a large flat floor space and two useful wells, one on each side of the spare wheel compartment. The lid is hinged at the top and counterbalanced by means of torsion bars. It has an interior light operated by a mercury switch in the locker lid. The lid itself is domed to increase carrying capacity, and provision is made to use the car with it in the slightly open position. The rear number plate is adjustable to allow it to be positioned vertical when the lid is in various positions.

In keeping with Bentley quality the interior of the car is beautifully finished. The rear compartment is of particular interest in that the sides of the body are also upholstered—rather on the lines of a wing-back armchair. The interior heating system is similar to that fitted to the pre-

vious 4½-litre Bentley, but it is supplemented by an extra duct to the windscreen for demisting. It supplies fresh air in hot weather. Arrangements for supplying hot air to the demister have also been improved. Misting of the rear window is now a thing of the past with the Bentley, as it is fitted with an electric demister; this consists of 936 wires of 0.008in diameter, spaced to cover an area 24 × 8in and placed in the sandwich formed by the Triplex laminated glass. The wires are, in fact, so fine that it is almost impossible for them to be seen.

BENTLEY SPECIFICATION

Engine.—6 cyl, 92 × 114.3 mm (4,566 c.c.). Compression ratio 6.3 to 1. Seven-bearing crankshaft. 30 per cent chromium-iron short inset liners. Side camshaft, operating overhead inlet valves and side exhaust valves. Full-flow oil filter.

Clutch.—11in diameter, single-plate; 9 springs; ball-bearing thrust.

Gear Box.—Four forward speeds, synchromesh on top, third, and second. Overall ratios: Top 3.73 to 1; third 5.0 to 1; second 7.5 to 1; first 11.1 to 1; reverse 11.8 to 1.

Final Drive.—Hypoid bevel. Ratio 3.33 to 1 (11:41).

Suspension.—Front, independent by coil springs and wishbones. Bentley hydraulic dampers and anti-roll bar. Rear, half-elliptic leaf springs, tension shackles. Bentley hydraulic dampers with variable ride control. Suspension rate (at the wheel), front 102 lb per in; rear 164 lb per in. Static deflection, front 8½in; rear 7in.

Brakes.—Drums, 12¼in diameter front and rear; 2¼in wide front and rear. Total lining area 196 sq in (98 sq in front).

Steering.—Cam and roller.

Wheels and Tyres.—India 6.50-16in on 5-stud disc wheels.

Electrical Equipment.—12-volt, 54 ampere-hour battery. Head lamps, single dip, 48-48 watt bulbs.

Fuel System.—18-gallon tank. Oil capacity 2 gallons.

Main Dimensions.—Wheelbase 10ft 0in. Track, front 4ft 8.6in; rear 4ft 10.6in. Overall length 16ft 7½in. Width 5ft 10in. Height (running trim with 18 gallons fuel), 5ft 5½in. Frontal area 25.22 sq ft approx. Turning circle 41ft 2in. Weight (in running trim with 18 gallons fuel) 37½ cwt (4,202 lb). Weight distribution 51 per cent front; 49 per cent rear.

The under-bonnet space is well filled with the engine and its auxiliaries. A long-established motto of two of everything electrical is now applied to the ignition condensers as well as the coils.

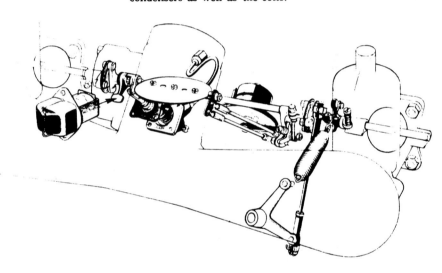

Arrangement of the components used in the automatic starting unit fitted to the latest Bentley. The two bi-metal springs are operated by heat conducted from the water jacket that surrounds part of the inlet manifold.

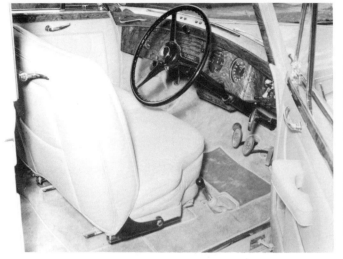

Grouping of switches, and the inclusion of the ammeter, oil pressure, fuel, and temperature gauges in one dial, leaves the walnut facia plain and dignified.

Below : The two small grilles are intakes for the heater-ventilator system. Head lamps are the latest Lucas Le Mans type.

NEW BENTLEY TOURING SALOON BY JAMES YOUNG

SPEED and COMFORT

IN the coachwork of a new Bentley, by James Young, of Bromley, Kent, the emphasis has been placed on long-distance touring, as regards seating, luggage accommodation, ventilation, lamps, driving visibility and fittings. Immediately it was built, the owner left for a tour in Spain.

The traditional radiator is two inches lower than standard, and seven inches further forward, giving a longer, lower bonnet. Noticeable in a side view, this is more apparent from the driving seat, both wings being completely visible, so that the big car can be placed and "aimed" with sureness. There are a wide windscreen of double curvature, screen pillars narrow enough to avoid a blind spot at each side, and a wide rear window, also double curved. The front wings sweep downwards gradually, and also inwards to a definite break at the rear wings, so that the sides of the car are not filled out to full width, and the two doors are not particularly thick. At the rear the corners are filled out, though the tail does not have a heavy appearance, and this has enabled the spare wheel to have upright stowage on the left side of the locker, where it rests in a recess located outside the chassis frame. A very large, deep locker with a flat carpeted floor results; the tool kit and touring spares are under a lid in this floor.

At both front and rear are deep rounded bumpers, of the coachbuilders' design, with over-riders, and well wrapped round the corners. They are 14-gauge and quite heavy, but represent a justifiable expenditure of weight. The slim handles and press-button locks of the doors and luggage locker are also of James Young design.

Lucas Le Mans head lamps are in-stalled, at present with yellow bulbs. These lamps have great range, and will bore right down a *route nationale*, although their beam is a little narrow. There is also a fan beam fog lamp of wide spread, and, matching it, a Lucas long-range driving lamp. At all four corners of the car are Lucas winking turn indicators, those at the front also serving as side lamps. An underbonnet switch effects a changeover from left-hand to right-hand dipping or vice versa. Between head lamp and radiator at each side is a fresh-air intake for the Smiths heater-ventilator, and these intakes have little grilles with plated slats matching those of the radiator. There is a sunshine roof.

Inside the body pale blue-grey leather upholstery and trim match the pale blue-grey of the coachwork, but seat covers are fitted. They are of a soft, fine woollen mixture weave, normally used in aircraft, and so is the headlining. Facia and fillets are of dark figured walnut. The rear seat is normal, with an armrest, and at each side are small lockers with sliding covers in the trim panels, containing clothes brushes and ashtrays.

The front seats are individual but of the divided bench kind, so that three can occasionally be seated there. The front seat armrest is divided into independently operated halves, allowing the passenger to use his section without interfering with the elbow of a driver who dislikes armrests. Besides the usual fore and aft adjustment, each front seat has a squab adjustable for rake, the adjustments being jacking bolts with plated milled-edge heads, accessible from the rear compartment. On long journeys the individual tastes of relief drivers are therefore catered for, or a change of attitude provided for a driver who spends long hours at the wheel. The cloth-covered vizors house extra blue Perspex panels, and a transparent anti-glare panel, which can be slid down as required. There are vanity mirrors on the cloth backs of the vizors. There are door pockets tailored for vacuum flasks and sandwich boxes.

Fittings include Radiomobile wireless, a windscreen washer, four interior lamps, and lamps for both facia and luggage lockers. There is also an underbonnet inspection lamp. The facia panel has a large Smiths speedometer situated in front of the driver. On the right are lighting switches and the ignition switch and lock, and a plug for a battery charger, all on the customary round black panel of the Bentley. Grouped below this are other switches, the push buttons for the electrically operated window opening gear, and the screen wash button. Next to the speedometer is a round dial, black, with white markings and needles, with segments for oil pressure, water temperature, fuel level and charging rate; pressure on a button causes the fuel gauge to record sump oil level instead. The radio occupies the centre of the facia, and on the left is the facia locker, with the clock in its lid. The facia is a neat one and is intended, as, indeed, is the whole body design, to be a standard James Young production.

The body was produced on jigs. It is framed in light alloy and panelled in aluminium throughout, except for the bonnet and scuttle, which are steel. The weight of the complete car is 38cwt, which is light in view of its size.

A bonnet both lowered and lengthened balances the long and capacious tail. The windscreen has a moderate slope.

No. 1512 BENTLEY SPORTS SALOON

The standard steel-bodied Bentley has a well - balanced line and the four-light window style is well suited to the traditional type of coachwork. The leading edge of the rear wing is covered by the door panel. Ventilators are built into the scuttle sides

The Autocar ROAD TESTS

A YEAR ago it was announced that the Bentley was to be fitted with an automatic transmission as optional equipment to meet the needs of export markets. A modified form of the well-known Hydra-Matic transmission was chosen as being the most suitable type available to meet the requirements of the car. The general layout and working principles of this system were described in the October 24, 1952, issue of *The Autocar*. It is a matter of no little significance that the designers of this car, which is traditional in very many ways—at least as regards appearance—should decide that the time has come to offer elimination of the clutch pedal and normal gear change, fine as these controls are on the Bentley. The export market influence must not be overlooked. This automatic transmission has now been made available for cars sold on the home market, but the normal clutch and four-speed gear box, with right-hand lever, remain available for those who prefer this system.

There are no doubt those who may think that a car fitted with " one of those new-fangled transmissions " cannot compete with a similar car fitted with a conventional gear box if the latter is skilfully handled; it may also be argued that the fuel consumption will of necessity be greater. To substantiate or disprove these arguments it is interesting to compare the performance figures obtained on a car that has been recently tested with the figures of a previous test carried out by *The Autocar* on a similar model having conventional transmission.

First, fuel consumption: in the previous test a fuel consumption range of 15 to 17 m.p.g. was recorded; in the present test a consumption range of 12 to 16 m.p.g. was obtained, showing that the automatic drive car does, under comparable conditions, tend to use slightly more fuel. Next, the question of maximum speed. Here there is very little difference in mean speed, although the automatic drive car did show a mean maximum speed of three-quarters of a mile per hour more. As regards the general performance, some comparative figures for the two cars are shown below and, very briefly, as regards both acceleration in any one gear or from rest through the gears, the automatic drive car has a better performance, although from rest to 90 m.p.h. it did in fact take 0.8 sec longer.

Acceleration from constant speeds				
	Manual Transmission		Automatic Transmission	
M.P.H.	Sec	Gear	Sec	Range
10-30	3.6	1st	3.6	(4)
20-40	4.4	2nd	4.7	(4)
30-50	5.5	2nd	5.9	(4)
40-60	7.1	3rd	6.7	(4)

From rest through the gears		
	Manual Transmission	Automatic Transmission
M.P.H.	Sec	Sec
0-30	4.5	4.4
0-60	15.2	13.8
0-80	28.4	26.3

As one expects with a car of this quality and price, the engine is particularly smooth and performs very quietly. The transmission consists of a fluid coupling and a four-

Left : Arm rests are fitted to the front doors, which are also provided with small pockets. The small rectangular duct between the front seat adjusting levers is part of the heating system.

Right : Fittings in the rear compartment include sloping foot rests, built-in tables and grab handles on the back rests of the front seats, and ashtrays built into the outside arm rests. The sliding control for the rear blind is seen above the driver's door.

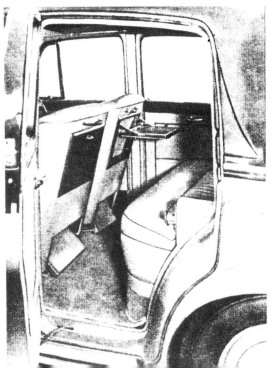

Semi-razor-edge styling is used at the rear and the body is particularly suitable for two-colour treatment. The combined brake and stop lights are flared into the rear wings.

speed and reverse epicyclic gear box, and, unlike the transmissions of American cars where the gear selector is labelled "Drive" or "Low Range," the Bentley selector quadrant is marked with the figures 4, 3, 2, and R for reverse. There is also a neutral position, N, and in this alone can the engine be started. To move off from rest the lever is normally placed in position 4, and as the throttle is opened the fluid coupling operates and the car starts in first gear. If the throttle is fully open it changes automatically to second gear at 20 m.p.h., third gear at 38 m.p.h., and top at 58 m.p.h. Gear changes can, of course, occur at speeds below those quoted, depending on load and throttle position. If position 3 of the lever is selected the transmission will operate similarly, except that the change from third to top gear will not occur at a speed below 62 m.p.h., irrespective of throttle position. If position 2 is used (equivalent to Low Range) the car will start in first gear and change to second gear at a speed of 20 m.p.h. (on full throttle), but it will not change up into third gear.

This system, then, enables the equivalent of second gear braking to be obtained; it also enables third gear to be selected (at speeds below 62 m.p.h.) so that the transmission will not automatically change up to top gear if the driver releases his foot momentarily. It may be argued that this transmission does not permit the use of third gear at speeds above 62 m.p.h., compared with a normal and maximum of 70 to 85 m.p.h. with the conventional transmission. This is, of course, true, but if the two sets of figures are compared, considering the acceleration from 0 to 90 m.p.h., there seems to be little, on a purely performance basis, to justify the need for a higher speed in the indirect ratio.

So much for the technicalities and performance aspect of the mechanism. Under normal conditions the take-off from rest is smooth; at full throttle the changes from gear to gear are noticeable but, bearing in mind that the resultant

performance is equivalent to that obtained by snatch change methods with a conventional transmission, this fact is perhaps excusable. Under part-throttle conditions very little snatch is noticed, particularly if the driver releases his foot very slightly at the instant at which the change occurs. In hilly country the second and third selector positions provide a very satisfactory measure of engine braking.

The Bentley is a particularly comfortable car both to drive and to ride in, and over all normal types of road surface the suspension produces a level ride without transmitting shock or causing the body to pitch. The well-known Bentley feature of a ride control (a lever on the steering wheel, which adjusts the rear spring dampers) does not produce any very noticeable change in the riding qualities, but it does stiffen up the suspension and give an added tautness that seems to improve the fast cornering qualities.

Steering and Brakes

The steering, with 3¼ turns from lock to lock, is a very satisfactory compromise which results in a sufficiently light control for low speed manœuvring and parking, yet it is also direct enough for fast driving. Road shocks are not transmitted back through the wheel, but it is not completely dead feeling. There is good self-centring action.

The brakes, with their system of operation comprising an hydraulic layout assisted by a mechanical servo, recorded a particularly good maximum efficiency figure (expressed in terms of a percentage of g) for a moderate pedal pressure of 80 lb. No fade was noticed under fast driving conditions, and over the test mileage the brakes did not show any sign of loss of balance or increase in pedal travel. There was, however, one feature about the system which was undesirable; at low speeds—when driving in close traffic, for

Twin ignition coils are fixed to the bulkhead, between the windscreen wiper motor and the demister fan. Both the engine oil and the radiator filler caps, together with the dipstick, are on the left-hand side of the neatly arranged and beautifully finished engine.

The large luggage locker is completely trimmed, and the balanced lid lifts high to allow full access. A separate compartment contains the spare wheel and tools, and therefore luggage does not have to be disturbed in order to change a wheel. The twin exhaust pipes will be noticed.

example—there seemed to be a slight delay in the servo action which was apt to be disconcerting on occasion.

The interior is well insulated and the passenger compartment is very quiet as regards both road-excited body noise and wind noise. There is what may be called a desirable amount of engine noise, not very much, but just enough to let the driver know if the engine is revving too fast in low range, for example. In keeping with the general character of the car, the driving seat is very well proportioned. It gives plenty of support, is very comfortable, and correctly positioned in relation to both the steering wheel and the pedals. From the driving seat there is good all-round visibility, both front wings can be seen, and the mirror view is also satisfactory.

There is ample passenger space in both front and rear compartments, and the rear seat is particularly comfortable.

The luggage locker is very spacious and trimmed in keeping with the very high standard of finish of the rest of the car, and its interior is shaped so that it will not damage luggage. The head lamps are very powerful and well up to the requirements of the car for fast night driving. They are also well above average when dipped; the dipswitch is conveniently positioned. The one-shot chassis lubrication system prevents the need for frequent attention with a gun. It is operated while running by means of a pedal placed conveniently under the facia.

The Bentley is an expensive car, but the more it is driven the more it is appreciated that the high cost is brought about by the desire of the manufacturers to supply a car that is second to none in its class, one that is robust as well as one with very much more than an air of quality, and, perhaps most important of all, one that still retains its qualities of performance and silence even when very many miles are shown on the speedometer.

BENTLEY SPORTS SALOON

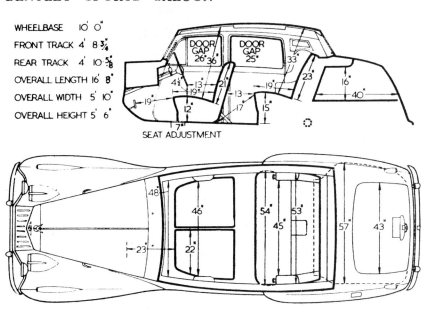

WHEELBASE 10' 0"
FRONT TRACK 4' 8¾"
REAR TRACK 4' 10⅝"
OVERALL LENGTH 16' 8"
OVERALL WIDTH 5' 10"
OVERALL HEIGHT 5' 6"

SEAT ADJUSTMENT

Measurements in these ¼in to 1ft scale body diagrams are taken with the driving seat in the central position of fore and aft adjustment and with the seat cushions uncompressed.

DATA

PRICE (basic), with sports saloon body £3,100.
British purchase tax, £1,292 15s 10d.
Total (in Great Britain), £4,392 15s 10d.
Extras: Automatic transmission £70, plus £29 3s 4d British purchase tax.

ENGINE: Capacity: 4,566 c.c. (279 cu in).
Number of cylinders: 6.
Bore and stroke: 92 × 114 mm (3⅝ × 4½in).
Valve gear: Overhead inlet; side exhaust.
Compression ratio: 6.75 to 1.
B.H.P.: — at — r.p.m. (B.H.P. per ton laden —).
Torque: — lb ft at — r.p.m.
M.P.H. per 1,000 r.p.m. on top gear, 22.

WEIGHT (with 5 gals fuel), 37¾ cwt (4,221 lb).
Weight distribution (per cent) 48.5 F; 51.5 R.
Laden as tested: 41.5 cwt (4,635 lb).
Lb per c.c. (laden): 1.01.

BRAKES: Type: F, Leading and trailing. R, Leading and trailing.
Method of operation: F, Hydraulic. R, Mechanical (mechanical servo).
Drum dimensions: F, 12¼in diameter, 2.6in wide. R, 12¼in diameter, 2.6in wide.
Lining area: F, 93 sq in. R, 93 sq in (90 sq in per ton laden).

TYRES: 6.50 — 16in.
Pressures (lb per sq in): 24 F; 33 R.

TANK CAPACITY: 18 Imperial gallons.
Oil sump, 16 pints.
Cooling system, 30 pints.

TURNING CIRCLE: 41ft 2in (L and R).
Steering wheel turns (lock to lock): 3¾.

DIMENSIONS: Wheelbase 10ft 0in.
Track: (F), 4ft 8¾in; (R), 4ft 10⅝in.
Length (overall): 16ft 8in.
Height: 5ft 6in.
Width: 5ft 10in.
Ground clearance: —in.
Frontal area 25.2 sq. ft. (approximately).

ELECTRICAL SYSTEM: 12-volt; 55 ampère-hour battery.
Head lights: Double dip; 48-watt bulbs.

SUSPENSION: Front, Independent, coil springs and wishbones; anti-roll bar. Rear, Half-elliptic springs.

PERFORMANCE

ACCELERATION: from constant speeds. Speed, *Gear Ratios and time in sec.

M.P.H.	4 Range	3 Range	2 Range
10—30	3.6	—	—
20—40	4.7	—	4.0
30—50	5.9	—	—
40—60	6.7	6.4	—
50—70	9.3	8.1	—
60—80	12.4	—	—
70—90	19.6	—	—

From rest through gears to:

M.P.H.			sec
30	..	..	4.4
50	..	..	10.0
60	..	..	13.8
70	..	..	19.1
80	..	..	26.3
90	..	..	39.8

*Gear Ratios 3.73; 5.4; 9.82 and 14.23 to 1.
Standing quarter mile, 19.1 sec.

SPEED ON GEARS:

Gear			M.P.H. (max.)	K.P.H. (max.)
Top	..	(mean)	100.75	161.4
		(best)	106.5	171.4
3rd	..	..	62	100
2nd	..	..	38	61
1st	..	..	20	32

(in 4 Range maximum on 3rd is 58 m.p.h.)

TRACTIVE RESISTANCE: 15 lb per ton at 10 M.P.H.

TRACTIVE EFFORT:

			Pull (lb per ton)	Equivalent Gradient
Top	..	..	295	1 in 7.5
Third	..	..	460	1 in 4.8
Second	..	..	550	1 in 3.9

BRAKES:

Efficiency	Pedal Pressure (lb)
94 per cent	80
72 per cent	60
52 per cent	40

FUEL CONSUMPTION:
12.3 m.p.g. overall for 206 miles (23 litres per 100 km).
Approximate normal range 12–16 m.p.g. (23.5–17.7 litres per 100 km).
Fuel, First grade.

WEATHER: Fine, dry surface; slight wind. Air temperature 64 deg F.
Acceleration figures are the means of several runs in opposite directions.
Tractive effort and resistance obtained by Tapley meter.
Model described in *The Autocar* of October 16, 1953.

SPEEDOMETER CORRECTION: M.P.H.

Car speedometer	..	..	10	20	30	40	50	60	70	80	90	100	110
True speed	..	..	9.5	20	30	39	48	58	67	77	86	94	106

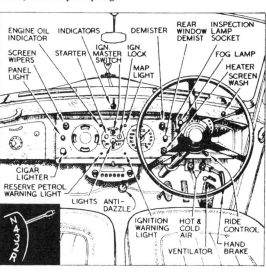

SILVER CLOUD AND

NEW ROLLS-ROYCE AND BENTLEY MODELS

W ITH the reputation for making the finest car in the world it is no easy task to introduce a new range of cars that will be better than the models they supersede but cost very little more. Yet with the introduction of the new Rolls-Royce Silver Cloud and the Bentley Series S this is just what has been done. That the nearer one approaches the ultimate the greater will be the standardization is evident by the similarity between the Rolls-Royce and the Bentley.

The automatic transmission, now made standard equipment on all models, remains unchanged. Chassis can be supplied for specialist coachwork. The engine is similar in design to that used on the Bentley Continental.

Cylinder bore diameter has been

of the journal. From there it is conveyed by another drilling to the crankpin, which is cross-drilled to lubricate the big-end bearing. The connecting rod is drilled throughout its length to lubricate the gudgeon pin, and is cross-drilled on the thrust side, below the piston skirt, for cylinder bore lubrication.

At the rear of the back main bearing an oil thrower is now incorporated in addition to the scroll type of oil return. A flange is formed at the rear of the shaft, and to this is attached the flexible disc flywheel which carries the starter ring, and to which is bolted the housing for the fluid coupling used in conjunction with the automatic transmission. At the front of the shaft there is a torsional vibration damper consisting of a metallic mass attached to a thin flange on the shaft by spring-loaded friction linings. In between this and the front main bearing there is the camshaft drive gear; again to reduce the effects of torsional vibration, a spring drive is incorporated in this. Both this

Larger Engine

New Front Suspension

Z-Bar addition to Rear Suspension

New Head and Porting

Automatic Transmission Standardized

Smaller Wheels—Larger Brakedrum Area

valve seats. To combat the effects of corrosion and reduce pre-ignition the heads of the exhaust valves are given a bright ray treatment. This coats the valve head with 80 per cent nickel and 20 per cent chromium applied with a welding torch.

The most noticeable change to the power unit has been redesigning the cylinder head, the four-port arrangement being replaced by a new six-port head to

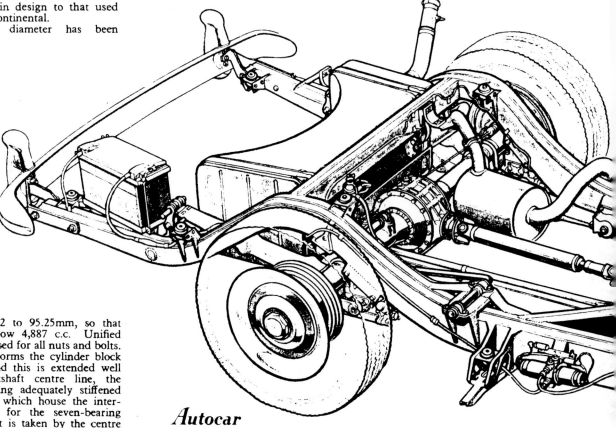

Autocar

increased from 92 to 95.25mm, so that the capacity is now 4,887 c.c. Unified threads are now used for all nuts and bolts. A single casting forms the cylinder block and crankcase, and this is extended well below the crankshaft centre line, the crankchamber being adequately stiffened by the five webs which house the intermediate bearings for the seven-bearing shaft. End thrust is taken by the centre main bearing, and all main bearings have 2.75in journals. The crankpins are 2in in diameter and have an effective width of $1\frac{1}{8}$in. Indium-coated lead-bronze steel-backed shells are used for both main and big-end bearings.

The forged crankshaft now has integral balance weights; these are placed on either side of the centre main bearing, on the outsides of numbers 2 and 6 main bearings, and on the insides of numbers 1 and 7 journals. Both main bearing and crankpin journals are hollow, the ends being sealed by bolted-in plugs of stainless steel. On earlier models these plugs were light alloy, but this was changed to prevent adverse effects from leaded fuels. Each main journal has radial drillings which allow lubricant to pass to the hollow centre

gear and the torsional vibration damper are mounted inside the engine front cover.

Full-length cylinder liners, pressed into the bores, provide wear-resisting surfaces for the long split-skirt pistons. These pistons have four rings, the top one being chromium plated.

The well-known Rolls-Royce system of overhead inlet and side exhaust valves is retained, the exhaust valves being produced from KE965 material with Stellite

improve the breathing and permit increased power output. Cast in aluminium, the cylinder head is attached to the block by 37 $\frac{3}{8}$in set bolts. By using these in place of the normal arrangement of studs and nuts it has been possible to increase the spanner clearance, particularly on the bolts adjacent to the rocker pedestals. The construction of the cylinder head is interesting: half of the manifold is actually formed in the head itself. The other half,

SERIES S

containing the flanges for carburettor attachment, is also a light alloy casting, the two parts being held together by 22 studs and nuts. This arrangement results in a fairly simple casting as far as the ports are concerned, and simplifies fettling and inspection.

The inlet valves are 1.85in diameter and have a lift of 0.4in. The corresponding figures for the exhaust are 1.625in and 0.375in. The inlet valves are produced from S65, a nickel chrome alloy steel, and a similar material is used for the inlet valve inserts; these are screwed into place and, once they are in position, the spanner lugs are machined off. Particular attention has been paid to the design of the inlet porting to improve flow, and the internal shape of the inserts is curved, to blend with the line of the inlet porting. This improves gas flow round the back of the valve heads.

Brass inserts are screwed into the head to take the sparking plugs, and these are locked in place by additional screwed rings to prevent the possibility of the insert being removed when the sparking plugs are unscrewed.

Both Bentley and Rolls-Royce models have twin horizontal S.U. carburettors in conjunction with the automatic cold starting device described in the September 19, 1952 issue. Both this unit and the carburettors are different from those previously used on Bentley models. The object of the cold-starting device is to eliminate the manual choke control and the need to raise and lower the carburettor jet block to provide mixture enrichment.

On previous carburettors the jet block was held in place by cork washers which enabled it to be adjusted and also provided a fuel seal. The bottom end of the carburettors has now been completely redesigned, and a new assembly is used with the jet block attached to a rubber diaphragm. This diaphragm permits vertical movement of the jet and provides a better seal. Because of the cold starting device variation of the jet position is required only for initial carburettor tuning.

The carburettors also include a new slow-running adjustment which does not rely on the setting of the main throttle valves in order to produce the correct tick-over. Instead, the linkage is adjusted so that when the throttle pedal is released the butterfly valves are closed and the tick-over speed is then adjusted by a taper-ended screw which controls the flow through a small port which by-passes the main throttle valve.

The cold starting device has been improved. On the previous model the solenoid which closes the choke valve was in circuit with the starter motor switch;

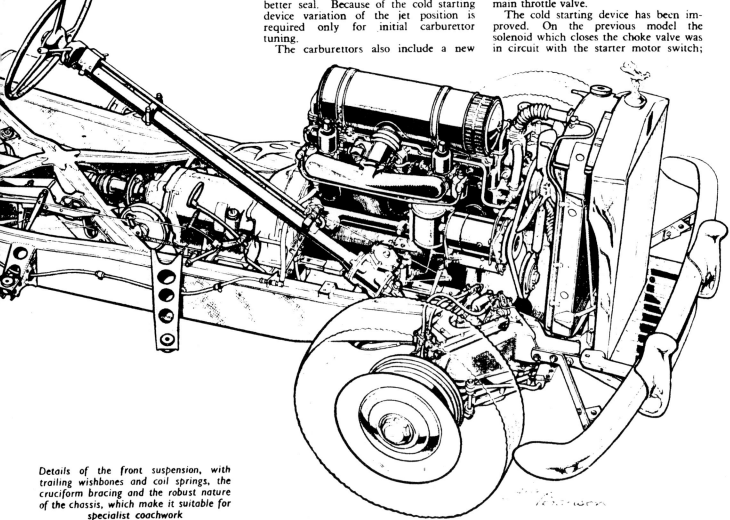

Details of the front suspension, with trailing wishbones and coil springs, the cruciform bracing and the robust nature of the chassis, which make it suitable for specialist coachwork

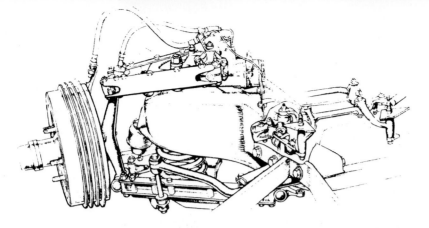

Rolls-Royce layout with single wheel cylinder and compensating link mechanism has been retained. In place of a high-rate spring, special low-rate springs are used on the shake-back stop assembly to enable the friction force to be controlled more accurately, and the friction surfaces for these springs consist of cadmium plating on the web of the brake shoe itself, in conjunction with chromium plated washers. In place of rolled section brake shoes, the linings are riveted to fabricated shoes on the new model.

Previous cars have sometimes been

SILVER CLOUD AND SERIES S .... continued

The independent front suspension units consist of half-trailing long and short wishbones, the inner fulcrum bearing for the upper wishbones being formed by the damper unit. The plate welded to the chassis frame and bolted to a plate on the inner end of the damper prevents deflections which could cause a change in castor angle under heavy braking

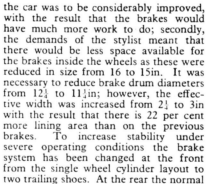

Although retaining a dignified style, the facia panel has been restyled to give a cleaner appearance

consequently, as soon as the engine fired and the starter switch was released, the circuit ceased to be energized. The effect could be to stall the engine after a few revs.

To overcome this the solenoid is placed in the ignition circuit; in addition, a pressure-sensitive switch is tapped into the oil gallery which breaks the circuit as soon as the pump produces a given pressure in the oil line. A temperature-sensitive switch is included in the cold-starting circuit to prevent the system from operating at under-bonnet temperatures.

On the new cars automatic transmission, identical with that optionally fitted to the previous model, is a standard feature. The drive from the transmission to the rear axle is by two-piece propeller-shaft with a flexibly mounted centre bearing. The rear section of the shaft consists of conventional Hardy Spicer couplings with a sliding spline just to the rear of the centre bearing. The front section, however, contains a special joint which will slide with the application of only a very light end load, even when it is transmitting full torque. This has been introduced in the quest for complete silence and freedom from vibration.

In designing the braking equipment Rolls-Royce engineers were faced with two problems: first, the performance of

the car was to be considerably improved, with the result that the brakes would have much more work to do; secondly, the demands of the stylist meant that there would be less space available for the brakes inside the wheels as these were reduced in size from 16 to 15in. It was necessary to reduce brake drum diameters from $12\frac{1}{4}$ to $11\frac{1}{4}$in; however, the effective width was increased from $2\frac{1}{4}$ to 3in with the result that there is 22 per cent more lining area than on the previous brakes. To increase stability under severe operating conditions the brake system has been changed at the front from the single wheel cylinder layout to two trailing shoes. At the rear the normal

criticized because of servo lag. This has been rectified by increasing the servo speed so that the motor now runs at $\frac{1}{5.6}$ of the propeller-shaft speed compared with $\frac{1}{10.5}$. This modification has also reduced servo noise and the slight judder that was sometimes experienced. In the new system the front brakes depend wholly upon hydraulic operation by the servo, and 60 per cent of the rear braking is so applied; the remaining 40 per cent at the rear is applied mechanically direct from the brake pedal (the old figure was 50 per cent). The total distribution of

A Z-bar pivoted to the chassis frame and the rear axle prevents road spring wind-up caused by torque reaction, and modifies the rear roll stiffness to produce the desired degree of understeer

The new S.U. carburettor has auxiliary drillings in conjunction with the needle valve to adjust the slow running, and a diaphragm member which forms the seal for the jet block assembly. A small lever with screw adjustment is used to vary the height of the jet block for carburettor tuning

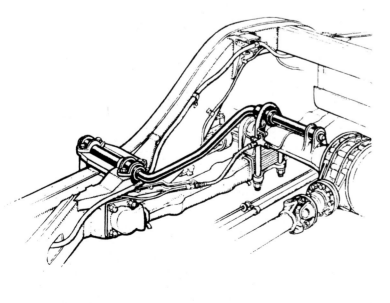

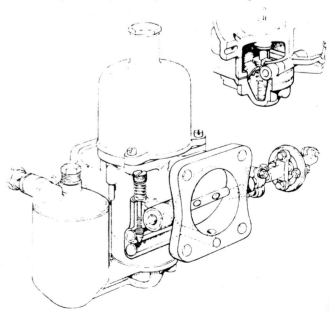

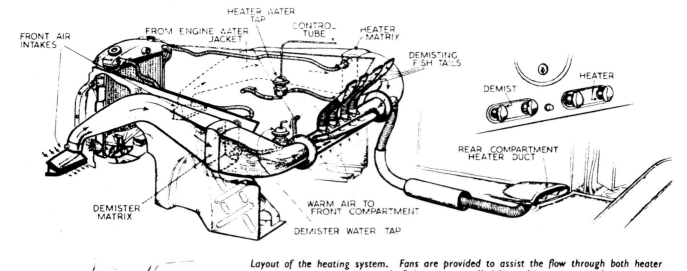

FRONT AIR INTAKES

HEATER WATER TAP

FROM ENGINE WATER JACKET

CONTROL-TUBE

HEATER MATRIX

DEMISTING FISH TAILS

DEMIST

HEATER

REAR COMPARTMENT HEATER DUCT

DEMISTER MATRIX

WARM AIR TO FRONT COMPARTMENT

DEMISTER WATER TAP

Layout of the heating system. Fans are provided to assist the flow through both heater units, and the speed of these is controlled by multi-position switches

SILVER CLOUD AND SERIES S .... continued

braking between front and rear is 1.23 to 1. Automatic adjustment is provided for the front brakes, and there is a special safety device to prevent the brake shoes from wearing out against the drums and to indicate when relining is necessary. This consists of a high rate spring which, in effect, over-rides the automatic adjustment, with the result that free pedal travel becomes noticeable after a predetermined amount of lining wear has taken place. Manual adjustment is necessary for the rear brakes, and this automatically adjusts the hand brake.

The most noticeable change in the front end is to be observed in the new suspension. A conventional independent arrangement with long and short wishbones and coil springs is now employed. This change has been brought about in order to increase the permissible amount of wheel movement. With the new system 3in of bump and 4in of rebound are provided.

In the new suspension the wishbones are half-trailing, with the inner fulcrum bearings set at an angle of 62½ deg to the longitudinal centre line of the chassis. The fulcrum bearings for the lower wishbones are bolted on to the main front cross member, while those for the upper wishbones are formed by the damper unit. Both upper and lower wishbones are channel section pressings with bolted-on bearing and attachment brackets, and additional bolted-on plates and pressings to form the spring mounting and attachment for the rebound rubber. The abutment for the road spring consists of a welded pressing located below the damper. Although the top end of the road spring is finished

flat, the lower end has a pig tail which fits into the pressing bolted to the bottom of the lower wishbone assembly.

Lubricant is piped to all front suspension pivots with the exception of those provided for the front damper, and screwed bushes are used in all suspension joints. Caster angle adjustment is provided by moving the inner ends of the top wishbones along the squared ends of the damper spindle and re-clamping in the correct position, suitably shaped steel blocks being placed between the channel section wishbone members, the centre flange of which is cut back to provide the necessary flexibility. Bolted-on lugs also provide attachment for the anti-roll bar, which is supported by rubber bushes and runs in front of the suspension unit. To prevent vibration the bar has a centre rubber bush bearing.

Steering and track rods are located behind the front wishbones, and the system consists of a three-piece track rod with two slave levers pivoted to the rear of the front cross member. To ensure that accuracy is maintained, lugs attached to the inner wishbone fulcrums provide the pivot points for the slave levers, thereby ensuring that the correct relative distance between the slave lever pivots and the wishbones is maintained. A lug extending back from the left slave lever is connected to a link pivoted to the forward facing lever on the steering box. The steering box itself is located inside the frame member, and has a forward facing lug on its casing so that the frame

attachment point is in line with the cross link (viewed from above), thereby preventing slight frame deflections from affecting the steering.

Although the rear suspension is conventional with half-elliptic leaf springs and a half-floating rear axle, a number of changes have been made. To simplify the frame and enable straight side members to be used, the springs are now placed closer together so that they are on the inside of the chassis frame. This arrangement also tends to make for greater interior body space as the frame side members run closer to the wheel arches. The new layout also increases the roll understeer characteristics. During the development stages it was found necessary to reduce the stiffness of the rear springs in order to improve the rear seat ride and this in turn reduced the rear roll stiffness, with the result that the car then had rather too much understeer. Further, it was found necessary to reduce spring wind-up brought about by torque reaction.

These two factors could have been controlled by the use of a rear anti-roll bar and torque arms, or some other form of link mechanism. However, it is very difficult to accommodate an anti-roll bar on the rear suspension (unless it is of a peculiar shape) and to provide, as well, clearance to permit rear axle movement. The Rolls-Royce engineers solved the problem by fitting a Z-bar, one end of which is pivoted to the frame, the other end to the top of the right-hand axle

Half of the inlet manifold is formed in the new cylinder head ; the other half is bolted to it.

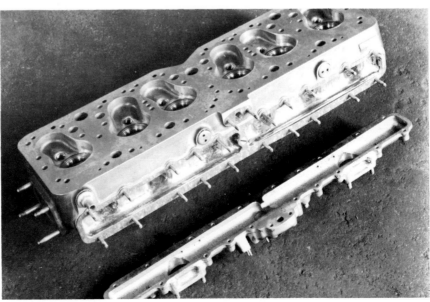

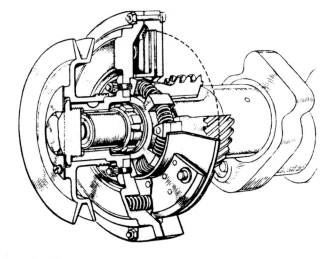

The crankshaft vibration damper and spring drive to the camshaft are located on the front of the crankshaft, and are enclosed by the engine front cover

ing plates spot welded to the upper and lower flange of each section before the main pressings are welded together to form a box. In the centre of the frame there is a deep box section cruciform, drilled to provide the necessary clearance for the propeller-shaft. In addition to the main front cross member, there are two cross members at the rear of the body behind the rear axle centre line.

On a car of this type smoothness and silence are two extremely important requirements. Particular attention has been paid to the body mounts, and these have

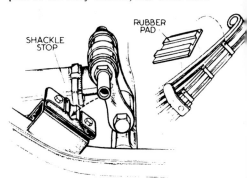

To prevent the rear spring shackle from going "over centre," a shackle stop is built on the top of the frame, and this engages with an extension on the outer end of the shackle bolt

casing tube. This bar, in effect, trims the car to provide the correct degree of understeer. The addition of the Z-bar caused a considerable increase in the loading on the front spring eye, located almost directly beneath it, under braking. It was, therefore, necessary to increase the size of the rubber bush, which is now housed in a wrapped and welded spring eye.

The leaf springs are double grooved. To reduce road noise rubber interlining is placed between the top four leaves. The leaves are Parkerized to assist retention of lubricant, and the complete spring is packed with Ragosine 204G lubricant containing 20 per cent molybdenum disulphide. The springs are, of course, enclosed in gaiters which greatly reduce wear by excluding grit.

Improved damping is provided on both front and rear suspensions, giving greater fluid flow, so that the whole of the fluid is circulated as opposed to a small quantity of it continuously. The ride control, which modifies the setting of the rear dampers, has been altered. It is now electrically controlled and alters the "slow leak" on the dampers; operating the switch on the steering column gives instantaneous change, and when in the hard position the damping is twice as

hard as that provided when in the normal position.

Produced in 16-gauge 20-ton steel, the chassis frame is 50 per cent stiffer torsionally between axles than on the previous models. This increase has been brought about without noticeably increasing the weight, the figures for the old and new frame being 286 lb and 300 lb respectively. The side members are of box section, composed of two "top hat" section pressings, with additional stiffen-

The crankshaft now has integral balance weights. This sub-assembly shows the shaft with a vibration damper and fan pulley at the front, and thin disc fly-wheel and a starter ring at the rear

A forward extension on the steering box brings its frame attachment point close to the ball joint on the steering lever, thereby reducing inaccuracies and vibrations that might occur as a result of frame deflection. Note the pipe around the lower end of the steering box which supplies lubricant to the steering lever joint

been placed at the greatest possible distance from the chassis longitudinal centre line in order to provide the maximum amount of rock control with relatively soft rubbers. Further, it has been found that to reduce noise all body mounts must be equally loaded. To solve this problem the housings for the mountings can be adjusted, and to ensure that all twelve mounts are equally loaded, the body is attached to the front pair of mounts, and air jacks are placed underneath the remainder. The air pressure then applies a uniform loading, and the mountings are then secured. Two additional body mountings are provided on the rear arms of the cruciform to prevent floor vibrations.

In producing the new body the aim has been to provide a car with faster and more modern lines, and also provide extra width in both front and rear compartments. The main body panels are in 20-gauge steel, although 18- and 16-gauge light alloy are used for the doors, luggage locker and bonnet panels. To resist corrosion, zinc-plated steel is used for the sills and bulkhead. To improve visibility and give the car a lighter appearance, thin, polished, stainless frames are used for the top halves of the doors. Like the door

A heritage from the coachbuilder's trade, the razor-edge treatment blends well with the curves and still the "finest car in the world" shuns the flush-sided treatment

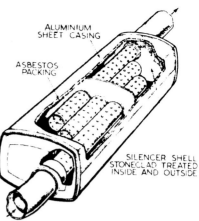

The first silencing chamber consists of a stoneclad treated steel box surrounded by asbestos, with an aluminium casing

panels, the fuel tank is also in light alloy, as are the fuel feed pipes.

Both the Rolls-Royce and Bentley now have completely new heating and demisting systems. In effect, there are two complete heat exchanger units, one on each side of the engine compartment. The combined output varies from 8 kw at 30 m.p.h. to 11 kw at 80 m.p.h. Both heating units have forward facing air intakes mounted low on each side of the main engine radiator. These are provided with special intake ducts which, in addition to the forward opening, have a diagonal grille and a rear outlet slot. The purpose of this is to prevent insects and foreign bodies from being drawn up into the main heater matrix. In addition, if the main forward facing grille becomes blocked with snow, the heater will still function because air can then be drawn through the narrow slot at the rear of the duct. The right-hand unit supplies air to the windscreen, the left-hand heater discharges it along the toe-board in the front compartment and via an additional tube into the rear of the body. This enables the temperature at the bottom and top of the car to be varied, and that very desirable combination of warm air at the bottom of the car and cool, fresh air around the driver's face can easily be provided. As on previous models, the electric element rear window demister is still retained.

In keeping with the remainder of the car, much thought and detail development have been given to the design of the seats. Basically the upholstery consists of a spring case with a Dunlopillo overlay, and in place of individual seats there is a single bench in the front. To increase the comfort and prevent the effects of weight on one side of the cushion being transferred to the other side (from driver to passenger, or vice versa), a measure of damping is provided by a vertical diaphragm fitted midway in the cushion. Another instance of detail development work is the use of a flexible panel under the tray behind the rear seats. This re-

To permit more accurate adjustment a low-rate spring is used for the shake-back stops on the brake shoes

duces boom. The new cars also have greater luggage carrying capacity. No part of the car can be analysed in detail without bringing to light a most interesting development story, and there is little doubt that these fine new cars will carry on the makers' tradition and reputation.

SPECIFICATION

Engine.—6 cyl, 95.25 × 114.3mm, 4,887 c.c. Compression ratio 6.6 to 1. B.h.p.—not quoted. Maximum torque—not quoted Seven-bearing crankshaft. Overhead inlet valves, side exhaust valves operated by single side four-bearing camshaft.

Transmission.—Fluid coupling and four-speed automatic transmission. Overall ratios: top 3.42 to 1; third 4.96 to 1; second 9.0 to 1; first 13.03 to 1. Reverse 14.7 to 1.

Final Drive.—Half-floating rear axle with hypoid gears; ratio 3.42 to 1 (12 to 41). Four-pinion differential.

Suspension.—Front: independent, wishbones and coil springs; anti-roll bar. Rear: half-elliptic leaf springs with Z bar. Rolls-Royce hydraulic dampers. Suspension rate (at the wheel): front, 92.5 lb per in; rear, 127 lb per in. Static deflection: front, 10in; rear, 9in.

Brakes.—Hydraulically operated two trailing shoe, front; hydro-mechanical interlinked leading and trailing, rear. Mechanical servo assisted. Drums: 11¼in dia, 3in wide, front and rear. Total lining area 240 sq in (120 sq in front).

Steering.—Rolls-Royce cam and roller. Ratio (straight ahead) 20.6 to 1. Five turns from lock to lock.

Wheels and Tyres.—8.20-15in tyres on 6L × 15in rims. Five-stud fixing.

Electrical Equipment.—12 volt, 57 ampere-hour battery. Double-dip head lamps. 60-36 watt bulbs.

Fuel System.—18-gallon tank. Oil capacity 16 pints.

Main Dimensions.—Wheelbase 10ft 3in. Track, front 4ft 10in; rear 5ft 0in. Overall length 17ft 8in. Overall width 6ft 2⅜in. Overall height 5ft 4¼in. Ground clearance 7in. Frontal area 26.4 sq ft. Turning circle 41ft 8in. Weight (with 5 galls fuel) 4,228 lb. Weight distribution 49.7 per cent front.

Price.—Bentley: Basic £3,295, British purchase tax £1,374 0s 10d, total £4,669 0s 10d. Chassis £2,465. **Rolls-Royce:** Basic £3,385, British purchase tax £1,411 10s 1d. Total £4,796 10s 1d. Chassis £2,555.

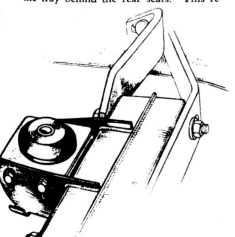

Adjustable body mountings are provided so that all the rubbers can be set to a predetermined load when the body structure is bolted to the chassis

Although the bench-type front seat has a one-piece cushion, the squab is divided. Both parts can be adjusted individually for rake, and this adjustment also results in a variation in available leg room

Cleanliness of line is emphasized by the two-tone finish. The appearance is essentially modern, but it remains restrained in the Bentley tradition. The simple grace will not quickly become dated

The Autocar
ROAD TESTS

No. 1578

BENTLEY SERIES S SALOON

A COMPANY as conservative as Bentley, known to develop and adopt changes in design only after prolonged experiment and consideration, produces new models infrequently. When the new Series S was announced, therefore, it was awaited by the motoring public with more than ordinary interest, even though the formidable price places that interest in an academic class for the majority of people.

The Series S, which succeeds the Mark VI, is, with the exception of the traditional radiator, of entirely modern appearance, incorporating the best of current standards of line and grace, yet excluding ultra-modern styling details that may fall suddenly from fashion. This approach is illustrated by the head lamps, which are faired in to the smoothly flowing wings but not cowled. Similarly the rear wings have a cleanly sloping line but are not swept up to prominent fins at their extremities. The car, longer by 1ft 1¾in than the Mark VI Bentley, has a delightfully balanced appearance. The Bentley tested was constantly admired by drivers and non-motorists alike in England and on the Continent, where much of the testing took place.

Performance matches the appearance, for the new model is a 100 m.p.h. car, reaching 50 m.p.h. from a standing start in 10.3sec and 80 m.p.h. in 28sec. After 80 appears on the car's exceptionally accurate speedometer, the speed can still be increased by nearly 1 m.p.h. per second to 90 m.p.h., after which it rises at an understandably slower rate, a considerable length of clear road being required for 100 m.p.h. to be achieved. In normal driving, speeds much in excess of a genuine 80 m.p.h. are unlikely to be seen, but this speed is as easily held as it is reached, its maintenance frequently made practicable by the reserve of safety provided by the incomparably good brakes.

These mechanical-servo-assisted brakes are the magic hand that grasps the car and strips it of its speed in a

twinkling in almost any conditions. On one occasion the car, quite heavily laden, was being driven at 85 m.p.h. down a completely open but quite steep hill when it was realized that a side turning almost reached would provide a better route. The result of firm, but not heavy, pressure on the brake pedal provided sheer joy even for a driver already familiar with the high standard of Bentley braking. The two tons of car and contents slowed smoothly to a crawl in a moment without noise from brakes or tyres, without the slightest deviation from course, and without even a tremor being detected. All that could be felt was the immensely powerful retardation.

During brake testing at lower speeds, it was found that only 25 lb pressure on the pedal produces a powerful braking effect, and that there is no advantage in exerting more than approximately 50 lb, which represents very little effort, for under this pressure deceleration is at its maximum at little short of 1g on smooth concrete. This deceleration was measured as 30ft per second per second, close indeed to the maximum of 32.2 permitted by the natural laws governing the braking by friction of a body subject to the normal pull of gravity. Incidentally, the brakes are not so efficient in reverse, although still effective. The pull-out hand brake lever holds the car in all conditions and the shortcoming of it not being ideally placed is of little consequence because automatic transmission and its attendant two-pedal control virtually reduces the hand brake lever to a safety device for parking.

Automatic transmission is standard equipment on the new Bentley and Rolls-Royce models; and it is now more refined than that used previously. As a safety precaution the engine cannot be started unless the quadrant lever is in the neutral position. Next to neutral is position 4, engagement of which provides the driver with fully automatic operation of the four forward gears in all conditions. If the throttle pedal is kept fully depressed, the gears change from first to second

BENTLEY SERIES S SALOON . . .

at 19 m.p.h., second to third at 32 m.p.h., and third to top at 60 m.p.h. When the car is travelling in top gear at speeds below 60 m.p.h., full depression of the throttle results in an automatic change down into third, or into second if the speed is in the twenties or below.

Sudden depression of the pedal in this way results in a rather fierce initial acceleration in either of the lower gears because they are engaged under full throttle. This technique of sudden, full throttle opening is primarily intended for emergency, however, for there are alternative methods of changing gear. In the ordinary way a driver simply opens the throttle smoothly and the gears will change almost imperceptibly according to load. But if below 60 m.p.h. the control lever is moved to position 3, third gear is automatically engaged, the change being made virtually imper-

The side lights high in the wings have red tell-tales, both of which are visible from the driving seat. Fog lamps incorporating winking-indicators are fitted as standard on each side of the traditional radiator grille

The french polished woodwork of the facia and window surround is very beautiful and, with the fine hide upholstery, helps to provide the luxurious appearance expected in such a car. Instruments and switches are laid out neatly, and the ride control switch is mounted conveniently on the steering column. Adjustable armrests are fitted to the doors. The backrests of the bench type seat can be adjusted independently. A pull-out table is fitted under the facia; it contains the ashtray drawer

ceptible if an appropriate touch of throttle is given simultaneously. With the lever in this position third gear is always held until 60 m.p.h. is reached. Above 60 m.p.h. top engages. In all other respects first, second and third gears operate as if the lever were in position 4.

For certain conditions—primarily the negotiation of prolonged, very steep hills—position 2 is provided to keep the car permanently in second gear. Position 2 is adjacent to reverse and, as a safety precaution, these two gears are in a different plane on the quadrant so that they cannot be engaged accidentally. When the lever is set at 2, first gear is by-passed and it is possible to hold second gear to something over 40 m.p.h., the gear being held up to maximum r.p.m. Position 2 is also useful for rocking the car, in conjunction with reverse, should the road wheels have sunk while stationary on a soft surface.

When the car is slowing gently, as when running up to red traffic lights, the changing down of the gears is imperceptible to the passengers. The changes are so smooth that they frequently pass unnoticed even by the driver. There is no tendency to creep when the car is stationary with the engine ticking over and the gear lever in one of the driving positions; the take-up when the throttle is opened in these conditions is delightfully smooth, even when maximum acceleration is required. When starting

from cold the smoothest take-off is achieved by letting the engine warm up sufficiently for low r.p.m. to be held while a driving range is engaged.

The performance provided by the new model calls for outstandingly good suspension and steering if it is to be used safely, and in a car bearing such a heavy price purchasers naturally expect very high standards indeed. Yet, in a car of such considerable weight, and in which comfort and silence are at least as important as high performance, the designers are faced with almost insuperable problems in trying to provide the best of two worlds. The Bentley engineers have been markedly successful in their compromises.

The steering has 4¼ turns of the wheel from lock to lock, and as a result it is light to operate, although the driver has to work rather hard when manœuvring in crowded streets. On the open road directional control is commendably precise, and the activities of the front wheels can be felt through the steering to a nicely chosen degree. When cornering fast on indifferent surfaces, movement of the wheels is translated into a slight reaction at the steering wheel that indicates pleasantly what is happening at road level.

It is easy to be misled by the softness of the ride into thinking that the steering and suspension fall short of the standards set by high-performance sports cars, such an

Two S.U. carburettors are fed with air through a massive cleaner and silencer. The six-cylinder 4,887 c.c. engine has an overhead inlet and side exhaust system, and the plugs and double-contact distributor are readily accessible

assumption being not unnatural having in mind the character of the car. In this connection it is interesting to note that on the decidedly poor surface of a straight road in northern France, the Bentley was kept to a speed of 85 m.p.h. in safety and with supreme comfort, the poor surface being indicated to the driver only through the reaction in the steering wheel and a lightness in the feel that indicated how hard the front suspension was being made to work. When recently the same road was used in similar conditions by two high-performance sports cars the equally safe speed was some 5 m.p.h. less and the effects of the rough surface were pronounced. Thus, in the new model is achieved a wonderful degree of comfort, combined with a standard of control that falls short only of the best of super sports cars. The only aspect of the suspension in which the car proved disappointing concerned the control of the rear spring dampers. Instead of the lever fitted to previous models to give the driver an adjustment at will of the rear dampers, there is a switch marked normal and hard, but virtually no difference in the ride could be felt when this was operated.

One fast run in the new car is sufficient for the driver to realize that the designers have surpassed themselves in making the interior silent. On previous models the effect of closing all the windows in town traffic was to encase the occupants in a soundproof room, but at high speed there was still appreciable wind noise. The interior of the Series S is utterly silent at 100 m.p.h. when the windows are closed. Should a window be opened the cracking noise of a hundred-mile-an-hour gale shatters the calm, but otherwise one is conscious of the speed only by watching the speedometer or the rapid approach of the horizon. On a Belgian *autoroute* speeds of more than 90 m.p.h. were held for some miles, the occupants of the

BENTLEY SERIES S SALOON

WHEELBASE	10' 3"
FRONT TRACK	4' 10"
REAR TRACK	5' 0"
OVERALL LENGTH	17' 7¾"
OVERALL WIDTH	6' 2¾"
OVERALL HEIGHT	5' 4"

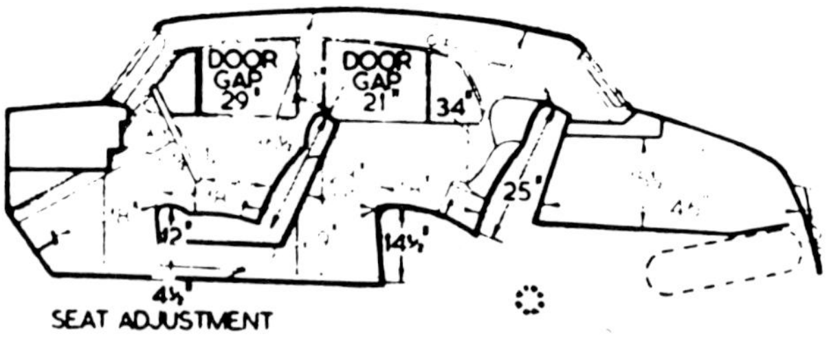

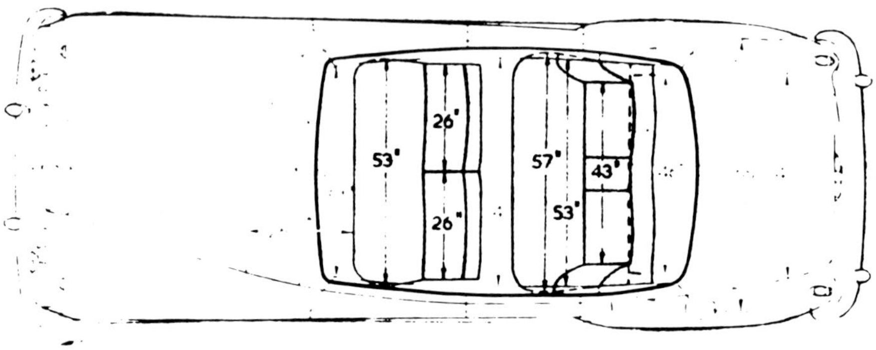

Measurements in these ¼in to 1ft scale body diagrams are taken with the driving seat in the central position of fore and aft adjustment and with the seat cushions uncompressed

DATA

PRICE (basic), with saloon body, **£3,295.**
British purchase tax, **£1,374 0s 10d.**
Total (in Great Britain), **£4,669 0s 10d.**

ENGINE: Capacity: 4,887 c.c. (298.2 cu in).
Number of cylinders: 6.
Bore and stroke: 95.25 × 114.3 mm (3¾ × 4½in).
Valve gear: o.h.v. inlet, s.v. exhaust.
Compression ratio: 6.6 to 1.
M.P.H. per 1,000 r.p.m. on top gear, 25.

WEIGHT: (with 5 gals fuel), 37⅞ cwt (4,242 lb).
Weight distribution (per cent): F, 51; R, 49.
Laden as tested: 40½ cwt (4,542 lb).
Lb per c.c. (laden): 1.08.

BRAKES: Type: Bentley Girling.
Method of operation: Hydro-mechanical, servo operated.
Drum dimensions: F, 11¼in diameter; 3in wide. R, 11¼in diameter; 3in wide.
Lining area: F, 212 sq in. R, 212 sq in (209 sq in per ton laden).

TYRES: 8.20—15in.
Pressures (lb per sq in): F, 19; R, 26 (normal).

TANK CAPACITY: 18 Imperial gallons.
Oil sump, 16 pints.
Cooling system, 30 pints.

TURNING CIRCLE: 41ft 8in (L and R).
Steering wheel turns (lock to lock): 4¼.

DIMENSIONS: Wheelbase: 10ft 3in.
Track: F, 4ft 10in; R, 5ft 0in.
Length (overall): 17ft 7¾in.
Height: 5ft 4in.
Width: 6ft 2¾in.
Ground clearance: 7in.
Frontal area: 26.4 sq ft (approximately).

ELECTRICAL SYSTEM: 12-volt; 57 ampère-hour battery.
Head lights: Double dip; 60–36 watt bulbs.

SUSPENSION: Front, independent, coil springs and wishbones. Rear, semi-elliptic. Anti-roll bar position front and rear.

PERFORMANCE

ACCELERATION: from constant speeds.
Speed Range, *Gear Ratios and Time in sec.

M.P.H.	4 range
10—30	3.5
20—40	4.5
30—50	5.9
40—60	6.9
50—70	9.5

From rest through gears to:

M.P.H.	sec.
30	4.4
50	10.3
60	14.2
70	19.9
80	28.0
90	39.4

* Gear ratios 3.42; 4.96; 9.00; and 13.06 to 1.
Standing quarter mile, 19.7 sec.

SPEEDS ON GEARS:

Gear		M.P.H. (max.)	K.P.H. (normal and max.)
Top	**(mean)**	**101**	**163**
	(best)	**101**	**163**
3rd		**62**	**100**
2nd		**32**	**51**
1st		**19**	**31**

(In 4 range maximum on 2nd is 40 m.p.h., 64 k.p.h.).

TRACTIVE RESISTANCE: 19 lb per ton at 10 M.P.H.

TRACTIVE EFFORT:

	Pull (lb per ton)	Equivalent Gradient
Top	253	1 in 8.5
Third	380	1 in 5.75
Second	550	1 in 4

BRAKES:

Efficiency	Pedal Pressure (lb)
75 per cent	25
96 per cent	50

FUEL CONSUMPTION:

14 m.p.g. overall for 261 miles (20 litres per 100 km.).
Approximate normal range 13–16 m.p.g. (21.7–17.6 litres per 100 km.).
Fuel, First grade.

WEATHER:

Air temperature 68 deg F.
Acceleration figures are the means of several runs in opposite directions.
Tractive effort and resistance obtained by Tapley meter.
Model described in *The Autocar* of April 29, 1955.

SPEEDOMETER CORRECTION: M.P.H.

Car speedometer	10	20	30	40	50	60	70	80	90	100
True speed	10	20	30	40	50	60	70	81	91	101

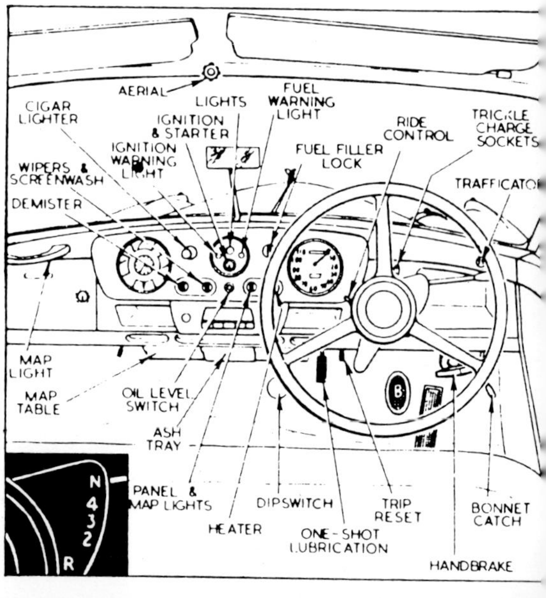

USED CARS

ON THE ROAD

No. 242 1955 BENTLEY CONTINENTAL PININFARINA

PRICE : Secondhand £2,750 ; New—£4,890 with tax £6,929

Petrol consumption	16-19 m.p.g.	*Date first registered*	3 June 1955
Oil consumption	140 m.p.pint	*Mileometer reading*	33,854

EVEN with a 10-year life behind it, the Continental version of a Bentley, with its much more modern-looking bodywork, can still command £1,000 more on the used car market than the concurrent R-type with standard steel body. The price of the car which forms the subject of this test, however, is almost as much again; it is believed to be the only Bentley Continental fitted with a two-seater fixed head body by Pininfarina.

Perhaps it may be on account of this scarcity value that the car has been meticulously maintained, and shows remarkably little evidence of its age. Its styling and condition throughout combine to make it very easy to pass the car off as being only three or four years old, whereas in fact the chassis was made in 1954, and it was not until the following year—perhaps after some motor show appearances—that the car was first registered in the U.K. It was made to special order for Rolls-Royce, on one of the first chassis produced with the then-new big engine, of 4¾-litres.

The golden-sand paintwork and impeccable chromium plate are almost entirely unblemished, as if the car had been driven straight from its show stand; and although revealing rather more signs of age and use, the maroon-finished

Ample carpeted space behind the seats supplements a small boot almost entirely occupied by the vast, covered spare wheel. Cold air vents have been taped up, perhaps because of draughts in winter, and somewhere under the facia there is a drip-leak in heavy rain

PERFORMANCE CHECK

Figures in brackets are those of the original Park Ward Continental Road Test, 21 December 1956)

0 to 30 m.p.h.	4·1 sec (4·3)	0 to 90 m.p.h.	31·0 sec (29·5)
0 to 40 m.p.h.	6·2 sec (—)	0 to 100 m.p.h.	42·7 sec (40·2)
0 to 50 m.p.h.	10·1 sec (9·3)		
0 to 60 m.p.h.	12·9 sec (12·9)	Standing quarter-mile 19·2 sec (18·8)	
0 to 70 m.p.h.	17·0 sec (17·1)	20 to 40 m.p.h. (top gear) 8·2 sec (—)	
0 to 80 m.p.h.	23·9 sec (21·3)	30 to 50 m.p.h. (top gear) 7·4 sec (—)	

Car for sale at: Offord and Sons Ltd., 154 Gloucester Road, London, S.W.7. Telephone: FREmantle 3388.

interior is also exceptionally clean and well-preserved. A strikingly modern appearance is given the car by its plain, leather-covered facia, but there is the odd contrast of the rather early Bentley instruments and minor controls scattered in a somewhat random way across the panel. Only the very cheap-looking painted metal surround of the windscreen is out of character with the lavish impression given by the interior trim.

A 6-cylinder engine of 4,887 c.c. with overhead inlet and side exhaust valves delivers its power exceptionally smoothly and quietly, accompanied by a mild crackle from the exhaust. It has the characteristic long-stroke impression of being reluctant to rev. fast. When taken up to 4,000 r.p.m. it begins to sound rather busy, but pulls extremely well, and belies its age with a rest to 100 m.p.h. acceleration time of only 42·7 sec. A more gentle touch brings out the superb Bentley refinements and effortless travel, and although at the 4,300 r.p.m. limit the high gearing and close-ratio gearbox allow over 70 m.p.h. in second gear, and up to 100 m.p.h. in third, it is more usual to slip into the next higher ratio at about 2,500 r.p.m.

Another oddity of this special model is that the gearchange linkage is modified to put the lever in the centre, instead of the classic right-hand change position. It still slips through from one gear to the next with delightful ease and precision, and the synchromesh remains thoroughly effective. The only faults which indicate a reasonable degree of wear are fairly pronounced whine in the indirect gears, and general transmission looseness shown up by a tendency to snatch at low speeds. There were some hot engine smells after a spell of 90 m.p.h. cruising, though the temperature gauge remained unshaken from its 85 deg. C. reading. The engine starts reliably, even if sometimes several turns on the starter are needed; and the automatic choke is working perfectly.

Clutch take-up is pleasantly smooth, and the pedal pressure is unexpectedly light, considering the amount of torque which the clutch has to transmit.

Only the brakes call for attention. The handbrake, with its umbrella handle under the facia, is very effective and holds securely on a steep gradient, but although the footbrake gives reasonable bite at speed, the response is not what it should be for a Bentley—even one of this age. Hard braking from high speeds brings a pungent smell from the linings, suggesting that fade would follow if the process were repeated too frequently. Delayed braking in reverse is a familiar weakness of this mechanical servo system.

No extras of any kind have been added to the car, but the equipment includes most of comfort's necessities such as a heater, a rather weak demister with outlets to the rear window, a clock and a windscreen washer. Only one of the two fog lamps is working, otherwise everything is in sound order. All tools, including a fine, fitted tray in the luggage locker, and the handbook and five near-new tyres (Firestones on the road, India on the spare) come with the car.

Appreciation of the comfort of the Bentley's ride, which really does respond to the ride control on the steering column, and enjoyment of its swift and deceptively effortless performance, remind one how very far ahead of its rivals the Continental was 10 years ago; and this example is still an admirable car today. As to its bodywork, with only two seats and a ridiculously small boot in so vast a car, it is an attractive extravagance, intriguing to many who want a really exclusive car.

REFINEMENTS

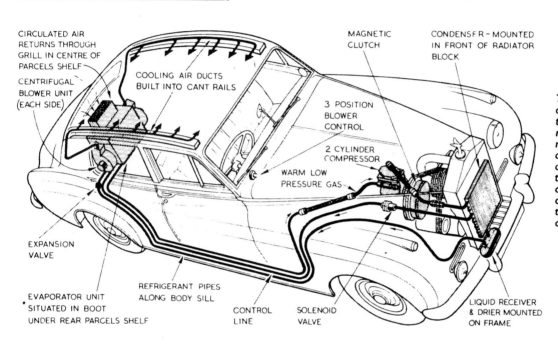

CIRCULATED AIR
RETURNS THROUGH
GRILL IN CENTRE OF
PARCELS SHELF

CENTRIFUGAL
BLOWER UNIT
(EACH SIDE)

COOLING AIR DUCTS
BUILT INTO CANT RAILS

MAGNETIC
CLUTCH

CONDENSER – MOUNTED
IN FRONT OF RADIATOR
BLOCK

3 POSITION
BLOWER
CONTROL

2 CYLINDER
COMPRESSOR

WARM LOW
PRESSURE GAS

EXPANSION
VALVE

EVAPORATOR UNIT
SITUATED IN BOOT
UNDER REAR PARCELS SHELF

REFRIGERANT PIPES
ALONG BODY SILL

CONTROL
LINE

SOLENOID
VALVE

LIQUID RECEIVER
& DRIER MOUNTED
ON FRAME

The cooling air of the conditioning unit is circulated through ducts built into the roof cant rails. Under maximum operating conditions the engine-driven compressor of the refrigeration system requires 5 h.p. to drive it. With the air-conditioning system inoperative, the compressor is disconnected by means of the magnetic clutch

AIR CONDITIONING AND POWER-ASSISTED STEERING FOR EXPORT ROLLS-ROYCE AND BENTLEY : INCREASED POWER FOR CONTINENTAL

WITH a large proportion of the Rolls-Royce and Bentley production sold in overseas markets, most of them crossing the Atlantic, it is not surprising that air conditioning and power assistance for the steering are to be made available. The air conditioning system is available as an optional extra on the Rolls-Royce Silver Cloud and Silver Wraith, and on the S series Bentley. Similarly, power-assisted steering is available as an export optional extra on all these models, but also can be supplied on any Silver Wraith chassis sold in the United Kingdom. The complete refrigeration plant for the air conditioning unit is imported from the U.S.A. On the Bentley Continental, for which increased engine power is now provided, only the power-assisted steering is available as an optional export extra.

The air conditioning or refrigerator unit works on the vapour cycle system, which uses a straightforward series layout of compressor, condenser and evaporator. The gaseous cooling medium (Freon 12) is quite harmless and practically non-toxic, though it requires a few simple precautions to guard against a higher-leak tendency than those of most other refrigerants.

It is not necessary for the refrigeration plant to provide a large drop of air temperature. In countries where the system is needed, the occupants of the car usually dress according to the climate—the ladies wear light filmsy dresses and the men cool linen suits, often without jackets. Investigation has shown that the inside air temperature of a car tends to run about 10 deg F higher than ambient. Thus, if the outside air temperature is between 78 and 82 deg F the comfortable inside temperature is around 68 deg F. The worst conditions are when a car is left standing in the sun with all doors and windows closed. Even under these circumstances, if the engine is running at fast idle, the inside temperature can be reduced to the normal operating range within three minutes with the blower control set in its high position. The air is changed at a rate of 300 cu ft per minute at this setting, which gives a complete change of the inside air every 1½ minutes.

On switching on the refrigeration unit, the engine is automatically set to fast idle, to prevent the engine from stalling, due to the power required to drive the compressor. Maximum refrigeration rate is reached at a road speed of 30 m.p.h.

The cycle of operations in the refrigera-

tion begins with the compressor inlet valve, through which the vapour enters at a relatively low temperature and pressure. On the down-stroke of the compressor piston the automatic suction valve is opened by the pressure differential, and vapour enters the cylinder. On the up-stroke the suction valve closes and the vapour is compressed until it opens the discharge valve, so that the high pressure refrigerant is forced into the condenser. Here the heat of compression and the heat absorbed by the refrigerant in the cooling coil is imparted to the air flowing over the tubes, and the refrigerant liquifies.

The liquid refrigerant next flows into the receiver, which acts as a storage tank and contains a strainer-drier to remove dirt and moisture. Still in a liquid state, the refrigerant enters the expansion valve, the function of which is to meter the flow to the evaporator by throttling it, so that some of the refrigerant flashes into vapour. The remaining liquid is cooled down to saturation temperature at the expansion valve outlet. This valve is also the dividing point between the high and low pressure and temperature sides of the system. No adjustment of the valve is provided, and it will maintain superheat from −30 deg F to +50 deg F.

Among the outstanding features of the chassis is the box section frame, cross braced for stiffness. There are two completely independent braking systems, each having a separate reservoir of transparent plastic for immediate visual check of fluid level.

FROM CREWE

Steering power assistance is obtained by a slight initial axial movement of the worm, which circulates the oil under pressure from the pump to a chassis-mounted actuating cylinder

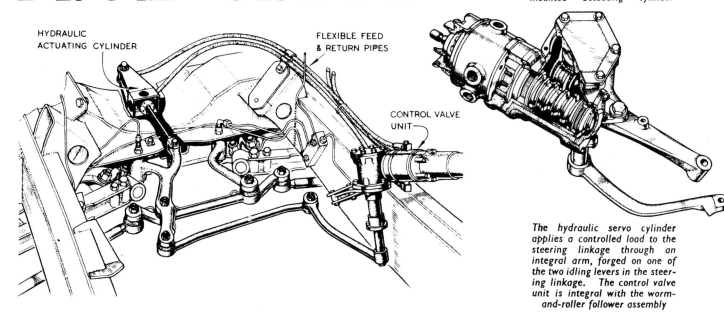

HYDRAULIC ACTUATING CYLINDER

FLEXIBLE FEED & RETURN PIPES

CONTROL VALVE UNIT

The hydraulic servo cylinder applies a controlled load to the steering linkage through an integral arm, forged on one of the two idling levers in the steering linkage. The control valve unit is integral with the worm-and-roller follower assembly

The liquid and vapour next enter the cooling coil of the evaporator unit, where the remaining liquid evaporates, absorbing heat from the air blown through it from the inside of the car. This is the refrigeration stage, in which the air is cooled by the latent heat of vaporization of the refrigerant in the coil. The completely vaporized refrigerant is finally drawn back to the compressor.

Triple wedge-type vee-belts from the crankshaft pulley drive the dynamo and fan pulley on the water pump shaft. The fan pulley has three additional grooves, two for the compressor drive and one for the power steering pump when fitted. A two-cylinder reciprocating type compressor with its own lubrication system is used. The suction and exhaust valves are of reed type, discharging through a common valve plate located between the block and head.

A magnetic clutch is provided in the compressor drive pulley, with a spring-

The two-cylinder compressor of the refrigeration system is belt-driven from the fan pulley. Great attention has been paid to the installation and fittings of the refrigerant pipes to eliminate possible leaks. The hydraulic circuit of the power-assisted steering has its own self-contained oil and filtration system

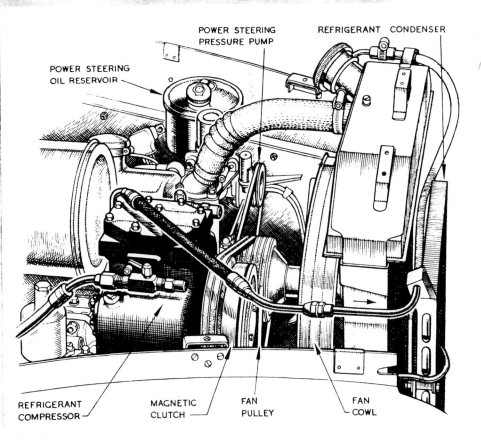

POWER STEERING PRESSURE PUMP

REFRIGERANT CONDENSER

POWER STEERING OIL RESERVOIR

REFRIGERANT COMPRESSOR

MAGNETIC CLUTCH

FAN PULLEY

FAN COWL

An example of the specialist coachwork fitted to the Bentley Continental chassis is this elegant two-door sports saloon by Park Ward. Engine power has been increased to enhance the already outstanding performance

Refinements from Crewe...

loaded drive plate attached to the compressor crankshaft. When the electromagnetic coil (mounted in the pulley) is not energized, the pulley assembly freewheels on a double roller ball bearing. With the car blower control switched on and the electromagnet simultaneously energized, the drive plate is attracted to the pulley and the compressor brought into action.

The condenser unit, made of finned tubes for rapid heat dissipation, is located in front of the engine radiator block to take maximum advantage of ram effect. For low road speed conditions, the engine fan has been increased in capacity and provided with a cowl. Housed under the parcel shelf in the luggage boot, the evaporator unit contains the twin air blowers and has a substantial filter.

The solenoid valve is fitted in a by-pass line between the pressure side of the compressor and the inlet of the evaporator. It controls the flow of gaseous refrigerant in the by-pass, and mixes it with liquid refrigerant from the expansion valve; the proportion of mixing regulates the degree of cooling imparted to the air in the car. The blower speed and temperature control switch is an integral unit, mounted on the dash; switching on energizes the magnetic clutch and the solenoid valve.

Power-assisted Steering

True hydraulic power assistance, as distinct from power operation, is achieved in the Rolls-Royce designed steering mechanism. It does not become operative until the driver applies one pound

of turning effort to the rim of the steering wheel; thereafter equal assistance is provided, i.e., for each pound of driver effort there is one pound of assistance. This ratio obtains until the driver exerts about 8 lb, after which an increased rate of assistance is provided. Under parking conditions with little or no motion of the road wheels, it might be necessary to exert a maximum rim effort of 12 lb which would not tax the frailest of drivers. The important feature of the Rolls-Royce system is that the driver retains a desirable degree of feel, even when motoring on ice or mud.

With power assistance, higher-geared steering is used with a steering box ratio of 18.7 to 1—the unaided manual ratio is 20.6 to 1.

Hydraulic pressure is supplied by a Hoborn-Eaton pump driven by a single wedge belt from the fan pulley, and it has its own built-in filter. There is a separate oil tank for the system, and when the engine is running 1¼ gallons of oil circulate continuously. With no steering wheel movement, this flow is by-passed through the control valve system.

The control valve assembly is mounted in tandem with a Marles hour-glass worm-and-roller follower. When the steering wheel is turned, resistance is met by the worm which is displaced axially (the movement is .008 to .010in), permitting the oil to flow through the distributor to the actuating ram which is mounted on the chassis and connected to one of the centre track rod idling levers. The hydraulic ram is mounted on a single pivot point to accommodate the small arcuate movement of its geometry.

The valves in the control unit are deliberately set to operate at high loads, so that they are not sensitive to any dirt which may escape the pump filters. A piston attached to the worm shaft presses

on a valve plate through a series of springs and plungers. These springs control the steering wheel rim load at which assistance becomes operative. Oil pressure on the valve from the piston thrust load tends to centre the valve plate and maintains feel in the steering.

Should the hydraulic assistance system fail, mechanical connection is still retained, with a slight increase in back lash at the steering wheel. This results from the 0.008 to 0.010in axial movement built into the worm to operate the hydraulic control valve. A safety valve in the circuit automatically cuts out the servo should the wheel be turned against a kerb or similar obstacle.

Continental Power

Power output has been increased on the Bentley Continental engine for this year. It is not the policy of Rolls-Royce to publish engine output figures, but the modifications have provided an increase of 13 per cent over previous power. The compression ratio has been increased to 8 to 1 (previously 7.25 to 1) and the inlet valve heads are larger. The twin S.U. diaphragm-type carburettors now have 2in diameter throats, instead of the 1¾in diameter on the earlier engines.

There are no changes in the Rolls-Royce Silver Cloud this year, but the six-cylinder engine of the Silver Wraith is now equipped with twin S.U. carburettors to improve engine breathing.

The bodies for the Silver Cloud and "S" Series Bentley are assembled at the Crewe factory of the Rolls-Royce Company from individual pressings and sub-assemblies supplied by the Pressed Steel Company of Oxford. In each range, specialist coachwork is available from H. J. Mulliner, Park Ward, James Young, Hooper, and Freestone and Webb.

BENTLEY S
CONTINENTAL
Park Ward
Drop-Head Coupé

No. 1619

The Autocar
ROAD
TESTS

In this drop-head version the Continental retains the sleek lines which tend to make the car seem smaller than it is. Lack of applied ornamentation is characteristic of this coachbuilder

IN its latest form the Continental Bentley is based on a modified Series S chassis and the engine also is basically similar to its Series S counterpart, but has larger valves and a much higher compression ratio to provide increased power output. (The b.h.p. is not quoted, in accordance with the long standing policy of the Rolls-Royce and Bentley companies.)

It is now four years since an earlier, pre-S-Series Continental Bentley with manual change was tested (*The Autocar*, September 12, 1952) but more recently we have been able to sample the actual Park Ward car now tried, in 1955 Continental form, before the improved 1956 engine and transmission had been installed.

The 1952 car was fitted with aerodynamic saloon coachwork, while the car now reviewed has a drop-head body: this may explain why the acceleration at high speed was found to be slightly less in this latest test, although in the lower ranges the new car is even more lively than its predecessors.

For a basic price approaching £5,000 the owner expects quality, and every design detail and fitting comes under the scrutiny of an unusually critical eye. From such meticulous examination the Bentley emerges with credit, but not entirely without grounds for criticism. And, having weighed up all the factors that make motoring safe, comfortable and fast it may be claimed without reservation that this Continental is unsurpassed among the world's currently produced cars.

This road test is mainly concerned with chassis and engine, for the coachwork and equipment would usually be produced to individual order and specification.

In the United Kingdom the model is not judged in its best environment, as its unusually high-speed cruising capabilities are limited by road and traffic conditions. Responsibility for such a luxurious and deceptively large car is heavy when manoeuvring in narrow, congested streets. Even so, its silence and lush comfort, and the ability to cover long distances at very high average speeds with a minimum of driver fatigue, cannot fail to impress. On the Continent, where much of the testing took place, enormous respect is won for the utterly effortless cruising at speeds of 100 m.p.h. or even more, in which circumstances peace of mind is provided by the precision response to brakes and steering, backed by stability at high speed on almost any surface.

Accepting then that luxury, silence and unrivalled quality are a *sine qua non* in Rolls-Royce and Bentley cars, the special interest of the Continental is in its performance. The sheer acceleration, measured by stop watch, is of a standard achieved only by a select class of sports cars, and a few transatlantic saloons in which the power is best used only on modern motorways. In spite of some drag from the drop-head coachwork, 120 m.p.h. can be obtained and used in safety on roads open to other traffic. On *autoroute* cruising, a speed of 100 m.p.h. is reached from a standstill in 40.2 sec, and 80 m.p.h., which may frequently be used for cruising with this car in England, is attained in 21.3 sec. All these figures, and the remainder quoted in the data table, were obtained with the transmission selector in the fully automatic position.

There is inevitably more wind noise from convertible body shapes than from a saloon, but the excellent fit of the hood helps to keep the noise level low when the windows are closed. Certainly one may listen to the radio or converse in normal tones at any speed.

This absence of fuss from wind or engine, while in itself admirable, may also mislead the driver unaccustomed to travelling at very high speed in relaxed comfort. Complete concentration is required consciously rather than instinctively to prevent a situation arising in which use even

There is a single, very wide door on each side, and at the rear the flashing indicators and reflectors are separate from the tail and braking lamps. Strong, deep overriders provide substantial protection

Above left and right: Armrests are fitted on the doors and beside the rear seat. The backrests of the front seats are adjustable for rake. Ease of entry is satisfactory for this type of coachwork and the floor is almost flat

Left : The purity of the lines, which include delicately finned rear wings, is unspoilt when the hood is down. The beautifully hung but heavy doors need more substantial open stops

of the finest controls is insufficient for the demands of safety. Although not unique in the history of our Road Tests, a *warning* concerning a car's excellence is rare. Yet it has to be recorded, just as it is passed from the manufacturer to each customer. Here "criticism" is probably the highest praise that a model can win.

None but the irresponsible would drive at very high speed if conditions were such that a sudden swerve might be required, yet even on the finest motorways the emergency can occur, and it is the car that has the reserves to cope with such a situation that earns the greatest respect. The S Continental is such a car.

The lightness of the steering is remarkable, achieved as it is with sufficiently high gearing for small movements of the wheel to have immediate effect on direction. Only in car park manœuvring is the steering heavy; from little more

than a walking pace it lightens until a touch alone is required, even though no power assistance is provided. Self-centring is positive and the driver receives plenty of information from the front wheels. The transmission of road surface feel through steering is welcome up to a point; on the long straights the Bentley provides just the right amount, but the return was considered to be excessive when cornering on a poor surface, severe shocks sometimes being transmitted through the steering wheel.

The simple, black steering wheel is of rather old-fashioned pattern and dimensions. A slightly smaller wheel would probably be preferred currently by the majority of drivers and, in the Continental, would slightly improve the forward visibility for a short driver. As the steering column holds the transmission selector, there is no telescopic adjustment for the wheel. The absence of adjustment, taken in conjunction with the lavish wrap-round support of the seat-back, means that unless the driver has longish legs he must sit close to the wheel and place his hands high if elbow movement is not to be restricted when cornering.

The suspension in itself calls for no adverse criticism, although the reaction from the wheels when the tyres are inflated to 35 lb front and 40 lb rear for sustained, very high speed provokes some rattles in the drop-head coachwork. In normal fast motoring on the Continent passengers do not enjoy quite the comfort that they might expect when, on the sort of marathon run made possible by this type of car, poor surfaces are encountered. A virtue of the car is that pronounced curves may be entered at 100 m.p.h. or more without concern, always assuming that traffic conditions are favourable. What other really big cars are there, one may well ask, that can be held confidently at such speed through sweeping curves with complete retention of stability and control?

When put to the test through a series of S-bends on a narrow road, the Continental suspension responds extra-ordinarily well for such a large car. Tyre noise is virtually nil unless the car is going so fast as to start sliding, and if this occurs the car remains stable without marked tendency to over- or understeer, although it is desirable to help the car round corners with the throttle pedal in extreme conditions. On the steering column is a switch

The facia is of walnut, and the overriding manual control for the automatic transmission is mounted on the steering column, with the speedometer and rev counter on the left and right of the column respectively. A wide ashtray drawer cum table is fitted centrally under the radio. Bonnet-locking levers may be seen below the facia on each side of the scuttle

The shape of the locker is irregular, but the carrying capacity is deceptively large, particularly if soft or fitted bags are used. Larger tools are contained in the floor under a lid beside the spare wheel cover. The black bag houses the tonneau cover. The lid is spring loaded

that remains perfectly taut at any speed, and that can be folded down in a moment and quickly concealed with a cover that fits well, without being so tight as to be difficult to fasten. There is a special bag for the cover in the luggage locker. With the hood down, wind protection—particularly for rear passengers—naturally is limited. On such a chassis there would be little difficulty in providing plenty of passenger space, but for reasons of appearance and character this model has been designed as a close-coupled model, with limited leg room for the rear passengers, who otherwise are provided with every luxury. The driving position is quite good, and it is an advantage that the backrests of the front seats are easily adjustable for rake. The seats have fore and aft adjustment, but none vertically. Both front wings can be seen, and the rear view is satisfactory. The rear quarters of the hood make vision difficult when the car has to be moved away from the kerb or filtered across a diagonally opposing stream of traffic.

Instrumentation is appropriate to a car of this type, but the water temperature gauge and the upper range of the rev counter are obscured by the transmission selector unless the driver leans forward. The range of instruments and accessories includes clock, lighter, wipers with screen washer control incorporated, two-brilliance panel light, speedometer with trip and total mileage recorders, oil pressure

which provides a normal or hard setting for the rear spring dampers. In normal driving, movement of the switch does not have a pronounced effect, although the ride is just a little softer with the switch at N. In the H position, however, there is a firm limitation of roll.

The mechanical servo brakes used on all Bentley and Rolls-Royce models have become a byword for sustained efficiency. Even during prolonged testing there was no fade, the formidable braking power remaining fully available in response to a really light pedal pressure. When it is realized that the energy which must be "lost" in bringing the car consistently to rest from 100 m.p.h. is equivalent to that required to lift about 115 tons ten feet from the ground, and that the Bentley will keep up this performance without deterioration, it can be understood why these brakes are so highly regarded.

On this particular car there was a slight movement to the left if the wheels were permitted to lock, and an occasional squeak when the brakes were very hot. In normal driving neither of these phenomena is likely to be encountered. The handbrake has a pull-out control under the facia. It works effectively but may be left partly engaged as the driver moves off, unless released with care.

The transmission system provides the best of two worlds. There is no clutch pedal, and with the selector in position 4, gear changing is fully automatic according to speed and load. In position 3, the car is held in first, second or third gears, again according to speed and load, and in position 2 second is retained. Thus the selector may be used to provide a clutchless, manual change, or a fully automatic change, or simply to retain a low ratio for long descents.

In practice the selector spends most of its time in position 4, but it should be used when required to give an instant change down into third (or even second if the driver is really "trying" on tortuous hills). If the selector is not used to change down, opening the throttle wide at speeds of under 80 m.p.h. will bring in third. Second gear will not engage on kick-down at speeds above about 30, and the maximum in this gear is only 39 m.p.h. unless the selector is moved to position 2, in which case the maximum may be increased to 46. When the automatic box is thoroughly hot, the kick-down is not always so readily obtained. It was felt during the test, particularly in English conditions, that a higher second would be desirable. This would also reduced jerk on kick-down.

The third ratio earns full marks, and on the Continent the ability readily to flick the lever into 3, at speeds between perhaps 50 and 75, helps greatly in maintaining very high average speeds, by providing immediate increase in acceleration or engine braking.

Park Ward have produced this drop-head with a hood

Water and oil fillers, distributor, sparking plugs and carburettors are all easily reached. Accessibility of the engine as a whole is of little account, few owners being likely to work on it without expert assistance. The unit is extraordinarily clean and free from oil

gauge, fuel and oil level gauge, ammeter, radio and heater fitted as standard. In some respects the radio falls short of the standard of those fitted in luxury Continental and American cars, which suggests either that the best coach-builders or the chassis manufacturers should demand a more ambitious specification, or that a better set should be made available in any case by one or more of the radio concerns for cars in which cost is of secondary importance to quality. The heater controls are elaborate, but correct use of them results in very efficient heat and fresh air distribution which could be improved only by a better supply of warmth to the rear passengers' feet.

Armrests on the front doors are adjustable, while those at the rear are fixed; there are twin fog lamps but they are not ideal, for in fog the spread of light is not of sufficiently precise outline. The head lamps are reasonably good in the main beam position, but the cut-off, when dipped, permits no more than a crawl in safety.

An exceptionally good handbook is provided, and when, for example, two fuses blew during the test it was found that the handbook indicated their location and precise functions in the simplest way. The fuses themselves proved characteristic of the attention to detail noted everywhere. They appear at first to be of old-fashioned design, repairable with bare fuse wire, yet, in conjunction with the bobbin of spare wire in the box, replacement proves very easy.

A day spent at the wheel of the Continental can result in a mileage being covered that is in itself an achievement. Yet, at the end of the day the driver looks forward to the morrow rather than to his rest.

An appreciation of the car on a fast drive to the Pyrenees and back will appear in a subsequent issue.

BENTLEY S CONTINENTAL PARK WARD DROP-HEAD COUPÉ

WHEELBASE	10' 3"
FRONT TRACK	4' 10"
REAR TRACK	5' 0"
OVERALL LENGTH	17' 6½"
OVERALL WIDTH	6' 0"
OVERALL HEIGHT	5' 2½"

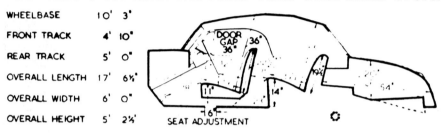

SEAT ADJUSTMENT

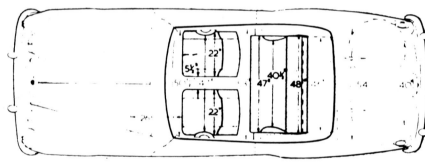

Measurements in these ¼in to 1ft scale body diagrams are taken with the driving seat in the central position of fore and aft adjustment and with the seat cushions uncompressed

DATA

PRICE (basic), with drop-head coupé body, £4,775.
British purchase tax, £2,388 17s.
Total (in Great Britain), £7,163 17s.

ENGINE: Capacity: 4,887 c.c. (298 cu in).
Number of cylinders: 6.
Bore and stroke: 95.25 × 114.30 mm (3¾ × 4½in).
Valve gear: o.h.i.-s.v.c.
Compression ratio: 8 to 1.
M.P.H. per 1,000 r.p.m. on top gear, 28.4.

WEIGHT: (with 5 gals. fuel), 35½ cwt (3,976 lb).
Weight distribution (per cent): F, 50.7; R, 49.3.
Laden as tested: 38½ cwt (4,312 lb).
Lb per c.c. (laden): 0.9.

BRAKES: Type: Bentley.
Method of operation: Hydro-mechanical, servo-assisted.
Drum dimensions: F, 11.25in diameter; 3.0in wide. R, 11.25in diameter; 3.0in wide.
Lining area: F, 212 sq in. R, 212 sq in (220.3 sq in per ton laden).

TYRES: 7.60—15in.
Pressures (lb per sq in): F, 27; R, 30 (normal). F, 30; R, 35 (for fast driving).

TANK CAPACITY: 18 Imperial gallons.
Oil sump, 16 pints.
Cooling system, 27 pints.

TURNING CIRCLE: 41ft 8in (L and R).
Steering wheel turns (lock to lock): 4¼.

DIMENSIONS: Wheelbase 10ft 3in.
Track: F, 4ft 10in; R, 5ft.
Length (overall): 17ft 6½in.
Height: 5ft 2½in.
Width: 6ft 0in.
Ground clearance: 7in.

ELECTRICAL SYSTEM: 12-volt; 57 ampere-hour battery. Head lights: Double dip; 42-watt bulbs.

SUSPENSION: Front, Independent, coil springs. Rear, Semi-elliptic. Anti-roll bar position front and rear.

PERFORMANCE

ACCELERATION: from constant speeds.
Speed Range, *Gear Ratios and Time in sec.

M.P.H.	4 range
10—30	2.9
20—40	4.0
30—50	5.2
40—60	6.6
50—70	7.3
60—80	8.4
70—90	12.2
80—100	17.9

From rest through gears to:

M.P.H.	sec.
30	4.3
50	9.3
60	12.9
70	17.1
80	21.3
90	29.5
100	40.2
110	51.8

*Gear ratios 2.92, 4.25, 7.69 and 11.17 to 1.
Standing quarter mile, 18.8 sec.

SPEEDS ON GEARS:

Gear		M.P.H. (max.)	K.P.H. (max.)
Top	(mean)	119.2	191.9
	(best)	120.5	193.9
3rd		79.0	127.1
2nd		39.0	62.8
1st		22.0	35.4

SPEEDOMETER CORRECTION: M.P.H.

Car speedometer	10	20	30	40	50	60	70	80	90	100	110	120
True speed	10	20	30	40	49	58	68	78	86	97	106	118

(At 4,250 r.p.m., gears retained manually, second 46 m.p.h., and third 82 m.p.h.)

TRACTIVE RESISTANCE: 19 lb per ton at 10 M.P.H.

TRACTIVE EFFORT:

	Pull (lb per ton)	Equivalent Gradient
Top	172	1 in 12.9
Third	339	1 in 6.5
Second	557	1 in 3.6

BRAKES:

Efficiency	Pedal Pressure (lb)
41.8 per cent	25
80.75 per cent	50

FUEL CONSUMPTION:
15.2 m.p.g. overall for 360 miles (18.5 litres per 100 km.).
Approximate normal range 14—18 m.p.g. (20.2-15.7 litres per 100 km).
Fuel, Premium grade.

WEATHER: Dry, slight breeze.
Air temperature, 50 deg. F.
Acceleration figures are the means of several runs in opposite directions.
Tractive effort and resistance by obtained Tapley meter.
Model described in *The Autocar* of February 29, 1952.

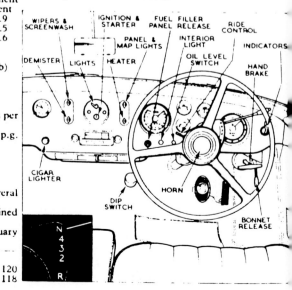

Flying Spur

HIGH PERFORMANCE FOUR-DOOR BENTLEY BY H. J. MULLINER

LUXURIOUS appointments and low weight do not generally go together. The high performance version of the Bentley—the Continental—has hitherto been fitted with two-door coachwork either by H. J. Mulliner or by Park Ward, since it is simpler to keep weight down with such a body and to achieve a sporting appearance, while still maintaining the traditional standards of equipment and finish.

The saloons by these two coachbuilders on the Continental chassis weigh some 4cwt less than the standard S-series Bentley with steel four-door body. The use of light alloy for framework and aluminium for panelling accounts for much of this saving. Now H. J. Mulliner have broken fresh ground with a four-door body on a chassis to Continental specification. In spite of an increase in passenger-carrying space, and the addition of centre pillars with extra hinges, catches and window-winding mechanisms for the rear doors, the weight of the new model is about the same as that of their two-door car.

This has been achieved by improved design permitting reduced weight in the lower part of the body structure and in the construction of the seats, which have a thinner Dunlopillo overlay on a stronger seat case, although the exceptional comfort is undiminished.

Generally the design follows that of the two-door body, except for the step at the rear window which replaces the sweeping roof line. Overall height is the same for both cars, but in the new model there is greater head room for rear-seat passengers, who also have an extra 1½in of leg room.

Compared with the alternative body, there are subtle changes in the shapes of the front and rear wings. In plan they are narrower, but the wheel arches have been flared to retain the original width

Above: Although bearing a strong similarity in design to the two-door Continental, the new four-door Flying Spur has higher swage lines in the wings which lighten the appearance. Right: Increased head and leg room for rear seat passengers. The rear doors, although not particularly wide, give improved access compared with the existing body. Finish, appointments and comfort are at the usual high standard of this coachbuilder

locally for protection against mud thrown up by the tyres. The horizontal swage lines, curving around the arches, have been raised which, together with a lower crown to the front wings, has given a considerably lighter appearance to the sides of this car. Side lamps, blending with the crowns, are an aid in gauging the position of the wings—particularly the nearside one—from the driving seat. Each lamp has a miniature red rear-facing lens.

The panelling between front wing and bonnet has also been lowered to improve the airflow over the front of the body. This gives the impression that the radiator is higher, but in fact its level is unchanged.

Luggage accommodation is greater than in the two-door car, for the rearward slope of the upper surface of the locker containing the lid is less steep. The spare wheel remains in a horizontal position,

within its cover, at one side of the boot floor, but the compartments beside it for tools, jack and tyre pump have been removed. The tools, set in sponge rubber, are in a tray which slides under the front passenger's seat cushion, the jack is housed under the bonnet and the tyre pump is clipped to the off-side wall of the boot.

The seats in H. J. Mulliner bodies are particularly well designed for correct support, and there are deep rolls at all edges of cushions and squabs to hold the occupants in place against cornering forces. Separate folding armrests at the inside edge of each front seat on the two-door Continental have been changed to a single-armrest between the seats on the four-door car, and this may be folded down to a position flush with the cushions. It also hinges upwards to reveal a locker of useful size. The door rests are adjustable for height.

Each front seat has a knurled handle at the outer squab hinge to adjust the squab to any angle between an erect and a semi-reclining position.

This handsome addition to the number of bodies available on Bentley chassis is likely to appeal to those who, while desiring performance approaching Continental standards, would appreciate greater rear passenger accommodation and luggage space and easy, independent access to the rear seats. The penalty—if that is the term—is a slightly less sporting but perhaps more dignified appearance. The price is £5,355 basic, £8,033 17s including British purchase tax, or £5,465 and £8,198 17s respectively when power-assisted steering is fitted.

Skilful blending of curves is evident in profile. While appearing to be of increased overall length, the new model is, in fact, two inches shorter than the two-door version

179

Continental Bentley drophead coupé by Park Ward. The wing line is carried through from front to rear lamps and the radiator shell is canted forward slightly

Continental Bentleys: VEE-8 ENGINES,

NEW FRONT BRAKES AND A NEW PARK WARD DROPHEAD COUPÉ

•• •• •• •• •• ••

This rear view demonstrates how the new wing line gives an apparent reduction in overall height

Instruments are well placed in a cowling in front of the driver and top and bottom edges of the facia are padded

NEW Continental Bentley models have been announced, built by H. J. Mulliner and Park Ward, following the introduction of the new Rolls-Royce vee-8 engine described in last week's issue of *The Autocar.* Two of these are at the Paris Salon, opening today—the Mulliner two-door hardtop and the Park Ward drophead coupé.

Latest version of the H. J. Mulliner Flying Spur four-door Continental saloon is also to be seen for the first time in Paris, but in showrooms in the Avenue Kléber. This particular car is to special order, and already sold. Of aluminium construction, it is finished in black, with tan leather upholstery, and fitted with the latest full air-conditioning system with refrigeration unit.

A few detail changes in design have been made to the H. J.

Mulliner Continentals. The fins on the rear wings have disappeared, while the front wings, which formerly had a rather complicated lamp housing, are now of plain design. Owing to some minor chassis changes concerned with mounting the new engine, the radiator shell has been moved forward a little over 2in, and is also canted slightly forward. Most important change is that the spare wheel is now mounted in a tray below the floor of luggage compartment, increasing considerably the space available in the latter.

Emphasis on length and width, by using a continuous wing shape from front lamps to rear, is the main styling change in the Park, Ward drop head Continental. This makes the car look lower than its actual height of 5ft, and hints at an Italian influence, in the current fashion.

Glass area has been considerably increased, and a fully wrap-round windscreen is used. The radiator shell, compared with that of the standard S.2 saloon, is shorter vertically by 3in and is mounted lower, with its upper edge canted forward, front bumpers being raised to match with the bottom of the shell as formerly. A welded sheet steel body structure includes scuttle, floor, rear seat pan, boot floor and rear wing and quarter panels, other panels being in light alloy.

Passenger safety has been given special consideration in this latest coupé. Instruments and switches, grouped in front of the driver, are cowled to prevent windscreen reflections, and the facia is edged at top and bottom with leather-covered padded rolls which extend along the door cappings. Window handles are inset into the doors, and the front seat guide rails are protected by a special design of cushion, so that with the seats fully forward there is no danger of injury from the exposed rails.

All models are fitted with an improved type of ventilation system, with optional refrigeration unit for full air conditioning.

Mechanically, the most important change on the new Continental Bentleys is to the braking system.

Basically the braking system is as used on the S series chassis, but the front brakes are equipped with four shoes, or, more precisely, two half-shoes per main shoe, with drums 11.250in dia. and shoe lining width of 3in. The size is unchanged, but the new shoe arrangement increases the total lining area for the four brakes by 25 per cent from 240 to 300 sq in.

Front brakes, as previously, are of the two-trailing-shoe type, an arrangement which reduces the tendency to fade and yet is light in operation, because the system (which has a duplicated hydraulic circuit) is assisted by the gear box-driven mechanical servo linked to the master cylinder.

Safety padded rolls are carried on from the facia along the top of the body sides

The two main shoes are of normal pattern, and the half-portions which carry the riveted and bonded linings can pivot freely on them for self-alignment. The shoes are aluminium castings, and at the point where the two halves come together the metal portion forms a lap joint. Thus, although the half-shoes can pivot freely when the drum is removed, they have sufficient freedom only for self-alignment on the car. This arises from the fact that the Girling brakes are of the autostatic pattern, in which the shoe remains in constant light contact with the drum.

In addition to the increased lining area achieved, which alone will improve life, the self-compensating action eliminates the tendency for the lining to wear more severely at one end. Furthermore, the pressures around the drum periphery are equalized, which should result in smoother, action, more even and therefore lower operating temperature, all of which substantiate the manufacturer's claim of greater efficiency and longer life.

New four-shoe front brakes on the Continental; they are self-adjusting for wear. Also seen are the new forged wishbones fitted to all Rolls-Royce and Bentley S series chassis this year

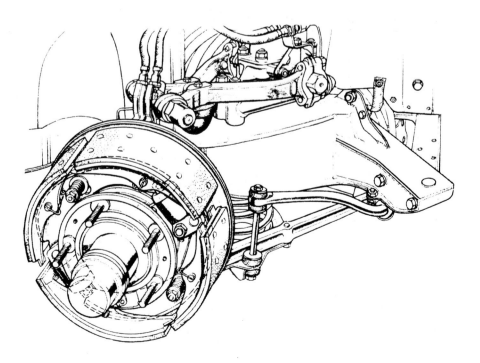

1802

BENTLEY S2 Continental

The radiator shell of the Continental Bentley leans forward slightly, and is 2·35 in. lower and 3in. farther forward than that of the S2. Scuttle height is 2in. lower. Badges and number plate on this car are, of course, special for the owner

VERY seldom indeed has a privately owned car been offered and accepted by *The Autocar* for full road test, but since Bentley Continentals are built only to order in very small numbers, and the waiting list is long, an exception has been made in this case. The car is the property of Jack Barclay—hence the registration JB 1—and Bentley Motors have checked the car and given their approval to the test.

S2 Continental Bentleys are not available with other than specialist coachwork. The chassis is very similar to that of the short wheelbase S2 Bentley, but there are optional final drive ratios, a slightly higher geared one being offered to give 28·4 m.p.h. per thousand r.p.m. in top gear instead of 27·0 m.p.h. However, the car tested retained the standard Bentley ratio, which is the lower of the two available.

All Bentleys have automatic transmissions. In addition, the Continentals have special Rolls-Royce Girling drum brakes, those in front being of four-shoe design. Continentals are also fitted with 8·00×15in tyres in place of 8·20×15 on standard models. The engine is the Rolls-Royce aluminium vee-8, fully described in *The Autocar* of 25 September 1959.

A light alloy four-door body, designed and built by James Young Ltd., of Bromley, Kent, is fitted to the test car; its lavish equipment is included in the model price quoted; only the white-wall tyres are extras.

In subtle ways, difficult to identify, this Continental is pleasanter to drive than the Rolls-Royce Silver Cloud tested last May. In particular, after an hour or two of familiarization, it gives the impression of being one of the smallest and most handleable large cars we have ever driven. As tested, it is only a matter of pounds lighter that the Silver Cloud and S2 Bentley, so the weight cannot have a significant effect. Part of the answer lies in the rather greater quietness and smoothness of the engine, perhaps resulting from more effective body sound damping materials.

Regarding the type of automatic transmission fitted, it should be sufficient to remind readers that its design is of American origin and that it comprises basically a fluid coupling and trains of epicyclic gears. The selector quadrant allows, in addition to fully automatic operation in position 4, 3rd to be held up to the maximum permissible speed in that ratio, and 2nd to be held for ascending or descending long and steep hills.

Engine braking is slight in top but more pronounced in 3rd. On this car, the adjustment is such as to make kickdown into 3rd quite reluctant unless the accelerator is fully depressed. Kickdown into 2nd, a marked change in ratio, also calls for full depression and does not occur above about 22 m.p.h. This is not altogether convenient in some circumstances; for example, when commencing an ascent immediately after a sharp turn. There is then an accompanying jerk and some engine roar. For this reason, the instruction manual recommends down changes into 2nd only on a light throttle. Maximum speed in 2nd is approximately 50 m.p.h., and there is no guard to prevent over-speeding of the engine, if 2nd hold is selected. Upward changes from 2nd to 3rd occur at a maximum of about 40 m.p.h. in the automatic range.

A great deal of torque is produced at low r.p.m. by the vee-8 engine and 3rd gear engages very sweetly if the lever is lightly flicked into position 3 on the quadrant. This seems to be the best technique for check braking into corners and

Of greater capacity than it appears, the boot, fore-shortened by the camera, is neatly trimmed. The spare wheel is under the floor

This Continental four-door has very pleasing lines, in no way interrupted by the sensibly massive bumper overriders. Note the small parking lamp provided on the centre door pillar

to obtain lively acceleration coming out. In all normal circumstances, out of town and city, driving is almost entirely in top gear.

Position R on the quadrant provides, in addition to reverse, a positive lock forward or backward for parking on an incline. In addition, if the car is stopped on a slope when in 4, another lock prevents it from rolling back.

Since the pressure lubrication system of the transmission depends on the rotation of the power input shaft, coasting in neutral must be avoided as must towing—other than for a very short distance for starting should the battery fail. For a tow-start Neutral is first selected and then at about 20 m.p.h. the lever is moved to position 4.

In spite of the size of the Bentley, the components and fittings are so numerous that there is little latitude in positioning the pedals or steering assemblies. This, no doubt, accounts in part for the steering column being angled slightly to the right, for the proximity of the two pedals and for the accelerator being placed close under the massive guide for the push-pull handbrake. The pedals themselves are small and of uneven height from the floor; the brake pedal cannot be operated conveniently by the left foot, and the welt of the driver's right shoe is apt to catch under it if a quick movement has to be made across from the lower-placed throttle pedal.

Exceptional Brakes

Few braking systems, disc or drum, are as effective as those of the Bentley, or give greater confidence. A mechanical servo giving instant response is provided, the hydraulic systems are duplicated for insurance against possible pipe fracture and the front drums have a special four-shoe arrangement as already mentioned. Frequent hard braking generated considerable heat but there was no fade and only a small increase in pedal effort. Check braking is always smooth, even and powerful in response to light pedal pressures; maximum retardation occurs at only 70lb pressure (the test track surface was damp at the time). When inching forward in a traffic stream there is negligible servo action, so the brake pedal must be pressed harder.

Bentley (and Rolls-Royce) steering is hydraulic power assisted. If the engine is stopped, and with it the power pump, the steering still operates quite normally, simply requiring more effort at the wheel. According to requirements, more or less power assistance is provided—the greatest amount for manoeuvrability at walking pace and the least when guiding the car at speed. Assistance is proportional to the effort of the steering wheel, which all makes for a very light-feeling and controllable car which may be thrown around like a small roadster should the driver so wish. Even if the tail is induced to slide, it does so progressively and predictably and may be checked at once. There is no impression of under- or oversteer, but the car corners more readily under power than on the overrun.

A slight shortcoming of the steering, which probably only a few owners would detect, may be noted when an unexpected demand is made on it. Examples of such circumstances during our test were correction at speed of the effect of a sudden cross-wind gust; steering the wheels out of tram tracks with which they coincided exactly in Sheffield and Glasgow; and holding course at certain times when

the road had heavy camber or an uneven pitching surface. In these rather extreme conditions our drivers found themselves correcting (or over-correcting) frequently and clumsily, and felt justified in blaming the car. For all normal driving the steering is exceptionally good. It is almost effortless, real feel is retained, yet road reaction at the steering wheel never exceeds a tickle in the drivers' palms. The thin-rimmed wheel itself is plain, slightly dished and of conveniently small diameter. In the large, almost flat boss is mounted the horn button.

With the exception of the slightly smaller section tyres, the Continental Bentley has no feature different from other models in the range which would affect the ride. A hard-soft switch controlling the rear hydraulic dampers is provided for suspension adjustments, and a distinctly firmer ride does follow the selection of Hard. This setting was found useful, in particular, for fast driving over the winding well-surfaced main roads of Scotland. With Soft selected the ride is still quite firm on this Bentley; there is practically no roll on corners, while vertical movements are damped out immediately.

Dunlop W.H.2 nylon tyres are fitted; they give good wet weather adhesion and are quiet and squeal-free. For maximum speeds tyre pressures were raised by 5 p.s.i. all round to 25 front and 30 rear.

Because the optional low-geared back axle was fitted to this car the maximum speed—a best figure of 114 m.p.h.—was not expected to be higher than those for the standard Bentley and Rolls-Royce. The overall fuel consumption figure for 1,440 miles—much of it fast driving—of 13.1 m.p.g., on the other hand, was particularly good. With a tank capacity of 18 gallons the green 3-gallon reserve tell-tale winked inconveniently often on long runs.

100 m.p.h. Cruising

On major roads, such as A1, the car cruised quietly and effortlessly between 90 and 100 m.p.h., and miles fell behind with remarkably little fatigue to the occupants. Engine noise was very slight indeed and the body was also silent, except for some wind roar which appeared to originate in the vicinity of the passenger's side screen pillar. The adjacent quarter light, which closed securely, was not the culprit.

At night the spread beams of the pass lamps proved to be very useful for showing up kerbs and obstructions in dimly lit residential areas, and in heavy traffic on the open roads. The main headlamps gave a powerful long-range beam, apparently of rather limited spread, since there were times when all four lamps would have been appreciated. The multiple light switch, however, does not permit this. On dipped headlamps, the cut-off is abrupt.

Workmanship of the highest order is seen in the James Young body and a minute search reveals nothing that is other than excellent. The fit and click-shut of the doors are a joy; the problems of body sealing have been mastered so that not a drop of water reached the interior during blinding rainstorms.

As already mentioned, the lavish equipment of the interior is almost all included in the price of the body, although this particular car had one or two personal extras, such as a pair of high-pitched wind horns and matching stop watch and chronometer on the panel. The normal Bentley radio had been replaced by a Motorola set (£7 for the change)

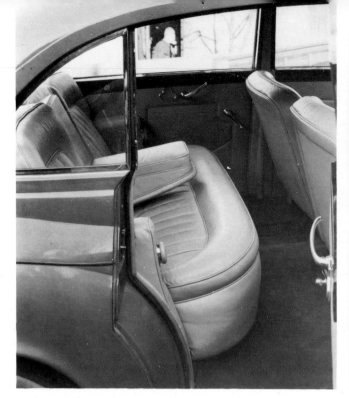

Exceptional quality of workmanship, as well as of materials, characterizes the luxurious interior of the James Young four-door body

which gave very pleasing reception through either front or rear speaker, or both together.

Only the front door windows are power operated on this car, but the two at the back may be, at an extra cost of £60. The rear window has built-in electric demisting which did not seem very effective; the quarter lights at the front swivel in response to small winders to give draught-free fresh air. Driving with main windows open is not pleasant because of air pulsation.

A very good view is obtained by all occupants and the well-curved (but not wrap-round) screen is plenty large enough, although it is not deep by the latest standards. The wipers are a little disappointing, both for the area they sweep and in the light blade pressures which do little to dispel screen smear. The rear view mirror, in conjunction with the wide rear window, gives an exceptionally clear view of following traffic.

Were we to order a car such as this Bentley, we should ask to have the main instrument dials turned through 180 deg, so that the most useful sector would appear at the top and so be easier to see at a glance. The r.p.m. dial on a car with automatic transmission is a traditional Continental feature of little value today. We should also ask for the subsidiary dials, particularly the fuel indicator, to register accurately in units, i.e., gallons, litres and degrees, rather than being marked only with sectors.

Among the luxuries of the Bentley are three cigar lighters —one in front and one at each side in the back—all accompanied by ashtrays. The front doors contain " pockets " with neat sliding doors, and there is a locker, with key, in the main panel.

On a car of this quality the driver's seat is usually made to suit the owner. The upholstery and soft leather covering are very comfortable indeed and the rake of the back rest, in addition to the fore and aft setting of the seat, can be adjusted with the aid of a knurled knob. Because of the attitude of the pedals, some drivers found that if the seat was set back for their comfort in relation to the steering wheel, its front edge roll supported their thighs too high. Between the front seats is a separate armrest, which swings up into position and contains another locker for small objects.

Heating, demisting and ventilation are provided by the basic dual system common to all the cars from Crewe, but no adjustable outlets are provided in the scuttle as there are in the case of, say, the Silver Cloud. For rear seat passengers, two ducts feed air from floor level beside the central

body pillars. The heating system of this car needed attention, both warmth and strength of air flow being below average. In the engine compartment are two three-way heater taps, marked for winter or summer operation, or cut-off.

Under the instrument panel are two switches, one of which selects either twin horns or headlamps for operation by the horn button; the other cuts out one of the horns for softer warning in towns. Also beneath the instrument panel is a socket for an inspection lamp or battery charger.

In addition to the seats, the doors and some panels are tastefully trimmed in light fawn leather. The floors have several layers of covering, topped at the back by a deep silk pile carpet and, in front, by reinforced carpets. The instrument panel and top, and window sills, are finished in fine walnut veneer. On its lower edge the panel has a padded leather roll to give protection to the front passenger, but at its upper edge there is a narrow lip of wood. The doors proper extend to waist level and above this the windows have slim metal frames. Wide access is given to the front seats; the rear door openings are more restricted. We should have expected both front doors to carry locks.

Few owners would find the capacity of the luggage boot inadequate; the floor area is considerable, although at the forward end the height is rather restricted. Under the boot floor, beneath a cover, is the spare wheel, and let in at the left side, a tray of tools. Wheel-changing equipment is also stowed here. The boot lid is balanced so that it is very easy to lift; like the doors, it clicks shut under gentle pressure. Master and limited keys are provided, the one operating all locks, the other ignition and door only.

Bentley owners will seldom attempt their own maintenance, but some of the recommendations are of interest.

Many will recognize the great cairn on Culloden Muir, near Inverness, the site of the famous battle of 1746. The white-wall tyres set the car off in the dull surroundings

Front suspension and steering needs greasing at intervals of only 10,000 miles, which to many owners means annually. At the rear, the assembly is lubricated for life, the grease packed springs being leather gaitered. The engine itself should be drained and refilled every 2,500 miles and the gearbox every 2,000 miles.

This must be one of the few remaining designs, the bonnet of which (with excellent latches) is divided and hinged down the centre line. The engine compartment is not very easy to get at and is filled to capacity. However, those few items which might need attention are placed where they can be reached immediately—fuses, carefully labelled in the box lid, high on the bulkhead; brake fluid reservoirs high on the driver's side; filler cap for the pressure cooling system (for which a spanner is provided) and sump dipstick on the passenger side.

Without doubt the Continental Bentley lives up to the traditional associations of its name: few cars would provide as rapid, restful and satisfying transport from, say, Paris to Nice. For owners who place special value on maximum speed, there is the alternative high-geared final drive, giving about 120 m.p.h. On arrival at its destination this potent vehicle at once reverts to the exceptionally docile and distinguished town carriage.

BENTLEY S2 CONTINENTAL FOUR-DOOR

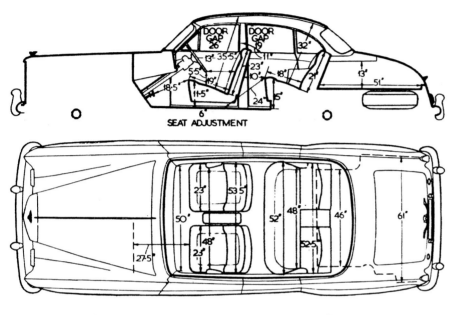

Scale ⅛in. to 1ft. Driving seat in central position. Cushion uncompressed.

SEAT ADJUSTMENT

------------ **PERFORMANCE** ------------

ACCELERATION TIMES (mean):

Speed range, Gear Ratios and Time in Sec.

m.p.h.	3·08 to 1	4·46 to 1	8·10 to 1	11·75 to 1
10—30	—	—	3·1	—
20—40	—	5·4	3·5	—
30—50	7·6	5·3	—	—
40—60	7·8	6·1	—	—
50—70	8·7	7·2	—	—
60—80	10·2	—	—	—
70—90	12·2	—	—	—
80—100	16·6	—	—	—

From rest through gears to:

30 m.p.h.	..	4·0 sec:
40 "	..	..	6·3 "
50 "	..	..	8·9 "
60 "	..	..	12·1 "
70 "	..	..	15·9 "
80 "	..	..	20·5 "
90 "	..	..	26·9 "
100 "	..	..	37·1 "

Standing quarter mile 18·6 sec.

MAXIMUM SPEEDS ON GEARS:

Gear		m.p.h.	k.p.h.
Top	.. (mean)	112·7	181·3
	(best)	114·5	184·2
3rd	.. .. ..	70	113
2nd	.. .. ..	50	80
1st	.. .. ..	21	34

TRACTIVE EFFORT (by Tapley meter):

		Pull (lb per ton)	Equivalent gradient
Top	..	310	1 in 7·1
Third	..	463	1 in 4·8
Second	..	636	1 in 3·4

SPEEDOMETER CORRECTION: m.p.h.

Car speedometer:	10	20	30	40	50	60	70	80	90	100	110	120
True speed:	10	20	30	39	48	57	66	74	82	90	98	108

BRAKES (at 30 m.p.h. in neutral):

Pedal load in lb	Retardation	Equiv. stopping distance in ft
25	20	151
50	63	48
70	90	33·6

FUEL CONSUMPTION (at steady speeds in top gear):

30 m.p.h.	20·2 m.p.g.
40 "	19·9 "
50 "	19·0 "
60 "	18·3 "
70 "	16·6 "
80 "	14·4 "
90 "	12·3 "
100 "	9·5 "

Overall fuel consumption for 1,440 miles, 13·1 m.p.g. (21·5 litres per 100 km.).

Approximate normal range 11-17 m.p.g. (25·7-16·6 litres per 100 km.).

Fuel: Premium grade.

TEST CONDITIONS: Weather: Fair, gusty, damp surface. 10-30 m.p.h. wind. Air temperature, 52 deg. F.

STEERING: Turning circle.
Between kerbs, L, 45ft 0·5in., R, 43ft 1in.;
Between walls, L, 46ft 11·5in.; R, 45ft 0in.
Turns of steering wheel, lock to lock, 4·25.

------------ **DATA** ------------

PRICE (basic), with James Young four-door saloon body, **£6,150.**
British purchase tax, **£2,563 12s 6d.**
Total in Great Britain, **£8,713 12s 6d.**

ENGINE: Capacity, 6,230 c.c. (380 cu. in.).
Number of cylinders, 8.
Bore and stroke, 104·1 × 91·4 mm. (4·1 × 3·6in.).
Valve gear, o.h.v., self-adjusting tappets.
Compression ratio, 8 to 1.
M.p.h. per 1,000 r.p.m. in top gear, 27·0.

WEIGHT: (With 5 gal fuel), 39·8 cwt. (4,460 lb).
Weight distribution (per cent); F, 49·6; R, 50·4.
Laden as tested, 42·7 cwt (4,786 lb).
Lb per c.c. (laden), 0·77.

BRAKES: Type, Rolls-Royce Girling drum. 4 shoes front, 2 L. & T. rear.
Method of operation, Hydro-mechanical, servo assisted and duplicated hydraulic systems.
Drum dimensions: F & R 11·25in. diameter; 3·0in. wide.
Swept area: F, 212 sq. in; R, 212 sq. in. (196 sq. in. per ton laden).

TYRES: 8·00-15in. Dunlop C Road Speed W.H.2.
Pressures (p.s.i.); F, 20; R, 25 (normal); F, 25; R, 30 (fast driving).

TANK CAPACITY: 18 Imperial gallons.
Oil sump, 13 pints.
Cooling system, 21 pints.

DIMENSIONS: Wheelbase, 10ft 3in.
Track; F, 4ft 10·5in.; R, 5ft 0in.
Length (overall), 17ft 8in.
Width, 6ft 1in.
Height, 5ft 1in.
Ground clearance, 7in.
Frontal area, 23·5 sq. ft. (approximately).

ELECTRICAL SYSTEM: 12-volt; 67 ampère-hour battery.
Headlamps, 60-36 watt bulbs.

SUSPENSION: Front: Independent, coil springs, with anti-roll bar.
Rear: Live axle on asymmetric half-elliptic leaf springs; hydraulic dampers controlled by two-position switch on control column.

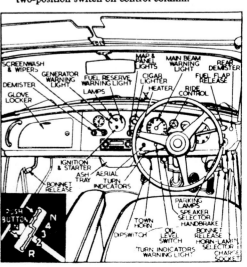

185

ROLLS-ROYCE SILVER CLOUD III

BENTLEY S3

Crewe-cut, 1963 style: Immediate recognition points for the new Rolls-Royce Silver Cloud III are the paired headlamps, bolder wings with recessed parking-signalling lamps, and more discreet bumper overriders. A second glance reveals that the classic radiator shell has been lowered by about 1⅛in

MORE POWER, MORE PASSENGER SPACE, BETTER LIGHTING, EASIER STEERING

VERY high grade cars such as the Rolls-Royce and Bentley are made in such relatively small numbers that the fruits of constant research and development can be embodied quickly on the production line. This is a more or less constant process, but modifications of a somewhat basic nature, in particular those which have a sufficiently marked effect on performance or appearance to justify a new series or model designation, are naturally introduced together.

Both the Rolls-Royce Silver Cloud and the S-series Bentley—identical in all except radiator shell and bonnet—advance a major step and are now designated the Silver Cloud III and S3 respectively. In brief, they have more power, an improved lighting system with paired headlamps, reduced steering effort, and increased passenger space in the back.

Firm to their tradition, Rolls-Royce do not reveal power output figures, but claim a seven per cent increase to this unknown quantity for the latest version of their 6,230 c.c. vee-8 engine. This results from a rise in compression ratio, now 9·0 to 1 instead of 8·0 (the lower ratio being optional to suit markets where 100 octane fuels are not available); and from the replacement of 1¾in. S.U. HD6 carburettors by 2in. HD8s. A new vacuum advance-retard mechanism for the ignition distributor, supplementing the centrifugal weights, together with the raised compression, are said by the makers to have lowered the specific fuel consumption.

To meet the higher power, the chrome molybdenum steel crankshaft is now nitride-hardened, and larger diameter gudgeon pins are fitted. These are now offset in the pistons, the better to withstand the increased thrust and contributing also to quieter running. Crankcase breathing is drawn into the engine intake through sealed ducting, to avoid the possibility of fumes escaping.

Extra power-assistance has been provided for the cam-and-roller steering gear, reducing the maximum load at the wheel rim to 6lb. While this brings about an appreciable saving in effort for normal driving, its effect is most marked during low-speed manœuvring and parking. Plenty of "feel" is retained in this system, and the hydraulic power valves remain closed up to ½lb load. There are

Above: This is the Bentley S3, which shares the senior partner's amendments. Driving vision is improved over the steeply sloping bonnet. From the rear only the overriders are new, and the earlier type is retained for export cars. Left: Sealed crankcase breathing into the induction is new, and the ignition distributor now has a supplementary vacuum advance-retard control

no further main modifications to the mechanical components, the complex drum braking system with all-trailing shoes, a gearbox-driven friction servo and three independent systems being retained.

A four-headlamp system is now standardized, all being Lucas sealed beam units of 5¾in. dia. The inner, long-range lamps each have a single filament, the outer units two filaments—one slightly out of focus to add spread to the main beams, the other for dipped beam. Wattage for the main beams is up from 120 to 150. Parking and direction-signalling lamps are now combined in neat oval units recessed in the wings; the twin fog-lamps are retained. Except for the North American market, smaller and simpler overriders are fitted to the bumpers.

More Seat Room

Inside the cars are important changes in that individual front seats, each with its own centre-folding armrest, have become standard equipment, although the one-piece bench remains optional. In the back two valuable extra inches of legroom have been found, the seat cushion being moved back by that amount. Most of this has resulted from making the backrest more upright—and certainly no less comfortable. Also, the previously rather "aggressive" corner padding has been reduced; this allows greater effective width for seating three abreast, as well as being more comfortable to lean against in any circumstances.

There are five new standard colours—Astral blue, Antelope, Dusk grey, Pine green and Garnet. The four discontinued colours (Velvet green, Midnight blue, Opal and blue-grey) can still be specified, but now at extra cost. Other listed supplementaries include electric window-lifts, a refrigeration system, tinted glass and fitted suitcases for the boot.

While this completes the particular innovations for the Silver Cloud III and Bentley S3, the later Silver Cloud IIs and S2s had quite a few features which had been progressively incorporated without any fanfares, and which are continued on the new cars. Those which follow are especially noteworthy. The heating and ventilating installation has two ventilating matrices for independent fresh air and recirculating systems, the latter with improved delivery to the middle of the rear floor. A ram position has been added to the fresh air circuit. A headlamp flashing button has been

Above: Interior innovations include a padded capping rail above the facia. Right: Less prominent corner bolsters save space, allowing three abreast in greater comfort. There is extra leg-room, too

incorporated in the direction indicators lever, and there is a tell-tale lamp in circuit with the ignition switch to warn the driver when the handbrake is on.

For the standard Radiomobile receiver (there is a choice between three) a second speaker has been added on the rear parcels shelf, with a balance control for adjusting the front and rear outputs. Footrests are provided for those riding in the back, who also have ashtrays of an improved design. There is a map reading lamp on the facia, the instrument panel lighting is more powerful, the switch for the electrical demisting element in the rear window is on the facia instead of in the back compartment, and the driving mirror is better supported to resist vibration. In the luggage boot there is a detachable metal panel covering the spare wheel, which lies horizontal below the boot floor.

Other Rolls-Royce and Bentley types—the long-wheelbase Silver Cloud III and S3, the huge Phantom V and the S3 Continental—naturally all incorporate the revised engine and other changes. Of the coachbuilt cars in series production,

there is a new two-door sports saloon by Park Ward on the Continental chassis, and the Phantom V seven-passenger limousine (Park Ward and H. J. Mulliner) has a modified rake to the screen as well as a completely redesigned boot.

Price increases have brought the Silver Cloud III and Bentley S3 standard saloons up to £6,277 17s 9d and £6,126 12s 9d respectively, the previous figures being £5,913 10s 3d and £5,769 2s 9d. Current chassis prices for these two cars are £3,135 and £3,035.

During an afternoon spent on the Oulton Park racing circuit in Cheshire, when examples of the latest products were tried in direct comparison with a Rolls-Royce Silver Cloud II, we were able to confirm the gain in performance and to appreciate the sensitive control provided by the unusually light steering. These fine cars have always felt smaller than they look to drive, and the increased close-range field of view over the lowered bonnet adds to this impression. Further remarks concerning the handling of the Silver Cloud III and S3 must await a full Road Test.

Autocar's representatives were given the run of the Oulton Park racing circuit for an afternoon, to sample the increased power and lightweight power-steering of the new cars

A FAR CRY FROM
CRICKLEWOOD..

or how Rolls-Royce erect a Bentley motor car

By Martin Lewis   **Photography by Ron Easton**

Bare bodies for the four door cars arrive at Crewe from Pressed Steel. At this stage only the difference in the bonnet pressings distinguish between Rolls-Royce (background) and Bentley (foreground). Engines are built up on a short production line, with only the rocker box covers to tell which is which. Only cars fitted with full air conditioning have an alternator.

WITH war clouds gathering in 1938, the government built the Crewe factory for the production of Merlin vee-12 two-stage supercharged aero engines, which powered the Spitfire, Hurricane and later the heavy bombers and even, in a modified form, the Churchill tank and motor gun and torpedo boats. In 1945, Rolls-Royce found that they had space to spare at Crewe and the Motor Car Division was moved across from Derby; in that year the first complete Bentley made by the company, the Mk. VI, rolled out to meet its public.

Although Rolls-Royce engineering standards are world famous, the Crewe factory has a second incentive to perfection, for, in the engineering section, many of the car components are machined alongside the Continental aero engine lines, where specifications are far, far higher than those found in most automobile engineering.

At present, about 42 cars a week are being made, with one in six of them Bentleys. Half the production goes overseas, and half of this again are destined for the USA. For British customers, the waiting list is about 18 months, with export customers having to wait about half this time. Even if one could jump the queue, it would be at least three months before you could have your car, for it takes this time to build. Today, most car manufacturers rely very largely on bought-out parts, and it is from parts that the greatest source of trouble arises. Rolls-Royce have decided that, unless outside suppliers can meet their standards, they will make the part themselves. This may appear somewhat old-fashioned and a case of tradition for tradition's sake, but when a customer is paying £8,000 for a car, he expects it to be as near perfect as possible. As a result, Rolls-Royce even make their own nuts and bolts; no lockwashers are used, the nuts being tightened to a precise degree so that the metal's natural elasticity provides enough clamping action to prevent undoing through vibration. In the same way, brake discs, wiring looms and even final drives are made in the factory.

The four-door bodies are made by Pressed Steel, and the basic floor pressing is used by Mulliner as the basis for their two-door saloon and convertible models. Even in this bare-metal form, the two marques have their identity, the Rolls-Royce bonnet having the Doric lines as opposed to the Bentley's slightly Gothic appearance. As the bodies are received, they are given their initial smoothing, and the doors are fitted by coachbuilders; these doors stay with that car, initially located on metal hangers, until they are removed for trimming.

In the paintshop, after de-greasing, the bodies go through six basic processes prior to their initial baking. This includes phosphate rust-preventative, acid etch, primer, filler and guide coats, which give the finishers an idea of how much filler they are removing during rubbing down. Inspection starts during this rubbing down, and what might appear to the lay eye a perfect finish is scrawled with marks, to go back time and again until it is perfect. Only then can the car receive its first of many coats of cellulose. Again, these are inspected, rubbed down, re-checked until the final finish is approved.

In the meantime, the engines are being built up. Each rotating or reciprocating part is ba-

In the trim shops, seats are made, while the carpenters prepare wood for facias and capping rails. Veneers are selected, so that graining will form a mirror image through the car's centre line. In the paint shops, bodies are hand rubbed, marks are put on by inspectors, indicating what action is to be taken. Only when the body is perfect can the car go on to road testing.

•• •• •• •• ••

lanced in the engine as it is built up, until it takes on the first sign of its marque, when the Rolls-Royce or Bentley rocker box covers are bolted on. The initial running in is done on town gas, and if any faults are even remotely suspected, it is put right through the mill on the dynomometer.

As each car is started, it receives its History Book. This book stays with the car right through its life in the factory, and contains minute details of paint colour, trim, carpets, headlamps and any special equipment. Within its pages are recorded every stage of inspection, and when the car is driven away from Crewe, the History Book goes into the files, a permanent record of the building of an individual car. Virtually every car is built to order, and there is no such thing as a "standard" Bentley, for until a customer places his order, no details could be put in the History Book.

In the main assembly shop, the bodies and sub-frames meet for the first time. Before this, the wiring, complicated hydraulic systems, bas-

(c internal sound proofing and so on are added. Eight times a day, a body is lifted into the air and lowered on to its engine and final drive sub-frames; then the whole unit is lifted on to the only moving assembly line—powered by a hand winch and length of rope! Again one meets detail perfection—the solid brass wheel nuts have handed threads; who else would go that far?

On the overhead line, the car is completed underneath and then comes back to earth, for its final trim—carpets, seats and doors, which have been at the trim shop. The only things missing are the brightwork and the radiator shell. They still look relatively dull, with the cellulose perfect, but still unpolished.

In a special bay, the cars are made ready for their first excursion under their own power, and then handed over to the test drivers. This is not the usual once-round-the-houses job, but an ultra-careful check on running, noise, adjustments going on until it is perfect. All the test drivers double as trouble shooters, so they are

highly experienced in both diagnosis and cure. Incidentally, everyone at Rolls-Royce who drives company cars has to pass their firm's own driving test—the only private test to carry a certificate recognised by the IAM.

When the cars hve been passed out mechanically, they go on to their final stage. The dull cellulose is given a coat of polish and then attacked with electric buffers until it glows. The car is wheeled into the inspection tunnel, where batteries of fluorescent lamps pick out any minute imperfections. That car will go through the tunnel as many as eight times before the inspector's signature goes in the History Book. Now the bright trim is fitted and the final touch comes when the radiator shells are bolted on, with the winged "B" proclaiming the car's proud ancestry.

There is still one final inspection, by Quality Control. These men have the roles of super-critical customers, and it is their job to accept or reject the final product. Only then is a Bentley considered fit to be handed over to its owner. □

The Bentley body meets its sub frames for the first time (right). The car is then put on an overhead line, where the final connections between running gear and the body shell are made. In the final stage, an inspector checks the coachwork after it has been polished. Only when he considers it as good as it can humanly be, will he allow it to go on to have the bright trim fitted. The finished car (this one is destined for the United States) after three months inside the factory

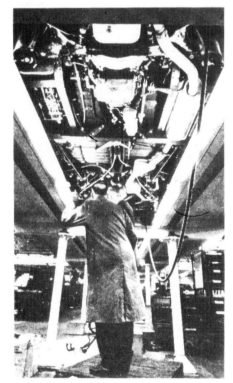

Bentley T2

Behind a different ▼ radiator

NOT EVEN strictly speaking, this Bentley T2 Road Test may be read without any reservations as that of the current Rolls-Royce Silver Shadow II. The test car bears a Bentley radiator — which to some eyes suits the Shadow shape better than the Royce one does, thanks to way its more rounded profile blends with that of the car — it has a winged-B mascot, and other minor changes.

So, although the last *Autocar* Road Test of a Bentley was as long ago as 1960 (Bentley Continental S2 by James Young), the last time we tested this car was effectively only three years ago, in the Rolls-Royce Silver Shadow test of 1 May 1976.

Bentley T2

Rolls-Royce's classic Silver Shadow II with a differently labelled radiator, headlamp surrounds, mascot, nave plates and tail marking becomes a Bentley — a lovely motor car, if a misuse of a once great name.

Rolls-Royce Motors Limited
Crewe
Cheshire

There was, it is true, the Silver Wraith II Road Test of a year ago (21 October 1978), but that car has 4in more wheelbase and is not therefore exactly the same mechanically, although it did incorporate the considerable Shadow Series II changes.

Since the Series II modifications, there have been other detail ones, not all of them found on the test Bentley — from a Road Test point of view, a commendably high mileage car — because some came after it was built. The electric gearchange mechanism automatically selects Park with the ignition off; a Pioneer KP292 stereo cassette player replaces the cartridge player; an extra switch allows the driver getting into the car on a hot day to direct refrigerated air direct to his face via the facia eyeball vents; the electric aerial switch is deleted, in favour of automatic radio switching; and brush-type wash wipe has been added to the paired headlamps.

Performance

Effortless obedience

Dealing with the actual performance figures first, the current Series II car weighs a shade under 43 cwt, 57lb (a negligible amount in 4,809lb) more than the 1976 Road Test Shadow I, which had the same capacity 6,750 c.c. engine with the lower same-as-today (8.0-to-1) compression ratio but the bigger HD8 SUs, and 149lb more than the first Shadow test car of 1967, which had the original shorter-stroke engine size of 6,230 c.c., a 9-to-1 compression, and HD8 carburettors. The current Bentley (and Silver Shadow) weight is given as 99lb less than the Silver Wraith II without division between driving compartment and rear.

For many years, Rolls-Royce have been famous for not stating engine outputs. The power figures are probably not by any means the highest for the engine size class, as the company have obviously sought quietness as well as enough performance. There is no rev-limiting device other than the driver's nerve and hydraulic tappet pump-up; in our case it was the former which pumped up first, at 49 and 82 mph in the intermediate gears, which corresponds to 4,650 rpm assuming no torque converter slip. The engine is clearly past its peak then, so that one would guess that that peak is not much more than the 4,000 rpm which is the average for similiar-sized vee-8's of American and European (Daimler-Benz) manufacturers. That being so, the car is almost certainly a mite undergeared, for the sake of good top gear acceleration; its maximum speed of 119 mph — the highest figure we have seen from any Shadow — is equivalent to a calculated 4,550 rpm, with a best one way of only 1 mph more (120 mph and 4,600 rpm) in pretty good testing weather.

In spite of its greater weight, as well as having the highest maximum, the test Bentley is the most accelerative Silver Shadow of the four we have now tested; for the sake of anyone interested, previous tests were published in the *Autocars* of 30 March 1967, 16 November 1972, and 1 May 1976. The test day weather may have helped a little, with 10 mph less wind than for any of the other cars, but there is no doubt that this car performs well. The Silver Wraith II had been the fastest Shadow variant previously tried, yet it is now displaced; here are the full set of standing start figures, done leaving the excellent GM400 box to its own devices— we could not beat it by changing up higher than the set points at 44 mph (4,150 rpm) and 72 (4,050) — which are strong hints that the power peak is close to 4,100 rpm; 0 to 30 mph in 2.9sec (3.6sec for the Wraith), 40 in 4.6 (5.3), 50 in 6.6 (7.4), 60 in 9.4 (10.1), 70 in 12.8 (13.3), 80 in 16.9 (17.7), 90 in 23.2 (23.7), 100 in 30.7 (32.4) and 110 in 44.6 (47.5).

The transmission can be over-ridden with Rolls-Royce's superb steering column electric selector, still unapproached by any other maker. In Low, there is no safety change up, nor is there any sort of freewheel, so that it may be used for engine braking at slow speeds. The box will not drop into Low (first gear) from too high a speed however. In Intermediate, the same applies, at higher speeds of course. Maximum kickdown speeds are 27 mph from 2 to 1 and 68 from 3 to 2. Changes are made beautifully smoothly, which together with an exemplary light yet ideally progressive throttle linkage makes fast sweet movement of the car remarkably easy. Big cars should be so, because their mass absorbs jerks, yet the Bentley is remarkably good all the same in these respects. The discerning driver derives enormous quiet satisfaction from the way one can hurry this large saloon along any sort of road, restricted only by width of course. When the engine is warm, the only transmission jerk noticed is an unavoidable, slight but perceptible one when selecting Intermediate on the move — it changes up again almost imperceptibly. Kick down changes are done very well indeed. It will be good when Crewe adopt fuel injection, as one small drawback of the present carburettor cold start device is the high engine speed from cold, which inevitably means a jerk on engaging Drive.

The engine is not however as inaudible as one might hope and expect. Amusingly, several drivers agreed that the noise it makes are unacceptable in a Rolls-Royce, but about right in a Bentley. It is beautifully quiet at town speeds when one is not using the acceleration too much; the way the car drifts along at 30 to 40 mph is one of the greatest delights of Rolls-Royce motoring. But quite a few cheaper cars can do the same thing notably Jaguar (see our interior noise comparison tests in *Autocar* of 15 September) — and on the open road, when the driver puts his foot down, even to maintain speed up a motorway gradient at 80, there is a subdued growl from in front, not unpleasing but definitely there. It grows louder on full acceleration.

Noise

You can hear the clock ticking

. . . But only at up to about 30 mph, partly no doubt because modern car clocks are much quieter than they used to be. There are other sources of noise besides the engine, which together mean, as on much lesser cars, adjusting the radio volume according to speed — and road surface. The car is still disappointingly sensitive to coarse road dressings, to a surprising extent until you consider how quiet some other usual noise makers are. The steering power assistance is inaudible, which is most unusual. There are no transmission noises. But that road noise is there, and it is the car's only real let down; bump-thump is there, and if you hit a particularly sharp bump, it is made slightly worse by a hint of boom resonance in the body. Brakes on the test car tended to make graunchy noises towards the end of a gentler slowing down, and the Avon tyres squeal too readily at low cornering speeds.

Economy

Surprisingly good for the size

If you make nearly two and a quarter tons of large, quite tall motor car accelerate from 0 to 60 mph in under 10 seconds, you are going to burn a fair bit of petrol. It is remarkable then with such performance, even if one

Apart from the radiator, only badging distinguishes the Bentley T2 from its Rolls-Royce sister. Black moulded bumpers are a distinguishing feature of the T2. Rear quarters are not as blind as they appear from the side

The T2 outside the automobile museum at Clères in Normandy. Note the spoiler beneath the front bumper

uses it only occasionally, that up to 15 mpg is possible at times, and, given gentle driving, that 16 mpg is fairly easily obtainable. Town driving takes a heavy toll, reducing the figure to around 13 mpg. The car's overall test consumption of 13.6 mpg is equal to the previous best figure obtained from the 1976 Silver Shadow test car. The 23½ gallons tank means a useful range of between 275 and 350 miles, and time is not wasted at petrol stops by that tiresome modern disease of too many cars, fuel fillers that blow back and are slow to brim; the Bentley one takes full delivery very

nearly all the way to the last quarter-gallon. A neat feature is the remote button which you press to release the fuel filler flap. As a safety measure, it only works when the ignition is switched off.

Road Behaviour
Superb direction

The change to power-assisted rack and pinion steering is perhaps the best thing that has happened to the design in its 14-year evolution. It puts to headlong flight the notion that rack and pinion is not suitable for very large cars, since the system combines the best of that simple mechanism's virtues — simplicity through a far less compli-

cated linkage, directness which gives real feel of what the front tyres are doing, accuracy and response — with the safeguards of more old fashioned steering gear, adequate insulation from road shock.

That last point may sound contradictory; it is not in this case, because the system doesn't kick back at all alarmingly, yet it does kick just enough to give the steering life and true feel without it becoming anywhere near out of hand, even in the most gentle driver's charge. The fact that it kicks at all on this sort of car is astonishing enough; and that the gearing is so delightfully high, at only 3½ turns — the same as for a really very handy-for-the-size-of-car 37ft turning circle. It is just the right weight, no longer tip-of-little-finger as on the old recirculating ball system, but light enough to take all real effort out of steering, regardless of what you are demanding of it (some power systems can be caught out, when manoeuvring for example, when they begin to lose their power temporarily). You find yourself sitting in the car, controlling it with wrist and fingertips, elbows supported by the adjustable door armrest and its mate which swings down from the left side of the seat squab. It self-centres well too,

making town driving in tight places a pleasure.

The car handles therefore pretty well for its size and class.

There is of course still some understeer when you start cornering at all quickly, but not too much. One cannot help suspecting that the construction of the Avon R-R Turbo Steep Speed 70 radials is biased towards ride rather than handling, since even when we pumped them up for high speed banking tests, they rolled over too readily on to their shoulders and the tops of their sidewalls as one approached the car's cornering limit, reducing the effect of the improved front suspension geometry on the uprightness of the loaded outside wheel. There is then quite a lot of roll, which doesn't help. The ultimate limit is set by break away in front if you keep your foot down, or at the back if you decelerate in the corner, when the camber change due to weight transfer and the semi-trailing arm rear-end geometry takes immediate but not unacceptably sudden effect. The quickness of the steering makes opposite lock correction of what can be a very undignified, wide slide relatively easy.

One must naturally be careful with the throttle in the wet; provided there is enough room on

the road, leaving right-angle junctions then makes one wonder whether a limited slip differential might not be a good thing. Harder than standard tyre pressures make response and accuracy of steering that much more pleasing, but if one takes such changes too far, one realises how much of the car's remarkable low-speed, sharp-cornered-bump ride is owed to tye deflection. The Bentley is wonderfully soft in ride, to an extent few if any other cars attain, without an unacceptable cost in steering response. Big bumps it rides well too, except that there is a suggestion of

under-damping on the far side of the bump, the car giving a long extra pitch — really a very slow bounce as the nose drops. It may, on some other cars so equipped, be a fraction of the Citroen-design self-levelling which is otherwise very much appreciated in the way it keeps the Bentley level.

Brakes are beautifully weighted, with a virtually linear response curve — retardation goes up almost exactly as pedal effort does — and an excellence enough 1g maximum stop for 50 lb pedal — slightly under the norm for big cars but not too much so. The all-disc system, ventilated in front, copes impressively well with our fade test. Stopping ten times in immediate succession at ½g from the car's standing-quarter-mile speed (79 mph) at quarter-mile intervals without anything worse than pad smoke and some shudder during the last two stops is good going when there is so much weight to arrest. The handbrake takes advantage of the Bentley's not too front heavy 52.6/47.4 weight distribution by returning an excellent 0.4g stop from 30 mph; you have to pull very hard on the umbrella handle, as you do for it to hold, just, on 1 in 3.

Far left: Rear legroom is good, as one would expect, and each door has its own cigar lighter and ashtray. Vanity mirrors and reading lamps are positioned in the rear quarters. Left: Upholstery is in best Connolly hide and door armrests are adjustable. Seat multi-way electric adjustment is worked from just behind central ashtray. Each front door has a switch for the central locking

Behind the wheel
That valuable thing, height

Rolls-Royces and Bentley's have one advantage that puts them usefully above all other cars — the height of the driver's eye level. You sit only a little above other cars, your eyes roughly level with your neighbour's roof — but it is enough to give one a commanding extra view around one.

The driving position is in any case good, and although paradoxically the car is available only to a minority, thanks to the electrically moved fore-and-aft and vertically adjustable seat, it will suit the majority of drivers. The armrests on each side have been mentioned; taller drivers may wish that the door one had another half-inch of adjustment range. The centre armrest provides, crudely, a rough sort of sideways location that is sadly lacking in the seat itself. The seat's rake adjustment is ideal, in that it can be moved fast to roughly where you want it, by pulling the usual lever, then adjusted finely with the rotary knob; the combination is a perfect answer.

Generally controls are done very well. We like the retention of a horn button in the middle of the steering wheel, which is still the ideal place for it, since in any emergency, whatever the driver is doing with the steering, that is the easiest place in which to find and work it quickly. It is high time on the other hand that Rolls-Royce put the wipers control on a stalk (easier to work quickly) instead of on an old-fashioned facia switch — and that they modernised the wiper action; at present it still insists on making that hesitant start, making three of four half strokes before settling into its stride with

the full cycle. The 82 wipe cycle per minute fast setting is excellent, but we would like a variable rate control for the interruption wipe. The Vintage style switch panel to the right of the comprehensive warning lamp one looks well amid the walnut of such a car, and its switches — the lamps and ignition key ones — like all others on the car work very pleasingly.

The driver's door carries both switches for all four electric windows and the central locking system. The windows open and shut exceptionally quickly as well as quietly, taking just over 2sec to wind up and 1.3sec down — the norm for most other cars so equipped is around at least twice those times. The central locking control locks all doors and the boot, but leaves the boot locked when used to unlock the doors; the boot remote lock release button is hidden inside the (key-lockable) glove compartment.

Visibility is generally good. The rear quarter panel is quite large, but too far behind one for its size to make anything more than a small blind spot. The car's pronounced shoulders at the front make it surprisingly easy to "place".

The highest compliment one can pay the automatic air conditioning-cum-heater system is to say that having selected the temperature which suits you, you forget about it thereafter. It works very well indeed, and is an enormous yet unnoticed contributor to the way the car relaxes one for the entire length of a long journey. The only other car we know to be the Bentley's equal in this respect is the Jaguar XJ family, which has the very slight advantage of being quieter in operation when first working to bring the temperature under control.

Living with the Bentley T2

The first of the many pleasures of such a life is the smell of leather on first getting in; it isn't overpowering, but just enough. Another is to find a foot dipswitch again, ideal on a two-pedal controlled car since whilst the hands may be busy when one needs to dip, there is always the left foot available. The hundreds of little details found in the car never cease to please; window switches which work when the ignition's off (handy for passengers left in the car); the oil level test switch which, although the handbook says you should treat as a rough indicator only, and then (by implication) only when ticking over at rest, in fact works quite well enough at steady straight-running speed; the outside air temperature gauge (which certainly only works accurately with the car moving); the ideally placed bonnet release, under the steering column, which instead of the stiff yet fragile-feeling action of so many other cars, works smoothly and firmly; the lensed map light which peers over the passenger's should on pressing a switch in front of him; the provision of an ashtray on the driver's right.

For back seat passengers, there is as there should be plenty of knee and leg room, with ideal support for the feet on inclined toe boards under each front seat. Behind, on top of the seat, there is a padded roll for a headrest. In front are elasticated pockets of decent size in the front seat backs. Roof grab handles are provided, with what some will use as coat hooks. There is enough headroom for a 6ft passenger, and just the right amount of visibility.

Not every detail pleases. We

twice cut ourselves quite messily on the unduly sharp-cornered catch for the petrol filler flap, when undoing the handsome screw cap; it is perfectly placed to skin the knuckle of the middle finger. The boot floor gets warm at its front six to eight inches when laden; a minor detail, of no importance until the day one left say, a box of chocolates there. The spaces between the cartridge holder in between the front seats and the seats themselves are just high enough to lose a pencil in, which is very difficult to get out again. Few drivers will encounter the tendency for the front window frames to start vibrating quite badly as one approaches maximum speed, but it happened on the test car nevertheless. The same probably applies to the way's one right knee, searching for the sideways location missing from the seat when cornering very fast, works the driver's switch for the door window.

The Bentley range

The car tested is the cheapest Bentley, at £36,652.42 — the same price as the equivalent Rolls-Royce Silver Shadow II. Two other models flying the winged B mascot are available: the more powerful Corniche and its very dashing convertible variant (£53,322 and £56,636 respectively).

Above: Boot is fully carpeted and houses the battery and fitted small tools as well as the jack. Spare wheel lives under the floor and winds down

HOW THE BENTLEY T2 PERFORMS

TEST CONDITIONS:
Wind: 0-12 mph
Temperature: 11 deg C (52 deg F)
Barometer: 29.3 in. Hg (993 mbar)
Humidity: 70 per cent
Surface. Dry asphalt and concrete
Test distance: 1,947 miles

MAXIMUM SPEEDS

Gear	mph	kph	rpm
Top (mean)	119	192	4,550
(best)	120	193	4,600
2nd	82	132	4,650
1st	49	79	4,650

ACCELERATION

FROM REST

True mph	Time (sec)	Speedo mph
30	2.9	32
40	4.6	42
50	6.6	52
60	9.4	63
70	12.8	74
80	16.9	85
90	23.2	97
100	30.7	97
110	44.6	119
120		129

Standing ¼-mile: 17.7 sec, 79 mph
Standing km: 32.3 sec, 101 mph

IN EACH GEAR

mph	Top	2nd	1st
0-20	—	—	1.8
10-30	—	—	2.4
20-40	—	—	3.3
30-50	—	4.2	—
40-60	—	5.2	—
50-70	—	6.4	—
60-80	—	7.7	—
70-90	10.2	—	—
80-100	13.6	—	—
90-110	22.0	—	—

FUEL CONSUMPTION
Overall mpg:
13.6 (12.0 litres / 100km)
Constant speed:

mph	mpg		
30	22.0	70	17.1
40	21.1	80	15.0
50	20.1	90	12.8
60	18.8	100	10.3

Autocar formula: Hard 12.2 mpg
Driving Average 15.0 mpg
and conditions Gentle 17.7 mpg

Grade of fuel: Premium, 4-star (98 RM)
Fuel tank: 23.5 Imp. galls (107 litres)
Mileage recorder reads 1.0 per cent long

Official fuel consumption figures
(ECE laboratory test conditions;
not necessarily related to Autocar figures)
Urban cycle: 11.1 mpg
Steady 56 mph: 19.5 mpg
Steady 75 mph: 15.9 mpg

OIL CONSUMPTION

(SAE 20W/50) 850 miles / pint

BRAKING
Fade (from mph in neutral)
Pedal load for 0.5g stops in lb

	Start/end		Start/end
1	25-20	6	25-35
2	25-25	7	25-38
3	25-30	8	25-35
4	20-20	9	25-35
5	25-30	10	25-30

Response (from 30 mph in neutral)

Load	g	Distance
10lb	0.21	143ft
20lb	0.41	73ft
30lb	0.60	50ft
40lb	0.78	39ft
50lb	0.98	30.7ft
Handbrake	0.40	75ft

Max. gradient: 1 in 3

WEIGHT
Kerb, 42.9 cwt / 4,809 lb / 2,181 kg
(Distribution F/R, 52.6 / 47.4)
Test, 46.5 cwt / 5,209 lb / 2,362 kg
Max. payload 1,063lb / 482kg

DIMENSIONS

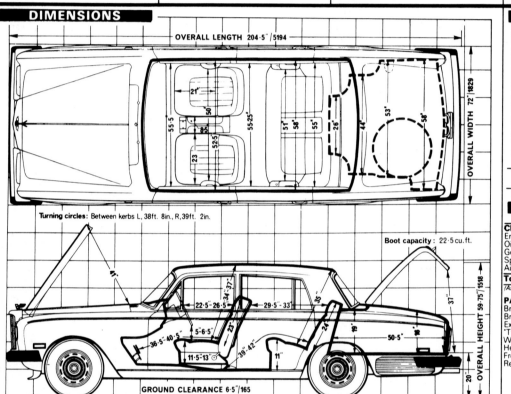

Turning circles: Between kerbs L, 38ft. 8in., R, 39ft. 2in.

OVERALL LENGTH 204·5"/5194
OVERALL WIDTH 72"/1829
Boot capacity : 22·5 cu.ft.
OVERALL HEIGHT 59·75"/1518
GROUND CLEARANCE 6·5"/165
WHEELBASE 120"/3048
FRONT TRACK 60"/1524
REAR TRACK 59·5"/1511
SCALE 1:35
OVERALL DIMENSIONS in. mm

PRICES

Basic	£29,420.00
Special Car Tax	£2,451.67
VAT	£4,780.75
(Total in GB)	**£36,652.42**
Seat Belts	Standard
Licence	£50.00
Delivery charge (London)	£70.00
Number plates (approx)	£20.00
Total on the Road	£36,792.42

(exc. insurance)
EXTRAS (inc. VAT) — selection only)

Mascot anti-theft alarm	£130.19
Chubb fire extinguisher	£37.06
Rear armrest compartment	£84.10
Front seat head restraints	£59.49
Picnic tables, per pair	£265.98
Non-standard paint	£495.22

*Fitted to test car

TOTAL AS TESTED ON THE ROAD	**£36,792.42**
Insurance	Group 7

SERVICE & PARTS

	Interval		
Change	**6,000**	**12,000**	**24,000**
Engine oil	Yes	Yes	Yes
Oil filter	Yes	Yes	Yes
Gearbox oil	No	Yes	Yes
Spark plugs	No	Yes	Yes
Air cleaner	No	Yes	Yes
Total cost	**£94.76**	**£143.18**	**£163.18**

(Assuming labour at £8.00/hour)

PARTS COST (including VAT)

Brake pads (2 wheels) — front	£28.75
Brake pads (2 wheels) — rear	£14.95
Exhaust complete (stainless steel)	£851.00
*Tyre — each (typical)	£102.53
Windscreen (laminated, tinted)	£143.75
Headlamp unit	£19.55
Front wing	£213.90
Rear bumper	£230.00

WARRANTY
Mechanical: 36 months / 50,000 miles
Body: 12 months

SPECIFICATION

ENGINE

	Front, rear-wheel drive
Head/block	Aluminium alloy
Cylinders	8, in 90 deg vee
Main bearings	5
Cooling	Water
Fan	Viscous fan drive, plus electric fan
Bore, mm (in.)	104.1 (4.098)
Stroke, mm (in.)	99.1 (3.902)
Capacity cc (in.)	6,748 (412)
Valve gear	Ohv pushrods, hydraulic tappets
Camshaft drive	Gear
Compression ratio	8.0-to-1
Ignition	Breakerless, transistorised
Carburettor	2 SU HIF7
Max power	Not stated
Max torque	Not stated

TRANSMISSION

Type	GM400 3-speed epicyclic automatic with torque converter
Clutch	

Gear	Ratio	mph/1000rpm
Top	1.0-2.0	26.2
2nd	1.48-2.96	17.70
1st	2.48-4.96	10.56
Final drive gear	Hypoid bevel	
Ratio	3.08-to-1	

SUSPENSION

Front—location		Independent, double wishbone
	springs	Coil, self-levelling
	dampers	Telescopic
	anti-roll bar	Yes
Rear—location		Independent, semi-trailing arm
	springs	Coil, self-levelling
	dampers	Telesciopic
	anti-roll bar	Yes

STEERING

Type	Rack and pinion
Power assistance	Yes
Wheel diameter	15.2 in.
Turns lock to lock	3½

BRAKES

Circuits	Two, split front/rear
Front	11.0 in. dia. disc
Rear	11.0 in. dia disc
Servo	Hydraulic, engine-driven
Handbrake	Umbrella handle, rear disc

WHEELS

Type	Steel disc
Rim Width	6.0 in.
Tyres—make	Avon (on test car) or Dunlop
—type	R-R Turbo Steel 70 radial tubeless
—size	235/70HR-15
—pressures	F24 R28 psi (normal driving)

EQUIPMENT

Battery	12V 68 Ah
Alternator	75A
Headlamps	4 lamp system 115/195W
Reversing lamp	Standard
Hazard warning	Standard
Screen wipers	2-speed and intermittent
Screen washer	Electric
Heater and air conditioning	Auto temperature control
Interior trim	Leather seats, cloth headlining
Floor covering	Carpet
Jack	Screw
Jacking points	One each side
Windscreen	Laminated
Underbody protection	Galvanised, phosphated, bitumastic

Bentley T2 (A) £36,652

Front engine, rear drive

Capacity
6.748 c.c.

Power
Not stated

Weight
4.809lb/2.181kg

Autotest
Rolls-Royce Silver Shadow 1 May 1976, Silver Wraith II 21 October 1978

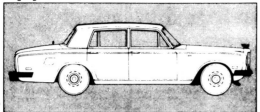

BMW 733i (A) £15,012

Front engine, rear drive

Capacity
3.210 c.c.

Power
197 bhp (DIN) at 5.500 rpm

Weight
3.585lb/1.627kg

Autotest
6 August 1977

Ferrari 400I (A) £31,809

Front engine, rear drive

Capacity
4.832 c.c.

Power
340 bhp (DIN) at 6.500 rpm

Weight
4.145lb/1.880kg

Autotest
Ferrari 365 GT4 2+2 4 October 1975

Daimler Vanden Plas 5.3 (A) £22,672

Front engine, rear drive

Capacity
5.343 c.c.

Power
285 bhp (DIN) at 5.750 rpm

Weight
4.310lb/1.955kg

Autotest
Jaguar XJ12 5.3 9 September 1978

Mercedes-Benz 450 SEL (A) £19,161

Front engine, rear drive

Capacity
4.520 c.c.

Power
225 bhp (DIN) at 5.000 rpm

Weight
3.904lb/1.772kg

Autotest
4 May 1974

Mercedes-Benz 450 SEL 6.9 (A) £30,476

Front engine, rear drive

Capacity
6.834 c.c.

Power
286 bhp (DIN) at 4.250 rpm

Weight
4.060lb/1.841kg

Autotest
24 March 1979

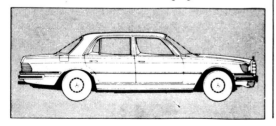

MPH & MPG

Maximum speed (mph)

Ferrari 400I*	150*
Daimler Vanden Plas 5.3**	147**
Mercedes 450SEL 6.9	140
Mercedes 450SEL	134
BMW 733i***	122***
Bentley T2	119

Acceleration 0-60 (sec)

Ferrari 400I	7.1*
Mercedes 450SEL 6.9	7.3
Daimler Vanden Plas 5.3**	7.8**
BMW 733i***	8.9***
Mercedes 450SEL	9.0
Bentley T2	9.4

Overall mpg

BMW 733i***	19.4***
Mercedes 450SEL	14.1
Bentley T2	13.6
Mercedes 450SEL 6.9	13.6
Daimler Vanden Plas 5.3**	13.2**
Ferrari 400I*	11.0*

Figures for 365GT4 2+2 manual gearbox (1.8 per cent lower power to weight ratio).
Figures for 1.8 per cent lighter Jaguar XJ5.3.
Figures for manual gearbox BMW 733i.

Even before one considers the price and quality of the Bentley, it has to be admitted that there are precious few cars made which are completely comparable with it, for all sorts of reasons. Big luxury saloons are, if not a dying breed — Rolls-Royce sell every car they make up to at least two years before it rolls out of the factory — a rare one today. Of the cars variously obvious or not which are available we have not tested the Lagonda (£39,931), Maserati Quattroporte (available here in left hand drive manual box form only at £28,900), de Tomaso Deauville (£24,418), or any of the odd Americans "legally" available here, the most obvious of which must be the Cadillac Fleetwood (£15,739). With the exception of the Ferrari, which though the biggest car Modena produces is only a 2 + 2, the cars chosen here are after something like the same market; as the figures show, the Bentley pays for its ride and quietness, to some extent achieved with sheer mass — it is 11½ per cent heavier than the next heaviest rival, the Daimler — in performance. It is only fair to point out that the less roomy Daimler does better than the Bentley in quietness and performance, thanks to less frontal area and weight, probably better shape, and a more powerful, smoother V12 engine, whilst the BMW wins easily on economy.

ON THE ROAD

Best all-rounder here is certainly the Daimler, with its superb ride, handling and roadholding, and its unrivalled quietness; its road manners are impeccable. For pure saloon car pedigree and entertainment, the Ferrari is of course tops — and you don't buy a Ferrari for quietness or the best of ride. Interestingly these two cars are the only ones with the near-ideal of double wishbone geometry front and rear, avoiding too much camber change with changes of attitude. The other four are all semi-trailing rear-ended, which sets a certain limit on their ultimate roadholding and behaviour (due to camber change at the back); but the Bentley must be singled out for its superb ride and, since the adoption of a rack and pinion steering set-up, its really magnificent direction, which is one area where Crewe still does build the Best (Big) Car in the World; the two Mercedes better it with their exemplarily high gearing, particularly in the case of the 6.9 (2.6 turns lock to lock for a 36ft turning circle), but haven't got quite such remarkable feel.

SIZE & SPACE

Legroom front/rear (in.)

(seats fully back)

BMW 733i	42/40
Mercedes 450SEL 6.9	43/39
Mercedes 450SEL	43/39
Bentley T2	40/41
Daimler Vanden Plas	39/36½
Ferrari 400I	41/29

Legroom dimensions are a little misleading here, since they take no account of headroom, where the Bentley and BMW are paramount; all of the four-door cars are in fact more than roomy enough, whilst the Ferrari does not pretend to be anything greater than a 2 + 2. In interior layout the German cars win, particularly the BMW with its very good clarity of instrument layout, though they have the least informative range of instruments. Best equipped in that respect is the Ferrari as you would expect; it has an oil temperature gauge which arguable necessity the others lack.

VERDICT

Final choice in this peculiar case boils down to a case of horses for courses; the man who wants something like the Ferrari won't look at any of the others for a start, though he might consider an Aston Martin Vantage (£30,878) not listed here. Amongst the five four-door cars, things are a little more even, with the Daimler winning on refinement and performance, value for money, the BMW followed by the 450SEL doing something like the same things the least thirstily, and the 6.9 offering something marvellously different in Mercedes motoring; sadly, it must be remembered that it is now extinct, with the coming of the new S-class — which will undoubtedly mean its financial canonisation as an appreciating classic of the 1970s. The Bentley is of course merely a differently labelled Rolls-Royce Silver Shadow; in passing we must say that we find such a cavalier misuse of a great name a mistake, about which rumour suggests the name's owners are eventually to do something. Names aside, it is nevertheless very impressive, and it undeniably offers a sort of progress about the place, nothing to do with motoring snobbery, which thanks to that height, that shape, that refinement and finish and that taste, is still unapproached by other cars made here or, even more so, abroad.

By Michael Scarlett and
Warren Allport
Drawings by Chris Plant

The Blower returns

Turbocharged version of Bentley Mulsanne saloon boasts 50 per cent more power and 0-60 mph in 7 sec

*Right:
Immediate
distinguishing
feature of the
Mulsanne Turbo
is the painted
radiator shell
finished in the
body colour*

*Below: Fitting the
turbocharger
installation under
the Bentley's
already crowded
bonnet was quite
a feat in itself. The
big central air box
with "Turbo" on
the lid houses the
carburettor, with
the turbocharger
itself at the front
of the engine on
the right. The
power steering
pump has been
re-located on the
left*

PERFORMANCE WAS the hallmark of the original Cricklewood Bentleys. After the takeover of Bentley by Rolls-Royce in 1931, the "Silent Sports Car" established new parameters for the marque, but performance was still important, and the new type of Bentley motoring was carried into the post-war era with the advent of the R-type Continental in 1952. By the 1960s, however, Bentleys had become little more than differently-badged Rolls-Royces. This step, deplored by *Autocar* and enthusiasts for the marque, was a departure from the philosophy laid down by Sir Henry Royce when the first Derby Bentley – which was originally to have been a supercharged car – was being developed. Since Rolls-

Royce Motors took over the production of cars from Rolls-Royce Ltd., we have sensed an increasing determination at Crewe to do justice to the Bentley name and heritage. Clearly for the production quantities involved, a Bentley with a completely new body was out of the question, so the only choice left was to endow an existing car with increased performance. The choice rested on the Bentley Mulsanne four-door saloon, and on turbocharging as the way of providing the extra performance. The decision to use the Corniche Solex carburettor arrangement also meant that in markets where strict emission requirements were met by fuel injection – USA, Australia, Japan – the Mulsanne Turbo would not be available. There were sound engineering reasons, as well as policy, behind the decision that there would not be a turbocharged Rolls-Royce.

So now, at last, the Bentley

marque has an unique model with a painted radiator shell and the emphasis on performance. In terms of total sales the actual numbers of Turbos will probably not exceed 100 cars a year, and in 1981 total Bentley Mulsanne sales were only 134 units. Nevertheless Bentley sales will account for a small but important part of Rolls-Royce Motors sales of 3,205 cars a year, and customers who buy the Turbo are probably unlikely to have bought a Rolls-Royce. The Mulsanne Turbo does not go on sale until September and no prices have yet been announced, but we would expect the price to be around £60,000.

Turbo choice

There are basically two ways of mating an exhaust-driven turbocharger to an engine. Probably the ultimate is to harness the frequency of exhaust pulses from each cylinder to give the best flow of turbine-driving gas by arranging exhaust manifold pipe lengths suitably -- a "tuned" manifold, with the pipes from each exhaust port remaining separate for as long as possible before arriving at the turbine. With a V8, that would ideally mean two turbos, one for each bank. The other way is to try to make the combined exhaust pulses from all the cylinders add together to provide a reservoir of pressurized gas to drive the turbine. When space under the bonnet is limited by a fat 6¾-litre V8 and the need to preserve a big car's minimum turning circle diameter (at 39ft 4in. not at all bad for a 10ft wheelbase), you have little choice; Rolls-Royce went for the reservoir system, with a single turbo. As John ("Jack") Read, project manager – future projects, puts it, "the final reason for the entire layout is what could be fitted under a bonnet that was already full."

The next decision is what size and match of turbocharger to use. Whilst the main point of the Bentley Mulsanne Turbo is

considerably better performance, the last thing wanted for such a car is the heavily stepped power curve with no bottom-end and a rush of power from 3,000rpm. Turbochargers use centrifugal compressors, which together with their turbine drive tend very strongly towards an exponential output, boost pressure increasing as the square of the engine speed (for a constant load). Crewe wanted both a worthwhile increase in top end power *and* appreciably more mid-range urge, by far more useful in most driving.

Rolls-Royce settled on a Garrett AiResearch T04 unit, with a very large turbine housing (thought to be the largest available) just big enough to suit the considerable exhaust mass flow, working a proportionately smaller compressor, which in contrast to the turbine is around the normal size for the job. It is mounted relatively high in front of the "A" bank (right hand seen from the driving seat) valve cover of the engine, the turbo spindle axis crossways in the car, its outer compressor end tilted upwards slightly. Both exhaust manifolds are of the simplest sort, each effectively a cast pipe with flanged openings opposite each exhaust port running flute-like forwards, and cast in nickel iron instead of the unblown car's grey cast iron. This more expensive material is used because it will run at higher temperatures without scaling or flaking internally from any free oxygen in the exhaust, which can obviously damage a hot turbine wheel turning at 80,000 or so rpm. The right hand manifold ends in what are effectively three branches, one carrying the wastegate valve assembly horizontally, pointing forwards, and another pointing upwards to flange-couple with the turbine housing and blending with the third branch which takes the exhaust feed from the left hand manifold via a 2in. dia stainless steel pipe. This pipe is shaped

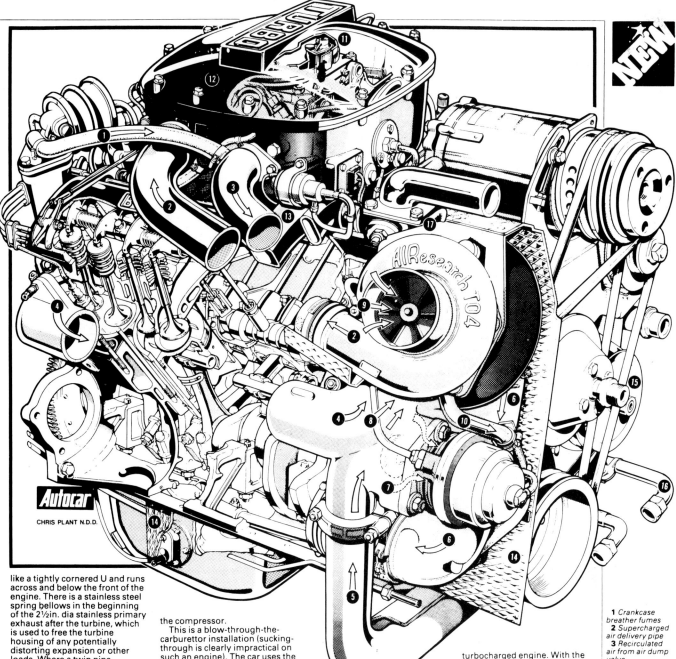

Autocar

CHRIS PLANT N.D.D.

like a tightly cornered U and runs
across and below the front of the
engine. There is a stainless steel
spring bellows in the beginning
of the 2½in. dia stainless primary
exhaust after the turbine, which
is used to free the turbine
housing of any potentially
distorting expansion or other
loads. Where a twin pipe
secondary exhaust system is
used on the unblown Mulsanne
(and Silver Spirit etc), with each
bank's exhaust running back to
emerge separately on each side
under the tail, the Mulsanne
Turbo system is single pipes (still
2½in.) until beside the
transmission when it forks into
two 2in. pipes which emerge as a
pair at the rear.

Sealed carburettor

As on the normal car, the air
intake from atmosphere is hidden
behind the right hand end of the
bumper, but it is 4¼in. bore
instead of 3in. The air cleaner
cum intake muffler is as before
behind the right hand headlamp
assembly but is simpler and
neater with no right-hand-
exhaust-manifold-heated air feed
(because of course of the inlet air
warming provided in the
turbocharger). Flexible trunking
(4in. dia) takes the filtered air to

the compressor.

This is a blow-through-the-
carburettor installation (sucking-
through is clearly impractical on
such an engine). The car uses the
same centrally mounted Solex
two-stage four-barrel
downdraught 4A1 carburettor
used on the nine per cent more
powerful Corniche and
Camargue engine, but with the
difference that it is sealed within
a cast aluminium air box which
dominates the engine
compartment, crown-like.
Besides the plethora of controls
– valves, solenoids, throttle
lever and so on – which encrust
its sides, barnacle-like to the
unaccustomed eye, two pipes run
from its right hand wall towards
the compressor.

The longer, larger of these
(about 2¼in. outside dia) lies low
and carries compressed intake air
at up to a design maximum of
7psi boost. The shorter, smaller
one (roughly 1⅝in.) runs from
what Rolls-Royce call the air
dump valve back from the
carburettor air box to the intake
side of the compressor; the
smaller flexible pipe to its side is

from the crankcase breather. The
working of the system is
explained below.

Modifications

Surprisingly little is done to the
engine, until one recalls how
Rolls-Royce tend to build things,
with plenty of strength and life in
reserve. The compression ratio is
not (as usual on many
turbocharger installations)
reduced, avoiding the tendency
to lose bottom end power with a
turbo, although this is not so
impressive as it might at first
seem when one learns that the
ratio is that standard on Rolls-
Royces up to roughly two years
ago, a comparatively modest 8-
to-1 (since then the normal cars
have gone up to 9-to-1); 8-to-1 is
however quite high for a

turbocharged engine. With the
boost provided, the effective
dynamic maximum compression
ratio is around 11-to-1 – more of
this anon.

The largest mechanical change
is to the Hepolite pistons, which
have what are called steel
"struts" cast into them. These are
H-shaped pieces of steel
strapping, two to each piston,
lying on their sides at gudgeon
pin boss height, whose very
much smaller coefficient of
thermal expansion than the
piston aluminium alloy is
designed to reduce the tendency
of the thicker boss sections of the
piston to cause out-of-round
distortion. The cylinder head
gaskets are slightly heavier duty
ones, although not as much as
you might expect; the exhaust
manifold gasketting is noticeably
stronger than before, because
where formerly it was subject to
little direct pressure, it is here
part of a high temperature
(around 950deg C) pressurized

1 Crankcase
breather fumes
2 Supercharged
air delivery pipe
3 Recirculated
air from air dump
valve
4 "A" bank
exhaust
5 Feed from "B"
bank exhaust
6 Exhaust outlet
from turbine
7 Flow past
wastegate valve
8 Exhaust to
turbine
9 Filtered air in
and breather
fumes and
recirculated air
10 Turbo oil drain
11 Four barrel
two stage Solex
downdraught
carburettor
12 Air box with
controls fixed to
outside
13 Inlet manifold
14 Radiant heat
shielding
15 New position
for power
steering pump
16 Oil cooler
pipes
17 Oil feed to
turbo

The Blower returns
continued

container subject to pressure variations.

The engine itself runs around 20deg C hotter, necessitating an oil cooler – which however thanks to thermostatic control is cut in only when needed – but not any radiator changes other than to ensure that the electric fan can switch itself on when the ignition is off, to cope with heat soak from the engine. As far as sparking plugs are concerned, normal Rolls-Royce wear is Champion, but to provide the wider heat range needed, copper-cored electrodes were needed, so Crewe interestingly plumped for a Japanese NGK plug. The overall weight increase is a very tolerable 51lb.

How it works – the control system

Persuading an exhaust-driven turbocharger to make an engine run more powerfully without destroying the engine, without irritating throttle response lag and a too top-end-ish power delivery is a fascinating job. Rolls-Royce go about it comprehensively and apparently thoroughly.

The aids and controls used in this role include a knock sensor – the first such application in a European market car – the wastegate, intake air circulation when boost is not wanted at low load, and a car maximum speed control.

The knock sensor (or "knock sensing accelerometer" as Rolls-Royce call it) itself is mounted behind the air box on the inlet manifold on the near side. That turned out to be the best place out of three or four positions tried, giving the most favourable "readings" of the eight cylinders. Supplied by AC Delco in the USA, (where knock sensing is increasingly used), it is effectively a microphone with ferrite core moving within a coil coupled to a circuit which can be tuned to a particular engine type's typical frequency of detonation, which is amongst other things a fundamental of the cylinder size. It is designed to "hear" only the noise of knock, when it progressively retards the Lucas magnetically triggered electronic ignition system by introducing an electronic delay into the ignition primary circuit between the trigger and the trigger signal amplifier. As soon as knocking stops, it attempts to advance the timing again, and so on; up to 8deg of retard is available.

This anti-knock feedback arrangement is not, according to Rolls-Royce, used full-bloodedly, since the ignition advance curve is set to the theoretical maximum – but that takes the engine very close to knocking at maximum mean effective pressure (maximum torque). The system is there to retard the ignition only if unusual conditions occur – poor fuel, awkward combinations of weather, or a heavy build-up of

combustion deposits after perhaps a lot of traffic crawling and cold starts.

One of the reasons for turbo lag is of course the time it takes after the throttle has been snapped open to accelerate the turbine to its working speed. That time can be reduced if there is the least drag on the turbine – in other words, by removing the restriction of closed or partly closed throttle against which the compressor normally works at idle and low load. The smaller diameter pipe between the carburettor air box and the upstream side of the compressor inlet is opened or shut by the air dump valve at the air box end. When there is some or a lot of vacuum in the air box, a vacuum switch switches off a solenoid which normally keeps the dump valve shut; the valve opens, and air being lightly urged on its way by the compressor is allowed back to the compressor inlet, recycling relatively unimpeded, permitting the turbo spindle assembly to spin much faster even when boost is not wanted.

The Solex carburettor itself is largely as found in the Rolls-Royce Corniche and Camargue, but has a vacuum-operated part-throttle mixture weakening device to improve cruise economy. Once the air box pressure rises 1psi above atmospheric, another pressure switch and solenoid arrangement allows boost pressure to the underside of the weakener piston, counter-acting it to return mixture to normal.

Safety measures to prevent engine overload are provided by the Garrett wastegate itself which is set to blow at 7psi boost, and also by the air dump valve which releases automatically if the wastegate hasn't already done so for any reason at 8 to 9 psi. As usual, the wastegate poppet valve is opened by boost pressure taken from near the start of the compressor volute and applied to one side of the wastegate-opening diaphragm. Less usually, the car has another limiter system which takes a signal from the electronic speedometer and restricts the maximum speed to 135 mph. As this figure approaches, a small electric vacuum pump normally used as part of the cruise control starts up; at 135 or so, it is allowed to apply vacuum to the other side of the wastegate diaphragm, opening the wastegate.

The fuel system is similar to American market fuel injection Rolls-Royces, in that it is a recirculating one using a moderate pressure Bosch pump placed near the tank under the car. This runs at 12 psi; a fuel pressure regulator in the air box maintains the supply to the pressurized carburettor at 4psi above the boost pressure.

Gearing it up

In the transmission, final drive output shafts are thickened, from 27 to 34mm dia, with Löhr and Brokamp constant velocity joints uprated and positive splined instead of taper fixing in the hubs. Relatively little happens to the General Motors THM 400 three-speed automatic gearbox. The torque converter has more fixing bolts than before (six, as on some more powerful GM cars),

and the change points are altered. Minimum throttle changes up to 1 to 2 and from 2 to 3 are at 12 and 26 mph; at full throttle, they are at 46 and 109 mph. Maximum kickdown speeds are 52 from 2 to 1 and 82 from top to 2. Automatic safety changes up are not included in the L and I over-ride ranges, the required maximum speeds being 56 and 88 mph respectively, corresponding, assuming no torque converter slip, to 4,400 and 4,650 rpm. Overall gearing is raised by 14½ per cent, using a 13/35 (2.692) final drive instead of the standard Mulsanne's 3.08, which as Jack Read puts it means that "although the car now goes faster, the drive line and engine don't notice any difference" – up to the final drive pinion at any rate.

This is confirmed by looking at the deliberately limited 135 mph maximum speed which at 29.97 mph per 1,000 rpm (and again assuming no converter slip) corresponds to 4,500 rpm, against the *Autocar* Road Test Rolls-Royce Silver Spirit's 119 mph at 4,550 rpm. Rolls-Royce admit that the unbridled Bentley Turbo as geared would achieve a slightly higher maximum.

How much horsepower and torque does the Turbo Bentley produce? As before, Rolls-Royce aren't saying. They do say that besides the "horsepower being sufficient and the torque very adequate", power is up by around 50 per cent installed, compared with the standard twin SU carburettor'd Mulsanne, that the Turbo engine reaches its maximum power by soon after 3,000 rpm, and that peak torque is nearly doubled and occurs at 2,500 rpm. We know from figures published in Germany (see *Autoview* this issue) that the standard car has a power peak of 198 bhp, so therefore the Turbo must be approaching 300 bhp. From what Crewe are prepared to say, and the evidence of the speed limiter, it is obvious that as before the car is undergeared, for good top gear acceleration.

The choice of the Bentley radiator shell is better aerodynamically as well as market-wise. Crewe will not divulge drag coefficients, but point out that the more rounded top to the Bentley shell is responsible for a 0.02 improvement in the C_d, relative to the Royce. Air flow through the radiator is better on the Bentley too, important with a hot underbonnet from the

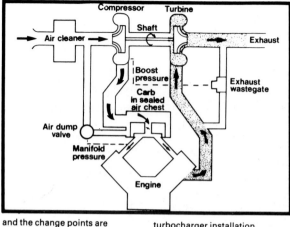

turbocharger installation.

By present day standards, the Bentley Mulsanne Turbo is probably the heaviest over-130-mph car made, scaling around 4,960lb (44.3cwt). With standing start acceleration claimed to 60 mph in 8sec instead of 10, and the 50 to 70 mph time improved by a spectacular 35 per cent (5sec instead of 7.8), the car imposes new demands on its tyres. So far, Avon, who have previously led all other tyre manufacturers in successfully tendering for Rolls-Royce custom first, particularly with steel-braced tyres, are the only suppliers of a new VR-rated 235/70-15in. tyre. Crewe's requirements have previously been accented towards a more flexible than usual sidewall, for optimum low speed ride, but a firmer compromise (probably slightly less quiet) has had to be adopted to cope with the higher speed of the Turbo, for understandable reasons. Avon, rightly jealous of their lead, will not give exact details of how the job is done, but do say that an important difference is that the VR tyre has wider and differently curved steel breaker plies which reinforce the tread and sidewall, avoiding sidewall vibration.

An unexpected further detail was that the considerably greater power at the wheel rims proved to induce the rear wheels to creep round inside the tyre slightly under certain severe circumstances, such as a succession of full bore 1-in-3 hill starts or a lot of high speed driving. Avon cured that by in effect tightening the bead wire to give the cover a tighter grip on the rim.

Otherwise, there are no suspension, steering or braking changes worth mentioning. High speed tyre pressures are interestingly different, at 27/35psi front/rear, instead of the standard car's HR tyre corresponding settings which dictate a much higher front pressure – 30/34psi. Bearing in mind that manufacturers, and especially Rolls-Royce, tend to go for the lowest pressure for the speed-load relationship compatible with good safety margins, this lower front pressure for the Turbo shows how much cooler the VR tyre is capable of running, because of its stiffer construction.

We have not yet had a chance to experience the Mulsanne Turbo on the road. No member of the Press will be allowed to drive one until May, and the first customer cars will not be ready for delivery before September. □

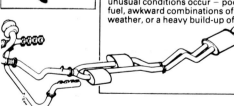

Sufficient isn't enough

Revealed — Rolls & Bentley bhp

TABLES OF specifications of the World's cars, including the *Autocar* Buyers' Guide, have always had some gaps where manufacturers were unable or unwilling to publish information that only they could provide. Notable among them are the power output and torque figures for Rolls-Royce and, more recently, Aston Martin ranges.

Ask Rolls-Royce how much power their cars have available and they will answer "sufficient". It is not because they don't know; as one would expect, Rolls-Royce are meticulous in their engineering detail and documentation. But it has never seemed fitting for them to indulge in a "power race" of the kind that the Americans with similar-sized engines to the Rolls V8 had in the 1960s and early 1970s.

Now, with the arrival of a new high performance car from Rolls-Royce — the Bentley Mulsanne Turbo, described in detail on page 16 of this issue — they have a dilemma. Even their normally confident publicity people were a little awkward at describing the turbocharger's effect as providing power that was "sufficient, plus 50 per cent".

Percentages, like other statistics, can be used to prove anything if you don't have the parameters on which they are based. The Mulsanne Turbo goes fast, we are told (for we have yet to try it), and the performance improvement is all the indication one needs of the power increase. So goes the official line.

Engineers and enthusiasts generally *do* want to know the figures. Thanks to a typically thorough German government department they now can. To gain Type Approval in Germany, full details of a car's specification must be declared, including power outputs and "homologated" performance figures. These figures are published by a Federal department based in Flensburg. From them we find that our estimate based on road test findings for the Silver Spirit and its predecessor of 200 bhp (net) for the standard car was remarkably accurate. The official German figure for the Spirit/Mulsanne is 148 Kw (198.5 bhp) at 4,000 rpm. And though the car is not yet on sale there or anywhere else, they also have figures for the Mulsanne Turbo which show that Rolls have been typically exact with their "plus 50 per cent" claim: 222 Kw (298 bhp) at

Rolls-Royce Silver Spirit has power enough for most purposes (above left) but how much is 50 per cent more for the Bentley Turbo?

3,800 rpm.

If one is mischievous enough to make the comparisons that Rolls-Royce have always sought to avoid, it is discovered that the Bentley Turbo fails by 1 bhp to exceed the maximum output of the 5.3-litre V12HE engine of the Jaguar XJ12 and XJ-S, and is also behind the quoted figures for the bigger Ferraris and Porsches. The standard Rolls and Bentley find that their beautifully smooth 6,750 c.c. V8 engine has less horsepower than Jaguar's 4.2-litre six-cylinder and several Mercedes and BMWs. But then Rolls-Royce and their customers know better than anyone else that power isn't everything. . . . ☐

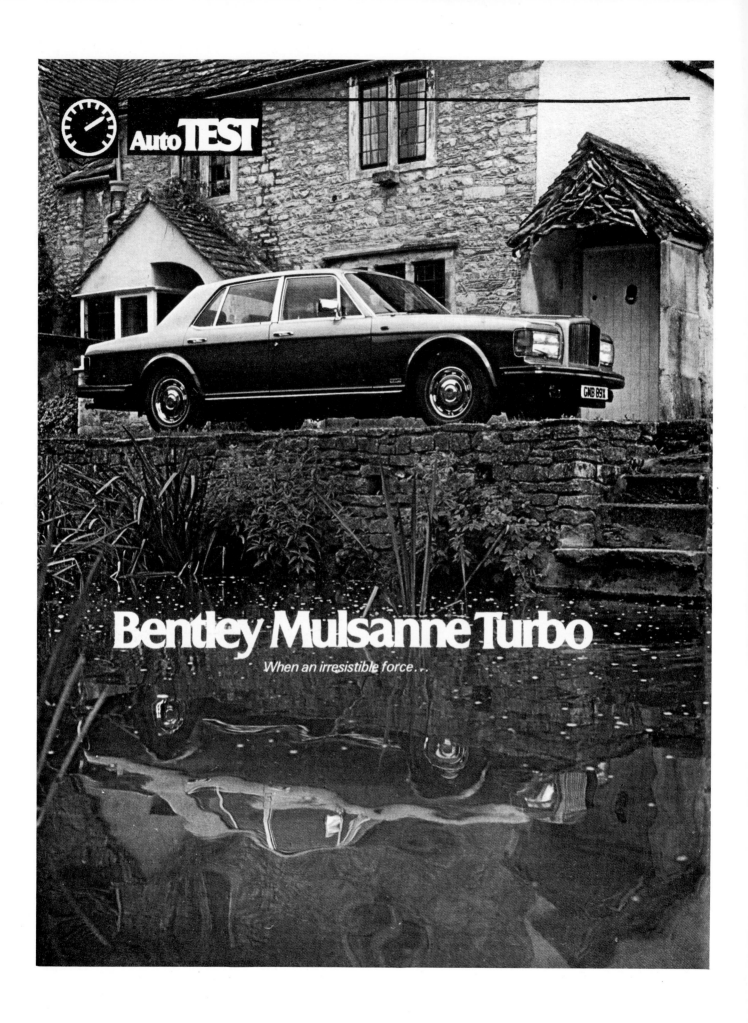

Bentley Mulsanne Turbo

When an irresistible force...

IF YOU'VE GOT a Bentley Mulsanne (or, for the same £55,240, the mechanically identical Rolls-Royce Silver Spirit), which is a car signifying power and prestige, it is understandable if you expected a little more substance to the power. The fact that at 119 mph (our Silver Spirit *Autotest* of 12 September 1981), it is between 24 and 31 mph slower in maximum speed than other less prestigious large cars might not rankle too much, but being up to 30 per cent less accelerative to 60 mph is, practically speaking, galling. For an extra £6,504, (£61,744), you can now put that right, with the Bentley Mulsanne Turbo, which if there were a prize for the world's most accelerative car considering its weight, would take the palm handsomely.

First, a brief reminder of the specification. Rolls-Royce could not afford, they say, to provide a unique body-chassis for the Bentley, even though it represents the first Bentley-only combination of engine and body since the R-type Bentley Continental of 1952. So it would be accurate to say that this more Bentley Bentley begins with the undeniable weight handicap of using the basic Rolls-Royce body-chassis, so that with the addition of the turbocharger equipment it scales 4,926lb in *Autocar* kerb condition (half-full tank, full oil and water, no occupants), which is 191lb more than the Silver Spirit we tested — in other words, it is effectively the same weight.

The turbocharger sits on the end of the right-hand (seen from the driver's seat) exhaust manifold front end, with a cross feed from the left-hand manifold. It blows into a massive cast aluminium air box — which dominates the underbonnet view — sealing the Solex carburettor in mid-rev at a maximum boost of 7psi. To encourage the turbine to keep spinning when the throttles are closed after being open, a valve in the side of the air box opens to permit the suddenly un-

Above left: From this angle only the observant will spot that this is a Mulsanne Turbo. Rear lamp clusters are arranged so that brake, rear fog and reversing lamps lift up with the bootlid.

Left: Distinguishing feature of the Turbo is the Bentley radiator painted in the body colour. Brush type headlamp wash/wipe and Lucas foglamps are standard equipment

Below: Paired exhaust outlets on the right distinguish this as a Turbo, and there is a badge on the left of the boot lid

wanted boost air to recirculate via a second pipe back to the intake side of the compressor. An exhaust wastegate is the basic boost control, and to prevent the car over-speeding into perhaps high speed tyre problems, the wastegate is, most unusually, opened by a vacuum applied by the cruise control pump to the wastegate-operating capsule, on receiving a signal from (in effect) the electronic speedometer at 135 mph. Further ultimate boost control is guaranteed if the wastegate misbehaves by the re-circulating compressor system, which opens automatically if boost rises to 8 psi. Finally, there is a knock sensor, which can retard the Lucas magnetically triggered ignition by up to 8deg.

The car is geared up, with a 2.692 instead of 3.08-to-1 final drive, and tyres are supplied solely by Avon at the moment, being a special VR-rated version of the 235/70-15in. standard tyre. They have to cope with what West German car type approval homologation papers reveal to be 298 bhp at 3,800 rpm.

Performance
Truly massive

As the body declares, this is still more of a Rolls-Royce than a Bentley should be, and it feels very much so when started up and driven with restraint. The first major difference is the time it often takes to start; frequently, particularly when hot, you have to keep the starter turning for much longer than usual before the engine catches, although it should be emphasized that it always starts reliably. There is no loss in engine refinement. The car pulls away as sweetly and superbly smoothly as it always has.

But once warm, try full throttle. It is a marvellous treat to feel such a large car surge forward as the Bentley Turbo does. There is a perceptible extra surge as the turbocharger really starts to get going, but with nothing violent about it; the car just goes and goes, its progress accompanied by the virtually imperceptible

gearchanges — the change in engine noise is more noticeable than any jerk — of the GM 400 transmission. This is a very quick motor car, especially considering its size and weight, and a great deal more accelerative than its standard original; the following figures make the point as well as any words:

Mph	Rolls-Royce Silver Spirit sec	Bentley Mulsanne Turbo sec
0-30	3.3	2.7
0-40	5.1	3.8
0-50	7.3	5.1
0-60	10.0	7.0
0-70	13.4	9.1
0-80	17.6	11.5
0-90	23.2	14.6
0-100	30.8	17.9
0-110	43.5	22.9
0-120	–	29.1
0-130	–	39.3

It is faster over its entire speed range than the Daimler Double-Six HE (0-60 mph in 8.1sec, 0-100 in 18.6 and 0-130 in 39.4), which is largely explained by the fact that the 14.4 per cent lighter and at least 10 per cent less drag-making 299 bhp Daimler is virtually ideally geared (in other words, neither over-or under-geared) whereas the Bentley is definitely under-geared by a considerable margin, and has appreciably lower intermediate gears too. If one trusts the German type approval source for the Bentley's normally unpublished power figures, the 3,800 rpm power peak in the Turbo corresponds to 46, 77 and 114 mph, (where the

corresponding Daimler figures for its 5,500 rpm power peak speeds are 60, 100 and 149 mph respectively).

Throttle response is excellent for a turbocharged car, with a maximum delay of not more than a second when one floors the pedal from lower speeds; lifting off briefly then accelerating again shows how well the boost recirculating system works, with hardly a hint of delay. Rolls-Royce have done a particularly good job as far as the choice of sparking plug (Japanese NGK) is concerned, since, as claimed by the makers, there is never any suggestion of plug fouling after a lot of town running. In town driving, there is the same perfectly progressive throttle control which exemplifies the normal Rolls-Royce or Bentley, but that urge is always there, ready to be tapped. The box will kick down into first at up to 34 mph and into second at up to 74 mph, yet it

Opposite page: Turbo reflections at Castle Combe, Wiltshire

Bentley Mulsanne Turbo

Long overdue justification of the Bentley name by its proprietors since 1931, Rolls-Royce. Using a single Garret AiResearch exhaust turbocharger blowing through a two-stage, four-barrel Solex carburettor (similar to Corniche one), with automatic recirculation of compressor air when throttles close (to help reduce turbo lag), power of largely standard 6.7-litre aluminium-alloy V8 is boosted from 198 bhp at 4,000 rpm (DIN) to 298 at 3,800 rpm, whilst peak torque is nearly doubled and occurs at 2,500 rpm. Car uses standard Mulsanne body, with higher gearing and painted radiator as main identification.

PRODUCED AND SOLD BY:
Rolls-Royce Motors Limited, Crewe, Cheshire CW1 3PL.

Right: The sealed airbox containing the downdraught four-choke Solex carburettor dominates the engine bay. Fuel supply and the power steering pump have been moved to the left of the engine

Below: The Garratt AiResearch TO4 turbocharger is mounted on the right of the engine at the front

Right: Ignition and lighting are controlled from the traditional circular Rolls-Royce panel to the right of the facia. The large knob immediately below operates the two-speed and intermittent wipers

Right: Facia is finished to the usual Rolls-Royce standard and differs only in the addition of the word Turbo. There is no rev counter, the paired circular instruments ahead of the driver housing the electronic speedometer (right) and oil pressure, oil level, water temperature, battery voltage and fuel gauges. The electric gearchange selector to the right of the steering column incorporates the cruise control and indicators; headlamp flashing and windscreen/ headlamp washers are controlled by a stalk on the left

does so with the greatest refinement, thanks partly to the jerk-absorbing weight of the car.

On the MIRA horizontal straight's good surface, traction was ideal, but whenever there is even the odd patch of wet road, one wonders whether a limited slip differential wouldn't be a good idea. Even if one has made a good initial full throttle getaway at, say, a dryly surfaced junction, but then encounters a shallow puddle with one back wheel whilst still in first gear, that wheel will spin somewhat easily.

Economy
What economy?

If you provide enough power to accelerate nearly 2½ tons laden

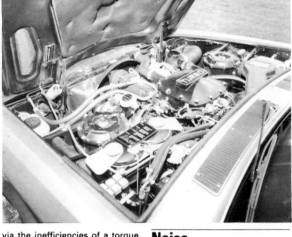

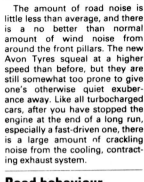

via the inefficiencies of a torque converter at around ½g initially, and commensurately quickly thereafter, and make the car generally under-geared as well — which doesn't help cruise economy — then you mustn't expect high mpg figures. Driving gently, avoiding more than half throttle and observing speed limits rigorously, one can achieve up to a best of 16.5 mpg; 14 to 15 mpg is more often seen, but if you run the car briskly, using its performance to a reasonable extent, 12 mpg is reached. It isn't difficult in hard driving, accelerating and braking to make the most of what is so willingly offered by the engine, to see just under 10 mpg.

We had experience of two cars, and both of them used appreciably more oil than normal for the Royce V8, at around 500 miles per pint instead of 1,000. Both fuel and oil fillers are typically pleasant details of the car; the fuel one has a slipping cap which prevents overtightening, and the oil filler has a racing style quick-release cap, which saves burnt hands when topping up a hot engine.

Noise
Still a Rolls-Royce

When we visited Crewe to learn about the mechanicals of the car for the Turbo's description *(Autocar* 6 March, 1982), the makers suggested that there had been a price to pay for the extra performance and the slightly less absorbent ride in noise. Judging by every Turbo Mulsanne we have tried, the price is a truly small one in all respects. No contemporary Rolls-Royce is quiet when its engine is worked, and you are certainly aware of some audible effort from under the bonnet. The sound is a low rumble, a typical V8 beat, not at all unpleasing, yet not really obtrusive, and neither, we suspect, appreciably louder than in the unblown car. Pulling away from 40 to 50 mph and using the power with moderate enthusiasm, one is just aware of turbocharger whine, but only just. We thought at one stage that we detected a suggestion of pneumatic hiss, presumably from the induction, under the same circumstances, but again this was only very low.

The amount of road noise is little less than average, and there is a no better than normal amount of wind noise from around the front pillars. The new Avon Tyres squeal at a higher speed than before, but they are still somewhat too prone to give one's otherwise quiet exuberance away. Like all turbocharged cars, after you have stopped the engine at the end of a long run, especially a fast-driven one, there is a large amount of crackling noise from the cooling, contracting exhaust system.

Road behaviour
Predictable

Driven normally, and after the first half hour, when one finds the steering and brakes a little too responsive, the high gearing and light effort required from both these controls is a delight, taking most of the effort out of driving. The steering is rack and pinion, and is remarkably responsive. The car has a remarkably tight lock for its size — 39ft 2in. mean diameter which when combined with only 3.3 turns lock to lock confirms how high the gearing is. Only when swinging from one direction to the other does one notice any slop due to cleverly arranged compliance in the suspension, and even then it isn't much. The car is, of course, basically an understeerer and has excellent straight stability. Cornered hard, as its performance

demands, it tucks the front sidewalls under appreciably less than the standard car, and provided one keeps the right foot down, understeer eventually predominates, unless the corner is a tight one, when power breakaway is obviously likely. The swing-axle effects of the semi-trailing arm rear end are more obvious on this than the normal car if you decellerate sharply in mid-corner taken too fast; the tail comes out markedly, but the quick steering plus the reasonably forgiving character of the breakaway makes collecting and tidying the slide relatively easy.

The car rolls somewhat less than usual for this body. One example tried during the test period had cloth rather than leather seats, and we would suggest to any Bentley Turbo purchaser that he or she specifies cloth, as it largely makes up for the to-some irritating breadth and lack of sideways location of the seat when cornering, by discouraging one's bottom from sliding.

Left: Interior is spacious and well appointed. Seats are upholstered in the best Connolly hide, with Jersey Kapwood polyester cloth as an option, and lambswool rugs are included. Rear seat passengers have removable sloping footrests

Ride is an interesting mixture, remembering that the principal difference is slightly stiffer tyre construction. One senses this in the car's increased sensitivity to small, high frequency sharp bumps, which are transmitted to the body, whilst long lower frequency inequalities are soaked up very well, with the exception of pronounced humps, over which the Bentley flops, Citroen-like (which isn't surprising bearing in mind what its suspension owes to Citroen). For the fast cross-country driving which the Turbo invites so winningly, the suspension needs to be less soft. We twice experienced bumps which brought the car to its bump stops, where other cars of similar character are not so troubled. There is also a perceptible amount of that sideways jogging, which moves the head from side to side at times, usually caused by anti-roll bar stiffness. It has a slightly loose feeling as one drives along, producing a gentle pitching motion reminiscent of a ship, and some sharp bumps provoke a suspicion that the body shakes, felt as well as seen in the movement of the interior mirror. The small tendency towards boom resonance provoked by noisy coarse surfaces is perhaps a product of the same thing.

Brakes are first class, pulling the car up very well without undue bias to either end, and resisting our exacting safe test successfully, even if the successive 0.5g stops from 91 mph at ¼-mile intervals did become somewhat rough towards the end of the test. We had a lot of wet weather during the test, and even after a long wet motorway run, the brakes always pulled up square as one first used them coming up the slip road – this is still not so for every fast car.

We mentioned traction earlier. It is worth emphasizing that with this power coupled to a semi-trailing arm suspension, it is well to respect what over-enthusiasm

can do in wet or greasy weather. This is not even to suggest that there is anything even faintly difficult about driving the Mulsanne Turbo in poor conditions, since keeping the car tidy is made so exceptionally easy by the smooth progression of the throttle control; there is no excuse at all for driving this car jerkily.

Behind the wheel
Stately

The driving position is not in the least different from usual in this body, so that one enjoys an exceptionally commanding view out thanks to the little bit of extra height of the car. Only to the side and three-quarter rear is vision poor, made more so by the width of the middle roof pillar and the rear head restraints, which combine uneasily with the thickness of the rear quarter pillar. The view forward is excellent, even somewhat stirring, given the subtle hint of the Bentley radiator shape, and the muscular and imperious shoulders formed by the tips of the wing fronts, which make placing this big car unusually easy.

Controls are unadulterated Rolls-Royce, and will be entirely familiar to Silver Spirit or Mulsanne owners. There is no boost gauge – just a fairly discreet "Turbo" badge under the digital display for outside temperature, stopwatch and clock. The minor switches look a little old-fashioned to people not used to Royces, but in fact they work particularly well, and are perfectly logical. One might criticise the rotary wiper switch mildly, placed under the key-cum-lamps-switch sub-panel, where the key fob obstructs it slightly; a well arranged stalk would be more convenient.

Seat comfort in cornering has been mentioned. The well-known electric adjustment is as refined and quiet as before, but has been somewhat overtaken by the S-class Mercedes arrangement,

which has a better, logical switch, and has the extra lazy convenience of seat back rake control. Drivers taller than 6ft may well demand a little more rearward adjustment than is provided, but for most sizes of person the car is most accommodating.

The automatic two-level heating and air-conditioning system is very satisfactory, and we were very impressed with the performance and reproduction of the standard Blaupunkt Toronto SQR32 stereo radio/cassette player, which is helped by unusually good loudspeaker installation, devoid of most of the too-usual boom problems.

Living with the Mulsanne Turbo

This is of course an immensely pleasing car to get to know. There are a myriad details which contribute to one's pleasure in it. Visibility in the wet is aided by the excellent pantograph linkage of the driver's side wiper arm, which allows it to sweep close and parallel to the screen pillar. Neither wiper blade is too short, so that the best possible area is swept.

All of the controls, both major and minor, are well harmonized – that is, they are all of similar character in the effort needed to work them; this plus the generally very high standard of smoothness and precision makes a subtle difference to the pleasure of using the car. The central locking system works very well, and is not noisy. The automatic transmission selector on the steering column with its electric action is as usual a delight to use.

As a carrier, the car is most satisfactory. For major items the boot is a good shape and very generous, its low sill making loading unusually easy. Oddment space is generous too, with a central open tray between the seats, full length door pockets in front, a

proper glove locker, big elasticated sleeve pockets in the backs of the front seats, and the large rear shelf.

Accommodation in the back is good too, as it ought to be, and of course the standard of luxury is high, with detail touches like the individual vanity mirrors in each side pillar.

The Bentley range

There are just three cars bearing the winged B; the standard Mulsanne, twin sister to the Rolls-Royce Silver Spirit, at the same £55,240, the Mulsanne Turbo at £61,744, and the Corniche convertible, which has the unblown but slightly more-powerful-than-Mulsanne Solex carburettor engine at £73,168. It is stressed by Rolls-Royce that the Bentley Mulsanne Turbo is and will remain unique, available only as a Bentley for good aero-dynamic reasons, given the more efficient Bentley radiator and front, in addition to marketing policy.

Left: The boot is capacious as befits a luxury saloon. The battery and a spare can of Castrol LHM fluid (for brakes and suspension) are housed on the right. Tools come in a fitted tray. The spare wheel is below the boot floor

Figures taken at 7,647 miles by our own staff at the Motor Industry Research Association proving ground at Nuneaton and on the Continent.

All Autocar test results are subject to world copyright and may not be reproduced in whole or part without the Editor's written permission.

TEST CONDITIONS:
Wind: 8-12 mph
Temperature: 18 deg C (64 deg F)
Barometer: 29.97 in. Hg (1016 mbar)
Humidity: 70 per cent
Surface: dry asphalt and concrete
Test distance: 1,313 miles

MAXIMUM SPEEDS

Gear	mph	kph	rpm
Top (mean)	135	217	4,500
(best)	135	217	4,500
2nd	104	167	5,150
1st	62	100	5,150

ACCELERATION

FROM REST
True mph	Time (sec)	Speedo mph
30	2.7	32
40	3.8	42
50	5.1	51
60	7.0	62
70	9.1	72
80	11.5	83
90	14.6	95
100	17.9	106
110	22.9	118
120	29.1	130
130	39.3	142

Standing ¼-mile: 15.1 sec, 91 mph
Standing km: 27.8 sec, 118 mph

IN EACH GEAR
mph	Top	2nd	1st
0-20	–	–	1.8
10-30	–	–	1.8
20-40	–	–	2.1
30-50	–	–	2.7
40-60	–	3.8	3.4
50-70	–	4.1	–
60-80	–	4.5	–
70-90	–	5.5	–
80-100	7.1	7.6	–
90-110	8.5	–	–
100-120	11.4	–	–
110-130	16.8	–	–

FUEL CONSUMPTION

Overall mpg:
12.1 (23.3 litres/100km)
2.67 mpl

Constant speed
Bentley fuel system incompatible with *Autocar* test equipment

Autocar formula: Hard 10.9 mpg
Driving Average 13.3 mpg
and conditions Gentle 15.7 mpg

Grade of fuel: Premium, 4-star (97 RM)
Fuel tank: 23.5 Imp. galls (107 litres)
Mileage recorder reads: 0.5 per cent long

Official fuel consumption figures
(ECE laboratory test conditions; not necessarily related to Autocar figures)
Urban cycle: 11.4 mpg
Steady 56 mph: 21.0 mpg
Steady 75 mph: 16.3 mpg

OIL CONSUMPTION

(SAE 10W/30) 900 miles/litre

BRAKING

Fade (from 91 mph in neutral)
Pedal load for 0.5g stops in lb

	start/end		start/end
1	24/24	6	24/26
2	22/26	7	28/28
3	24/28	8	28/32
4	28/28	9	32/32
5	30/38	10	32/32

Response (from 30 mph in neutral)

Load	g	Distance
10 lb	0.20	151 ft
15 lb	0.32	94 ft
20 lb	0.50	62 ft
30 lb	0.75	40 ft
40 lb	1.05	29 ft
Handbrake	0.30	100 ft

Max. gradient: 1 in 3

CLUTCH

WEIGHT

Kerb, 44.0 cwt/4,926 lb/2,234 kg
(Distribution F/R, 53.0/47.0)
Test, 47.6 cwt/5,336 lb/2,420 kg
Max. payload, 992 lb/450 kg

DIMENSIONS

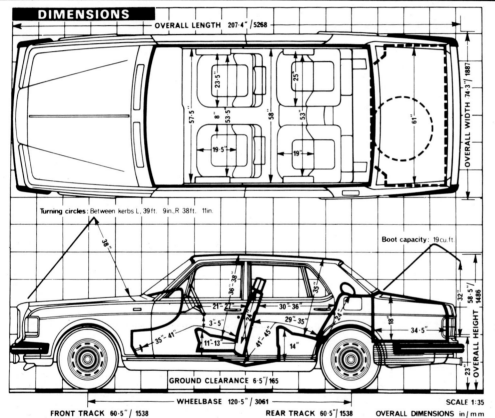

OVERALL LENGTH 207·4" /5268
OVERALL WIDTH 74·3"/1887
Turning circles: Between kerbs L, 39 ft. 9in., R 38ft. 11in.
Boot capacity: 19 cu. ft.
OVERALL HEIGHT 58·5"/1486
GROUND CLEARANCE 6·5"/165
WHEELBASE 120·5" / 3061
SCALE 1:35
FRONT TRACK 60·5"/1538
REAR TRACK 60·5" /1538
OVERALL DIMENSIONS in/mm

PRICES

Basic	£49,560.00
Special Car Tax	£4,130.00
VAT	£8,053.50
Total (in GB)	**£61,743.50**
Licence	£80.00
Delivery charge (London)	£70.00
Number plates	£20.00
Total on the Road (exc. insurance)	**£61,913.50**

EXTRAS *(inc. VAT)*

Vinyl roof	£957.42
Air horns	£187.50
*Fire extinguisher	£54.20
Hide headlining	£544.43
Picnic tables	£386.84
Non-standard paint finish	£720.41

*Fitted to test car

TOTAL AS TESTED ON THE ROAD	**£61,967.70**
Insurance	Group 8/9

SERVICE & PARTS

Change	Interval 6,000	12,000	24,000
Engine oil	Yes	Yes	Yes
Oil filter	Yes	Yes	Yes
Gearbox oil	No	Yes	Yes
Spark plugs	No	Yes	Yes
Air cleaner	No	Yes	Yes
Total cost	**£171.72**	**£244.91**	**£288.04**

(Assuming labour at £17.25/hour inc. VAT)

PARTS COST *(including VAT)*

Brake pads (2 wheels)—front	£178.62
Brake pads (2 wheels)—rear	£125.40
Exhaust complete (stainless)	£1,213.12
Tyre—each (typical)	£159.60
Windscreen (laminated)	£347.19
Headlamp unit	£32.63
Front wing	£499.87
Rear bumper	£886.39

WARRANTY

36 months/55,000 miles

SPECIFICATION

ENGINE
Head/block	Front, rear drive
Head/block	Al. alloy
Cylinders	8, in 90 deg V, wet liners
Main bearings	5
Cooling	Water
Fan	Viscous plus electric
Bore, mm (in.)	104.1 (4.10)
Stroke, mm (in.)	99.1 (3.90)
Capacity, cc (in.³)	6,750 (412)
Valve gear	Ohv, hydraulic tappet
Camshaft drive	Gear
Compression ratio	8.0-to-1
Ignition	Breakerless
Carburettor	Solex 4A1, 2 stage
Turbocharger	Garrett AiResearch TO4
Max boost pressure	7 psi
Max power	298 bhp (DIN) at 3,800 rpm

TRANSMISSION

Type	Automatic GM 400 3-speed, torque converter

Gear	Ratio	mph/1000rpm
Top	1.00-2.2	29.97
2nd	1.48-3.26	20.25
1st	2.48-5.46	12.08
Final drive gear	Hypoid	
Ratio	2.69-to-1	

SUSPENSION

Front—location	Independent, double wishbones
—springs	Coil
—dampers	Telescopic
—anti-roll bar	Standard
Rear—location	Ind., semi-trail. arms
—springs	Coil+gas; auto. level control
—dampers	Gas
—anti-roll bar	Standard

STEERING

Type	Rack and pinion
Power assistance	Hydraulic
Wheel diameter	15.2 in.
Turns lock to lock	3.3

BRAKES

Circuits	Doubled, powered hydraulic
Front	11.0 in. dia. disc
Rear	11.0 in. dia disc
Servo	Power system
Handbrake	Foot operated, hand release, separate rear calipers

WHEELS

Type	Steel
Rim width	6 in.
Tyres—make	Avon
—type	Radial, tubeless
—size	235/70VR15
—pressures	F 27, R 35 psi (normal driving)

EQUIPMENT

Battery	12V 68Ah
Alternator	75A
Headlamps	60/55W
Reversing lamp	Standard
Electric fuses	28 plus 3 thermal cut-outs
Screen wipers	2-speed
Screen washer	Electric
Interior heater	Auto. air blending 2-level
Air conditioning	Standard
Interior trim	Hide seats, cloth headlining
Floor covering	Pile carpet and lambswool rugs
Jack	Scissor
Jacking points	Two each side
Windscreen	Laminated
Underbody protection	Galvanised steel, phosphate dip, rubber compound in seams

Bentley Mulsanne Turbo (A) £61,744

Front engine, rear drive

Capacity
6,750 c.c.

Power
298 bhp (DIN) at 3,800 rpm

Weight
4,926 lb/2,234 kg

Autotest
23 October 1982

Aston Martin Lagonda (A) £56,500

Front engine, rear drive

Capacity
5,340 c.c.

Power
300 bhp (DIN) at 5,000 rpm

Weight
4,219 lb/1,914 kg

Autotest
18 July 1981

Daimler Double-Six HE (A) £20,748

Front engine, rear drive

Capacity
5,345 c.c.

Power
299 bhp (DIN) at 5,500 rpm

Weight
3,836 lb/1,740 kg

Autotest
18 July 1981

Ferrari 400i (A) £35,300

Front engine, rear drive

Capacity
4,823 c.c.

Power
310 bhp (DIN) at 6,400 rpm

Weight
4,303 lb/1,952 kg

Autotest
365 GT4 2+2 (manual)
4 October 1975
(400i not yet tested)

Maserati Kyalami 4.2 £25,998

Front engine, rear drive

Capacity
4,136 c.c.

Power
270 bhp (DIN) at 6,000 rpm

Weight
3,836 lb/1,740 kg

Autotest
8 July 1978

Mercedes-Benz 500 SEL (A) £25,570

Front engine, rear drive

Capacity
4,973 c.c.

Power
240 bhp (DIN) at 4,750 rpm

Weight
3,570 lb/1,620 kg

Autotest
11 October 1980 (500 SE)

MPH & MPG

Maximum speed (mph)

Daimler Double-Six HE(A)	150
Ferrari 365GT*	150
Maserati Kyalami	147
Mercedes-Benz 500 SE (A)	145
Aston Martin Lagonda (A)	143
Bentley Mulsanne Turbo (A)	135

Acceleration 0-60 (sec)

Bentley Mulsanne Turbo (A)	7.0
Ferrari 365GT*	7.1
Mercedes-Benz 500SE (A)	7.5
Maserati Kyalami	7.6
Daimler Double-Six HE (A)	8.1
Aston Martin Lagonda (A)	8.8

Overall mpg

Daimler Double-Six HE (A)	16.4
Maserati Kyalami	15.3
Mercedes-Benz 500SE (A)	15.2
Aston Martin Lagonda (A)	13.7
Bentley Mulsanne Turbo (A)	12.1
Ferrari 365GT*	11.0

* 400i not yet tested

There are inevitably difficulties when it comes to finding cars comparable to the Mulsanne Turbo. There are ones with engines nearly as big or equally powerful, but none of them however mechanically equal or superior quite combine the power with the refinement *and* the still very Rolls-Royce character of the Bentley. As we have tried to make clear in the *Autotest* itself, the Mulsanne Turbo may certainly be remarkably accelerative for its weight and size, but because of the body-chassis in which the engine finds itself, in spite of the maker's declaration that this is a Bentley and nothing else, it is still much more a faster Royce than anything else. However, as someone is bound to point out, a cat may look at a king, and there are cars with which this machine can be compared. Our list suffers from the lack of an opportunity so far to test the current 400i automatic Ferrari, and the fact that the 500SEL figures shown are in fact those for the earlier, conventionally geared 500SE (it is now higher-geared, and much more economical). But given that the 365 GT4 was a manual box car, so that the automatic 400i is unlikely to accelerate better, and that the higher gearing of the current Mercedes won't improve its acceleration, the 0-60 top of the table position for the Bentley is not challenged by any of the others.

ON THE ROAD

Talking about a recent comparison in *Autocar* between the Jaguar (here read Daimler) and 500SE Mercedes, someone wondered how it could be that a 14-year-old car could still be found to have a more satisfactory combination of performance, refinement, ride and handling than the three-year-old-one. The uncomfortable answer is, of course, that some designers get it right, and another lot get it not so right in every way even with the advantage of all that hindsight. The point applies here for several of the Daimler's rivals; the Coventry-built Double-Six HE still has

the best compromise between ride and handling for all road purposes. The Bentley's softness is very pleasant in town and at slow speeds, but limits the extent to which its performance advantage can be used out of town, on country roads. None of the others have the ride comfort at boulevard speeds of the Bentley although the Mercedes is close, whilst the two Italian cars are likely to be more fun. The Lagonda's length and overhangs are sometimes limiting in narrower ways, but it nevertheless handles surprisingly well for such a large car.

SIZE & SPACE

Legroom front/rear (in.)

(seats fully back)

Aston Martin Lagonda	45/37
Mercedes-Benz 500SE	42/40
Bentley Mulsanne Turbo	41/41
Maserati Kyalami	43/35
Daimler Double-Six HE	39/36.5
Ferrari 365GT	41/29

The first five in the list here are all generous cars, with no space problems for the majority of sizes of occupant. Some very tall drivers might want a little more rearward adjustment in most of these, including the otherwise very capacious Bentley, but for most there is no problem. The Bentley boot is very practically shaped and accommodating, and loading it is made easier by the low sill. The Daimler's elegant tail is bought at a little cost in boot room, since height is not so great. The Lagonda boot is small for the size of car; the Mercedes one is huge. Kyalami accommodation is better than one expects from Italian cars.

VERDICT

As always when spending a lot of money, the final choice boils down entirely to personal taste. For the man who wants Continental glamour of a powerful kind, both the Ferrari and Maserati offer surprisingly restrained extravagance; in the case of the Maserati, there is now the added appeal of rarity — the car has just ceased production in Italy, although examples are still available. The Lagonda offers undeniable extravagance, in its appearance as much as anything else. The most closely comparable cars are the Mercedes, Daimler and Bentley, in that they share more of the same aims, the common denominator being refinement. The Daimler wins hands down on value for money, and those who point to its comparative common-ness must be reminded that it is the best all-rounder of the bunch, and top in its combination of roadholding, ride and handling. In this company, the Mercedes doesn't look as expensive as usual, and in its current form offers the greatest (an impressive greatest) efficiency in a very marvellous car. If fuel costs don't matter, the Bentley is immensely attractive and enjoyable — quite, if one may be so vulgar about a car from Crewe, the most point-and-squirt near-limousine ever to come from that factory. It's up to you, the lucky buyer.

NEW CARS
A STIFFER UPPER LIP

Rolls-Royce has taken the Bentley Mulsanne Turbo and given it the stiffer suspension its 135mph performance potential deserves. Michael Scarlett drives and describes Turbo R

Announced at Geneva in March, the Bentley Turbo R is basically the 135mph, 7secs 0-60 Mulsanne Turbo with the stiffer suspension its performance deserves. As *Autocar* pointed out in the October 1982 Road Test, the original Turbo suffered unduly from its too-soft springing, both in too much roll, and, more seriously, far too little resistance to bottoming on roads which did not trouble an XJ12.

It is very encouraging to find that Bentley's proprietor, Rolls-Royce, realised this, and has done something generally pretty impressive to correct the weakness.

According to Rolls-Royce engineer Phil Harding, the company has been examining the question of less boulevard suspension for the Bentley for some time, apparently for up to five years. The coming of engineering director Mike Dunn two years back pushed both the idea and the severity of the change even further.

Moving nearer the handling side of the inevitable ride-handling compromise than before immediately dictated the only outward sign differentiating the R from the standard Turbo — the fitting of 275/55VR15ins Pirelli P7 tyres (the size already existed for Aston Martin) on low pressure die-cast aluminium alloy wheels made by the German Ronal company (suppliers to BMW and Audi).

A lot of experimenting was done with all the major suspension variables, although the time available limited any really large changes. The upshot is interesting. No changes were made to the coil springs, which are as normal Rolls-Royce Silver Spirit, as are the gas spheres and struts.

The things that did alter were (a) anti roll bar stiffness, up by 100 per cent front and 60 per cent rear, (b) the dampers — bump slightly stiffened but rebound by a factor depending on wheel movement speed of up to four times, (c) rear sub-frame sideways location — anchored later-

With Bentley Turbo R Rolls-Royce has done something pretty impressive in its attempts to tackle the unduly soft springing and excessive body roll

ally by its own hard-rate rubber bushed *Panhard rod*, (d) the self-levelling, (e) engine mounts, to which a damper was added to eliminate a 13 Hz resonant shake excited by the other alterations, and (f) slightly higher effort steering, achieved by fitting a 50 per cent stiffer torsion bar in the power assistance.

Work with Pirelli at the Nardo bowl·in southern Italy emphasized that, although the car ultimately was no faster — it is road-speed limited by the lack of a suitably wide ratio range gearbox and the 4500rpm speed limit of the engine, and not by the tyres as we were originally led to believe — high-speed stability could be better. Revisions to the front air dam were made, reducing drag by 7 per cent and front lift by 15 per cent.

The self levelling on the standard Royce works independently on each rear wheel so that, if the load is asymmetric, the car levels laterally as well as longways. Because changes in suspension height due to load variations are countered by pumping up each rear strut, however, the ride *and* roll rates change, which alters the handling character. To avoid this, the struts are linked hydraulically, so that levelling is applied to the 'axle' as a whole. The loss of the lateral attitude correction is countered by the increased roll bar stiffness. Finally, the cast wheels have Pirelli's safety rim section, which improves cover retention in any rapid puncture. The slightly smaller rolling diameter of the Pirellis means a small reduction in the top speed.

DRIVING THE R

You immediately notice the loss of low speed bump absorption, which is marked, and made more noticeable by what seems to be a vibration in the body itself, betrayed by the steering column. Again at low speeds, up to 40mph, potholes or other sharp bumps produce an unpleasantly noticeable jarring — most un-Rolls-Royce but no worse than average for some other cars. There is also, at higher speeds, that obvious sideways rocking familiar from many cars with stiff anti-roll arrangements. Bump-thump has increased, but not as

much as one might expect.

These are the prices paid for what is otherwise an infinitely more satisfactory motor car to drive fast on a twisting road. It is now the size of the beast which limits it, not the suspension. There is still that superb rack and pinion steering, more responsive and so delightfully and unexpectedly precise, now with better 'turn-in' and backed up by a reduction in roll that is both very welcome and remarkable. Anyone perceptive who is familiar with the old car or with normal Rolls-Royces cannot help but notice the greatly improved reduction in the car's lateral sloppi-

ness, which makes fast or tight S-bends vastly tidier to take. The improvements point up the car's power-on understeer more in a corner; I didn't find enough road to investigate how much the medium tail-happy semi-trailing arm lift-off cornering behaviour has been tamed, but suspect that it is better.

There is still the marvellous surge of quiet power — it seemed quieter than before — so nearly instant by turbo standards, backed up by the entrancing smoothness and quick kickdown of the GM box in this 2¼cwt machine. The combination of this with the new tautness may cost something

After extensive reworking of the suspension, test sessions with Pirelli at the Nardo bowl in Italy resulted in revisions to the front air dam. Other distinguising external features are the 275/55VR15 Pirelli P7 tyres, mounted on low pressure die-cast aluminium alloy wheels

notable in slow speed ride, but the price is less noticeable at speed, making the car's cross-country travel a revelation. If you are in the £68,420 class, can afford the typical 13mpg consumption I saw and enjoy driving yourself, tell the chauffeur to move over and get one.

This is a Bentley that is fun. ∎

ROAD TEST   BENTLEY TURBO R

| **PRICE** £79,397, **TOP SPEED** 143mph, **0-60mph** 7.0secs |
| **FOR** Performance, build quality **AGAINST** Ride, price, ergonomics |

ADDING FUEL TO THE FIRE

With the addition of fuel injection has come sensational performance and a price tag to match for the Turbo R. But to whom will this Bentley appeal?

There was a time, not so long ago, when Bentley played a faint second fiddle to Rolls-Royce. That is no longer the case. Rolls-Royce's management now recognises the value of the Bentley name and tradition and has developed the image — along with the sales — to take advantage. In a terribly upmarket way, Bentley is now the enthusiast, high performance partner, and never more so than in the turbocharged Bentley R.

Rolls-Royce has long built its reputation on superb build standards and exceptional refinement. One of the cornerstones of that refinement is an engine that is understressed by any normal standard. It was therefore a natural choice, once the decision has been made to build a higher-perform-

ance Bentley image, that turbocharging should be the chosen route. The adoption of a turbocharger boost system gave far more power and torque than Rolls-Royce owners could ever previously have dreamed of, but the application was — and is — strictly Bentley. The Turbo R is one of four listed Bentley models (there are also four Rolls-Royces); it lies between the 'ordinary' Mulsanne (the direct Bentley equivalent of the Rolls-Royce Silver Spirit) and the Bentley Continental, the Corniche's opposite number.

It lies between, on price that is, but certainly not on performance. By any standards, the performance figures we quote hereafter are quick: by the standards of a car weighing well over

two tons at the kerb, they are sensational. They are a guide not only to the benefits of turbocharging but also to fuel injection, one of the two major technical innovations which justify our retest of the Turbo R since our original definitive test of September 1985, the other major change is the introduction, as standard, of anti-lock braking. In addition, the governor which originally held the maximum speed to 'only' 135mph has been removed.

Without anticipating the conclusion of this test, it has to be said that the standards by which one judges an £80,000 car have to be different. Nobody seriously questions the fact that such price levels take one well beyond the point of diminishing

returns, so far as the normal parameters of motoring efficiency are concerned. Half that price will, beyond dispute, buy you a car of generous accommodation and impeccable behaviour, superb comfort, high performance and excellent equipment. So why should anyone spend twice as much?

The answer to that fascinating question is what this test, hopefully, is all about. If there is a yardstick, it is the raw results of the 1985 test which showed a maximum speed of 134mph, 0-60mph time of 6.9secs and overall test consumption of 13.4mpg. The adoption of fuel injection in place of carburettors sometimes benefits performance, sometimes fuel economy, sometimes both: but an

By any standards, the two-ton Bentley Turbo's performance is quite sensational

improvement of some kind must clearly be expected, if only to help justify a price increase of £10,500 — handsomely in excess of the inflation rate in the intervening two years.

Price will not, one suspects, be the main consideration for Bentley Turbo R buyers, any more than fuel consumption. You may agree with Rockefeller that if you have to ask the price, you can't afford it; or you make take the view that most millionaires got rich by knowing the price (and value) of everything they ever bought, to the last penny.

▶

209

TECHNICAL FOCUS

You have to be observant to tell the difference between the Silver Shadow chassis of 1965 and the Bentley Turbo R chassis of '87. Wheelbase has scarcely changed, though the track is wider and the tyres are bigger; the suspension is still double wishbones at the front and semi-trailing arms behind. The engine is still a big all-alloy V8 driving through a three-speed General Motors GM400 automatic.

Yet the changes are there. The most important are the adoption of turbocharging, via a big Garrett TO4 unit, and now of Bosch KE-Jetronic electronic fuel injection. This helps lift power to 328bhp (as always, Rolls-Royce remains officially coy about power outputs, but that is the quoted figure in Germany where the figure is legally required to be published). Torque output remains a matter for conjecture but can scarcely be less than 400lb ft.

Bosch also provides the other car's other major innovation — the ABS anti-lock brake system. Installation was eased by the fact that Rolls-Royce already used a fully powered brake system rather than one which was mere-ly power-assisted.

When the Bentley Turbo first appeared there was confusion about the deliberate limitation of maximum speed to 135mph. Rolls-Royce said it was out of respect for the tyres; the tyre manufacturers said it wasn't. In any event, the limiter has now been removed and the Turbo R is free to find its natural maximum in an awesome contest between power, gearing and CdA. The car is much higher geared overall than previously, the final drive ratio having been lifted all the way from 2.69 to 2.28-to-1.

PERFORMANCE

Part of the interest of the fuel-injected engine is to see how it starts and idles. Our test took place during one of the hottest weeks (so far!) of the year. Starting was always immediate, warm-up appeared to be rapid, and there was no suggestion of heat-soak fuel vaporisation problems even when restarted at the end of a long, hard drive — often a tricky moment for turbocharged engines. Idling was smooth at all times; the fuel injection plays its part here but the engine has also been modified with a 'real' flywheel to supplement the inertia of the torque converter and housing.

With the taller final drive acceleration should have suffered a 15 per cent decline — were it not for the claimed 10 per cent extra output of the fuel-injected (and otherwise improved) engine. Against this is weight: and the car proved nearly 100lb heavier than the previous model.

The higher gearing does have the small advantage of making 60mph within the scope of the GM400's low ratio at the 4500rpm red line (backed up, as usual, by a 'safety change' upwards if the driver transgresses). By the same token, 100mph now falls within reach of intermediate. In practice, however, it's best to leave the transmission to sort itself out, in which case full-throttle upchanges come at 57 and 91mph while downshifts are possible at up to 32mph from intermediate to low, and 84mph from high to intermediate.

The injected car comes close to matching the times recorded by its lower-geared, carburettored predecessor, showing how carefully the balance between extra power and higher gearing has been struck. To 50mph the times are identical; thereafter the 'old' car creeps away until it reaches 130mph in 38.7secs against the current model's 43.1. But with times like 7secs to 60mph, 19.5ses to 100mph and 15.4secs for the standing quarter-mile, the Turbo R still approaches super performance standards for all its two-and-a-quarter tonnes.

The weight and gearing do tell, though, in flexibility as our figures show. Although the turbo is a bigger unit than usually encountered, it is well matched to the size of the engine and there is no suggestion of turbo lag. However, at most normal overtaking speeds, where the transmission stays resolutely in intermediate, the figures do not match those of the old car. The 60-80mph time of 5.2secs (compared with 4.4secs) is an example. It could hardly be otherwise, now that intermediate ratio is geared to pull 24mph per 1000rpm compared with 'only' 19.4mph. One seeks compensating benefits in even more relaxed cruising.

To a degree there is a benefit in more relaxed cruising although under hard acceleration the Turbo R exhibits a muffled yet hearty V8 throb reminiscent of the American muscle-cars of a generation ago. But there is so much in hand at, say, 120mph — which now represents just 3400rpm — that cruising is indeed relaxed as it should be.

Freed from artificial constraint, the Turbo R eases its way to a mean maximum of 143mph, corresponding to 4000rpm. Our best one-way speed of 146mph, helped by a light wind and achieved at close to peak power revs, suggests that the car might well be undergeared to reach its true maximum in mechanical comfort.

ECONOMY

The higher gearing and the efficiency of fuel injection helped the Turbo R achieve a better result here. Our figures show a best of 17.4mpg for a mainly motorway cruise, against 12.5mpg for a fast cross-country journey. Our overall figure of 14.2mpg is poor by current standards, but must be balanced against that massive weight and crushing performance. It is also some six per cent better than that of the previous model's 13.4mpg.

Stated fuel capacity is 108 litres, just short of 24 gallons, giving a range of more than 300 miles if the car is driven with restraint. The low fuel warning light begins to flash much earlier in spirited driving — when 40 litres remain — and the fuel gauge, which doubles as an oil contents gauge at the push of a selector button, is sufficiently pessimistic that no tester was brave enough to push his luck beyond an 87-litre rebrim.

REFINEMENT

This is where any Rolls-Royce or Bentley must score well, but, as in our previous test, the Turbo R falls short of the highest standards. There are three problem areas: the ride, some aspects of noise, and the quality of the transmission.

One has to accept that when so large a car is set up for more sporting handling the ride is likely to suffer. In the Bentley, the standard Rolls-Royce spring and damper settings have been retained and the handling modified by fitting much stiffer anti-roll bars. One looks in vain for the sharp sideways acceleration at head level as the car passes over bumps, the hallmark of excessively stiff anti-roll bars, but there is certainly some sharp torsional reaction through the body — heard as well as felt — when a large bump is encountered. There is also a constant muted grumble, of both noise and vibration, on anything but the very best surfaces, and some bumpthump over road joints and ridges. In other words, while the Turbo R rides well by most standards it will disappoint those who are used to the very best.

Apart from the engine and road noise the test car suffered an urgent whisper of wind noise from the top of the driver's door. At 100mph this was the loudest noise though it was not sufficient to call for raised voices.

The transmission presents a more worrying aspect of refinement. It is not that the venerable GM400 has grown worse, simply that other units have improved. Three speeds instead of four, especially when they are spread this far apart, imply there will be problems in smoothing over the shifts and so it transpires. In part-throttle conditions — the full-throttle shift quality remains outstanding — the driver must learn to be careful with the accelerator if the shift points, both up and down, are to be smoothed out.

In automatic transmission terms, the Bentley is lacking; the standard is now the ZF HP24 of the BMW 750i.

ROAD BEHAVIOUR

It is no good pretending the Turbo R handles like a sports car, however well its performance matches sports standards. Two and a quarter tonnes and a high centre of gravity are no recipe for agile cornering even on tyres as capable as Avon Turbospeeds.

The power steering is geared at 3.4 turns between locks for a 39-foot turning circle. This is not quick in the sporting sense but in fact the turn into a corner feels crisp, which is a credit to the tyres' initial response. Steering effort is always light, probably too light for a sporting enthusiast, but one learns that a gentle grip reveals a consistent if rather distant sense of feel.

Straight-line stability is good, even though on poorer surfaces the driver is conscious of the steering wheel moving slightly. It seems however that this stability is achieved at the expense of over strong understeer which is revealed as soon as the Turbo R is driven briskly on a winding road. At other times, as when powering through a favourite roundabout, the understeer simply becomes so strong that the only solution is to back off the power.

The Turbo R also has a trick, not unfamiliar among large, powerful cars, of going more quickly than the driver realises. This is most usually evident in the need to brake more positively than anticipated, but it can have more serious implications. A driver deciding to shed a lot of speed when entering a corner will be reminded that Bentleys like all other cars are subject to the laws of physics, and to the less than perfect behaviour of semi-trailing rear suspensions in front-engined cars which are simultaneously braked and turned. It is to the car's credit (or perhaps that of its very high polar moment of inertia) that the resulting swing of the tail is easily held with a twitch of the steering wheel.

The much increased roll stiffness, by comparison with the rest of the range, makes for tidier behaviour through S-bends. Even when going absurdly fast there is none of the difficulty caused by the roll of the body getting out of phase with the direction of turn. If difficulties are encountered they are more likely to be — yet again — those of excessive understeer.

The brakes occasionally feel overservoed in their lightness. A 40lb push is enough to produce the limiting 0.96g stop, an average performance for a lighter than normal effort. There was some fade towards the end of our 10-stop series from 90mph, the last three stops showing sharply rising pedal pressure. The ABS system works in typically reliable fashion, with the usual thumping reminder at the brake pedal. The parking brake is foot-operated in Rolls-Royce (and American) tradition, and it fails badly as an emergency backup, delivering no more than 0.1g deceleration when stamped on at 30mph. It's fit only for parking.

AT THE WHEEL

The Turbo R has no problem providing seat adjustment for a wide range of drivers. Another of its new features is seat position memory, the adjustments (up/down, fore/aft, tilt and squab angle, all electrically powered by manipulating miniature seat diagrams on the centre console) for four different people being set up at the touch of a button.

New seats have a more sporting appearance, with more positive side rolls to cushion and squab to give better support during fast cornering. Somewhat in the German tradition they are well shaped rather than deliberately soft but nonetheless comfortable for that, especially in the long term.

The driver is confronted by a large, leather-trimmed steering wheel, a traditional wood dashboard with a scatter of controls and instruments, and an expanse of bonnet through the wide, deep windscreen. There are two stalk controls on the steering column, one the (electric) transmission selector which also houses the (too easily activated) cruise control selector, the other a conventional indicator/dip/flash/screenwash control. Other minor controls are randomly scattered across the dashboard and centre console.

It has to be said that compared with the stark tidiness of a Mercedes control layout, the Bentley is different but hardly attractively so: the next time the Turbo R comes up for a facelift, some replanning will be in order. Likewise the instruments: a full set but scattered widely and, it would seem, indiscriminately. The big tachometer and speedometer sit directly ahead of the driver — the speedometer is an unworthy 11mph fast at a true 120mph.

The pedal layout favours the operation of both accelerator and brake with the right foot, leaving the left with no task beyond that of operating the archaic and ineffective parking brake.

Visibility from the driving seat presents no problems and in this respect the Bentley is probably better placed to exploit its performance safely than many supercars of similar performance but half the overall height.

CONVENIENCE

The Bentley is a roomy car, though the sports design of the back seat makes four rather than five the practical number of people to have aboard. Given its size, it would be astonishing if there was not the room for a very large passenger to sit behind an equally large driver, and there is, though we are surprised that the margin of kneeroom is not larger. In Rolls-Royce tradition, the back seat is set high with properly chosen cushion and backrest angles: passengers do not have to sit upright, knees under chin. Once installed — very easily, thanks to the wide-opening doors — rear passengers are decently looked after, each side of the car providing a cigar lighter, ash- ▶

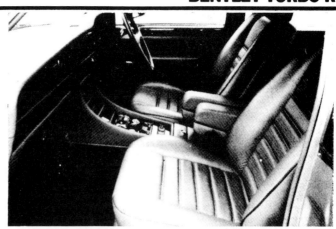

Seats, *electrically moved, now offer much improved support*

Individual *rear seats are as comfortable as fronts, but only for two*

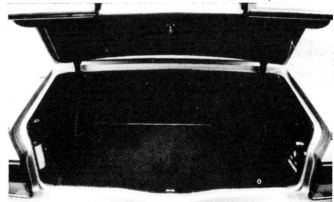

Boot *is notable more for low sill and good shape than outright size*

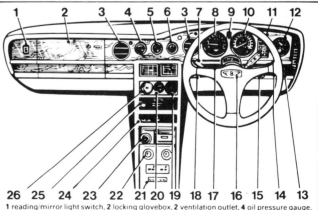

1 reading/mirror light switch, 2 locking glovebox, 2 ventilation outlet, 4 oil pressure gauge, 5 water temperature gauge, 6 fuel contents, 7 indicators/main beam/wash and wipe column stalk, 8 rev counter, 9 warning lights, 10 speedometer, 11 warning lights, 12 lights/ignition switches, 13 oil level button, 14 wiper control, 15 fog light switch, 16 horn push, 17 hazard flashers, 18 air conditioning/temperature controls, 19 outside temperature, 20 battery condition, 21 seat memory controls, 22 electric door mirror controls, 23 cigar lighter, 24 warning light and electric/air horn selector, 25 radio/cassette player, 26 analogue clock.

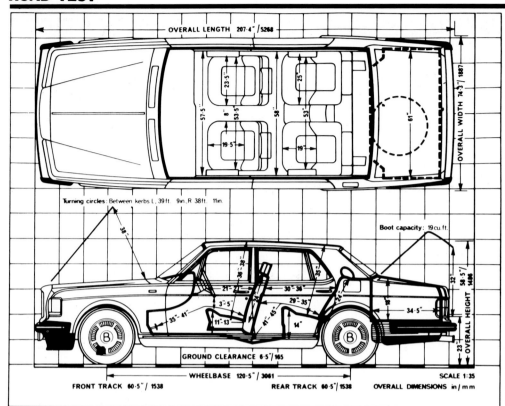

OVERALL LENGTH 207·4" / 5268

OVERALL WIDTH 74·3" / 1887

Turning circles: Between kerbs L, 39 ft. 9in. R 38 ft. 11in.

Boot capacity: 19 cu.ft.

OVERALL HEIGHT 58·5" / 1486

GROUND CLEARANCE 6·5" / 165

WHEELBASE 120·5" / 3061

FRONT TRACK 60·5" / 1538   REAR TRACK 60·5" / 1538

SCALE 1:35   OVERALL DIMENSIONS in / mm

COSTS

Prices

Basic	£63,730.00
Special Car Tax	£5310.83
VAT	£10,356.12
Total (in GB)	**£79,396.95**
Licence	£100.00
Delivery charge (London)	£230.00
Number plates	£20.00
Total on the Road	**£79,746.95**
(excluding insurance)	
Insurance group	OA
EXTRAS (fitted to test car)	
Front fog lamps	£143.27
Total as tested	
on the road	**£79,890.22**

SERVICE & PARTS

Change	Interval 15,000
Engine oil	Yes
Oil filter	Yes
Gearbox oil	Yes
Spark plugs	Yes
Air cleaner	Yes
Total cost	**£300.00**

(Assuming labour at £25.00 an hour inc VAT)

PARTS COST (inc VAT)

Brake pads (2 wheels) front	£144.60
Brake pads (2 wheels) rear	£88.35
Exhaust complete	£1175.45
Tyre — each (typical)	£264.50
Windscreen	£503.00
Headlamp unit	£163.86
Front wing	£729.40
Rear bumper	£894.00

WARRANTY

36 months/unlimited mileage.

EQUIPMENT

Ammeter/Voltmeter	●
Automatic	●
Cruise control	●
Economy gauge	N/A
Five speed	N/A
Limited slip differential	N/A
Power steering	●
Rev counter	●
Self-levelling suspension	●
Steering rake adjustment	N/A
Steering reach adjustment	N/A
Trip computer	N/A
Headrests front/rear	●
Heated seats	N/A
Height adjustment	●
Lumbar adjustment	N/A
Seat back recline	●
Seat cushion tilt	●
Seat tilt	●
Split rear seats	N/A
Door mirror remote control	●
Electric windows	●
Heated rear window	●
Interior adjustable headlamps	N/A
Sunroof	DO
Tinted glass	●
Headlamp wash/wipe	●
Central locking	●
Child proof locks	●
Radio/cassette	●
Aerial	●
Speakers	●

● Standard N/A Not applicable DO Dealer Option

TEST CONDITIONS

Wind:	5mph
Temperature:	19deg C (66deg F)
Barometer:	29.7inHg
	(1006mbar)
Humidity:	42per cent
Surface:	dry asphalt concrete
Test distance:	844miles

Figures taken at 6668 miles by our own staff at the General Motors proving ground at Millbrook.

All *Autocar* test results are subject to world copyright and may not be reproduced in whole or part without the Editor's written permission.

MODEL

BENTLEY TURBO R

PRODUCED AND SOLD BY:
Rolls-Royce Motor Cars Ltd,
Crewe, Cheshire,
CW1 3PL

SPECIFICATION

ENGINE
Longways, front, rear-wheel drive.
Head/block al.alloy/al. alloy.
8 cylinders in 90 deg V, wet liners, 5 main bearings. Water cooled, viscous and electric fans.
Bore 104.1mm (4.1in), **stroke** 99.1mm (3.9in), **capacity** 6750cc (411.8 cu in).
Valve gear ohv, hydraulic tappets, 2 valves per cylinder, gear camshaft drive. **Compression ratio** 8.0 to 1. Electronic ignition, Bosch KE-Jetronic fuel injection. Garrett AIResearch TO4 turbocharger, boost pressure 7 psi.
Max power 328bhp*.

*Estimate, official figure not released.

TRANSMISSION
GM 400 three-speed automatic, torque converter.

Gear	Ratio	mph/1000rpm
Top	1.00	35.6
2nd	1.48	24.0
1st	2.48	14.3

Final drive: Hypoid, ratio 2.28.

SUSPENSION
Front, independent, double wishbones, coil springs, telescopic dampers, anti-roll bar.
Rear, independent, semi-trailing arms, Panhard rod, coil and gas springs, gas dampers, automatic self-levelling, anti-roll bar.

STEERING
Rack and pinion, hydraulic power assistance. Steering wheel diameter 15.5in, 3.4 turns lock to lock.

BRAKES
Dual circuits, hydraulic system with anti-lock. **Front** 11.0in (279mm) dia ventilated discs. **Rear** 11.0in (279mm) dia discs. Handbrake, pedal acting on rear discs.

WHEELS
Al.alloy, 7.5in rims. Radial tyres (Avon Turbospeed on test car), size 255/65VR15, pressures F27 R35 psi (normal driving).

EQUIPMENT
Battery 12V, Alternator 108A. Headlamps 55/60W. 54 electric fuses. 2-speed plus intermittent wipers. Electric screen washer. Air conditioning standard. Hide seats, hide headlining. Carpet with heel mat floor covering. Scissor jack; 4 jacking points each side.

PERFORMANCE

MAXIMUM SPEEDS

Gear	mph	kph	rpm
Top (Mean)	143	230	4000
(Best)	146	235	4100
2nd	108	174	4500
1st	64	103	4500

ACCELERATION FROM REST

True mph	Time (sec)	Speedo mph
30	2.6	31
40	3.7	41
50	5.2	53
60	7.0	65
70	9.4	76
80	12.0	87
90	15.0	98
100	19.5	109
110	25.0	121
120	31.9	131

Standing ¼-mile: 15.4sec, 90mph
Standing km: 28.3sec, 114mph

IN EACH GEAR

mph	Top	2nd	1st
10-30	—	—	2.0
20-40	—	—	2.1
30-50	—	—	2.7
40-60	—	3.5	3.2
50-70	—	4.3	—
60-80	—	5.2	—
70-90	—	6.0	—
80-100	—	6.7	—
90-110	10.2	—	—
100-120	12.7	—	—
110-130	18.1	—	—

CONSUMPTION
FUEL
Overall mpg: See text

Grade of fuel: Premium, 4-star (97 RM)
Fuel tank: 23.8 Imp galls (108 litres)
Mileage recorder: 0.7 per cent long
Oil: (10W/40) 900 miles/litre

BRAKING
Fade (from 90mph in neutral)
Pedal load for 0.5g stops in lb

	start/end		start/end
1	20-24	6	30-36
2	24-30	7	36-40
3	24-32	8	44-50
4	26-32	9	44-54
5	28-34	10	64-68

Response (from 30mph in neutral)

Load	g	Distance
10lb	0.14	215ft
20lb	0.48	62ft
30lb	0.66	45ft
40lb	0.96	31ft
Handbrake	0.1	301ft

WEIGHT
Kerb 44.3cwt/4965lb/2252kg
(Distribution F/R, 52.2/47.8)
Test 47.9cwt/5375lb/2438kg
Max payload 992lb/450kg

ASTON MARTIN LAGONDA £87,500

Extravagant car, extravagantly styled in angular William Towns fashion, based on Aston Martin V8 mechanicals. First appeared in 1976. An £87,500 essay in space efficiency which falls rather uneasily between two stools — it's not truly quick or nimble enough to be a performance supersports coupé and it is neither quiet nor refined enough for a luxury saloon

Tested	18 Oct 1980
ENGINE	5340cc
Max Power	313bhp at 5500rpm
Torque	318lb ft at 4000rpm
Gearing	23.8mph/1000rpm
WARRANTY	12/UL, 6 anti-rust
Insurance Group	9
Automatic	●
5-Speed	N/A
Radio/cassette	●
Sunroof	£1993.33
WEIGHT	4622lb

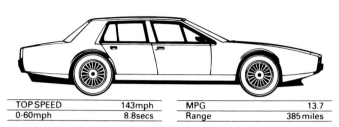

TOP SPEED	143mph	MPG	13.7
0-60mph	8.8secs	Range	385 miles

BRISTOL BRIGAND TURBO £64.783

Petite fabrique anglaise de voitures de grande classe is how the French label the Bristol marque; the petite-ness refers to the factory output and rarity of this aluminium-alloy bodied Chrysler V8-engined 5.9-litre machine, only available in automatic form. Uses non-integral chassis with torsionbar, and Watts linkage live rear axle

Tested	N/A
ENGINE	5900cc
Max Power	N/A
Torque	N/A
Gearing	28.6mph/1000rpm
WARRANTY	12/UL
Insurance Group	9
Automatic	●
5-Speed	N/A
Radio/cassette	DO
Sunroof	£1955
WEIGHT	3856lb

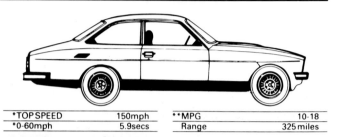

*TOP SPEED	150mph	**MPG	10-18
*0-60mph	5.9secs	Range	325 miles

DAIMLER DOUBLE SIX £30,200

Most lavishly equipped, rebadged version of Jaguar's deservedly renowned XJ-12, with May-head 5.3-litre V12 mated only with automatic box giving superb performance and refinement in a body-chassis whose standards of handling, roadholding, ride and quiteness still remain the target by which all other rivals are judged. Good value in this company

Tested (HE)	18 July 1981
ENGINE	5345cc
Max Power	299bhp at 5500rpm
Torque	318lb ft at 3000rpm
Gearing	26.9mph/1000rpm
WARRANTY	12/UL
Insurance Group	9
Automatic	●
5-Speed	N/A
Radio/cassette	●
Sunroof	●
WEIGHT	4219lb

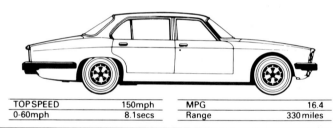

TOP SPEED	150mph	MPG	16.4
0-60mph	8.1secs	Range	330 miles

FERRARI 412 £69,999

Classically elegant in the traditionally Italian (Pininfarina) way, with that blend of purpose and grace which this coachbuilder is so good at. In automatic form considered here, not as quick as its 4.9-litre double ohc V12 specification with claimed 335bhp output might suggest. Well equipped by Ferrari standards but never as popular as it might have been

Tested	N/A
ENGINE	4942cc
Max Power	335bhp at 6000rpm
Torque	332lb ft at 4200rpm
Gearing	23.9mph/1000rpm
WARRANTY	12/UL
Insurance Group	9
Automatic	●
5-Speed	ONC
Radio/cassette	●
Sunroof (electric)	£2012.50
WEIGHT	3989lb

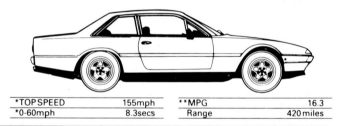

*TOP SPEED	155mph	**MPG	16.3
*0-60mph	8.3secs	Range	420 miles

MERCEDES-BENZ 560 SEL £50,970

Once you have sampled Mercedes S-class motoring to the full it is difficult to imagine travelling in a higher degree of comfort or style. The large V8 engine is smooth and effortless in its power delivery and overall refinement levels are high. The ride may be a little on the firm side for British tastes, but the 560 SEL handles and feels like a much smaller car

Tested	30 Jul 1986
ENGINE	5547cc
Max Power	285bhp at 5000rpm
Torque	335lb ft at 3750rpm
Gearing	28.3mph/1000rpm
WARRANTY	12/UL, 6 anti-rust
Insurance group	9
Automatic	●
5-Speed	N/A
Radio/cassette	●
Sunroof	●
WEIGHT	3934lb

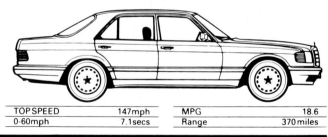

TOP SPEED	147mph	MPG	18.6
0-60mph	7.1secs	Range	370 miles

PORSCHE 928 S4 £50,306

The Series 4 version of the 928 has a 5-litre 32-valve V8 that delivers 320bhp and 160mph even with the automatic gearbox. Roadholding and brakes are well up to this performance although ride and refinement levels are definitely on the sporting side. The Series 4 is a 2+2 Grand Tourer that is almost unmatched as a mile-eater, yet still lacks appeal to the real enthusiast

Tested	3 Dec 1986
ENGINE	4957cc
Max Power	320bhp at 6000rpm
Torque	317lb ft at 3000rpm
Gearing	28.0mph/1000rpm
WARRANTY	24/UL, 10 anti-rust
Insurance Group	9
Automatic	●
5-Speed	ONC
Radio/cassette	●
Sunroof	£1257.04
WEIGHT	3505lb

TOP SPEED	160mph	MPG	17.0
0-60mph	6.2secs	Range	325 miles

● Standard ○ Optional at extra cost ONC Optional at no extra cost N/A Not applicable DO Dealer Option * Manufacturer's figures ** European Legislative Average

There are *major flaws in design and layout of instruments*

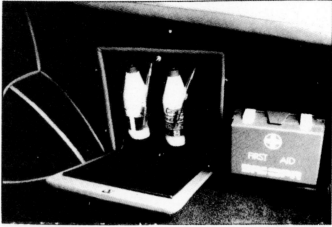

Reserve supply *of brake fluid and first aid kit are stored in boot*

Discreet turbo *badges and add-ons play down performance image*

Body roll *is well checked but there's understeer aplenty at limit*

◄ tray, overhead light and wedge-shaped footrest. One looks in vain for the cocktail cabinet, though.

Boot space is best described as adequate. It will take four suitcases and some soft bags though one wonders if that would be enough for the needs of four Bentley-type people on a two-week holiday. There are plus points, though: the sill is low and the interior shape is free from awkward intrusions. The massive spare wheel is slung in a carrier beneath, with the equally large fuel tank forward of it. a practical touch is the provision, behind a panel in the boot wall, of two containers of the rather special LHM fluid on which the power braking system runs.

Like all current Rolls-Royces, the Bentley comes with a standard air-conditioning system whose outward simplicity belies its inward complexity. Two thumbwheels enable the desired temperature in the upper and lower levels of the cabin to be dialled separately. The system is extremely effective, quickly reducing the car's interior temperature and being quiet in operation.

Convenience equipment like central locking and electric windows are standard, and they strike a common chord in their butler-like efficiency.

SAFETY

The body shell is designed with ample crush zones front and rear, and has substantial beam-strength against side impact built into the door. The massive bumpers, though not to full

American 5mph standard, should be capable of absorbing minor bumps without significant damage.

Inside, there is a notable absence of sharp features which might injure occupants in a crash. The control layout, which removes all major controls from the centre console area, helps here and the roof area is smoothly padded and finished. Front and rear headrests are, of course standard, and the steering column provides the necessary energy absorption in an impact.

The Bentley's sheer massive bulk is an advantage in the event of front or rear impact with another vehicle. There's little indeed in the car line that can 'out-bulk' this vehicle.

VERDICT

One has to judge the Bentley in two ways: as a car, and as a possession. In judging it as a car, we will ignore the price because, as we've said, cars which are just as all-round capable can be had for half the money, if not less. And as a car it does not fail. The performance can only be described as remarkable, especially now that it is delivered from gearing high enough to provide about the most relaxed high-speed cruising there is, despite the absence of a four-speed transmission. One result of this has been a small but useful gain in economy, while the new fuel injection system gives an eagerness of engine response which was not the case in the days of the carburettor.

Stability and handling complement

the performance well enough, even though the Turbo R's weight, and its understeer, betrays itself in extreme situations. As a grand tourer, but not a sports car it acquits itself well, taking corners far more crisply than any other model in the Rolls-Royce range. But there is a penalty for this — the disappointing ride. Nine out of 10 ordinary people given their first trip in the Turbo R, would say it rode superbly. The Bentley's problem, however, is that the people who buy it are not ordinary.

This leads us to the second part of our assessment. Driving such a car confers occasional benefits, notably in the way one is treated when one arrives. On the road the reaction is mixed. Some drivers treat it with forelock-tugging deference, others take pleasure in reminding the Bentley owner that he is no more than their equal.

It is part of the Bentley's charm, insidiously overcoming one's initial personal feeling about the car, that it encourages the driver to take a relaxed and detached attitude to either reaction. It is no mere accident that one never sees any Rolls-Royce, even the Bentley Turbo R with its tempting level of performance, being driven with the bad tempered competitiveness and aggression of lesser cars. There is no need: merely the implied encouragement (however reprehensible in its own way) resignedly to label certain of one's fellow drivers as peasant or bolshevik, in the original meaning and context of

either word.

That must be justification enough for some buyers. There is also that much aired aspect of the Bentley, or any of its cousins, that it is indeed beautifully built, with a skill and care greater than those lavished on genuine works of art—particularly in this day and age. Whether that justifies the traditional ergonomic shambles (that really is the only word for it) of the minor controls and instrument layout, or makes it even more of a pity is open to (inconclusive) debate.

It is a more obvious pity that the car has some drawbacks of refinement. Surely it cannot be long before Rolls-Royce beats a path to the door of some purveyor of smooth four-speed automatic transmissions—and the Turbo R would be the ideal toe to stick in the water of such a change. There are times, too, when the car makes a quick driver begin to wonder about the body's overall rigidity, and whether it would be further improved by adding still more to that already massive weight. Or is that it's the weight itself that's really the problem?

Is it possible to combine Turbo R performance, image and genuine air of quality in something smaller, lighter and therefore more nimble and economical? Or is it that people buy cars like this precisely *because* of 6.7-litres of engine, 17ft of overall length and two and a quarter tonnes at the kerb? Once upon a time, perhaps, but not today. ■

Bentleys make a comeback

A lower price for the new Bentley Eight (above) as Rolls-Royce increase model range

ROLLS-ROYCE have launched a new cut-price Bentley. Based on Silver Spirit running gear and bodywork, the Bentley Eight costs £49,497 in Britain, £5,743 less than the Mulsanne, the normal Bentley equivalent of the Rolls-Royce Silver Spirit, and £12,246 less than the Mulsanne Turbo.

After a management shake-up that has rocked the Crewe establishment, and its sales network throughout the world, Rolls-Royce have recently discovered what motoring magazines have been telling them for years: that the Bentley name has been under-played, that in Britain and Europe – if not in America – its image is not only quite different from that of Rolls-Royce but well worth exploiting.

Forty years ago, when Rolls-Royce resumed production after the war, 90 per cent of the cars they made carried the Bentley label, acquired in 1931. By the early 1980s, the percentage had dropped to a mere four per cent. The Bentley name was rescued from oblivion by the Mulsanne Turbo, launched in 1982, which this year will account for roughly 10 per cent of the 2,200 cars Rolls-Royce forecast they will make. That's 700 more than last year, a black one for the company when production was reduced to 1,500 units to help shift the previous year's stock.

All told, the Bentley percentage has risen now to around 22 per cent, and is likely to increase to 40 per cent in the near future as more owner-drivers (as opposed to business buyers) foresake their Mercs. At least, that's the hope of RR's new sales chief, Peter Ward.

Ward sees the jump from a Jaguar as too big. But from a top Mercedes, nudging £35,000, the new Bentley Eight is at least within sight. Dealer discounting, unheard of before (and largely over now), caused disruption and disquiet at the top end of the luxury market in 1982-83, not

least because depreciation, traditionally very low on Rolls-Royces, escalated sharply, slashing the value of used cars over night.

Rolls-Royce are now trading profitably, and going from strength to strength, they say. Worldwide sales in June totalled over 300 – their best month for years. The United States is still the company's strongest market (half this year's output is destined for North America) but to begin with the new Bentley Eight will be sold only in Britain.

By lowering their threshold price, RR hope to attract new customers – young entrepreneurs they call them – who want top-quality comfort and prestige in a car that doesn't have the sedate image (or price tag) of a Silver Spirit.

The Bentley Eight is distinguished by its chromed mesh grille, calling to mind the legendary pre-war Le Mans cars that swept to victory in the 24 Hours five times.

Most of the running gear, including the 6.74 litre V8 engine, automatic transmission, powered rack and pinion steering and all-disc braking system is identical to the Mulsanne's and Silver Spirit's. But the suspension has been simplified and stiffened – it is actually less resilient than the Turbo's, which RR say is under review – and the standard of cabin furnishings and equipment has been lowered, though it is still very high by absolute standards.

Further to strengthen the Bentley name ("We shall ensure that potential customers are aware of Bentley as a separate identity and not simply a name on the radiator," says Ward), the Corniche Convertible has been re-badged as a Continental, reviving perhaps the most revered of all Bentley nameplates, last used in 1966. With colour-keyed bumpers, restyled seats and a new facia, it costs £76,108.

MR. BENTLEY AT 80...

...talks to Peter Garnier

1920, and the start of it all. W. O. Bentley, then a young man, takes the road in the first Bentley, an open 3-litre. Matching tyres on the same axle didn't seem to matter much in those days!

IT IS GIVEN to very few artists in any sphere to see in their lifetime their creations become valuable collectors' pieces. Yet W. O. Bentley's cars, built upwards of 28 years ago, are now changing hands at more than double their original value, and are among the most sought-after Vintage cars in the world. Like so many other treasures, their value went unnoticed at first; in pre-war days they changed hands for a song, often being allowed to delapidate beyond salvation. After the war, £100 a litre was about the price; now, £1,000 a litre would buy only a few—the rare ones can fetch twice this sum. They are the raison d'être for one of the strongest one-make clubs in existence, and an almost magical glamour has built-up around them and the people who raced them in their heyday; thousands upon thousands of pounds have been spent on restoring them to better-than-new; and unfortunately, large sums of cash are still being spent by people who should know better than to convert them into "hot-rods". For 50 years they have travelled the roads of the world, seldom able to stretch their legs nowadays, despite the tremendous advances in road engineering they have witnessed, abiding—in the UK—by the snowballing legislation of Transport Minister after Transport Minister.

Each December, their admirers gather at the Bentley Drivers' Club party at London's Dor-

chester Hotel—four or five examples of the marque standing silent in the ballroom—presided over by W. O. Bentley himself—the man who brought all this about. In September this year, this quiet, gentle person celebrated his 80th birthday—flatly refusing, as he has done all his life, to make a speech. He was persuaded, however, to say a few words to a tape-recorder, which were played-back to the assembly of his one-time employees and a host of his friends —while he sat with them and listened.

Diffidently, he talked to me a few days ago about the old Bentley days, refusing to admit to any pride that he has given so many people so much pleasure through the years—"Those cars," he says, "are a team effort, not mine alone. I can't take the credit." But his wife Margaret confesses for him that in fact he is deeply proud when people invade their home in Surrey's tucked-away Shamley Green to talk Bentleys. Locomotives were his first love, and even by the age of eight he had decided his future lay in this direction. He became an apprentice at Doncaster; but in five years he realized that there was more money to be made in the growing world of motor cars, so he moved on to a taxi-cab company where he learned about petrol engines, becoming agent for the DFP car after another 18 months or so until the outbreak of war in 1914.

During the war he designed the Bentley

Rotary engine, on which aluminium cylinders with steel liners were used for the first time. As a member of the RNAS he used to visit, every five weeks, the battlefields in France where his engines were in use. "The pilots felt a bit lonely and neglected out there, and it used to cheer them up—also I learned a lot. One day I volunteered to go on a dawn patrol with one of them. The CO asked me if I'd ever used a machine gun, and when I told him I hadn't, he said, 'Oh well, that's all right. You'll have to get up a bit earlier and we'll teach you.' It was a Nieuport scout-fighter, and we went out over the sea to do a reconnaissance. When we turned back there was a very strong headwind, and as we sat there with the engine turning over at full throttle and not making any headway, I realised the importance of reliability. I think that trip did the Bentley Rotary a great deal of good."

After the war he returned to the world of motoring, founding the Bentley company on 18 January, 1919. Having completed the first 3-litre chassis, he summoned Autocar artist F. Gordon Crosby. "Draw me the sort of body-work you think would go with a fast, open four-seater sports car—and design me a badge for it while you're at it." To this day, Gordon Crosby's painting hangs in W. O.'s bedroom, the only Bentley relic (save for an original Bryan de Grineau cover for Motor, that hangs in the "loo") to be seen at Shamley Green—and the radiator badge continues on Bentleys to this day. The design for the bodywork, and for the "gothic arch" radiator, save for a few modifications, took shape, and became the first 3-litre which was in production by 1921.

"People wonder why we made such big cars," W. O. said. "But you see, our sort of customers simply wouldn't get into anything lower in those days—they needed dignity, and plenty of room above their heads, which meant a thundering amount of wind-resistance. To do 100 mph in one of those cars you needed slightly over 200 bhp—which is why we went up to $6\frac{1}{2}$ and 8 litres. I kept the original head design because I didn't think there was anything finer—and I still think so; so do one or two other people to this day, though we used four valves and they use two. We used four because you can cool the exhausts better; and for the same valve acceleration you can get a much quicker opening.

"Eighteen months before we went into liquidation in 1931 we were making a very good profit—which will surprise you—due largely to the $6\frac{1}{2}$- and 8-litre, notably the 8. The amount of work involved wasn't terribly much more, but we charged a lot more. In fact, we put on an extra £50 to make it more than the Rolls-Royce —it gave us prestige, and didn't mean a thing to the sort of people who bought our cars. We never produced a sporting 8-litre—they were big, fast, comfortable saloons with really comfortable seats.

"Shortly before we went into liquidation we were going to become a public company and the capital was practically underwritten. We were thinking about building a smaller car at the time—down to $1\frac{1}{2}$ litres perhaps—but then the slump arrived. It wasn't a case of sales going down but of sales being cut off—not only for Bentleys but for other luxury cars. We simply couldn't go on. The only alternative would have been to get rid of all but a skeleton staff—which we didn't want to do. If we'd been able to continue, and become a public company, we'd have built our own machine shops and certainly produced a little Bentley. You see, in those days we had to design everything on our cars except the electrics—there were no off-the-shelf universal joints, axles, steering, steering joints and so on, and everything cost us so much to produce. It wouldn't have been a cheap small car, but we'd have made one."

W. O. is extremely interesting on the subject of Le Mans, which brought the big cars so much of their glamour with their five wins—and the three-in-a-row for Woolf Barnato, who won every Le Mans he entered, once with Rubin, once with Birkin and once with Kidston. "Le Mans to us was purely and simply a means of getting known to the public. Incredible though it may seem, the *whole* of our racing cost us only £3,500. The cars came off the production line, were rebuilt carefully, everything being split-pinned, by the racing department who were convinced the production people couldn't build an engine properly—then they were usually sold to private owners after the race. We got good bonuses from the fuel companies and so on, even before we started a race—that was after we'd made our name, of course. And, you see, we didn't even pay our drivers—we just paid their fares and their bills at the Hotel de Paris. We put the mechanics at the Moderne, with the cars in the yard. We didn't want to

W. O. Bentley sits quietly in his drawing room at Shamley Green, discussing with the author the heroic days. Below: One wonders what far-away memories this 1922 3-litre Bentley conjured up for its creator—nearly 47 years after it left the works

One of the rare 9ft chassis, 100 mph 3-litre cars (of which, between 1925 and 1927, only 14 were built), driven here at a VSCC Oulton Park meeting by Mrs. Christopher Jennings. As Margaret Hall, she was a well-known Bentley driver before the war.

The ex-Birkin single-seater track car, now rebodied as a 2-seater and owned by B. M. Russ-Turner. Originally the first-ever blower 4½-litre car, this was rebodied by Birkin as a single-seater and held the Brooklands Outer Circuit lap record at 137.96 mph in 1932.

Not original, but still giving pleasure on the racing circuits—the 3-6½ litre hybrid which has scored many successes in the hands of Harvey Hine and owner David Llewellyn.

interrupt their pleasures—they worked very hard indeed, and we thought it was best to let them be on their own.

"People have said we wasted money—but we didn't. Our Le Mans successes were absolutely everything—they *made* the car. We would have been nowhere without them."

I asked W. O. how he had chosen his drivers who, as men, seemed to fit the Bentley image so well. "Well, you see, we had already got Frank Clement in the company—first in the experimental department then in sales. He and Duff had driven Duff's privately owned car in the 1923 race—and I told him that he was absolutely cracked to run in a race that lasted 24 hours. But he insisted, and I went over to have a look. Although they had no end of trouble with the electrics, and a stone holed the fuel tank, they finished equal fourth with a Bignan, and I was tremendously impressed. The following year we prepared Duff's car ourselves, fitting protection for the lamps and tank. He drove again with Clement, and they won the race.

"We thought it was all pretty easy—but we were caned for this light-hearted attitude. We entered works cars the following year, and didn't even finish; it took until 1927 before we won again, and then we won four in a row. The blower cars were nothing to do with us—an entirely separate affair. I felt we had more chance with a big engine that wasn't pushed. But Tim Birkin and Babe Barnato thought a blown 4½ would be absolutely magnificent and win it easily. But the 6½ was a *very* good car for Le Mans and it gave no trouble at all . . . and the blower 4½ never won a Le Mans race.

"We had people who'd driven at Brooklands and whom I knew personally—people whom I thought were the right type and circulated in the right quarters. I told them that provided they were obedient they'd go on driving for us; if not they'd go out straight away, whoever they were. We had no trouble at all. They used to call me 'The Schoolmaster'; they weren't hard to control, but it was their females . . . they all had them, and they all came over. They all got on each other's nerves and quarrelled—and I had to make it up for them. The drivers used to grumble a bit at being slowed down but we never won a race at a mile an hour faster than we had to. They thought I was silly—but I told them that next year we wanted nobody to know what we really could do. We fooled even Caracciola that way—he told me so."

W. O. reminisced about "battles long ago"—the memorable campaign in the 1930 race when Caracciola's blown 7-litre Mercedes was hounded first by Birkin's blower Bentley, then by the works Speed Sixes until, through excessive use of the blower, the Mercedes faded out after 12 hours. "They told me that his lights had failed and that his accumulator had gone. But I was very hurriedly round to their pit and I saw water streaming from the engine. I told them I thought their accumulators were rather curious."

"Birkin was very good, and he always got the Press. Barnato won three times—his three races at Le Mans—but he wasn't even noticed. The Press and spectators meant nothing to him; all he thought of was winning. He never put on the drama at corners, like a young man would do."

It was fascinating hearing this very great man, in the quiet of his home, recalling achievements that had made motoring history—and men who, as the "Bentley Boys", had been credited with wealth and a way of life that scarcely exist now. But, in W. O.'s quiet voice, they sounded almost "standard"—as standard as the cars they drove, perhaps, on which only the compression ratios had been altered, and the ports polished. "It didn't do any good, but the mechanics loved doing it."

TRIBUTE TO "W.O."

WE HAVE ALREADY recorded the death, on Friday, 13 August, of Walter Owen Bentley. On Monday of last week, a Memorial Service was held for "W.O." at Guildford Cathedral, to which no fewer than 68 of his great cars—all of them built 40 or more years ago—helped to carry his many friends and admirers. We felt readers might appreciate the full text of the Address given by Stanley Sedgwick, president of the Bentley Drivers' Club, on this occasion. No words of ours could express better, or more sincerely, the feelings of those who knew him—or wish they had done so.

THE part played by "W.O." in the advancement of automobile engineering is well known to all of us. So is the measure of his contribution to the well-being of this country in time of war and to its prestige in peacetime.

I am not going to cover again this well-trodden ground. Rather shall I try to put into words what "W.O." has meant to me and—in doing so—hope that I shall be voicing some of the thoughts which are in all our minds today.

I was not among those fortunate enough to have witnessed the Bentleys racing in their heyday, but the Bentley tradition was well-established when I left school. For me there was only one motorcar—the Bentley. "W.O." was an enigmatic, unknown figure whose name ranked in one's teenage hall of fame with Louis Armstrong, Jack Hobbs and the like.

When I met "W.O." for the first time after the war and told him that I was helping to revive the Bentley Drivers' Club it was clear to me that the idea of encouraging ownership and preservation of the old Bentleys was an enterprise which he regarded with little enthusiasm and considerable misgivings.

The country was emerging from the darkness and difficulties of the war years and seemingly the great old Bentleys had disappeared into the limbo of breakers' yards and long-forgotten garages. No one could have foreseen that the name and fame of the "Vintage" Bentley would yet again become something of consequence wherever motoring meant more than mere transportation.

New cars were unobtainable and almost anything which could be made to move under its own power was seized upon by those seeking a return to some sort of normality. Many young men feeling the need for a substitute for the exhilaration and companionship of Service life remembered the glamour of the "Bentley Boys" and the innate quality of the old Bentleys and sought out these cars. These chaps, and the fortunate owners who had stored their Bentleys throughout the war, found in the reviving Bentley Drivers' Club a means of sharing their enthusiasm and knowledge with like-minded motorists and triggered off a movement which has grown beyond belief in the ensuing years.

"W.O.", disillusioned by the adversities which he had endured in the 'thirties, was in no hurry to reopen a chapter of his life which he had tried to forget, but in September 1947 he accepted the committee's invitation to become our patron. As the club grew and grew to its present size—so blossomed its association with

"W.O." He began to enjoy coming along to sporting and social gatherings up and down the country. I find it difficult to avoid sounding like a "commercial" for the B.D.C., but the club and its members played such a large part in "W.O.'s" life in recent years—and vice versa—that to speak of one is to speak of the other.

"W.O." has said that the pleasure he derived in the post-war years from club activities; from making new friends among its members; and from seeing the loving care bestowed upon "his" cars has more than compensated for all his earlier disappointments.

The cottage at Shamley Green was the Mecca of Bentley enthusiasts who beat a path to his door from all corners of the globe. He was too kindly a man to turn away even the most importunate visitor.

Humility and a sense of humour were, perhaps, his most endearing attributes. He could never understand the hero-worship apparent at gatherings of Bentley owners and was embarrassed when those meeting him for the first time thanked him for the pleasure he had brought into their lives. He was a man who never sought the limelight and would never make a speech in public. To have insisted on his doing so would have spoiled his enjoyment of the occasion, but it is characteristic of him smilingly to have found refuge in recent years in the philosophy that people would have been disappointed if he had changed his Trappist image. Nevertheless, overcoming his natural shyness, he yielded to pressure to appear on Television and radio programmes on several occasions and proved himself a match for the most "experienced" interviewers.

To the last he followed developments in the automotive field with a keen and critical interest and himself drove regularly until earlier this year.

The current issue of the *Autocar*, of which he had been a regular reader since the first issue in 1895, was at his bedside when I visited him a few days before he died.

It is said that behind every great man, there is a great woman. I know of no instance where this is more true than in the case of "W.O."—though I prefer to say that behind this

great gentleman stood a great lady. "W.O." and Margaret has almost become a compound noun, for they were inseparable. Not only did Margaret encourage "Bent"—as she has always called him—to come out into the light when his inclination would have been to withdraw from the public eye, but she was there beside him on all occasions to support him. Those of us who were at Le Mans two years ago when the *Merite Sportif Francais* was conferred on "W.O." by the Minister of Youth and Sport, will never forget how Margaret stepped forward on behalf of the speechless "W.O." and thanked the president of the *Automobile Club de l'Ouest* in impeccable French. Here I would say that there are many among us who consider that the honour bestowed upon "W.O." by a grateful government at home was less than his desert. That he was held in high esteem far beyond the immediate circle of Bentley owners is evidenced by the presence here today of those who worked at Cricklewood in the 1930s and of the many representatives of various aspects of the motor industry and of motor racing.

"W.O." has earned a place in our hearts which none will supplant—Margaret has earned our admiration and affection and I hope that she will wish to join us on many occasions in the future. Wherever "W.O." and Margaret have been welcomed in the past, Margaret can be sure of an open door in the years to come. We have lost a patron and gained a new honorary life member.

We mourn the passing of "W.O." from our midst, but, recognizing the frailty of the human frame, we rejoice that he should have lived so long, and count ourselves fortunate to have known him.

Few people are known widely by their initials alone—those of "W.O." will long be remembered and his memory is enshrined in the cars which bear his name and show every sign of sharing the longevity of the man who conceived them. Some of these cars now stand here today in silent tribute to their creator—soon they will give tongue again and go forth as living memorials to our patron—and our friend. □

NEW BREED OF BENTLEY BOY

Peter Ward is a Bentley Boy, of that there is no doubt. He is just the sort of potential buyer Bentley is trying to catch — the young, successful businessman, company chairman or MD, for whom a top level Mercedes-Benz or Jaguar is really rather common, a Porsche impractical and a Rolls-Royce something rather stuffy.

A Bentley, on the other hand, is grand without being ostentatious, is sufficiently sporty without sacrificing comfort and yet still shows that its driver has arrived. Peter Ward *does* drive a Bentley, a Turbo R. In his position he could drive — or be driven in — a Rolls-Royce, but the choice has been a Bentley.

It's a decision that would make the top man at Rolls-Royce smile, a conquest sale that proves the Bentley image is making a comeback as a sporting alternative. Thing is, Peter Ward *is* the top man at Rolls-Royce. Since April he has been the chief executive of the world's most prestigious car maker, having started at Crewe in the dark days of 1983 as managing director of sales amd marketing.

If there is one man who can claim much of the credit for having put Bentley back on its feet, it's Ward. And by driving a Turbo R instead of a Silver Spirit, he is practising what he preaches. "If you look at people who grew up in the '60s on Beach Boys' music, Frogeye Sprites and TR3s, then you are looking at ideal Bentley material. Assuming they've made it and can afford the sort of car we are talking about, they are unlikely to consider a Rolls-Royce . . ."

In the 1960s a typical Rolls-Royce owner was perceived by the young as having one foot in the grave, or if young himself, called it a Roller and painted it to resemble a gypsy caravan. Sales of 'radiator-clone' Bentleys were minimal. Now aged 41, Ward was an impressionable 21-year-old during the 1967 'Summer of Love'. A '60s kid, his values were determined by that time. He doesn't say as much, but you get the impression he drives today's Bentley because he doesn't want people to think he's getting on in years, rather than getting on in business.

Bentley's re-emergence has been startling . . . even Ward is surprised at the speed with which sales of the two marques have reached almost 50/50 in the UK. "The market was ripe for the picking," he says. "Despite all that tradition and heritage, a Bentley was no more than a badge-engineered Rolls-Royce. The heritage was being thrown away."

It's not fair to suggest, however, that Ward has brought the winged 'B' back from the dead single-handed, and that without him the Bentley and the Turbo R wouldn't exist. There was a Bentley Camargue Turbo (no, that's not a misprint) that paved the way for the Mulsanne Turbo, but it *is*

Rolls-Royce chief executive Peter Ward had a hunch that the world was ready for a new strain of sporting Bentleys, cars that were true to the Bentley heritage. As he explains to Matthew Carter, that hunch has proved quite correct

fair to say that it's his marketing flair that has been at the heart of the turn around.

That Camargue Turbo prototype proved two things; that it was possible to turbocharge the faithful V8 and get the right results, and that there was a

Project 90 *appeared at Geneva '85 and stole the show*

Eighty years *on from the Silver Ghost the company is thriving*

future for the bentley marque.

The turbo car was the brainchild of Sir David Plastow, then managing director of the Motor Car Division of Rolls-Royce; he wanted a Bentley version of the coach-built Camargue that "went like crackers." Initial turbocharging development of the

engine was entrusted to Broadspeed and the prototype, complete with widened Bentley grille, covered more than a quarter of a million miles before being scrapped in 1982.

It had served its purpose, though. It proved that turbocharging a Rolls-Royce was feasible and if the car was presented as a Bentley, customer interest could be as high as 150 cars a year — far too many for a coachbuilt car like the Camargue. In January 1981 the go-ahead was given for a turbocharged version of the four-door Mulsanne.

Ward is well aware that those early Turbos were good only in parts, mostly when driven in a straight line. "We've done a great deal to those cars since launch. They may look the same, but they're quite different underneath — I challenge anyone to drive an '87 car and one of the originals and tell me any different."

They don't *look* very different, however, which leads to frustration, the frustration of being unable to consider a new car until the mid-1990s at the earliest. "The cost of producing a new body shell is no different for us from the way it is for GM, Mercedes or any of the others. The difference is that we don't have the volume to recover costs as quickly as they do," says Ward.

"We are looking at a life span of between 10 to 16 years for a body shell, 10 years production to amortise the costs and the next few years as profit — how long that period is, depends on how buoyant that shape is in the marketplace at the time."

To look on the bright side though, you can place your order for a new Mulsanne or Spirit now without the fear it's about to become obsolete! As the Spirit was launched at the end of 1980, the shape will be with us until around 1995. But that's not to say further changes won't be made. When Ward arrived at Rolls-Royce from Motaquip, the parts division of Peugeot-Talbot, he found a divided and dispirited Crewe. It was in the aftermath of the recession; there had been high levels of redundancy and , naturally, the cars weren't selling. When there's no money around, the last thing a company chairman will do is buy a new Rolls-Royce. People know how much they cost.

Ward also found the company heirachy split in two. There was a sales and marketing division and an engineering and manufacturing division. And, it appeared, the two never spoke to one another, "I believe much of the recession redundancies were caused by the company being lead by the manufacturing and engineering requirements, without that being tempered by the marketing side who knew what the world needed at that time."

Coincidentally, Ward and Mike Dunn, Rolls-Royce head of engineering, started working at Crewe on the same day. Ward immediately tackled the marketing problems, and Dunn supplied the engineering answers. The Bentley Eight, the 'poor man's Rolls' was a joint effort. The Turbo R, with suspension to match the power, is a perfect example of how Ward listened to criticisms, gave Dunn the go-ahead to find the solution, and then sold the idea to the buyers . . . pulling Bentley and Rolls-Royce further apart as a result.

The latest round of changes, which includes fuel injection, anti-lock braking and yet stiffer suspension for the Turbo R, indicates that though ▶

People who grew up in the '60s on Beach Boys music, Frogeye Sprites and TR3s are ideal Bentley material

Rolls-Royce *was not afraid to let journalists lap the Hungaroring at speed to prove the Bentley Turbo R's worth*

◀ the cars may look the same as they've always done — air dams and wide wheels apart — constant changes and improvements *are* being

What's next? A V12 with active ride and four-wheel-drive, perhaps. Ward smiles a 'I'm not going to give away our secrets' smile but does admit that technical trends are always being monitored and tested at Crewe. "We do have to be careful of what is a passing fad and what has genuine merit," he says. "We have been criticised for only just bringing ABS onto our cars but that was preceded by a huge debate on whether the system was good enough to replace the dual circuit system, the 'double H' we had before. You can't have that failsafe system with ABS. We have been messing around with ABS since 1973, but we had to be sure it would give us the safety reserves and the reliability we demand to preserve the quality and integrity of the car."

Should GM's old 400 three-speed auto be replaced by a newer four speed 'box, for example? Ward professes himself happy with it. "It's a big engine putting out tremendous torque and there aren't many transmissions around that can handle that and give us the smooth change requirement we need. The four speeds that we know of get very fussy. Our Spirit requirements are catered for by the three-speed and we don't

think the Turbo is lacking in not having a four-speed."

But that's not to suggest Rolls-Royce feels the cars have reached perfection. "We will always be looking for improvements," says Ward. "And we will have the inevitable discussion over four-wheel-drive and traction control systems. There will be all sorts of on-board navigational aids that will come and go — whether they are appropriate to Rolls-Royce is another debate — and so forth. And, according to a race report from the Detroit Grand Prix, it looks as if we might not need to consider active ride; the report said that Senna stepped out of his Lotus looking as though he had just been for a drive in a Rolls . . ." Ward, tongue planted firmly in cheek, smiled that smile again.

There will not be a V12 engine, however. "Just because BMW and Mercedes have got, or are getting, them, and Jaguar is putting more work into its V12, it doesn't mean we have to follow suit. Apart from the fact our engineers don't like the V12 concept, there is still plenty of life in our V8. More development work has been carried out on that engine in the past three years than in the whole of the preceding 22 years. And there's more to come — we have cars running around now giving in excess of 20mpg.

At the mention of fuel consumption Ward goes in for the kill.

"People consider Rolls-Royces socially unacceptable because of fuel economy. I tell them they had better ask Range Rover to cut 70 or 80 per cent of its production as it is making more gas guzzlers a year than we could produce over the next 10," Ward says. Talk about the future for Bentley, however, and Ward warms to the subject with youthful enthusiasm. Newspaper reports that the next Bentley will be a small, coupé-like sportscar with its own identity have been a little wide of the mark. But something along those lines would be the ultimate dream he admits.

"Even to consider that we would have to be very successful over the next few years developing sufficient funds. But what we have done already is show that simply by creating a different image for Bentley, the market is there. There is huge recall in this country for the glory of the name, but what is more amazing is that we have launched Bentley in the States where there is no recall at all. And Bentley has taken off."

He's on the right track to make that dream come true. After a £4.5 million loss in 1983, the following year saw a £12 million profit. It was £14 million in 1985, £16.5 million last year . . . "and the sun's shining today, too."

The US remains Rolls-Royce's biggest market, taking 1155 cars in 1986, compared with the UK's 808 — which itself represents almost a 14 per cent increase over 1986 — and 640 for Europe and the rest of the world. But while the Bentley/Rolls-Royce share is almost neck and neck in the UK, Ward believes it will settle around 70/30 per cent, in Rolls's favour. An early pointer that distancing Bentley from Rolls-Royce was the right thing to do, was the success of Project 90, the hastily conceived GRP body taken from a styling buck that stole the 1985 Geneva Show. "After a bad day I go home and dig out the press cuttings about Project 90 — it's a guaranteed lift. We were centre-stage for the full 10 days . . . and the hardest thing was convincing people we weren't going to make it for real!

"But it did prove what we were doing was right. In the old days Rolls-Royce traded on repeat business. The recession and the collapse of the Middle East market showed how shaky that could be. By creating a new image for Bentley we spread our base — you know, most Bentley sales have been conquest ones."

It's a long way from the Beach Boys and Frogeye Sprites but as a Bentley Boy '80s-style, Ward is having as much fun as he ever had then. Rolls-Royce's top man has a great deal to smile about. ∎

Just because BMW and Mercedes have got V12 engines doesn't mean we have to follow suit. There's plenty of life in our V8

221

HIGHLIGHTS
1919-1988

1919   Bentley Motors formed by W.O. Bentley, and first 3-litre car completed.

1921   First production 3-litre completed.

1922   Bentley's first major sporting achievement, when three team cars finished second, fourth and fifth in the Tourist Trophy, and won the team prize.

1923   J.F. Duff's Bentley covered fourth-greatest distance in first Le Mans 24-hour Race, this independent entry sparking W.O.'s interest in the race.

1924   A 3-litre driven by J.F. Duff and F.C. Clement won the Le Mans 24-hour Race

1926   The 6½-litre 'Big Six' introduced.

1927   The 4½-litre introduced.
3-litre driven by J.D. Benjafield and S.C.H. Davis won the Le Mans 24-hour Race. 4½-litre driven by F.C. Clement and G. Duller won the Grand Prix de Paris.

1928   Speed Six version of the 6½-litre introduced (this was reputed to be W.O. Bentley's favourite car).
4½-litre driven by W. Barnato and B. Rubin won the Le Mans 24-hour Race.

1929   Speed Six driven by W. Barnato and H.R.S. Birkin headed a Bentley 1-2-3-4 in the Le Mans 24-hour Race. Two weeks later the Speed Six was driven to victory in the BARC six-hour race at Brooklands by W. Barnato and J. Dunfee. Late in the year F.C. Clement and J. Barclay won the BRDC 500 mile race at Brooklands in a 4½-litre.

1930   W. Barnato and G. Kidston won the Le Mans 24-hour Race in a Speed Six. Barnato and F.C. Clement won the Brooklands Double Twelve in a Speed Six.
8-litre announced at the London Motor Show.

1931   4-litre announced.
Bentley Motors Ltd acquired by Rolls-Royce.
J. Dunfee and C. Paul won the BRDC 500 mile race at Brooklands in a 6½-litre.

1933   First 'Derby' Bentley announced. A 3½-litre car using a twin-carburettor version of the Rolls-Royce 20/25 engine, it was dubbed the 'Silent Sports Car'.

1935   W.O. Bentley left Bentley Motors (1931) to join Lagonda.

1936   4¼-litre version introduced.

1946   Bentley production resumed, at Crewe.
              Mark VI 4¼-litre saloon introduced.

1951   Mark VI engine enlarged to 4½ litres

1952   R type launched, the first Bentley to be offered with automatic
              transmission, as an optional extra.
              Two-door Continental introduced, with tuned version of 4½-litre
              engine.

1955   S series announced, the last Bentleys to be powered by a straight
              six.

1959   S2 announced, with a 6.2 litre V8 and automatic transmission.

1963   S3 announced. All 'S' models complemented by Continental
              versions.

1965   T series introduced. First Bentleys with monocoque construction;
              specification included independent self-levelling suspension, power-
              assisted disc brakes and an improved V8.

1971   W.O. Bentley died, a month short of his 83rd birthday.
              Corniche introduced.

1977   T2 series launched.

1980   Mulsanne introduced.

1982   Mulsanne Turbo announced at Geneva Motor Show.

1984   Eight launched at the lower end of the range.
              Corniche became the Continental.

1985   Turbo R launched.

1986   Stiffer suspension introduced on all Bentley models except the
              Continental

1987   Fuel injection and anti-lock brakes fitted to all models, except
              Corniche (which had these items from 1988) and Continental, where
              anti-lock were brakes fitted to US models for 1988.

1988   Turbo R introduced.